The Intimate Environment

The Intimate Environment

Exploring Marriage and the Family

Arlene Skolnick

University of California, Berkeley

Little, Brown and Company   Boston

Library of Congress Catalog Number: 73-9120

THIRD PRINTING

Published simultaneously in Canada
by Little, Brown & Company (Canada) Limited

Printed in the United States of America

CREDITS AND ACKNOWLEDGMENTS

Production and design supervision: *Kenneth R. Burke*
Copyediting: *Judith Fillmore*
Design: *Michael Rogondino*
Photo research: *Kay James*
Proofreading: *Marjorie Hughes*

PERMISSIONS

Pp. 92–93, 182, 334, 336, 338, 343, 344: From *Centuries of Childhood* by Philippe Aries, translated by Robert Baldick. Copyright © 1962 by Jonathan Cape Ltd. Reprinted by permission of Alfred A. Knopf, Inc., and Jonathan Cape, Ltd. **Pp. 268–269:** From *Beliefs, Attitudes, and Human Affairs* by Daryl J. Bem. Copyright 1970 by Wadsworth Publishing Company, Inc. Reprinted by permission of the publisher, Brooks/Cole Publishing Company, Monterey, California. **Pp. 143–144, 146, 317, 425–426:** From Bennett Berger, Bruce M. Hackett, and R. Mervyn Millar, "Child-Rearing Practices in the Communal Family." A progress report to the National Institute of Mental Health, 1972. Reprinted by permission. **Pp. 218–219, 221:** From Jessie Bernard, "The Adjustments of Married Mates," in Harold T. Christensen (ed.), *Handbook of Marriage and the Family,* © 1964 by Rand McNally and Company, Chicago, pp. 705, 706–708. **Pp. 106, 107:** From J. Demos, *A Little Commonwealth* (New York: Oxford University Press, 1970), p. 186. Reprinted by permission of Oxford University Press. **Pp. 294–295:** From H. Ginott, "Being a Parent," *San Francisco Sunday Examiner and Chronicle,* February 11, 1973. © King Features Syndicate, 1972. Reprinted by permission. **Pp. 222, 224–227, 252:** From Jay Haley, *Strategies of Psychotherapy* (New York: Grune & Stratton, Inc., 1963). Copyright © 1963 by Grune & Stratton, Inc. By permission of the publisher and author. **Pp. 180, 211, 227, 375:** From *Self and Others,* 2nd edition revised, by R. D. Laing. Copyright © 1961, 1969 by R. D. Laing. Reprinted by permission of Pantheon Books, a division of Random House, Inc., and Tavistock Publications. **Pp. 283–285:** From "Checks on Population Growth: 1750–1850," William L. Langer. Copyright © 1972 by Scientific American, Inc. All rights reserved. **Pp. 379–381:** From Jean Macfarlane, "Perspectives on Personality Consistency and Change from The Guidance Study," *Vita Humana* 7 (1964), pp. 121, 122–123. Reprinted by permission of the author and Karger and Basel. (New title of this journal: *Human Development.*) **Pp. 6, 7, 21, 436:** From David M. Schneider, *American Kinship: A Cultural Account,* © 1968, pp. 33, 35, 116. By permission of Prentice-Hall, Inc., Englewood Cliffs, N.J. **Pp. 7, 8:** From J. Spiegel, *Transactions: The Interplay between Individual, Family, and Society,* pp. 144–145. Copyright © 1971 by Science House, Inc. Reprinted by permission of Jason Aronson, Inc. **Pp. 11, 85–86, 88–89, 188, 257, 300, 334:** From *The Family in Cross-Cultural Perspective* by William N. Stephens. Copyright © 1963 by Holt, Rinehart and Winston, Inc. Reprinted by permission of Holt, Rinehart and Winston, Inc. **Pp. 164, 186, 195, 209, 261:** From *The Social Context of Marriage* by J. Richard Udry. Reprinted by permission of the publisher, J. B. Lippincott Company. Copyright 1971.

PREFACE

In the past few years we have witnessed a remarkable transformation in the public image of family life. Since the late 1960's the notion that the American family is in danger, trouble, or a state of crisis has been an increasingly prominent theme in the mass media. The nuclear family, once generally held to be the backbone of society as well as an expression of instinctual tendencies programmed into human genes, was described in one magazine as "the most maligned institution of 1972."

Those who are worried about the "survival" of the family point to statistics showing an increase in divorce rates, a dramatic decline in birth rates, and a less-marked but still noticeable decline in marriage rates. On the other side of the ideological fence, the same statistics have been hailed as indicators of liberation from oppressive family and sex roles, and adaptation to the need to stop the population explosion.

The emergence of family life and sex roles as controversial public issues has been curiously disconnected from family scholarship. No new theories or research findings have provoked the current questioning of family life, nor have social scientists been very active in interpreting it. Indeed, most family sociologists have stressed stability over change in interpreting American family patterns.

The origins of the questioning mood about the family can be traced to the social upheavals of the past decade rather than to social science. The public protest that erupted during the mid-1960's has all but disappeared from the streets, campuses, and television screens. Yet the deeper currents set off by the youth revolt and the counterculture still reverberate among us. Ironically, of all the institutions that were challenged during the 1960's—the universities, the schools, the military, the government itself—it is the American home that has been shaken most profoundly. It is no longer possible to take the family for granted as a haven of stability and togetherness.

The main fact about family life today is that formerly sanctified beliefs and practices have come to be openly challenged. Everything that used to be taken for granted as part of human nature—definitions of masculinity and femininity, the necessity of marriage, the desirability of having children, the rights and obligations of children and parents to each other—is open to question and debate.

The social sciences themselves have been thrown into disarray by the unrest of the past decade. A sense of dislocation, if not of crisis, pervades all fields of social science, and it both includes and transcends such issues as political and moral relevance of social theories, the ethics of research methods, and the uses to which research findings are put. There is also a crisis of knowledge, a realization that the conceptual underpinnings of each field may be weaker than had generally been assumed. In sociology, for example, there is a growing awareness that the entire sociological enterprise, the whole structure of theories and findings, may rest "on a soft substratum of human biases and assumptions."

One particular casualty of recent history is the assumption that human activity functions to maintain the stability and harmony of the social order. Starting out from this assumption, which dominated the social sciences during the 1950's and '60's, one is inevitably driven to conclude that the family plays a key role in assuring social stability, continuity, and consensus. If, however, one assumes that change and conflict are natural conditions of social life, that social institutions are maintained by sanctions, rewards, and social pressures rather than by consensus, and that values and ideals are a poor guide to how people actually behave, then one is free to construct an alternative vision of family life. This book is an attempt to begin to construct such a vision.

In contrast to the prevailing assumptions about the necessity and naturalness of the family, this book begins with the assumption that the family is problematic in every sense of the term. We do not really know, for example, whether, and in what ways, it is useful to think of the family as a constant in all human societies. The very concept of the family is also problematic because it exists at several levels of reality. At one level the family is the stream of behavior that flows in families; but the family is also a mental construction in the heads of family members and observers of family life. The relations among the different levels of reality are neither direct nor constant in their indirection. For example, it would be wrong to assume that family ideologies are always maps of behavior, but it would also be wrong to conclude that they are always smokescreens. Besides, what people think is happening is an important part of what really is happening.

Finally, the family is problematic in an emotional sense. Family life is the place where, as one writer put it, "you're dealing with life-and-death voltages." Dramatists and novelists, from the Greek tragedians to Eugene O'Neill to the writers of soap operas, have always portrayed the intimacies of family life in terms of love *and* hate, devotion *and* cruelty, sacrifice *and* spite. Until very recently, however, students of marriage and the family have tended to overlook the inconsistencies and ironies of family life in favor of such orderly conceptions as family harmony on one side and breakdown on the other.

In the past decade the special psychology of intimate relationships has been rediscovered by family therapists and researchers observing family members in face-to-face interaction. This book has been strongly influenced by concepts of family life emerging from that approach. Particularly influential has been the notion that the family cannot be understood only in terms of the individual personalities of family members, nor as merely a small unit of the larger society. Rather, families need to be analyzed as behavioral systems — as environments larger than the individuals in them. Furthermore, all families, normal and pathological, are problematic, difficult environments with their own rules, myths, taboos, secrets, patterns of alliance and communication, and loves and hates. The resemblances between the behavior patterns of normal families and those of disturbed families are often more striking than the differences.

Research into the history of the family has provided a second influence in the writing of this book. Recent historical studies have suggested — despite the vast differences between historical research and observational psychiatry — a similar vision of family life. Departing from concepts of the normal, typical, or model family, historians have tried to look at everyday family life in past times as it varied with social class, population movements, and social change. Unfettered by the balanced, consensual society model, historians tend to treat such issues as illegitimacy, premarital sexuality, infanticide, and generational conflict as part of family life itself rather than as a separate category of deviance.

Paradoxically, by emphasizing the problematic nature of the family, this book is able to be unpessimistic about the future of the family. If there is no definition of the family that will hold across all cultures and periods, and if the family is a concept rather than a biological reality, then novel forms of the intimate environment may be equally valid. If conflict between the generations and the sexes is part of human history, then today's situation is not such a radical departure from the past. If the normal family is a myth, then perhaps the craziness we observe in family life is also part of the human condition. What we are witnessing may not be so much the breakdown of the family as an institution, as the destruction of myths and assumptions about family living that were never true in the first place. The analysis of these assumptions, their historical development, and the evidence and logic supporting them form the structure around which this book is organized. It is a textbook in the sense that it attempts to be systematic in organization, understandable to the introductory student, and reasonably comprehensive. At the same time it does not shrink from criticism or controversy, and its author firmly believes that a textbook lacking in such qualities will prove not only dull but misleading.

Arlene Skolnick

Berkeley, California
May 1973

ACKNOWLEDGMENTS

I would like to thank first of all the institution, which shall remain nameless, that indirectly led me to enter the field of family studies by failing to come through with jobs promised during the time my husband was being courted. As I have since come to learn, my experience was not unusual for dual-career academic couples. I am now grateful for what seemed at the time a personal crisis, for if I had not been pushed by adversity, I would never have left the narrower paths of social and developmental psychology for the wider interdisciplinary wilds of family studies.

I am also, and unironically, grateful to my husband, Jerome H. Skolnick, for the countless number of ways he has supported and encouraged me through the inception and writing of this book. It was his suggestion that we embark together on a study of the family, which solved the unemployment problem for me. The result of our joint efforts that year was *Family in Transition*, which raised some of the issues that this book attempts to explore more deeply. Throughout the writing of this book, Jerry has been, as always, my severest critic and best friend, a difficult feat in view of the complications my writing introduced into our domestic life. I would also like to thank my children, Michael and Alexander, who had to share me and our household with a demanding sibling, this book. I am grateful in a special way to Ingrid Brown, whose sensitive care provided Alexander with pleasure and security, and me with the peace of mind required by the task of writing.

I owe a special debt of gratitude to the people who read the manuscript and provided valuable comments: Patricia K. Allen, Dale Hoffman, Janet Z. Giele, Blaine E. Mercer, and Lenore Weitzman. Also, I would like to thank Ken Burke, the production supervisor, who transformed the manuscript into a book and made it possible for me to enjoy the process of bookmaking, as well as Milton Johnson and Chris Hunter, the editors at Little, Brown who provided so much support and encouragement.

My thanks also to the various people who helped with the research and typing: Janet Kiniry, Cecily Tighe, Georgeanne Austin, Emily Knapp, Gay Englezos, and especially to my mother, Rosalie C. Silberstein, who helped in various ways during the writing.

Finally, I wish to express my thanks to two research organizations of the University of California, Berkeley: to the Center for the Study of Law and Society for providing typing and research assistance at critical moments; and to the Institute of Human Development, whose studies of family life over four generations represent the point where I began my professional career, and where I have returned, full circle, to find I have not gone so far afield after all.

Arlene Skolnick

CONTENTS

The Intimate Environment

The psychology and sociology of personality and interpersonal relations have been in the past, and still are, vitiated by three sets of assumptions and tendencies. The first is a rigid ideal of scientific exactness which produces in the minds of many social scientists a bias toward selecting . . . those facts and aspects of reality which lend themselves best to a precise, if possible, quantitative investigation. This results in the neglect of those facts and aspects which resist or elude precise analysis. The second is the set of silent assumptions rooted in the ideological or cultural background of the society to which the particular psychologist and sociologist belongs. These silent assumptions often induce the social scientist to ask only those questions and to select only those problems suggested by the accepted ideology. . . . The third is the tendency to neglect, or even to ignore, certain very important facts and problems because . . . [they] . . . appear to be quite obvious.

Gustav Ichheiser, *Appearances and Realities*

IN SEARCH OF
THE FAMILY

Chapter 1

One difficulty in the psychological sciences lies in the familiarity of the phenomena with which they deal. A certain intellectual effort is required to see how such phenomena can pose serious problems or call for intricate explanatory theories. One is inclined to take them for granted as necessary or somehow "natural."

Noam Chomsky, *Language and Mind*

Chapter One   Nearly everyone has grown up in a family and thus come to have a deceptive sense of knowing what the family is. In no other field of study is there such a great temptation to use one's own experience as a basis for wide-ranging generalizations. Yet, rather than being the easiest of subjects to study, the family may be one of the most resistant to analysis. Like anthropologists who find their own culture harder to study than an exotic one, perhaps only a person who has never lived in a family is really qualified to study families. As R. D. Laing puts it:

> The first family to interest me was my own. I still know less about it than I know about many other families. This is typical. . . . (1971, p. 67)

> We speak of families as though we all know what families are. We identify, as families, networks of people who live together over periods of time, who have ties of marriage and kinship to one another. The more one studies family dynamics, the more *un*clear one becomes as to the ways *family* dynamics compare and contrast with the dynamics of other groups not called families, let alone the ways families themselves differ. . . .

> The dynamics and structures found in those groups called families in our society may not be evident in those groups called families in other places and times. . . . (1971, p. 3)

The anthropologist Ray Birdwhistell argues that the family is an extremely difficult form for social scientists to study, not only in their own culture but in other cultures also. He concludes that everywhere family processes are both idealized and camouflaged (1966). The social scientist looks out through the blinders and filters imposed on him as a member of a particular culture. He deals with people who may hold unrealistic assumptions about their own family systems. As an anthropological field worker, Birdwhistell was struck by the discrepancy between the actual behavior of people in their family life and the accounts people gave of their family systems. He found this discrepancy in interviewing Indians in Canada as well as Americans in "Border County," Kentucky:

> What even the most sophisticated interviewer gets when he asks about the family is a set of personalized stereotypes—the

stereotype obscured by anecdotes which purportedly report personal experiences, but which are no less banal by virtue of this pseudo-individuality. (p. 211)

Thus it is more than familiarity that makes it hard to use our own experience as a basis for understanding the family. As Laing notes, even the psychiatrist or the family therapist may know less about his own family than he knows about others. We enter our complicated family worlds not as adults, obviously, but in the state of "blindness" and "prolonged panic" that is childhood (Sartre, 1963). Each of us lives out a unique childhood inside a particular family, in a particular set of circumstances, in a particular segment of a given society. These early experiences are never fully outgrown and they condition many of our beliefs and ideas, including our ideas about the family.

Families, like governments or organizations or even individuals, do not find complete candor a necessary ingredient for their day-to-day functioning. Quite the opposite. One of the discoveries of recent family research is that families have myths, secrets, and information-processing rules that determine the kind of communication that goes on—what can be said and, more important, what can't be said. Families not only filter information about the wider culture, but about their own functioning. Or as Laing puts it, families practice mystification: they have complicated stratagems for keeping people in the dark about what is going on, and in the dark that they are in the dark.

Sanctity and Secrecy

Besides familiarity and mystification, other obstacles handicap the study of the family: it is morally sacred, and it is secret. The family in America includes two moral dimensions, a religious one based on Judeo-Christian family ideals, and a legal one relating to the laws of marriage, economic obligations between husband and wife, parents and children, etc. (Ball, 1972). Thus the happenings of family life are the concern of others besides the family members themselves; they have a public dimension. Yet, paradoxically, because privacy is also a cherished value, the family is perhaps the most secret institution in American society. To a greater extent than in other societies and in our own historical past (see B. Laslett, 1973), American family life goes on behind closed doors. The home is a "backstage area" (Goffman, 1959, pp. 106–140) where people can be relaxed, informal, and off guard precisely because they cannot be observed by outsiders.

As a result of this privacy, family life in America is marked by what sociologists call "pluralistic ignorance," a term usually applied to sexual experience. We know what goes on in our own household or bedroom, but we have little or no direct knowledge of what really goes on in other peoples'. Thus we know where our own family life falls short of the *ideal* norms — the way family life is supposed to be — but we do not know where it fits in *statistical* norms — the extent to which other families also may be departing from prescribed behavior. As Goffman puts it, people are aware of how their own "backstage" behavior differs from how they act "in public," but they are not in a position to come to the same conclusion about others (1959, p. 132).

Until very recently family scholarship has paid relatively little attention to the "backstage" aspects of family life. Despite the vast literature on family life spreading across several disciplines, practically everything social scientists know about the family has been derived from questionnaires and interviews obtained from family members seen alone (Framo, 1965, p. 410). Often only one member of a family serves as an informant about the rest of the family.

There are of course some very good and obvious ethical reasons for respecting family privacy. Keyhole peeping and eavesdropping, electronic and otherwise, would be hard to justify as research methods. In the past decade and a half, however, researchers have found a compromise between privacy and research. They have begun to observe live family interaction with the consent of those being observed. Although these glimpses of family life do not give a view that is truly "backstage" or unobserved, they nevertheless have led to new conceptions of what families are, and how they are to be understood. Viewing live family interaction has reclaimed for social science some of the insights into family life that previously had been found only in the writings of novelists and playwrights (Henry, 1971, p. 456). We shall explore these insights later on.

The Definition Problem

In much of this chapter we are going to explore what people mean when they speak of families and "the family." The family has proved to be an elusive concept, in spite of our conviction that we know what families are all about. Trying to pin down the meaning of the term is not just an intellectual game. There is, as we shall see, genuine doubt among those who have thought about the matter just what it is that distinguishes families from nonfamilies, and whether there is a single definition of family that applies to all times and places.

Definitions of the family have important consequences in peoples' lives. Family definitions are like Marianne Moore's description of poetry; they are imaginary gardens with real toads. The toads represent the negative consequences that flow from labeling as deviant those families that depart from a narrow definition of a family. The assumption that one form of "the family" is not only the most desirable but also the most real and observable form avoids interesting intellectual issues, dictates social policies that stigmatize certain family and sexual behaviors as pathological deviance, and at the same time fails to direct attention to the potentials for psychological and physical harm in ordinary family life.

The definition problem is important for another reason. There is a widespread belief, encouraged by family textbooks and popular writings on the family as well as by some distinguished scholars, that the family is universal, found in every known human society. Many people interpret this belief to mean that the family as we know it or would like it to be in our society occurs everywhere. Yet the very term "family" is ambiguous. Murdock, one of the leading anthropological students of the family, observes that "the layman and even the social scientist often apply it to several social groups which, despite . . . similarities, exhibit important points of difference" (1949, p. 1).

Does "the family" mean the nuclear family—the married couple and their offspring? Is the husband-wife relationship the core of the family, or is it the mother-child pair? Does "family" include the family tree—the aunts, uncles, cousins, grandparents? Does it include the dead, whose influence some researchers have detected two generations beyond the grave? If "the family" means the nuclear family, is the whole family as a unit "the unity of interacting personalities," as Burgess (1926) put it? Or is the family a separate reality for each member—the child's view of the family may not be the parental view; the wife's view may not be that of the husband.

What is the irreducible basis of the concept of family: blood ties, marriage, living together, a sense of identification, a sense of obligation? Some combination of these? How does the quality of experience in groups called families differ from that in nonfamily groups? Will any definition apply across all cultures and historical periods?

The American Definition   For family textbook writers, many social scientists, and the American public "the family" is the nuclear family—a married couple and their children. Society seems to be divided into nuclear-family groups, each living in a home of its own. Any deviation from the parent-child unit living together is not quite a family and needs explanation. It may be a "broken home" or some other variation from the expected pattern.

One may say, "I have no family," and mean that perhaps one is not married and has no spouse or child, or that one's parents are no longer alive. Or, one may point to certain persons and say of them, "This is my family," or "I would like you to meet my family." One may also say, "I have no family," meaning that one is separated from one's spouse and therefore not living with a spouse and children.

A married couple without children does not quite make a family. Neither do a married woman and her children without a husband nor a married man and his children without a wife. For the married couple without children, one may say, "They have no family," or "Their family has not arrived yet," if they are very young. "Family" here means that the addition of children will complete the unit. . . . And of course one may say of an older couple, "Their family has all grown up and is married, each has a family of his own now."

This last example makes clear another condition which is part of the definition of the family in American kinship. The family, to be a family, must live together. (Schneider, 1968, p. 33)

This description of American kinship usages may strike the reader as obvious to the point of being funny. But that is exactly the purpose of Schneider's study. The essence of any system of cultural symbols and definitions is what people in that culture take for granted. Schneider is trying to apply the anthropological methods used in exotic cultures to the contemporary American scene.

As Schneider points out (1968, p. 9), the anthropologist must act like a child. He has to learn the names for things, how to use the names correctly, and the values and dangers that lurk around them. Thus Schneider is spelling out the basic cultural premises of the American system which a native or anthropologist from another culture would have to know in order to understand the kinship system.

One of the striking features of the way Americans think about the family, Schneider notes, is the emphasis on the family as natural.

. . . The family is defined by American culture as a "natural" unit which is "based on the facts of nature." . . .

The family is a cultural unit which contains a husband and a wife who are the mother and father of their child or children. . . . (1968, p. 33)

. . . This is the sense in which Americans see a family when animals mate and rear their young in a place which they occupy and protect—their nest, their cave, their home. (1968, p. 35)

John Spiegel, a psychiatrist, and his associates decided to learn as much as they could about the structure and function of family life in the United States, in order to define "the normal American family." Spiegel (1971) describes a remarkable search for "the family" amid the welter of real families in their varied day-to-day existence:

. . . We decided that the first step toward our goal would be to inform ourselves with regard to the structure and function of the family. But this apparently simple task brought us face to face with whole new series of complications. Instead of finding a clear-cut definition of the family easy to achieve, *we discovered families exhibited the most astonishing variance in their structure and function.* (Spiegel, 1971, p. 144) (Italics added)

Just within the United States alone, disregarding the rest of the world, the researchers found tremendous variation based on regional, ethnic, and social-class differences. It was difficult, for example, to know where to draw the boundaries around the family. Some families seemed to extend laterally —that is, to include relatives such as aunts, uncles, and cousins—whereas others extended vertically to include grandparents and great-grandparents.

Small family groups were associated with the urban middle class and its continuous demand for maximum mobility, both geographical and social. Continuity of generations was found in the upper-class families with their family portraits, traditions, and hierarchical systems. (Spiegel, p. 144)

The complexities reached into the very heart of the nuclear unit itself — the relations between husbands and wives, and parents and children. Spiegel writes:

Not only were various and differing functions assigned to the family in different social milieus, but even those functions which were apparently universal, such as the socialization of children, the satisfaction of sexual needs, or the biological and material maintenance of the members of the family, were carried out in such various ways with such differing implications that it proved impossible to obtain meaningful patterns without reference to the surrounding social system. The responsibilities and attitudes of a father toward his child, his wife, and his mother-in-law could not be divorced from his other roles in the society. . . . For example, different functions were expected of him, depending on what his occupational role was — whether he owned a farm, worked in a factory, or piloted an airplane. A mother's attitude toward and relations with her children varied, among other factors, with her ethnic origin as well as with her decision to stay at home or to increase the family income by going to work. (pp. 144–145)

But the complications did not end there. Beyond the occupational structure, Spiegel writes, was another level of human behavior: the level of cultural and subcultural values. For example, middle-class families in the United States emphasize planning for the future, hard work, and individual initiative. But the United States has a mixed cultural heritage that complicates the picture. Each ethnic group seems to relate to the dominant value system — in its own way.

Are these differences among families interesting and worthy of study in themselves, or are they obstacles or masks hiding "the family"? Clifford Geertz, an anthropologist, has criticized the search for universals such as "the family" as a misguided effort that "drowns living detail in dead stereotype." He continues:

. . . The notion that the essence of what it means to be human is most clearly revealed in those features of human culture that are most universal is a prejudice we are not obligated to share. Is it in grasping such general facts — that man has everywhere some sort of religion — or in grasping the richness of this religious phenomenon or that — Balinese trance . . . Aztec human sacrifice or Zuni rain dancing — that we grasp him? Is the fact that "marriage" is universal (if it is) as penetrating a comment on what we are as the facts concerning Himalayan polyandry, or those fantastic Australian marriage rules, or the elaborate bride-price systems of Bantu Africa? (Geertz, 1965, p. 105)

Conceptions of the Nuclear Family

Discussions about the nuclear family are often confused because the term is used in a variety of ways. The nuclear family that some anthropologists have claimed to be universal is not the same nuclear family that Schneider found elaborated in American culture. In American society the nuclear family refers to an observable group of people who live together and are set off from the rest of society in a number of tangible ways; the universal nuclear family of the anthropologists is more abstract. The distinguishing feature of the *abstract nuclear family* is some form of recognition of the nuclear group as a unit. It is "abstract" because it does not imply that the nuclear family lives together, or acts as a unit, or is behaviorally similar from one society to another.

The classic statement as to the universality of the nuclear family was made by Murdock in 1949:

The nuclear family is a universal social grouping. Whether as the sole prevailing form of the family or as the basic unit from which more complex familial forms are compounded, it exists as a distinct and strongly functional group in known society. No exception . . . has come to light in the 250 representative cultures surveyed for the present study, which thus corroborates the conclusion of Lowie. "It does not matter whether marital relations are permanent or temporary; whether there is polygamy or polyandry or sexual license; whether conditions are complicated by the addition of members not included in *our* family circle: the one fact stands out beyond all others that everywhere the husband, wife and immature children constitute a unit apart from the remainder of the community." (Murdock, 1949, pp. 2–3)

In addition, Murdock postulated the following characteristics of the family: common residence, economic cooperation, socially approved sexual relationships, reproduction, and child rearing.

Since Murdock's assertion that the nuclear family is a cultural universal, an imperative found in all societies, anthropologists have been debating the validity of the statement. In general, even those who argued for the idea of a universal nuclear family were well aware that family life as a day-to-day reality was not the same everywhere.

Murdock himself argued that the nuclear family is one of three distinct family organizations found in human society. The other two were the *polygamous family*, formed by the marriage of one man to two or more women, or one woman to two or more men, and the *extended family*. The extended family forms when a married couple joins the parents of one of the spouses, and three generations live under one roof or close to each other. Murdock argued, however, that the nuclear families were still separate units in these complex forms of the family:

> Whatever larger familial forms may exist, and to whatever extent the greater unit may assume some of the burdens of the lesser, the nuclear family is always recognizable and always has its distinctive and vital functions—sexual, economic, reproductive, and educational. . . . (Murdock, 1949, p. 3)

Other scholars disagreed that these larger family organizations could be viewed as being made up of nuclear families; rather, it seemed, the nuclear families were submerged in them (see Levy, 1955).

Other arguments about the universality of the nuclear family involve changing or stretching definitions. For example, the collective living and child-rearing arrangements of the Israeli kibbutz can be seen as an exception to the nuclear-family principle, or as a confirmation of it, depending on how the family and its functions are defined (see Spiro, 1954). Another series of debates concerns the Nayar, a warrior caste in India (Gough, 1959). Among these people, households consisted of brothers and sisters, and the children of the sisters and their daughters. One of the remarkable features of the Nayar was the complete separation between the roles of husband, biological father, and legally designated father. That is, marriages in this society were formal rituals, after which the spouses need never have anything more to do with each other. In fact, if a husband did develop a fondness for his wife, this would cause fear and concern among the relatives of each spouse. Men and women were free to take lovers. Neither the woman's husband nor the biological father had any rights over the child; the legitimate father of a child was one of the mother's lovers who agreed to pay for the birth expenses.

In viewing the customs of the Nayar, it is possible for one group of anthropologists to argue that these people do not have the institutions of marriage, fatherhood, and legitimacy, and for another group to argue with equal fervor that they do, however differently these institutions may be defined. Both sides would agree that there is little resemblance between the contemporary nuclear family as a group of people who live together and the family life of the Nayar.

One anthropologist, trying to sort out the arguments concerning the universality of the family, concluded it was a hopeless task:

. . . It looked as if the question of the universality of the family was a rather pointless argument, depending on the arbitrary choice of definitions.

However, as I delved more deeply into the problem, I found it was even more hopeless than this. I was not able to give even an arbitrary answer to the question because I was unable to arrive at a clear definition of the term "family." "Family" is really terribly hard to define properly. We all use this term. Doubtless we all have the illusion we know what we mean by it. But when one sets about trying to separate families from nonfamilies, he begins to realize how very hard it is to say just exactly what a "family" is. (Stephens, 1963, p. 4)

Another anthropologist, Marvin Harris, scathingly refers to the tendency of some of his fellows to argue that the nuclear family is the same everywhere and yet different as a "miracle, a kind of holy duality. . . . The concept of the nuclear family makes sense only if we know that fa(ther), mo(ther), so(n), and da(ughter) behave in certain ways. It would almost seem as if Family is a Platonic essence. Take away the shadow families on the wall of the cave . . . and Family is still there burning bright in some realm of superior reality" (Harris, 1964, pp. 180–181).

The Actual Nuclear Family   The nuclear family may not be universal, but it is observable in many societies. As an independent living group it is called a "conjugal" or "neolocal" family. The term "conjugal" implies that the husband-wife relationship is the usual basis on which the household is formed, as opposed to the parent-child relationship in the extended family. The term "neolocal" represents another way of expressing the fact that a married couple should form their own household, rather than move in with or near his father (patrilocal) or her mother (matrilocal). Such a household typically does not contain anyone besides mother, father, and children. Conjugal households can be observed in at least three different social circumstances. The first occurs in simple hunting societies, such as the Eskimo, where family structures tend to be nuclear in fact and in principle. The second occurs where the extended family is supposed to prevail but circumstances prevent it. Thus among European peasants the household is supposed to be extended; that is, the three generations are supposed to live together under one roof or nearby. In past centuries in Western Europe and America, however, people married relatively late, and life expectancy was short (see P. Laslett, 1965). Hence on the average there were only a few years between the marriage of a couple and the death of the in-laws. During those years extended-family households prevailed. Yet an observer visiting the society at one point in time would find only a relatively small number of extended-family households (Berkner, 1972). The formation of a three-generation household might also be prevented by poverty (see Goode, 1963): if a farm could not produce enough to support a large household, the son might not marry, or he might have to look elsewhere for work.

The nuclear family is the prevailing form of the family in modern society. William Goode (1963) has described a worldwide revolution in family patterns: in every country now in the process of becoming modern, industrial, and urban, traditional kin obligations are giving way to the familiar Western nuclear or conjugal way of life. Goode emphasizes that the change to the modern family pattern involves more than a change in household composition or economic obligations between blood relatives. The modern family forms are accompanied by an ideology, and indeed the ideology of the conjugal family may appear before the changes in actual life circumstances. The ideology emphasizes the values of individualism, freedom, marriage for love, and strong emotional ties between family members. Privacy also plays an important part in the nuclear-family ideology — in the concept of the home as an enclave separated from the rest of society. Goode and other scholars see a distinction between the nuclear or conjugal family as empirical fact and the nuclear-family ideology:

> The ideology of the conjugal family proclaims the right of the individual to choose his or her own spouse, place to live, and even which kin obligations to accept, as against the acceptance of others' decisions . . . . The *individual* is to be evaluated, not his lineage . . . . A strong theme of "democracy" runs through this ideology. It encourages love, which in every major civilization has been given a prominent place in fantasy, poetry, art and legend as a wonderful, perhaps even exalted experience, even when its reality was guarded against. Finally, it asserts that if one's family life is unpleasant, one has the right to change it. (Goode, 1963, p. 19)

The Idealized Nuclear Family   In American society the mass media and many family professionals have tended to confuse the empirical nuclear family with its idealized counterpart in the nuclear-family ideology. Thus we come to the final usage of the term "nuclear family" — the idealized or "sentimental" (Birdwhistell, 1966) model of the nuclear family. Like the abstract nuclear family, this model assumes that the nuclear family is found everywhere; but unlike the abstract model, it assumes that the emotional bonds between family members are constant. This model of the nuclear family is, in effect, the one Schneider found in his study of the American kinship system. However, it may be found among family professionals as well as laymen. The key aspects of the sentimental model of the nuclear family include assumptions about the naturalness, emotional intensity, self-sufficiency, and balance of the nuclear-family unit. Birdwhistell writes that he "knows of no cases in which the ideal model [of the American family] has been observed" (1966, p. 211). By this he means not only the household group of parents and children, but also what he sees as the psychological premises of the ideal model: that parents and children constitute a self-contained unit in which all the significant emotional needs of each family member are satisfied within the inner family circle. In short, he argues, the "family" is a collective

myth that might be harmless were it not used by professionals to "manipulate the lives of their fellows."

The marriage counselor, the social worker, the psychiatrist or
the family doctor, if he unquestioningly accepts the ideal model
of the family as "healthy," has no recourse but to direct his clientele
toward unreality or toward passive or "philosophical" acceptance
of their failure in familial relationships. (Birdwhistell, 1966, p. 211)

House, Home, and Family

One of the main assumptions in the American definition of
family is that a family lives together in a home. The terms
"home" and "family" are used almost interchangeably. We
know of course that in reality some families do not live
together, and some people live together who are not families.
But we tend to define these situations as abnormal and
unfortunate or immoral.

Until recently most social scientists also tended to
assume that home and family were equivalent. Common
residence was one of the defining attributes of the family.
For example, Murdock defined the family as a social group
characterized by common residence, as well as economic
cooperation and reproduction (1949, p. 1). Households were
thought of as containers or shells for family members, not
as something to be considered separately.

Yet including the notion of household as part of the
definition of the family has created many problems. For one
thing, home and family are logically different, as Bohannan
(1963) has pointed out. Family has to do with kinship relations, whereas home is a place, a spatial concept. Bohannon
argues that households or homes perform the functions
usually ascribed to the family — they provide food and shelter
and raise children. The distinction between household and
family must be made because in many societies around the
world families do not usually form households, and households may not be composed of families. Nuclear-family
members often do live together, but it is also very common
for husbands and wives and even for children not to live
together under the same roof. Thus situations regarded as
unfortunate, if not unusual, in our society turn out to be
regarded as the usual and normal way of living in many
other societies (Bender, 1967, p. 493).

Most often it is the father-husband who lives apart from the rest of the family. Among some peoples — the Iroquois, for example — households consisted of mothers and daughters and daughters' children, while the men engaged in hunting or warfare. In some societies adult men may live in men's houses, apart from their wives and children; and sometimes all-male households consist of brothers. In most of these male living situations the father lives nearby his wife or wives and their children, and visits fairly often. Such an arrangement would be considered "common residence" by many anthropologists. But Stephens raises this question: how close must the father be in order to be counted as living with a wife and children? Fifty feet? A mile? Perhaps the extreme of distance is that found among a people in Kenya, where the mother-child households are located on widely separated farms (Stephens, 1963, p. 16). Among the Navaho also, a man may marry unrelated women who live at considerable distances from one another (Bender, 1967, p. 494).

Another question can be raised: how often must a father visit, and how long must he stay, in order to be considered part of the household? Or, to put it another way, how long must he be gone in order not to be counted as a member of the household? Sometimes work or warfare take the father-husband away for years at a time. Is he then to be considered as "living with" his wife and children? It is also unclear whether the father should be counted in the household if his job requires him to live away from the rest of the family and maintain a separate residence.

Besides those instances when father lives apart from the rest of the family, there are many cases of children normally living separate from their parents. The Israeli communes (kibbutzim) are probably the best-known example. But in societies where the mother-child household prevails, boys usually move away from home at or before the onset of sexual maturation. The boys may merely sleep out and eat at home, or they move to the village of another relative (Stephens, 1963).

Even younger children sometimes live away from home. Among the Ibo, boys of five or six leave their mothers' houses and live with boys their age from the same compound (Bender, 1967). Samoan children wander around from one relative's household to another, choosing where they will stay and for how long (Mead, 1928, p. 36). Closer to home, in Europe and America in past centuries it was a common practice for children past the age of seven or so to leave home to become apprentices or servants in other households (Aries, 1962; Demos, 1970; E. S. Morgan, 1944). And, of course, seven-year-old boys in upper-class British families are to this day sent off to boarding schools. Finally, there are instances where infants do not live at home. During most of European history, when of course there were no feeding bottles, many babies were sent off to wet nurses or to baby farms to be nursed; they returned home, if they survived, after weaning, during the second or third year. Stephens notes two societies where infants leave home after weaning; among these two African peoples, the Hehe and the Thonga, the grandmother typically takes the child to her home after it has been weaned, and returns it to its parents several years later (1963, p. 17).

Nonkinsmen in the Home   Another reason for analyzing family and household separately — besides the *absence* of nuclear-family members — is that the household can also *include* people who are not members of the immediate family. Households of European peasant and craftsmen families in the distant and recent past commonly contained servants, apprentices, and lodgers. Servants, usually young people employed by the family with whom they lived, shared the family's food and shelter as part of their wages. They were not a distinct social class; being a servant for several years during one's youth was part of the experience of the most respectable and well-off families (Berkner, 1972; E. S. Morgan, 1944). Lodgers typically worked outside the family with whom they lived. In peasant households these servants and lodgers tended to be part of the family rather than simply "employees" or "tenants."

The legal definition of the household was very precise in Austria; it meant all the people living in the same house under the authority of the head of the household, whether or not they were members of the family. Moreover, as Otto Brunner has pointed out in his marvelous essay on the concept of the household in European history, *the word "family" was not commonly used in German until the eighteenth century — before that people spoke of belonging to a house or a household.* The Universal Lexicon (1735) for example defined the family as "a number of persons subject to the power and authority of the head of the household either by nature or by law"—"nature" referred to children, "law" to wife and servants. The idea that the entire household and not only the nuclear family group was the real basis of the peasant family organization was championed in the nineteenth century by the German sociologist Wilhelm Riehl. . . . (Berkner, 1972, p. 411) (Italics added)

In preindustrial England the households of craftsmen also included more than the immediate or nuclear family.

In the year 1619 the bakers of London described a typical bakery and its expenses (P. Laslett, 1965). The bakery was a household as well as a workshop; it contained about thirteen or fourteen people, including the baker and his wife and children, plus paid employees, apprentices, and servants. This group too was called a family:

. . . All these people ate in the house. . . . Except for the journeymen [paid employees], they were all obliged to sleep in the house at night and live together as a family.

The only word used at that time to describe such a group of people was "family." The man at the head of the group, the entrepreneur, the employer, or the manager, was then known as the master or the head of the family. He was father to some of its members and in place of father to the rest. There was no sharp distinction between his domestic and his economic functions. His wife was both his partner and his subordinate. . . . (P. Laslett, 1965, p. 2)

The key to the size of the household in preindustrial times was economic need. Homes were workplaces. When the farm or the craft needed and could support more hands, the household group expanded. In hard times, it contracted. The baker's household described above was atypically large.

In the American Household   The idea of outsiders living in the family is alien to most Americans. Even relatives such as in-laws tend to be defined as outsiders. It is taken for granted that households should consist only of husband, wife, and their minor children. As Margaret Mead described it:

The belief that every family should have a home of its own seems like a truism to which almost every American would assent without further thought. . . . Furthermore, each family should consist only of a husband, wife, and their minor children. All other forms of living are seen as having great disadvantages. (1949, p. 309)

Despite the truism, the presence of "outsiders" in the home has not been uncommon in America, even in recent times. In the seventeenth, eighteenth, and early nineteenth centuries, when homes were also workplaces, apprentices were part of the master's household. More recently—well into the twentieth century, in fact—boarders and lodgers were found in a sizable proportion of families at some point in their lives. And although taking in boarders was more common among poorer families, the practice could be found among the more affluent also (Modell, 1972).

The decline of boarding seems to have been associated with the rise, during the twentieth century, of a belief that the household should contain only the nuclear-family group, and the practical conditions that enabled this value to be acted upon—the availability of private homes and apartments, and the widespread ability to pay for them. One sociologist, Barbara Laslett (1973), has argued that family privacy, in principle and practice, distinguishes the modern nuclear family from its counterpart in the past. With the rise of communes and a variety of other new life styles in recent years, households have once again become more complex and open: adolescents leave home, other peoples' children may move in, husbands leave, and single people—male and female—form households. The evidence from anthropology and history suggests that such "deviations" are not rare and, further, that the private, self-contained nuclear-family household is a modern life style that has occurred only within the twentieth century, and mainly in America.

A House Is Not a Home   Recently some of the same problems that plagued the concept of the family have been raised with regard to the household. Consider, for example, the situation of a group of college students who share an apartment or a house, but have all their meals out and send all their dirty clothes to the laundry. Should this group be called a household? Or consider this situation: among the Ashanti, an African people (Fortes et al., 1947, p. 168), husbands and wives do not live together. Each partner lives with his or her relatives on the mother's side. Yet the wife prepares meals for the husband and children, and he provides his wife and children with clothes. The nuclear family doesn't form a household, yet they seem to be involved in household activities in a way that the college roommates are not. Then there is the situation in which households carry on domestic functions but are not composed of families. The arrangement of the two divorced men on the "Odd Couple" television show illustrates this kind of household.

In order to deal with distinctions like these, Bender (1967) has suggested that we ought to distinguish between "coresidence"—the roommate or dormitory situation—and "domestic" functions or activities, which have to do with the basic day-to-day necessities and trivia of living—the provision and preparation of food, the cleaning and mending of clothing, and the care of children:

> One is dealing, then, not with two distinct social phenomena—families and households—but with three distinct social phenomena: families, co-residential groups, and domestic functions. All three frequently correspond, both ideally and in fact (this is reflected in at least one meaning of our folk term "home," which implies a family residing together functioning as a domestic unit). The three also can and sometimes do vary independently. . . . (Bender, 1967, p. 495)

In sum, then, Bender proposes that the term "family" be reserved for kinship relations. Family members may or may not live together and may or may not engage in domestic relations. People can live together and carry on domestic functions without being families. Or people can simply live together without sharing in domestic activities.

In modern societies, of course, domestic functions need not be performed by the family. Indeed, this is one of the most important features that set off modern societies from traditional or preindustrial ones. Laslett, for example, describes how institutional life in preindustrial England was almost unknown; most people spent all of their days in small familial groups:

> There were no hotels, hostels, or blocks of flats for single persons, and very few hospitals and none of the kind we are familiar with, almost no young men and women living on their own. (P. Laslett, 1965, p. 11)

Yet the concept of domesticity seems to capture an important part of the essence of what we mean by family, and it is useful to distinguish it from kinship on one side and living under one roof on the other. Domesticity involves both intimacy and trivia. Sharing meals, for example, appears to represent a higher degree of intimacy — of communion — than merely living together under the same roof. Berkner (1972, p. 412) notes that servants in peasant households usually ate with the family, out of the same pot. Later, when the relation between master and servant became less patriarchal and more like that of boss and worker, the practice of eating together stopped.

This is not to suggest that intimate environments are necessarily better and pleasanter than less intimate ones; not only our deeper joys but our most painful miseries are enacted in them.

The Meaning of Kinship

Perhaps at this point the reader is bothered by all this scholarly nit-picking about the definition of the family and household. Surely the family and kinship are based on the solid bedrock of biology: parenthood and sexual intercourse! Some scholars do argue that family relationships reflect underlying biological realities, but a number of others reject the idea of direct reflection. The social facts of family life often violate the biological facts in various ways. In some societies, for example, it is necessary to distinguish between the *genitor* — the biological father — and the *pater* — the man who plays the father role. Thus, among the Tallensi, an African society, any child a woman bears belongs to her husband's descent group. Even though he knows he is not the biological father of the child, the husband is said to experience all the emotions of true fatherhood, while the genitor is said to feel no fatherly emotions at all (Zelditch, 1964, p. 465).

Kin relations also violate biology through fictional relationships such as adoption and godparenting. Such relationships are both meaningful and common in many societies, although only recently have they been studied to any great extent. Two kinds of fictional relationships occur. In one kind the fictionalization is so complete that everybody involved "forgets" the relationship isn't real. For example, an orphan might join the household of a relative, treat its members as parents and siblings, and be treated as a "real" child (Fallers, 1965, p. 77). The other kind of fictional kinship maintains the distinction between fictional and real, as in the godparent relation, which was widespread in Mediterranean Europe and is important in Latin America. Some scholars are coming to believe that such fictional relations tell us more about the true nature of kinship than those instances where the biological facts and the social facts coincide.

David Schneider, for example, has argued that kinship has as much to do with real biological facts as supernatural beliefs have to do with the real nature of ghosts and spirits (1965). Both kinship and religion, he argues, are systems of cultural beliefs that originate in people's heads, rather than in some reality out there.

To be sure, there are biological facts, but kinships systems make use of these facts in various symbolic ways. The biological relationships involved in kinship and marriage

represent something other than what they are . . . they represent diffuse, enduring solidarity. They symbolize those kinds of interpersonal relations which human beings as biological beings must have if they are to be born and grow up. They symbolize trust . . . they stand for the fact that birth survives death, and that solidarity is enduring. . . . (Schneider, 1968, p. 116)

Schneider does not suggest that actual family life is characterized by perfect love, trust, and solidarity, only that the family symbolizes these ideal qualities. For example, the symbolic meaning of kinship is shown when people in social movements call themselves brothers and sisters, and people in communes call themselves "families."

The Politics of Family Definitions

Much research in the social sciences, especially that about the family, is guided by concern with social problems of one kind or another. What one defines as a problem, however, depends greatly on what one defines as normal and what as problematic (see Skolnick and Currie, 1973). The definition of the normal family as a married couple with their children residing together leads to conceiving of any variation as a social problem—for example, common-law unions, husband and wife living apart, illegitimacy, homosexual unions, bachelorhood, spinsterhood, communes, even childlessness (see Ball, 1972). In the same way, definitions of age and sex roles dictate what is to be defined as normal and what as problematic. In general the family literature is full of concern about such "problems" as broken homes, working mothers, illegitimacy, dominant wives, weak fathers and husbands, and children being given too much or too little love, independence, or discipline. Many of these problems derive what are essentially political assumptions about normal sex and power relationships within the family, and how people should live.

There may indeed be much that is problematic about atypical family situations, but the assumption that the heart of the difficulty lies in deviations from the usual family forms and norms obscures what the real problem might be. Rodman discusses the prevailing assumptions concerning family problems as follows:

> Are interfaith marriages the problem or is it organized religion and its demands that is the problem? Are "illegitimacy," "desertion" and "common law" unions *problems* of the lower class, or are they *solutions* of the lower class to more basic problems? Do we take the fact that there are few interracial marriages and few fulltime career women to indicate that these matters are somehow against human nature and therefore best to avoid? Or do we take these as indicative of cultural obstacles that should be removed?
>
> Are the findings of role differentiation between the sexes sufficient grounds for continuing to advocate a traditional system of such differentiation? (Rodman, 1965, p. 450)

The issue of illegitimacy provides a particularly useful instance of the way value judgments enter into social-science concepts and methodology. At first glance illegitimacy would seem to be an easy concept to define and measure. A child is either legitimate or not at birth, and this fact enters into the birth records. Most people define a child as illegitimate at birth if its mother is unmarried, as do the public agencies who calculate illegitimacy rates. Actually, however, illegitimacy can come about in other ways. For example, the mother may be married to one man, but have her child fathered by another. Or the mother may be separated or divorced at the time of birth. A child is also illegitimate if the parents live together as a stable couple but are not married. Some researchers have argued that illegitimacy statistics are not as "hard" and accurate as they are generally supposed to be. Teele and Schmidt (1970), for example, argue that official statistics tend to underreport illegitimate births to white women and to married women, and thus to overestimate the degree to which illegitimate births occur among blacks and the unmarried. They also question the practice of labeling children as illegitimate. Philip Hauser, himself a demographer, argues that demographers and statisticians use "inherited and probably inaccurate conceptual frameworks." He states:

I think it is important to remember that the standards we employ are based on our own categories of legitimate and illegitimate births. According to our standards, half the population in Latin America is illegitimate, and all of the population with whom I lived for two years in Burma is illegitimate and I'm not sure what that means. (Hauser, 1970, p. 148)

What *does* "illegitimacy" mean? Is it a social problem, and if so, why? Is illegitimacy itself the problem, striking at the very basis of the social order and jeopardizing the "continuity of society"? (Goode, 1964, p. 21.) Or is illegitimacy only a symptom of other social problems such as poverty and discrimination? Or is the problem of illegitimacy located in those who label children as illegitimate in order to "punish" and "brutalize" unwed mothers and their children? (Teele and Schmidt, 1970, p. 144.) A local minister recently introduced his new grandchild to his congregation. His daughter and the father of the child had decided— responsibly, he thought—that they didn't want to marry.

His only regret about the baby, he said, was that the child was valued less by the society than other infants, as indicated among other things by the word "bastard" as a term of abuse. There is no way to decide "scientifically" on the correct answers to the preceding questions. How one answers them depends on basic assumptions about society and human nature.

Malinowski, the distinguished anthropologist, has written of the principle of legitimacy as a universal social law:

. . . The most important moral and legal rule concerning the physiological side of kinship is that no child should be brought into the world without a man—and one man at that—assuming the role of sociological father, that is, guardian and protector, and male link between the child and the rest of the community.

I think this generalization amounts to a universal sociological law and as such I have called it in some of my previous writings *The Principle of Legitimacy.* (Malinowski, in Coser, 1964, p. 13)

Sociologists and anthropologists have built an extensive literature trying to show that the numerous exceptions to Malinowski's law were only apparent and not real. For example, there has been a debate concerning woman-headed households, particularly in the countries of the Caribbean (see B. N. Adams, 1968; Goode, 1964, p. 28; Smith, 1956). In these areas illegitimate births are as high as 70 to 80 percent of total births. On one side of the argument, the proponents of the universal nuclear family and the principle of legitimacy argue that these woman-headed or matriarchal households are abnormal, incomplete, or disorganized forms of the family. Further, the argument goes, the people who live in such arrangements think so too, because they value the nuclear family as an ideal in spite of their inability to live up to it. The other side of the argument states that to assume a variant family form must be abnormal is scientifically untenable: "The first job of science is, after all, to study what *is*, not what might be or could be" (B. N. Adams, 1968, p. 47). Rather than assume at the outset that a given family form is universal, we should assume that any variations we find are equally viable alternatives, at least until the contrary is demonstrated.

The Family, Science, and Values

It is questionable whether it is possible to study the family in the same way that natural scientists can study chemical reactions, the movement of the earth's crust, or the actions of DNA. In recent years the idea that the physical sciences can serve as models for sociology and psychology has come under increasing criticism. In this view the notion of a "value-free" social science is a myth that allows values to operate covertly, to sneak in the back door. That social scientists differ among themselves on basic assumptions points to important differences between the study of human social life and the natural sciences. Gordon Allport writes in the introduction to *The Handbook of Social Psychology:*

> The theories of social psychology are rarely, if ever, chaste scientific productions. They usually gear into the prevailing political and social atmosphere. Dewey (1899) has shown that this is so. For example, an aristocracy produces no psychology of individual differences, for the individual is unimportant unless he happens to belong to the higher classes. Dewey has likewise pointed out that dualistic psychology flourishes best when one group holds a monopoly of social power and wishes to do the thinking and planning, while others remain the docile, unthinking instruments of execution. And apologists for the status quo, he added in another context, are those who most readily declare human nature to be unalterable. (Allport, in Lindzey and Aronson, 1968)

Even the most scientific-minded and determinedly neutral social scientist must choose what to study and analyze, and in so choosing inevitably becomes involved in value judgments concerning human nature and society. Gouldner (1970, p. 29) writes that social and social-psychological theories contain at least two parts or elements. One is the set of statements that make up the theory itself—for example, Freud's theory of psychosexual development, Parsons' theory of the nuclear family, the various theories of personality and learning in psychology. The other part of any social theory is a set of tacit beliefs about the world, society, and human nature. These beliefs or "domain assumptions," as Gouldner (1970) calls them, rarely if ever enter into discussions of the theory, but they help determine why the sociologist or psychologist finds certain theories convincing and others not.

It is impossible to write about the family or do research in the field without choosing among contrasting assumptions about society and human nature. For example, is society a necessary curb on people's impulse—the only force that keeps people from murdering, raping, and plundering each other—or is "the whole of our present civilization . . . a captivity that man has somehow imposed on himself?" (Laing, in Boyers and Orill, 1969, p. 245.) Is the individual realized most fully by forming ties with other people, or are all social bonds a form of bondage? Is the family a refuge from the pressures of society, or is it the psychological agent of society, transmitting those pressures to the family members? Are people inexorably shaped by their life events and circumstances, or do they retain some freedom of choice in their actions? Are human beings creatures of purpose, choice, and reason, or is their behavior determined by the contingencies of reinforcement to which they have been exposed? Does "science" demand that human behavior be explained without making any statements about people's thoughts, feelings, and intentions? Or is it impossible to understand behavior without such statements? These sorts of questions can't be answered by going out and doing research; they have to be answered before any research can be done. How the researcher answers them determines what he will choose to study and the kind of interpretations he will make.

Thus value judgments and assumptions enter into methodology in fairly direct ways. They dictate what questions shall be asked and how they shall be answered. For example, the concept of the universal nuclear family as the basic social atom or unit dictates that researchers hunt for the similarities among family systems, both in our own culture and others. Differences in family forms and functions must be handled mainly as apparent challenges to the universal nuclear-family doctrine. Also, in looking at how sex and age rules are carried out in different cultures, the emphasis is on forcing divergent practices into a framework of universal male and female roles, and universal age grades.

Scientific arguments often concern not so much facts but how facts are to be interpreted. For example, we noted the debates about how to interpret the statistical facts concerning the prevalence of woman-headed households in the Caribbean. Does such prevalence indicate social disorganization? An adaptive response to poverty? A subculture with different values? Or does it merely indicate an alternative way of living? Should the researcher focus attention on how people actually behave, how they think they behave, how they think they ought to behave, or all three of these? Sometimes arguments center around what is or is not a fact: Has there been a sexual revolution in the United States in the last decade? Is the nuclear family found in all societies?

Social scientists who disagree about these matters often find it hard to carry on a discussion with each other. It is very much like a political disagreement—they find themselves talking past each other, and using the same terms with very different meanings. They just don't speak the same language. They differ ideologically. They have different paradigms or models of reality.

Paradigms

The paradigm concept has been elaborated by Thomas Kuhn in a work that is becoming a modern classic: *The Structure of Scientific Revolutions* (1962). In this book Kuhn attempts to explain the historical development of the natural sciences, but his ideas have an even greater generality. Kuhn argues against the popular assumption that the natural sciences have progressed by the gradual building up of more and more facts. Rather, he argues, science advances by a series of conceptual and ideological leaps which change the definitions of the facts themselves. Kuhn calls the process "paradigm change." Within the natural sciences, some of the most important paradigms have been Copernicus' theory that the sun, rather than the earth, is the center of the solar system, Newton's dynamics, and Einstein's theory of relativity. Kuhn argues that new paradigms replace old ones by revolutionary conceptions that transform the way the world looks, as well as the rules by which science is carried out.

A paradigm is not so much a theory as it is a taken-for-granted way of looking at things and doing things. A paradigm may start out as a theory—as Copernicus' theory or the theory of gravity—but after acceptance it becomes part of perceived reality. A paradigm also acts like a blinder. A scientist, for example, when immersed in a particular paradigm, will reject or misperceive facts that cannot be fitted into the paradigm. Research on extrasensory perception serves as a recent example of a field that has been ignored by many scientists because its findings, even if valid, cannot easily be fitted into existing paradigms.

For Kuhn a paradigm involves much more than just a set of verbal statements that people agree or disagree about: the earth revolves around the sun versus the sun moves around the earth. A paradigm tells us what to look at and what to ignore, what is central to the phenomena under study, and what belongs in the background.

Perhaps the best illustration of the idea of a paradigm and paradigm change is the way ideas about the stars have changed. Like family life the basic observations of the sky can be made by anyone. Unlike the family the heavens do not change according to the historical period or culture from which they are observed. The sun and moon stand out from a background of stars. Some of these stars seem to keep the same relative positions, some of them move among the other stars at varying speeds. Most theories before Copernicus assumed that the earth was the center of the universe and did not move. The stability of the earth was not regarded as a theoretical statement but, rather, as a simple perceptual fact. However, the everyday experience of living on the earth and looking up at the sky could give rise to a number of very different theories. One theory, for example, postulated a three-layered dome arching over a flat earth. Another theory postulated spheres within spheres. Today, when we look up at the sky, we feel comfortable with the view that the sun is the center of the solar system. We can look at a sunset and see it either as the sun going down, or the earth turning away from the sun.

In somewhat the same way, we can look at a community of people and see it as a collection of nuclear families. Or we can see it as composed of sets of blood kin who have exchanged children in marriage. Or we can look at the community as consisting of dyads or pairs of people—husbands and wives, mothers and children, fathers and sons, mothers and daughters, sisters and brothers. Or we can look at the same society as a collection of essentially isolated individuals who have convinced themselves and each other that they have certain bonds with and claims upon each other.

Kuhn argues that paradigm changes do not come about through the gradual building up of bits of information which eventually form a more accurate picture of the part of nature under discussion. Instead, he sees the change as a sudden, revolutionary transformation of the way the world looks. The process of paradigm change resembles the perceptual switch that occurs in the demonstration pictures of the Gestalt psychologists: a shape that may be seen as either a rabbit or a duck, two profiles that turn into a vase, an old witch who becomes a young woman, a box that may be seen from the top or the bottom. It is possible to switch back and forth between one interpretation and the other, but you cannot see both clearly at the same time: each image "uses up" all the lines and spaces.

Besides serving as models for interpreting experience, scientific paradigms are also models of how research is to be done. Studies study, and research centers around, a particular set of problems and questions. For example, all physicists begin by learning to experiment with and to explain such problems as inclined planes and pendulums. Psychology students used to learn how to run white rats through mazes.

Family Paradigms   In the study of the family, there are no paradigms in the sense of distinctive, contrasting theories, such as those in the natural sciences. Nor are there "schools" such as the Gestalt, the behaviorist, the psychoanalytic in psychology. The difference between various approaches to the family is more elusive. In 1960, for example, Hill and Hansen identified five basic approaches to the study of the family. Later scholars condensed the five into three (see Broderick, 1971). One approach looks at the family as a social institution in relation to society as a whole; the second looks at the family in terms of the group interaction of the family members; the third looks at the family as it changes over the life cycle. Contrasting definitions of what the family *is* may also be said to be paradigms, or pictures of reality.

There seem to be at least four paradigms or programs or schemata for interpreting the experiences of family life in a society. As in the Gestalt pictures and the scientific paradigms mentioned earlier, they tend to be incommensurate with each other. They subdivide reality in different ways, define and group objects differently, and employ different concepts of space, time, and human nature. These paradigms include, first, the familiar nuclear or conjugal family model—

what we mean in America by the term "my family" (Goode, 1963; Schneider, 1968). The second model of the family, based mainly on blood ties, is termed the consanguine family by anthropologists. It is also known as the extended family.

Some of Birdwhistell's (1966) Kentucky subjects, for example, who lived in interdependent or extended families, had very different conceptions and definitions of "family" from their friends, neighbors, and even spouses who had grown up in more nuclear or, as Birdwhistell calls them, segmented families. The interdependent family member seemed to define family in terms of blood kinship. He expected to continue all his life the intense involvement with kinfolk he had known as a child. He would not expect this involvement to be affected by reaching maturity, marrying, or work. In fact, the main purpose of Birdwhistell's research was to learn why some rural Kentuckians would migrate to other areas of the country and try to be "successful," while others who seemed much like them would remain behind in their hometowns. He believes he found the explanation in the different family patterns of the movers and nonmovers.

The family in the traditional extended-family model is a very different entity from the series of separate units in space and time that make up the nuclear-family model. The traditional family is continuous in space and time, unbounded by household walls, and immortal. Marriage, birth, maturity, even death do not reduce the central unit. The genetic family tree defines not only genetic connections, but ongoing obligations and involvements. Rather than the marriage of grown children leaving behind an empty nest, the in-law line may add additional family members:

> If the marriage is, in family terms, a good one, the affinal relatives/in-laws of the family member become one's own "almost like family." And as these affinal relatives meet at funeral, church, and family gatherings, they gain kinship status and are called by kinship terms. (Birdwhistell, 1966, p. 209)

Furthermore, in the traditional-family system, the husband-wife pair is by no means the obvious core of the family. As a 39-year-old English mother of five put it:

> I couldn't get on without me mother. I could get on without me husband. I don't notice him. (In Kerr, 1958, p. 40)

Yet Birdwhistell's interviewees did not perceive the unique quality of their family life. When asked directly about their family relationships, the "interdependent" family people talked in the stereotyped terms and imagery of the nuclear-family model. It was as if the nuclear-family imagery had blotted out the experiences of those who had had a very different life style from the standard husband-wife, parent-child unit. And if there was any awareness of being different, it was stated with a sense of shame.

People who hold to one of the foregoing models may doubt that the other one is really a viable family. They are likely to see people in the other family model as not quite healthy or normal psychologically. For example, Birdwhistell (1966) notes that his nuclear-family subjects tended to define people with traditional-family ties as immature, dependent, and lacking in ambition. The traditional people, on the other hand, were likely to feel that people with the nuclear-family

definitions were cold, selfish, and too driven by ambition. As for the family models we shall turn to next, the holders of both the traditional model and the nuclear model probably would think them mad and unworkable.

The first of these "deviant" family models is the communal one. The recent rebirth of the communal movement in the United States and other places has brought to many people an awareness that there are indeed alternatives to family life based either on blood kinship or the married couple and their children. This alternative is based on primary ties of mystic brotherhood or communion (Schmalenbach, 1961; Zablocki, 1971). The spread of the communal movement has also brought to light the fact that this form of family has a long and prolific history, reaching back to early Christian times at least. Within recent centuries the communal tradition has been associated in Europe with a number of Protestant sects as well as Utopian socialists and other idealists. The communes are often compared by both members and observers to the traditional extended family. Many contemporary communes consciously try to recreate the extended family on a nonkinship basis.

The fourth family pardigm is defined more by exclusion than by a focus on a particular family form. It makes no assumptions about a particular form of the family, or the family itself being necessary as the basic building block of society. The key difference between this paradigm and the others is that the individual is not defined by his place in a network of kin. He or she is not primarily a member of this clan or that tribe, as in the traditional family, nor primarily a son or father, mother or daughter, husband or wife, as in the second paradigm, nor a communal brother or sister. The family exists, of course, but it does not occupy all of the social space, nor is it the primary source of sociability. The two basic elements in this paradigm include the individual, considered apart from either blood or marriage ties, and an urban society, which supplies social density and a fairly high level of technology. Perhaps we should call it the "cosmopolitan model." Ralph Linton, the anthropologist, has written of how all kinds of family bonds are weakened in modern urban settings:

Breakdowns of kin ties and of the close social integration of individuals and conjugal family groups are no new thing in history. They were an accompaniment of urbanization and suddenly increased spatial mobility in ancient as well as modern civilization. Nevertheless, there is another factor in the present situation which, if it is not altogether new, is at least of unprecedented importance. This is the progressive diminution of the economic dependence of spouses upon each other. . . .

In the modern urban community the delicatessen, the steam laundry, ready-made clothes, and above all the opening to women of attractive and well-paid occupations have done more to undermine the sanctity of marriage than has any conceivable loss of faith in its religious sanctions. Under present conditions, adult men and women are at last in a position to satisfy their basic needs in the absence of any sort of familial association, either conjugal or consanguine. In the anonymity of city life and with the development of effective techniques for contraception even the sexual needs of both can be met without entering into permanent unions or entailing serious penalties. The revolutionary effect of these developments upon the family as an institution can scarcely be overrated. (Linton, 1959, p. 48)

Thus a person may be living in a torrent of social life, as in Aries' description of medieval life, or may combine public sociability with friend sociability, with family life and privacy. The common core underlying these models is the *individual* as the irreducible social atom, not the *family*. This model does not assume the close interdependence of family and society as in the other models. It does not assume a correspondence between kinship, living together, sexuality, and domestic functions such as child care, care of the sick, meal preparation (Bender, 1967). The emphasis on the individual implies that the family is *not* the building block of society.

Summary

The most familiar subjects are often the most difficult to study because we take them for granted. This is especially true of the family. In America the nuclear family — two parents and their minor children — in a home of their own is defined as *the family*. Variations from this pattern are seen as unfortunate and abnormal. It also has been widely believed that the nuclear family is universal.

When we look at family life in other societies, however, and our own historical past, we find that variations in family form and living arrangements are rather common. Nuclear-family members are often found living apart. The household may contain nonkin living together as a family. Households themselves may only be places where people sleep, while eating, child care, and other domestic functions occur elsewhere.

In trying to understand family life, family scholars have used a variety of different approaches or frameworks of interpretation. As in the rest of social science, family scholars disagree on basic assumptions concerning the nature of the individual, the family, and society.

IDEAL AND REALITY
IN FAMILY AND SOCIETY

Chapter 2

Social thought, unlike natural science, tends to be cyclical, returning to its roots periodically for sustenance, reassessment, reformulation. The study of man is passing through such a period now. . . . The comfortable assumption of the social sciences that human activity functions to assure the continuity and stability of the structures of society has fallen victim to the evidence of the recent past.

Robert Murphy, *The Dialectics of Social Life*

Chapter Two

Every theory of the family implies a set of assumptions about human nature and about the nature of society. As a matter of fact, all of us employ such assumptions whether we are aware of them or not. For example, many people would agree with such statements as the following: the family is the basic unit of society; a civilization cannot "survive" if its family system does not work well; the family reflects a natural division of power between parents and children. Thus the family seems to represent both social necessity and individual biological inclination. This duality has led one writer to describe the family as a "slippery" concept:

> The study of human life—or of behavior in general—has focused on three classes of elements (or systems): the individual, the family or small intimate group, and the society or culture. In this kind of classification, the family is inevitably in the middle. Perhaps because it is in the middle, it tends to be a slippery concept. It is slippery not only in definition, but also in focus. It is rare to complete an article or book whose title indicates it is about the family without finding the discussion sliding away from the family either to the individual or to the society, or even both. (Troll, 1969, p. 222)

In short, the study of the family often seems to be an extension of the study of the individual on the one hand, or the society on the other. Thus psychological and psychiatric writings emphasize the individual, and how the family serves individual needs and shapes the personality of children. In sociology the family tends to be viewed as part of the larger society. The emphasis is on the society and how it functions; the family is looked at in terms of how it meshes with the larger social order. Both of these approaches to the family may impede understanding family life as a distinct social phenomenon.

> Is it possible . . . to study the family without reference to either the individual or the society? Sometimes, faced with the difficulties of sticking to a framework for viewing the family, one is led to wonder whether . . . the concept of the family is a reification. Is it perhaps less "real," particularly in the context of modern social conditions, than the concept of society itself? (Troll, 1969, p. 223)

In this chapter we will explore how both approaches to the family—the individual and the societal—have tended to lead to unreal notions of family life. More specifically, we are going to examine how the sociological approach known as functionalism, and the psychological and psychiatric approaches to the family based on Freudian theory, have given rise to idealized conceptions.

Functionalism and the Family

Like the character in the play who was surprised to learn that he had been speaking prose all his life, most people are probably unaware that the set of ideas they take for granted about the family and the relations within the family represent a particular brand of sociological thought. When we speak of the "survival" of a society, or the "need" of a society for a stable family life, or for the orderly replacement of one generation by another, we are speaking in functional terms whether we realize it or not. It is impossible, of course, to summarize a complex body of thought like functionalism in a few paragraphs. Functionalism itself is not a unified body of thought, but has several opposing schools within its general outlook. Nevertheless, the basic assumption of functionalism is that human activities are integrative—that is, so organized as to assure the continuity and stability of society. Society is viewed as a structure—an organization of interrelated parts—rather than as a collection of discrete elements. The "parts" of society may be thought of as *institutions,* such as the family or the schools, *social roles,* such as mother, father, worker, manager, or *social practices* and *customs.* The way these parts fit together in functional thought is not, however, like a clock or some other complex mechanical structure, but rather like a living organism.

If we were to examine the body of an animal, any organ we found would be assumed to play some vital role in keeping the animal alive. The functional analyst similarly assumes that social customs or institutions persist because they serve a necessary social function, some ongoing usefulness to the society as a whole. Further, a living organism tends to be in a state of dynamic equilibrium or homeostasis: for example, a warm-blooded animal maintains a constant body temperature in spite of changes in the surrounding temperature. The functionalist sees society as also maintaining such a dynamic equilibrium; the society is not static, but changes are adjusted to smoothly.

Functional statements tend to pertain to a universal, timeless present—as in the idea that the nuclear family has existed everywhere since time immemorial, or Malinowski's rule of legitimacy. Accordingly, functionalism raises generalizations into universal laws. The assumption is often made that what has been true in the past must be true in the future as well. Thus when a functionalist states that no society has ever had social or sexual equality, he implies that such inequality must always be a part of human society.

Functionalism began in anthropology as one way of making sense out of the strange—to Europeans—ways of primitive societies. Earlier generations of anthropologists had sometimes explained certain customs as "survivals" from an earlier period in that society. Functional anthropologists such as Malinowski and Radcliffe-Brown opposed any such historical explanations; if a custom persisted, they argued, it must have some ongoing usefulness, serve some "function" in the integration of society or the maintenance of social order.

There is some confusion about whether functionalism is a particular theory or whether all social theories are functional theories. For example, it has been argued that functional analysis is nothing more than the basic operating procedure of any social scientist—he looks at aspects of social life and tries to determine how they are related, their causes and effects, and so on. This is true, but it is also misleading. Lumping all social scientists together as analysts of social functions obscures the differences between them. There is no name of consequence in the history of the social sciences who is not in some measure concerned with relationships between parts of culture.

> The contrast between different kinds of sociocultural theories is not built around the question of whether sociocultural systems have parts which are integrated with or affected by other parts, but rather, which parts, and how often, and with what kind of effect, and for how long? (Harris, 1968, p. 521)

In short, we have to distinguish between different kinds of functionalism — of Parsons, Marx, Freud, to name only a few. For Parsons social institutions like the family and religion function to maintain social stability and consensus. For Marx social institutions serve the interests of the dominant class. For Freud social institutions control human instincts and anxieties. Thus religion, for example, can be interpreted as an institution binding people in society together, as the opiate of the masses, or as an "illusion," as Freud put it, created by the childish dread of being alone in the world. The family may be seen as performing the functions necessary for the survival of society, as perpetuating the power structure, or as satisfying basic instincts.

Functionalism has come under increasing criticism in recent years. For example, the habit of thinking of society as an organism has been attacked as arbitrary and misleading. The assumption that certain practices and institutions are like vital organs predetermines that they are both necessary and sound.

If a social institution is as necessary to society as the liver is to the body, it would be dangerous to change it or remove it. By ignoring alternatives to contemporary social structures, functionalism tends to assume that things *must* be as they are, especially in the area of familial and sexual statuses and roles. Moreover, by implying — without arguing the point — that the fundamental goal of society is the same as that of an individual organism — surviving and maintaining a steady state — the organismic metaphor turns out to support politically conservative positions.

Perhaps the most pointed criticism of functionalism has been offered by sociologist Ralf Dahrendorf (1958), who argues that functional sociology employs a Utopian vision, in the tradition of a long line of writers beginning with Plato. Dahrendorf's point-by-point comparison of "Utopia" with the social system as posited by functional sociology is important in two respects: first, it enlarges our understanding of the relation between the institution of the family and society; and, second, it suggests what is basically wrong with conventional understandings of family life.

Utopia and Its Discontents

Most Utopias, whether "good" ones like Plato's Republic, or "bad" ones like Orwell's 1984, tend to have a number of common features. Dahrendorf says they are "societies from which change is absent" (p. 116). Utopias are suspended in time, beyond or outside history. They have no past or only a vague one, and no future. Not only are Utopias isolated in time, but they are also isolated in space. Outside influences are simply irrelevant—in no way is it possible to disrupt their essential tranquility.

There is nothing to argue about in Utopia. Everybody agrees on goals and values, and on the ways and means for reaching these goals. Most Utopian writers, says Dahrendorf, make it clear that in their society, conflict about values and institutional arrangements simply cannot arise or is just unnecessary. Thus there are no strikes or revolutions, or even parliaments in which opposing groups compete for power. Equality is not a feature of most Utopias; in fact, they are often caste societies—for example, the people in *Brave New World* who were genetically engineered to be the working drones of the society. But again, harmony prevails since everyone accepts the power arrangements as they are. The oppressed in Utopias do not see themselves as oppressed, and do not revolt.

In some of the literary Utopias, such as *Brave New World* or *1984*, the plot centers around a nonconformist who does not go along with the system. This nonconformist is often an outsider of some kind, such as a survivor from a previous society. It is something of a problem for the Utopian writer to explain how a dissident can arise in a "perfect" social structure: ". . . 'outsiders' are not (and cannot be) products of the social structure of utopia, but deviants, pathological cases infected with some unique disease" (Dahrendorf, 1958, p. 117).

In addition to social harmony, timelessness, and uniformity of values, a fourth feature of Utopias concerns what might be called their metabolic properties—that is, how they maintain equilibrium and replace worn-out parts. Since Utopias consist of mortal beings, they face the problem of producing and training new generations of Utopians. This creates a major risk to the stability of Utopia, and Utopian writers have given a good deal of attention to such matters. They have to figure out how sexual intercourse and reproduction will be managed, how children will be cared for and educated, and how these children will be assigned to their work positions. Dahrendorf points out that the inventors of Utopias could solve all these problems in one stroke by making people immortal, but they usually avoid this solution. Nevertheless, the Utopian world operates *as if* people were immortal—that is, new generations replace their parents just as body cells replace each other, preserving the intactness of the body. Everything that happens in Utopia serves to uphold the existing state of affairs, the value consensus and general agreement about the way things are done. Dahrendorf writes:

All processes going on in utopian societies follow recurrent patterns and occur within, and as part of, the design of the whole. Not only do they not upset the status quo: they affirm and sustain it, and it is in order to do so that most utopians allow them to happen at all. (p. 117)

Dahrendorf embarked on his travels in Utopia to advance a major critique of structural functionalism, particularly the work of Talcott Parsons in *The Social System*. Dahrendorf argues that the vision of society in this brand of sociology corresponds point by point with all the elements of Utopia. Any social system—for example, American society—is seen by the functional theorists as a community with a self-correcting equilibrium, based on consensus and isolated in time and space. In the social-system model of society, change is not absent but is seen as abnormal or unusual, something that has to be explained. Dahrendorf and other critics take functional sociology to task for generating a conservative complacency about society and its problems, and also for being boringly unconcerned with "riddles of experience." He feels that both theory and research "have both largely dispensed with that prime impulse of all science

and scholarship, the puzzlement over specific, concrete, and . . . empirical problems. Many sociologists have lost the simple impulse of curiosity . . ." (p. 123).

There is no need to go into details of Dahrendorf's indictment of sociological theory as essentially Utopian. It should be noted, however, that Dahrendorf admits the comparison does an injustice to Utopian writers. They constructed their ideal societies to make moral criticisms or even indictments of existing societies. Functional sociologists, by contrast, implicitly justify the status quo in their models of society.

What does Dahrendorf suggest as an alternative to the Utopian social system of functional sociology? Along with a number of others, he has suggested a conflict model of society. Dahrendorf suggests that Utopian definitions of the normal and expectable, as opposed to the unusual and in need of explanation, be turned on their heads. Thus change and conflict are to be seen as constants in society. Instead of assuming that social organizations remain the same until something happens to change them, Dahrendorf suggests we assume that change is constant unless something intervenes to stop it. The task of the sociologist should be to try to determine what is interfering with the normal process of change.

In the same vein, Dahrendorf argues that conflict is always present in social life. We should become suspicious or curious to find a social organization or society that exhibits no conflict, although the conflict need not be violent or uncontrolled.

Finally, the conflict model of society is based on the notion of constraint. Rather than being held together by consensus, societies and social organizations are based on the coercion of some by others. This is the source of conflict and change. Constraints lead to conflict, and conflict leads to change. Dahrendorf acknowledges that the idea that conflict is always present in social life is not a pleasant one, but it is indispensable for an understanding of social problems.

The Family as a Little Utopia We have devoted so much space to this issue because of its direct relevance to the study of the family. The image of the nuclear family in much of psychology, psychiatry, anthropology, and sociology corresponds with the model of Utopia outlined above.

The social scientist's views of the family fit the Utopian model in two distinct ways: as part of the Utopian social system as a whole, and as a miniature Utopian system in itself. As part of the social system, the family carries out vital functions: it helps maintain the equilibrium of the system by replacing and training new generations. As we saw earlier, Utopian writers from Plato on have been preoccupied with the family and education. The introduction of children into the social system brings with it an element of risk. There is always the possibility of a generation gap to threaten the stability of the system. Social theorists have also been strikingly preoccupied with the family and with the "problem" of socialization, including both education and assignment of people to occupational slots. Like the Utopian writers, functional sociologists speak in terms of the survival of the society.

It is readily apparent that what will terminate a society will not disintegrate an individual, at least not when he is viewed mainly as a biological organism. It should be evident, however, that the ways in which society meets its imperatives for survival have implications for the individual's socialization and that in actuality the requisites of continuing social life come down to what is largely a set of requirements for individual socialization. (Inkeles, 1968, pp. 81–82)

In short, the functional view of the family fits the Utopian model of regulated, orderly change: "Children are born and socialized and allocated until they die; new children are born, and the same thing happens all over again" (Dahrendorf, 1958, p. 121).

As a little world unto itself, the family in both popular and professional thought is also a Utopia. The family is suspended in time and isolated in space; it is outside of history, and not deeply affected by social surroundings. Major historical changes, such as the industrial revolution, do have their effect on the family, but these are only a matter of changing the relative importance of one of the basic functions. The family, like society, is assumed to adapt to change. In advanced industrial societies, for example, the state takes over the education of older children, but the nuclear family emphasizes infant care and emotional support for its members. In the same way, cultural differences in kinship patterns and so forth are explained as surface differences which do not change the separateness and distinctiveness of the nuclear-family group. Mother, father, and children still constitute the basic unit.

The family as a little social system also fits the model of Utopian harmony and consensus. There is basic agreement on values, and how these values are to be achieved in practice. Like most Utopias the family is a system of unequal statuses, a hierarchy in which the order of priority is men/women, adults/children. Yet in the conventional assumptions this class or caste system does not give rise to conflict, nor is it even recognized as such by the family members. For in living up to their prescribed roles, they are presumed to be carrying out their natural functions. Thus, in acting out the roles of male, female, and child, each person acts out his or her own biological and psychological predestination. Further, mother and father are also acting out the cultural rules learned in their own families: they are replacing their own parents. In short, the family is envisioned as a system of perfectly interlocking needs.

The infant's need for care matches the mother's need to mother. The needs of mother and children for economic support match the need of the husband-father to fulfill his masculine nature by providing for his family. All of this is familiar to anyone living in America who reads popular or professional writings on the family, but perhaps a sample will illustrate the way these ideas are usually presented. The following description of the nuclear family comes from a book by a well-known professor of psychiatry, one of the leading theorists of the family in that field. This description of the normal nuclear family serves to introduce the author's theory of the family origins of schizophrenia, which he assumes results from a failure to live up to the following norms:

1   The nuclear family is composed of two generations, each with different needs, prerogatives, and tasks. . . . The parents . . . seek to merge themselves and their backgrounds into a new unit that satisfies the needs of both and completes their personalities in a relationship that is permanent for them. . . . The parents serve as guides, educators, and models for the offspring. They provide nurturance and give of themselves so that the children can develop. . . .

2   The family is also divided into two genders with differing but complementary functions and role allocations as well as anatomical differences. The feminine role derives from the woman's biological structure and is related to nurturance of children and the maintenance of a home, leading to emphasis upon interest in interpersonal relations and emotional harmony—an expressive-affectional role. The male role is related to the support and protection of the family and leads to an emphasis upon instrumental-adaptive leadership characteristics. . . .

3   The bonds between family members are held firm by erotic and affectional ties. . . .

4   The family forms a shelter for its members within the society and from the remainder of society. . . . However, the family must reflect and transmit the societal ways. . . . (Lidz, 1963, pp. 51–53)

The family system outlined above can in no way give rise to serious strain or conflict. It contemplates no conflict over age and sex roles and power relations. Nor does it even recognize that roles are a matter of definition and negotiation. Instead these are preordained and natural functions. There is no room for any distance between the person and the role. Dissent from these role norms places the dissident outside the system as it normally functions. And, in fact, that precisely is Lidz's theory of schizophrenia: it arises from parental failures to observe their proper age and sex positions. For Lidz and many other psychiatrists, it is all perfectly clear: there are sick families over here and well families over there. This family system, like any Utopian social system, has to introduce deviance from the outside—in this instance from the dark depths of individual psychology.

Psychoanalysis and Utopia   Psychoanalysis has contributed to Utopian views of family life from two directions: its conception of society or "civilization" and its conception of individual human nature. Freud's notion of "civilization" corresponds to the Utopian social system of sociology, with one exception: Freud's civilization has as its fatal flaw innate sexual and aggressive drives. These drives, which Freud referred to as libido, or the id, play the role of original sin in the fall from paradise. "Every individual is virtually an enemy of culture," wrote Freud in *The Future of an Illusion* (1898, p. 4). In Freud's thought the fundamental contrast is between immoral man and moral society. The superego, or conscience, represents the forces of civilization inside the person, but a constant struggle takes place between these social restraints and impulse. The idealized social order of civilization or culture is always precarious, always in danger of being smashed by the repressed impulses that constantly strive for expression. Thus psychoanalysis abets the conservative thrust of the functional view of society in two ways. It accounts for social conflict and pathology in a way that does not challenge the legitimacy or perfection of the social system. And, second, it suggests that, since the troubles that beset us arise from dark unruly forces in human nature, there is little use in trying to change social conditions.

In the writings of Parsons, Freudian ideas have been used in another way to support the idea of a balanced social system. Parsons finds in psychoanalysis a set of ideas comparable to his own theory of social systems (1951). In particular, Parsons finds in Freud's concept of *internalization* an explanation of how the social system perpetuates itself smoothly from one generation to the next. In Freudian theory, a major step in the development of the child is its identification with the parent of the same sex. The moral dictates taught by the parents, according to Freud, are taken into the child's own personality, where they become the superego or conscience. Parsons expanded the concept of internalization. Instead of just moral dictates, the child incorporates all of the culture, including values, roles, and knowledge. The child's personality becomes a mirror image of the social world around him or her. Thus the requirements of the society are translated into individual motivation; people come to want to do what they have to do, and the society functions smoothly (Parsons and Bales, 1955).

This view of internalization has been criticized as a distortion of Freud's own thinking. As Dennis Wrong (1961, p. 192) puts it, "The concept of internalization as it is used by many social scientists presents an oversocialized view of human nature, one that is infinitely malleable and capable of accepting the demands of any social system."

Values and Ideals

The relationship between people's values and attitudes on the one hand and their actual behavior on the other is one of those perennial problems that plague the social sciences. Are people's ideals and images of family life, for example, reliable guides to their behavior? Or are norms and behavior two separate realms that have nothing to do with each other? Or are norms a kind of smoke screen that obscures what is really going on?

Social scientists have disagreed in their answers to these questions. Some, in particular those functionalists who assume society tends toward a state of balance, assume that there is a close fit between values and behavior.

The defects of such assumptions about the relation between ideal and reality are pointed out by Marvin Harris (1968). Warning anthropologists to avoid the temptation to write descriptions of exotic cultures in terms of the ideals of those cultures, he offers the following ethnography of American life, written in ideal terms:

If permitted to develop unchecked, the tendency to write ethnographies in accord with the . . . rules of behavior will result in an unintentional parody of the human condition. Applied to our own culture, it would conjure up a way of life in which men tip their hats to ladies . . . unwed mothers are a rarity . . . chewing gum is never stuck under tables and never dropped on the sidewalk; television repairmen fix television sets; children respect their aged parents; rich and poor get the same medical treatment; taxes are paid in full; all men are created equal; and our defense budget is used only for maintaining peace. (Harris, 1968, p. 59)

The problem with assuming that the norms are descriptive goes beyond that of inaccuracy. They prevent us from seeing that the behavior in question has rules and a logic of its own. For example, despite the notion of the "mother-child family," probably very few households fit that description. Most unwed mothers, particularly young ones, live with their own mother and perhaps a grandmother or aunt. Thus a child may grow up with two or three mothers rather than one.

Counternorms pose another problem with using norms as guides to behavior. These may turn out to be stronger in practice than the ideal. What is a counternorm? Jules Henry illustrates one with his observations on the pervasiveness of cheating in the American high schools. In spite of the lip service paid to the idea that cheating is wrong, there is a great deal of pressure to engage in it. This pressure comes from the grading system, from the children as a group, and even from the teachers who seem to be indifferent to the cheating going on under their noses. Henry notes that a child who refuses to share test answers with a classmate would be the real deviant in the social system of the high school he observed. Further, he notes, "An honest adolescent life could be a crippling preliminary for many phases of contemporary culture" (1963, pp. 205–206).

Likewise, Goode has recently written that the family *preaches* nonviolence but *teaches* violence:

. . . parents and other moral authorities constantly exhort young children against violence, but their own behavior belies that advice. We are all trained for violence. The child does learn that force is very effective at stopping others, and that force or its threat can change other people's calculations of profit and loss. The child experiences this directly, and watches it in others—the fright of his mother when his father is furious, arguments and threats among the neighbors, battles with his own siblings, and so on. (Goode, 1971, p. 630)

Similarly, the norms of marital faithfulness have a highly problematic relation to actual behavior. Again, the rules and pressures against observing the norms often seem to dominate those in favor of the norms. Extramarital sex seems to be an institutionalized part of American life that coexists, however uncomfortably, with the monogamy principle. Morton Hunt's recent book, *The Affair* (1969), describes the social system of extramarital affairs and the discomforts caused by the discrepancy between people's beliefs and behavior.

Hunt's book and such works as the study of upper-middle-class marriages by Cuber and Harroff (1965) reveal considerable social and environmental pressure on people to have extramarital affairs. Advertising and the mass media eroticize everyday life in America. Flirtation games are often played in work settings as well as at parties. Travel and business provides the opportunity for liaisons with minimal risks of embarrassment and entanglements. In some social and business circles, an insistence on strict monogamy would render one as deviant as the high-school student who refused to offer examination answers to a classmate.

The reader should not leap to the conclusion, based on these examples, that American society is necessarily marked by a greater discrepancy between norms and behavior than is found in other societies. Because of social science and the mass media, however, we may be more aware of such discrepancies.

There is little evidence anywhere of a culture whose ideal norms are reliable guides to what people actually do. Harris (1968) points out that even the kinship rules of primitive peoples, sometimes described as the most binding of social norms, often fail to be carried out in practice. For example, there are kinship systems whose rules state who is to marry whom. A rule may dictate that a young man has to marry his mother's brother's daughter. However, some anthropologists, when actually tabulating who was married to whom, have found more exceptions to the rule than cases where it seemed to have been followed.

In at least one culture, Harris notes, there seems to be an inverted relation between commitment to kinship principle in word and commitment to it in deed. He speculates that a kinship dogma may be strengthened by the failure of people to abide by it.

There is a vast literature in anthropology and related disciplines which indicates that . . . norms and . . . events never quite match, and that not infrequently the main function of the norms is to obscure the . . . reality. (Harris, 1968, p. 592)

As a research strategy and a general approach to the family, asking the question, "What is actually going on?"

will generally lead to a different set of findings, and a different view of the phenomena, than asking, "What are family norms and roles?" Questions about norms and roles are important, but they should not be taken as descriptions of observable behavior.

Writers on the family sometimes assume that norms derive from immutable instincts. For example, the norms for parent-child relations are often assumed to be governed by a set of interlocking instinctual needs. The child's need for loving care is assumed to be matched by the parents' "generativity" and need to fulfill masculine and feminine role requirements. In many research studies the parent is accordingly perceived — although not observed — as a kind of teacher, trying to shape the child's behavior or instill a set of values.

The sociological concept of role — as, for example, "the mother role," "the father role" — may be similarly misleading as a guide to understanding actual behavior. The term "role" was utilized to emphasize that people often seem to follow cultural scripts, rather than merely expressing their particular personalities. Thus one can analyze the roles of mother, salesman, college president, policeman, and so on, as something apart from the individual personalities of the particular people who occupy those roles. Accordingly, societies and cultures may be described as being made up of "role relationships."

Like many other valuable constructs in the social sciences, however, the idea of role is sometimes overextended. People may play several and conflicting roles. Does the role of "mother" accurately describe actual mother-child interaction in a culture? Often the "mother role" is assumed to dominate the existence of the woman occupying it. Presumably it overrides other roles:

Granted that mothers have idiosyncratic differences — the personality peeping through — nevertheless it is held that the role of mother can be separated from individual mothers. . . . But the mother is also a wife . . . and mother-wife may be president of the women's club. . . . What are the criteria for telling when she is wife, when mother, when president, in the contexts of situations making up her daily life?
. . . The "role of mother" requires symbols at such high levels of abstraction . . . that one is forced to minimize the realities of

observation in order to create one stereotype for an entire society. (Chapple, 1970, p. 272)

In the studies that have observed and measured what goes on in households between parents and children—that is, in the natural habitat of family life—a very different picture emerges of the "mother role." A child may receive its mother's undivided attention no more than a half-hour or an hour a day. The rest of the time the mother is busy with other things. What goes on between mother and child seems to be a by-product of the horde of small and seemingly trivial events and pressures that make the parent's day a good or a bad one, a harried or a calm one, a tired or an energetic one. Such studies emphasize the daily realities of household life rather than ideal roles in trying to understand parent-child relations. To those investigators who have been observing the complex realities of family life—from events such as the preparing and eating of meals, putting children to bed, greetings and leavetakings, to patterns such as the organization of household time and space—norms and roles are, as concepts, simply too broad and abstract to be useful.

Although ideals and images and role definitions cannot be taken at face value as guides to behavior, they cannot be left ignored either. Looking at behavior only, without some idea of what the behavior means to the participants, is misleading also. Consider the behavioral fact of a parent spanking a child. To understand the meaning of this event, one would have to know its context—why it occurred. If the parent were a modern, permissive parent who did not believe in spanking, the situation would signify a different meaning for both parent and child than if, say, the parent belonged to a culture teaching that physical discipline was good for children, that a parent who did not spank children was neglecting duty. In broader terms the modern nuclear family differs from its historical counterparts in ideals and images of family life. The beliefs in close emotional bonds between husbands and wives and parents and children, and in personal happiness as the chief justification for marriage, enter into people's perceptions and experience of the daily events of family life. So these beliefs and norms cannot be ignored. They influence relationships even if they do not accurately describe them.

Psychiatry and the Idealization of Family Life   It is easy to see how defining family life in terms of cultural norms can lead to a Utopian view of the family. And it is easy to see how sociologists and anthropologists, interviewing people about their family values and practices, can arrive at often idealized conceptions of family life. Interviewees tend to present themselves in a favorable light. Besides, they may sincerely hold to certain values, but have trouble carrying these out in real life. Finally, of course, people are not completely aware of how they are acting, of how their family behavior would look to an observer.

At first glance it would seem that psychiatrists, social workers, marriage counselors, and other clinicians who help troubled families would be in a much better position to make unidealized assessments of family life. In fact, one might expect that coming into daily contact with family miseries kept private from the rest of the world would lead clinicians to exaggerate the dark side of family life. Paradoxically, however, clinicians have contributed to the Utopian or sentimentalized model of the family: the clinicians' experiences with troubled families seem to reinforce idealized conceptions of "the family," rather than challenge them. Thus the idealized model of the family remains the standard by which the "sick" families are judged:

> Studies of the family have, with a few memorable exceptions, accepted the sentimental model—statistics are made of units derived from this model; anecdotes are collected; and formalistic abstractions are derived from it. . . . Focusing upon the family's pathologies serve(s) to *reinforce the sentimental model by the assumption that the pathology-less family has the shape of the sentimental model.* . . . The pathologies are defined as variations from the sentimental model, and the sentimental model is reinforced in its supposed shape by the shape of its supposed pathologies. (Birdwhistell, 1966, p. 211) (Italics in the original)

The Medical Model   The medical model of pathology stands behind the psychiatric assumption that normal families differ considerably from the families whose children become psychiatric patients. In recent years there has been a great deal of debate about the habit of applying concepts of physical health and illness to matters of thoughts, feelings, and personalities. The issue has many ramifications, but the aspect that concerns us here has to do with the kind of thinking the medical model leads to — the kinds of inferences the psychiatrist draws about normality by observing patients. Suppose, for example, a patient (child) were to describe a parent as acting in some way that parents are not "supposed" to act — for example, cruel, irrational, neglectful, bizarre, impervious to what the patient says. What conclusion can the psychiatrist make about the normality of these parents? Assuming that the psychiatrist believes the child, can he infer that the parents are very different from most parents, only a little different, or typical?

Actually, the psychiatrist cannot legitimately draw any conclusion about prevailing child-rearing practices and parental behavior from patients. There is no way of knowing whether and how much and in what ways patients differ from the general population. The question is a matter for scientific investigation. To answer it, a study would have to be carried out comparing families having children in psychiatric treatment with families having children who had never been psychiatric patients. As a matter of fact, several such epidemiological studies have been carried out. They generally conclude that people who become psychiatric clients or patients represent only the tip of an iceberg:

> Studies from many countries confirm the picture of a high and persistent burden of neurosis in the population, the differences in rates between different studies probably reflecting differing criteria, rather than real differences in prevalence. (Ryle, 1967, p. 135)

Even if one did find differences between the families of schizophrenics and other families, there would be no way of knowing whether the differences came after the schizophrenia or before, unless the family had been studied before the patient got "sick."

When using a model of thinking borrowed from physical medicine, the psychiatrist may fail to perceive any problem in comprehending the normal family world. Thus the medical model leads to Utopian conceptions of family life without any help from social theories! Medicine is based on the popular opposition of health and disease: if a patient comes to a doctor complaining of a symptom such as an itchy rash, the doctor easily understands "normality" — it is the absence of the symptom. In the realm of behavior such thinking can lead to the erroneous conclusion that normal behavior and family life must be the exact opposite of what the psychiatrist hears of in his office:

> In order to understand the psychiatrist's thinking one must bear in mind that his daily activities revolve around mental abnormalities and that concern with the psychological norm falls into the periphery of his endeavors. . . . The diagnosis of normality is made by exclusion, and if a psychiatrist can label a feature it is by implication pathological and undesirable. Therefore *anything that is called by a name is implicitly abnormal.* . . . Since the psychiatrist's attention is focused upon deviation, and since he has little or no training in normal psychology, *he tends to construct a hypothetical norm by averaging the exact opposite of those features he sees in his patients.* (Ruesch and Bateson, 1968, p. 71) (Italics added)

Freud and Family Psychology

Freud and his followers have made an enormous contribution to the understanding of the family. Freud's discoveries of the impact and lasting significance for the individual of early experiences within a particular family must be included in any serious understanding of the family. Freud's discoveries derived from his invention of a new social situation, a new form of human interaction and communication.

In psychoanalysis the patient talks at length about whatever comes to mind, to a fully attentive and sympathetic listener who will not interrupt or censure, no matter how socially outrageous the thoughts expressed might be. Using this method Freud made significant discoveries, many of which are taken for granted today. Most important perhaps was his discovery of the child as a person, capable of sensuous feelings, fantasy, and suffering. The prevailing view during the nineteenth century was that the child was essentially a nonperson, someone whose view of things should not be taken seriously. As women were placed on a pedestal, the child was sentimentalized as an adorable innocent. Such sentimentalization coexisted with economic exploitation of children in mines and factories, and savage disciplinary measures in homes and schools (see Coveney, 1967).

Freud destroyed Victorian illusions about childhood innocence and family serenity. His discovery of infantile sexuality was perhaps the most shocking of all his findings; it aroused the most indignation. Yet Freud also discovered—

or rediscovered—passions in adults that had been denied by idealized conceptions of family life. Freud was fond of stating that the essential themes of his theories were based on the intuitions of poets and playwrights (Ellenberger, 1970, p. 460). The conflicts and strivings Freud found lurking beneath the surface of ordinary family life were the same passions dramatized by Shakespeare and the Greek tragedians. The lustful, murderous impulses between husbands and wives and parents and children that one could see acted out in Hamlet, King Lear, Oedipus Rex, Medea, and other classic works are ever-present but secret undercurrents in ordinary family life.

The Freudian theory of the family is thus a conflict theory, with conflict not only between family members but also within them. Freud's most important concepts are those of *repression* and *ambivalence*. Repression is the mechanism by which a person keeps wishes and fantasies outside his awareness; it explains why we may not be aware even in ourselves of the passions we see acted out overtly on the stage. The concept of ambivalence points to the duality and incompatibilities of many of our wishes and fantasies. We not only love *or* hate, we can love and hate at the same time. We want intimate relationships, but we want our freedom and individuality; we want deep sexual intimacy with one person, but at the same time we want to sample sexual experiences with as many people as possible.

Despite Freud's anti-Utopian vision of family relations, psychoanalysis on the whole has reinforced the sentimental model of the nuclear family because Freud and his followers tended to ignore the everyday realities of family life in favor of inherited instincts—this despite Freud's stress on child rearing in the formation of personality. Nathan Ackerman, himself a psychoanalyst, has pointed to such incongruities in Freud's approach to the family:

The Freudian theory focuses attention on the role of the family in the shaping of personality, but it gives priority to inborn instincts. It dramatizes the biological core of man, while diminishing the role of society. . . .

Child-parent relations are the core of the psychoanalytic view of human development . . . Yet in psychoanalysis direct observations of family interaction have not been carried out until recently, and only now is their importance beginning to be recognized. (Ackerman, 1958, pp. 27–30)

In large part the lack of concern on Freud's part for the everyday realities of family life stemmed from his emphasis on the child as a biological organism. He defined development as a progression through a series of innate maturational stages. These stages Freud conceived to be universal, hence only partly influenced by differences in individual experiences or social conditions. Parents, in Freud's theory, also have a relatively fixed part to play; they are the tamers of the child's instincts:

Freud conceived the family as the instrument for disciplining the child's biologically fixed instinctual urges and enforcing repression of their spontaneous release. He described the child as a polymorphous, perverse little animal. The child epitomizes animal pleasure. The parent personifies reality and the restraints of society. . . . In this aspect of family relations, parent and child are . . . virtual enemies to one another. (Ackerman, 1958, p. 28)

The emphasis on parent-child relations as the taming of impulse has several implications. For one thing it implies that a certain amount of suffering on the part of children is inevitably part of growing up. Psychoanalytic writers often argue against the notion that childhood can ever be a happy, conflict-free time of life. Even the most loving and beloved parents can be transformed in the child's imagination into witches and monsters:

If we look closely into the life of a small child, we find that such transformations take place . . . when we are compelled to interfere with the child's pleasure. . . . The child begins life as a pleasure seeking animal; his infantile personality is organized around his own body. In the course of rearing, the goal of exclusive pleasure seeking must be modified drastically. . . .

So there are no ways in which a child can avoid anxiety. If we banished all the witches and ogres from his bedtime stories and policed his life for every conceivable source of danger, he would still succeed in constructing his own imaginary monsters out of the conflicts of his own life. (Fraiberg, 1959, pp. 14–15)

The problem with this point of view is that it assumes that all the witches and monsters in a child's life are imaginary. It implies that in family government the virtues are with the rulers, and the vices with the ruled. The assumption of parental virtue, however, was wryly challenged by Herbert Spencer, the nineteenth-century philosopher whose career overlapped Freud's:

The current assumption respecting family government, as respecting national government, is that the virtues are with the rulers and the vices with the ruled. Judging by educational theories, men and women are entirely transfigured in their relations to offspring. The citizens we do business with, the people we meet in the world, we know to be very imperfect creatures. In the daily scandals, in the quarrels of friends, in bankruptcy disclosures, in lawsuits, in police reports, we have constantly thrust before us the pervading selfishness, dishonesty, brutality. Yet when we criticize nursery management and canvass the misbehavior of juveniles, we habitually take for granted that these culpable persons are free from moral delinquency in the treatment of boys and girls. (Spencer, 1946, p. 87; originally 1858)

The psychiatric idealization of the family in fact contradicts the analyst's clinical knowledge of parental behavior. It also contradicts the psychoanalytic view of persistent human nature. Thus the witches and monsters of the child's imagination may reflect accurate perceptions of veiled or not so veiled parental hostility (see Bakan, 1971a, pp. 64ff).

Freud seems to have been curiously blind to realities concerning the parents of his patients. Far from blaming his patients' families for their children's disorders, Freud overlooked or rejected much negative information, even in his own published case histories. He blamed his patients' troubles on their own wayward impulses, rather than on parental treatment.

The case of Little Hans (1909), for example, is considered the classic statement on the Oedipus complex. It describes Freud's analysis of a phobia in a five-year-old boy. Erich Fromm (1970, pp. 90–100) uses the published case to show Freud's bias in favor of parental figures. Freud, he argues, attributes qualities to Hans's parents as models of enlightened parenthood which contradict the facts he presents. Both parents were among Freud's closest adherents. Little Hans was treated by Freud, with his father as an intermediary, because he developed a strong fear of horses. According to Freud the boy's parents were determined to raise him without coercion, bullying, or ridicule. They were, in short, rebelling against the prevailing child-rearing practices of their time and place—turn-of-the-century Vienna.

As often happens when people set out to raise their children by new principles, the old ones have a way of persisting. For example, Little Hans's mother, according to

Freud, told Hans the following at various times: that she would have his penis cut off, that she would abandon him, and that she had a penis. She also threatened to beat him with a carpet beater. At the same time Hans's mother was described as acting seductive in various ways. Yet none of what the mother did entered into Freud's diagnosis of what troubled Hans. Freud attributed the phobia only to Oedipal wishes that arose from Hans's inner depths. His amorous feelings toward his mother and his fear of castration were not related by Freud to his mother's seductiveness or actual threats! The case is a remarkable demonstration of how concrete incidents in day-to-day family life can be at odds with the professed beliefs and values of the parents, as well as with professional estimates of the parents as people.

Similar observations have been made of the case of Dora, an eighteen-year-old girl who was brought to Freud for treatment of hysteria (Chesler, 1971). Once again Freud overlooked the family situation as a source of Dora's troubles and attributed her problems solely to her unrecognized sexual wishes toward her father, and toward her father's friend and his wife. This family situation was more extreme than Little Hans's. Dora's father was having an affair with the friend's wife and was trying to offer Dora to this man so his own affair could continue. Freud was aware of this situation but considered it irrelevant to Dora's problems and to her treatment. He was concerned only with tracing her hysterical symptoms to their presumed origins in sexual wishes.

New Directions in Family Studies

New trends in the fields of psychiatry and of history suggest some profound changes in our assumptions about ordinary family life. Each of the new trends in its own way is undermining traditional concepts of family normality. As we noted earlier, both the average person and the family expert tend to think of family problems as a kind of pathology attacking an otherwise healthy system, like a germ invading the body. This way of looking at the family forces us to think of problems as separate from normal family life, and of normal families as separate from pathological families. Tolstoy once wrote, "Happy families are all alike, but each unhappy family is unhappy in its own way." Like Tolstoy many observers put normal families in one pile, and schizophrenic families or child-battering families in another. Then they develop a theory of what goes on in normal families and a different theory to explain what goes on in pathological families. They keep the two or three kinds of families in airtight logical compartments, paying little or no attention to the similarities, as opposed to the differences, between the types of families or to the process by which one type changes into another.

Newer studies in history and psychiatry are undermining this polarized way of looking at families. In different ways they suggest that definitions of family normality and pathology are much harder to draw than had been thought. Further, these new approaches emphasize variations among families rather than similarities.

Perhaps the major contribution of the new historical studies is to show that although the nuclear family has existed for many centuries, the set of ideas and practices that make up the nuclear-family ideology is a relatively recent invention in Western society. French historian Aries (1962) has traced the rise of the private nuclear family out of the "torrent" of general sociability in the Middle Ages. Aries draws an important distinction between the family as a biological unit and the ideas about that unit in a particular society or historical period. Thus there are mothers and fathers and children in every society, but the importance of the nuclear unit in social life can vary.

Aries' most striking contribution, however, is the notion of childhood as a social invention. The idea that the psychological bonds between husbands and wives have changed over time is a familiar one. Most people know, for example, that in the past in our culture, and in many other places today, marriages are not based on love but are arranged by families. We are not surprised to learn that the emotional aspects of marriage are conditioned by the historical and cultural setting. It is more surprising to learn that parental feelings toward children may be equally variable.

When infant- and child-mortality rates are extremely high, as they were in the early years of the modern era, infants do not count for much in their parents' feelings. That children were born to die was taken to be a fact no one could do much about. "'All mine die,' said Montaigne casually, as a gardener might speak of his cabbages" (Plumb, 1972).

Although infants were not quite human in these times, children over the age of seven were considered miniature adults. People did not think of childhood as a separate stage of life, with its own distinct psychological nature.

The historical evidence also undermines certain ideas about parenthood, childhood, and society that have been almost axiomatic among many anthropologists, sociologists, and psychoanalytic writers. Some examples of these ideas include the notions that parents have an innate desire to care for their young children; that there is an intuitive wisdom about the child-rearing methods of any culture; and, finally, that every society has a vested interest in children and in the child-rearing process, and therefore provides rewards and support for parents' efforts. On all these points, as we shall explain in more detail later, the historical evidence suggests that, unfortunately for children, none of these supposedly built-in benevolent forces can be counted on.

Other historical studies indicate that even deeply concerned and well-off families used child-rearing methods that were not only harmful but downright lethal. Writing of seventeenth-century France, David Hunt finds that, without bottles or good baby foods, there was great difficulty in nourishing infants during the first months of life. In a world where life was short and uncertain, and resources of all kinds were scarce, the infant was regarded as less than human, a gluttonous little animal who sucked away his mother's blood as he nursed (D. Hunt, 1970, p. 121).

Hunt had started his research with the expectation of finding that parents intuitively followed their own instincts and the wisdom of their culture in raising their children. He found instead a society-wide "breakdown" of parental care: parents were unprepared to deal with their children, the conditions of daily life seriously hindered their efforts, and children suffered. Hunt notes that when we are dealing with a distant society like seventeenth-century France, it is easy to see the plight of children and to accept the notion that this plight relates to the political and social order in which they live. "We lack the corresponding understanding of parenthood and society today" (p. 196).

Such an understanding can be found, however, in two recent branches of psychiatric study whose findings have not received as much general attention as they deserve. These studies involve the families of battered children and of schizophrenics. Actually these two kinds of studies have been carried out independently of each other by different researchers, using different methods and a different vocabulary. Both sets of studies began with groups of people who were thought to represent extreme forms of pathology: in one instance, people who had caused severe bodily injury to their children; in the other, families who had presumably driven their children into the most severe and debilitating form of mental illness. Yet each set of studies ended with findings that made it harder than ever to draw the line between normal and pathological. In particular they revealed a dark side of "normal" family life which in the past had been explored only in literary works.

The Perils of Family Life—Child Abuse   We tend to think that anyone who could deliberately injure a child enough, for example, to break a bone or to draw blood must be some kind of depraved, disreputable person. But the research on child battering points to a continuity rather than a sharp break with normal child-rearing methods. Some battering parents seem only to have exaggerated notions of obedience and of the capacities of very young children to respond to commands. Such parents are likely to be righteous about their acts. They may argue that they were only trying to teach their child not to be spoiled or disrespectful. For other parents the injuries that bring in the authorities are more like momentary outbursts of anger in the course of "normal" discipline.

In looking for the causes of child abuse, research points beyond the motives and weaknesses of the particular parent. It directs attention to the physical and social environment surrounding parents and children. What happens to the child in the course of a day often seems to be a by-product of what happens to the parent in his or her adult life outside the realm of parenthood—a fight with the spouse, troubles with the boss, money worries, the household workload, illness. If stresses mount too high, the parent may be overwhelmed and explode at the child. In short, a host of actors apart from the child determine the mood and the time and energy a parent has for child care. All this seems obvious; we see it even in television commercials—"I'm not going to let a headache MAKE ME SCREAM AT MY KIDS!" Yet this knowledge tends to be ignored in most family research and in the sentimental mythology of family life as a refuge from the stresses of the outside world.

Rather than being a refuge from the stresses, strains, and irrationality of the outside society, the family often seems to transmit or even magnify these strains. The isolated nuclear family seems to be a particularly efficient magnifier of strain because so few people are involved. Husband and wife look to each other to make up for whatever deprivation they have suffered in their social and work lives, and the adults have absolute power over the children. A good deal of truth appears in the comic strip showing the boss yelling at the husband, the husband coming home and yelling at the wife, the wife yelling at the child, and finally the child kicking the dog.

Anthropologists have pointed out how American culture is extreme in letting parents and children be alone together, shut off in their own houses, away from the watchful eyes and sharp tongues that regulate parent-child relations in other cultures. This isolation sets the stage not only for physical abuse but for the more usual and common psychological abuse. The isolated nuclear household forms a fertile medium in which irrationality can grow.

Madness and the Family   Like the studies of the battered child, the studies of families of schizophrenics began with a group of people in a category clearly labeled "pathological" and "not like other families." And like the battered-child studies, they have concluded with a set of concepts that make the line between the normal and the pathological, "them" and "us," harder than ever to draw. The studies of the families of schizophrenics form one part of an important shift in psychiatric thinking that has taken place in the past fifteen to twenty years. The issues surrounding schizophrenia, its nature and causes, remain unclear. But the concepts that have come out of these studies have produced profound and revolutionary implications for understanding family life, as well as human behavior in general.

These studies developed a new therapy, a new methodology, and ultimately a new set of concepts that have been hailed as major scientific discoveries (Henry, 1971, p. 455; see also Rabkin, 1970). The new therapy was family therapy. Rather than seeing the individual patient alone, psychiatrists started to observe and to treat whole families. The new methods of research grew out of the new therapy. With whole families coming together in hospitals and clinics, it became possible to observe the intimate conversations and interactions of family members in ways that had never before been available to researchers. Furthermore, a whole new technology was now available to record and preserve the record of what people said and did. Movies, tape recorders, videotape, and so forth caught the words, looks, and gestures of family members, so it was no longer necessary to depend on anyone's memory. "Instant replay" became possible in the study of family interaction — and endless replay also. The researcher could study a family scene again and again, picking up the more subtle aspects that had been missed the first time, or changing his definitions of what had gone on.

The new techniques transformed the family psychiatrist into a kind of anthropologist. Each family was like a newly discovered tribe, with its own language, rules, roles, and rituals. In looking at families this way, the researchers discovered that they lacked a vocabulary to describe what they saw. Psychiatry and psychoanalysis had many terms to describe the behavior and inner states of the single person, but very few terms to describe the interaction between two or more people. To fill this information gap, concepts were borrowed from many fields, some seemingly far removed from psychiatry — information theory, logic, ecology, general-systems theory, sociology, existentialism, and Marxism. Oddly enough, no name has yet emerged for this new science. Several have been suggested, but none has stuck. "Communication theory" is perhaps used most often, but it refers mainly to one particular version of the new approach, that of Gregory Bateson and his associates. Other suggested names are "clinical sociology" (Lennard and Bernstein, 1969), "social psychiatry" (Rabkin, 1970), and "interpersonal psychiatry" (Sullivan, 1953). Perhaps the lack of a general term reflects the novelty of the approach. It is not yet well known outside its own community of researchers and therapists. R. D. Laing is the only one widely known to the public, and even his readers seem unaware that he is a part of a larger group within the psychiatric community, rather than a solitary figure.

"Communicational psychiatry" failed to prove its initial assumptions: it did not discover a set of behavior patterns unique to schizophrenic families. Rather, it seems to have discovered patterns common to many families. The following features are some of those first found in families with a schizophrenic member:

The "politics of experience": struggles over definitions of what is really going on, over whose experience is to be defined as real, and whose experience is to be invalidated

Imperviousness: ignoring what the other person says

Mystification: doing something that is really in your own interests, but insisting you are doing it for the other person's good — for example, a parent tells a child "You're sleepy, dear — go to bed" when in fact the child is not tired, and the parent merely wants the child out of the way

A parent caring for a child only as an extension of himself or herself, not as a separate person

Mother and father as enemy camps; a cold war in the household

Mother and father united in a "holy alliance" against the rest of the world

Double-bind or paradoxical communications, such as glaring at a child and ordering him to kiss you at the same time; saying such things as "Don't take me seriously" or "Be spontaneous"

Too great a boundary between the family and the rest of the world — everyone outside the family is a suspicious character

Too little boundary between the family and the rest of the world: outsiders or other relatives constantly intruding on intimate family matters

Family secrets that everyone is aware of but doesn't dare discuss

Topics that are so taboo that there are rules against even thinking about the rules against them

A parent being preoccupied with the child's inner state: his moods, feelings, and general happiness

A parent mislabeling the child's inner states — telling him he is hungry or sleepy when he is neither

> A parent reacting to a child's statements or acts by belittling the child with sarcasm: "You can always depend on John—to do the wrong thing"

These findings were not so much discoveries as a rediscovery of what intuitive observers of the human scene had known all along: most families have small and large skeletons in their closets; the most mature-seeming people have foibles and weaknesses that emerge only in the presence of members of their family; family members conspire together to create a favorable impression for the outside world; family members may say one thing but imply another—"Don't worry about leaving me with all the dinner dishes—go and enjoy yourselves"; every family has its own unique set of rules, myths, communication networks, secret alliances, loves, and hates (see Framo, 1965, 1972).

Accordingly, the concept of a psychiatrically "normal" family is coming to seem as abstract and empty as the concept of a "universal" nuclear family that is the same everywhere. The more family interaction was studied, the harder it became to think that there was a normal "type" of family that could be contrasted with an abnormal "type."

The enthusiasm engendered by the new research gave way to disillusionment among those who had been hoping for an answer to the riddle of schizophrenia. Organic explanations have once again become acceptable. But the less the new findings tell us about what is unique to schizophrenic families, the more they tell us about family life in general.

Jules Henry, an anthropologist who studied families of schizophrenics by living in their homes, raises the question as to how far these newly discovered patterns reach among families never labeled as "sick." Are they the inevitable result of people living together? Are they peculiar to Americans? To the isolated, urbanized nuclear family? He writes, "I worry that we have here, perhaps, a sudden discovery of the contemporary *family* rather than the pathologic family, unless of course we urge that in our culture, most families are pathogenic, in some sense—a position I take in this book" (Henry, 1971, p. 455).

A somewhat different way of looking at family interaction is suggested by Lennard and Bernstein (1969). Rather than defining most families as "pathogenic," these researchers suggest that though ordinary family life can often be a difficult interactional environment, most people can cope with these difficulties most of the time. Just as our bodies have immune systems enabling us to live in a germ-filled environment without being sick constantly, so most of us are psychologically robust enough to deal with the emotional ups and downs of family interaction. Pathology such as schizophrenic reactions may occur when the level of interactional difficulty in a family exceeds the ability of a family member to cope with it. Some persons may be especially vulnerable to conflict, hostility, or emotional demands, and some families are more difficult interactional environments than others. When a vulnerable person finds himself or herself in a particularly difficult family, chances are that he or she will either try to withdraw from the family or develop symptoms that will lead to becoming a psychiatric patient.

Lennard and Bernstein were led to their conclusion concerning the difficulties of the family context by research comparing small-group interaction in families and other groups. They looked at "schizophrenic families," "normal families," and a variety of groups of unrelated people—for example, small groups that had participated in psychological experiments or therapy or discussion. One of their major measures was the ratio between positive interactions—agreeing, supporting, affirming—and negative interactions—disagreeing, contradicting, criticizing. As anticipated, they found that the "schizophrenic" families had lower ratios of positive to negative interactions. But to their surprise the differences between the "normal" families and those with a schizophrenic member were not as wide as previous clinical descriptions had led them to believe. Furthermore, family groups, whether with a schizophrenic member or not, contrasted with the groups of unrelated people:

. . . Family contexts as a whole, whether or not they involve families with a mentally ill member, exhibit lower concordance ratios than any other form of social context on which we had data available. Moreover, family interaction process does not meet the criteria set forth by Bales for a viable, task-oriented system. . . . The family interactional environment then must be considered as a difficult context for interaction—an observation that is, needless to say, not inconsistent with common experience. (Lennard and Bernstein, 1969, p. 185)

Summary

The family often has been studied from the point of view of either the society as a whole or the individual. Both of these approaches can lead to idealized conceptions of family life. The view of society as a balanced social system leads to a Utopian vision of family and society as conflict-free and harmonious. Clinical work with individuals and families often leads the clinician to assume that the patients he sees are troubled only by personal failings rather than by social strains besetting families in general. Recent work in history and psychiatry is undermining such idealized models of family life.

SOCIAL CHANGE AND
THE INTIMATE ENVIRONMENT

Chapter 3

The sociological imagination enables its possessor to understand the larger historical scene in terms of its meaning for the inner life and the external career of a variety of individuals. . . . The first fruit of this imagination—and the first lesson of the social science that embodies it—is the idea that the individual can understand his own experience and gauge his own fate only by locating himself within his period. . . . We have come to know that every individual lives, from one generation to the next, in some society, and that he lives it out within some historical sequence. By the fact of his living he contributes, however minutely, to the shaping of this society and to the course of its history, even as he is made by society and by its historical push and shove.

The sociological imagination enables us to grasp history and biography and the relations between the two within society.

C. Wright Mills, *The Sociological Imagination*

Chapter Three How does our own family life compare with family life in other times and places? Leaving aside for the moment that we actually know little about family life as it is lived in contemporary families, what can we say about the experience of motherhood and fatherhood in the Middle Ages or of being a child in a band of hunters? Is family life essentially "the same" everywhere or does it vary significantly from time to time and place to place?

History of the Family

The study of family life in other places, of course, is very different from the study of family life in other times. No matter how remote or exotic an existing group, it is conceivable to study their family behavior firsthand. The historian, by contrast, faces the task of reconstructing history. Before the past decade there was a great deal of skepticism about trying to reconstruct family life and family change in past eras. William Goode, a leading sociologist of the family, asserted that "not a single history of the U.S. family would meet modern standards of historical research" (1964, p. 105). Goode noted that there were great technical problems in analyzing family behavior of the past:

. . . Most family events do not ordinarily leave traces in the form of laws, documents, or treaties, much less systematic continuous records. Formal events such as births, deaths, marriages, divorces, adoptions, and lawsuits about inheritance are likely to be recorded, but these yield only few insights into family patterns. The comments of literary or philosophical figures about their times are at best the guesses of wise but untrained amateurs. Moreover, both records and comments focus on the top social strata only, leaving nearly in obscurity the family behavior of the majority of the population.

Faced with these handicaps, we must adopt a skeptical stance with reference to most of our assumptions about how the family changed in the past. (Goode, 1964, p. 105)

Until recently most historians avoided studying the family, ceding the field to anthropologists and sociologists. This avoidance can be attributed in part to the practical problems mentioned by Goode: the scarcity of documentary materials and the hesitancy of historians to venture into the alien territory of the social sciences. More important perhaps was the general tendency of historians to focus on public events rather than private experience, and on elites rather than on ordinary people.

In the past decade, however, a renewed interest in the history of the family has resulted from new methodologies as well as new definitions of the task of history. Many of the new historians of the family are young; their interest is stimulated in part by a commitment to understanding what life was like in all segments of society in past ages, not just the top social strata. The current interest in the family has also been stimulated by the generation gap, the women's movement, and anxieties about the future of the family.

For the new scholars of the family in history, reconstructing the intimate environments of past family life does not appear to be an impossible task. As Tamara Hareven (1971) points out, historians neglected the family not only because materials were lacking but because they failed to ask the right questions.

Now new ways of using existing materials have been discovered. A number of important techniques have been borrowed from the field of demography, enabling historians to trace population changes, mobility, fertility, birth control, infant mortality, illegitimacy, and even marriages with pregnant brides. One highly significant development is a technique known as family reconstruction; using records of births, deaths, marriages, land transfers, and wills, the historian can reconstruct the family and household patterns of large numbers of ordinary people who had previously been considered lost forever in the depths of time. Using the family-reconstruction technique, Philip Greven (1970) was able to trace the structures of individual families in Andover, Massachusetts, beginning with the first settlers and continuing through four generations. Greven emphasizes the role of the land in the family lives of farmers—the subtle ways inheritance patterns and the availability of land influenced relations between fathers and sons.

John Demos' (1970) study of the Plymouth colony presents another attempt to reconstruct the intimacies of everyday family life in the colonial era. Demos tries to depict the concrete realities of the family by a detailed study of colonial houses, who lived in them, their furnishings, clothing, child-rearing methods, the tasks carried out in the households, and the relations between households and the larger community.

Not surprisingly, the further such studies get from such facts as births, deaths, and household arrangements to make interpretations about the experiences of family life, the more debate their conclusions elicit. For example, Demos and Greven disagree about the quality of emotional life in colonial households: Greven sees life in the first generation of Andover settlers as harmonious in part because of the abundance of land; Demos suggests that the crowded households built frustrations and resentments that were expressed in disputes with other families. Since the history of the family is just beginning to be explored, it is not surprising to find such controversy.

Even so, the new techniques have shown that a number of previous ideas about the family were wrong; for example, there is much more variability in family structure and behavior at any one period than had been believed. It is not true, as commonly believed, that up until recent times everyone lived in extended-family households. Nuclear-family households have existed in Europe since the fifteenth century. In general, it appears that a variety of family structures prevails at any one time.

The idea that mobility is a modern phenomenon has also proved wrong; in preindustrial Europe, it turns out, people moved around from place to place much more than had been believed. Further, generational conflicts, sexual behavior outside prescribed channels, and women's resistance to their traditional roles are not modern innovations. Nor, as some sociologists would have it, are they constants representing some fixed proportion of deviants who must inevitably crop up in any society. Instead, they seem to rise and fall in response to a variety of social changes.

The most important contribution of the historical studies, however, is their revelation of the shortcomings of previous social-science approaches to the family, and their suggestion of an alternative approach. It is ironic that the two leading fields of family study, anthropology and sociology, were unable to supply the tools that historians needed. Instead, they have beset historians with problems (Hareven, 1971). For one thing, they have offered historians no clear definitions of family; as noted in a previous chapter, sociologists have tended to use the terms "family" and "household" interchangeably, a practice that can only confuse. Historians trying to decide whether to categorize the families they were studying as extended or nuclear found the following definitions of extended family in sociological writings: a single household containing grandparents; a single household containing two or more related nuclear families of any generation living under one roof; a nuclear family with any relative living in; related nuclear families living in separate households but on the same farm; related nuclear families living close to each other in cities; related nuclear families living far from each other but keeping in touch by mail (see Greven, 1970, p. 16).

Most misleading, however, has been the reliance of sociology and anthropology on normative models of the family. Anthropologists tend to portray the typical or ideal family structure of a given society, and how it functions in the total structure of society. Moreover, the emphasis on the universality of the nuclear family leads some social scientists to try to explain away differences in family structure and functioning rather than understand them.

As for sociology, the historian Tamara Hareven makes the following complaints:

. . . Sociologists have beset historians with several problems.

First, they relied on general census computations to determine trends in family patterns over time, instead of studying such changes in relation to specific groups, classes, and patterns of settlement. Second, they used historical data to illustrate sociological theory, thus divorcing most of its evidence from its historical context. Most importantly, however, their biases as to the nature of the ideal family dictated their historical interpretations. They typed all families that deviated from the middle class American family as symptoms of social disorganization. . . . (Hareven, 1971, p. 407)

Thus, while sociologists tend to look at the black families in American cities in terms of breakdown and social disorganization, historians can consider alternative interpretations such as the possibility that many different kinds of family structure are workable in urban environments. Similarly, while sociologists look at illegitimacy and nonmarital sexuality as symptoms of a breakdown in vital social controls, historians are free to interpret them as forms of expressive protest against the "dismal grind of daily life" (Shorter, 1971).

The point is not whether the sociologist or the historian is correct; the point is that the typical family sociologist does not even argue that illegitimacy represents social disorganization—he takes it for granted. Sociologists and historians generally employ different paradigms of society; as noted earlier the functional approach looks at society as an organism, a closed system, sealed off from change. So when functional sociologists do try to deal with change, they tend to treat it as something unusual, something set in motion by special circumstances. Change for many sociologists is something that transforms one equilibrated social system to another. The historical vision of social change is, like a movie, a continuous process. The functional sociologist treats change as a slide projector would, but with a few slides: here is preindustrial society, there is industrial society, here is the family structure of preindustrial society, there is the modern nuclear family. Even this concession to change is more apparent than real, for family roles are still assumed to be rooted in biology and hence outside the historical process; in every society since the dawn of humanity, the functionalist argument goes, man's role has been instrumental while woman's has been expressive and nurturant. This fundamental division of labor is constant, whether the man is a hunter, a farmer, a factory or office worker, and whether home is a cave, a thatched hut, or a high-rise apartment.

While the functional sociologist looks at variety and change and sees "the family," the historian looks at the seemingly unbroken surface of life in particular places and sees families as part of the endless process of social change. Philip Greven writes:

By studying the families of four successive generations of residents of Andover, I have sought to answer one of the most crucially important questions that can be asked about the nature and history of the family: Did the structure and the character of families change through time and place to place? The answer, as this study demonstrates, is affirmative; families did change, and patterns of family structure, patterns of relationships between fathers and sons, patterns in the transmission of land, and patterns in demographic experience all gradually altered in the course of the seventeenth and eighteenth century. Because of these complex and almost continuous changes . . . one can describe the family as having a history. The nature of the family was as mutable as the circumstances shaping the lives of the men, women, and children who were born, matured, and died in this community and others. (Greven, 1970, pp. 16–17)

Evolutionary Theories of the Family

To understand the development of the study of family change in the social sciences, we should recognize the dominance of two overlapping controversies: the debate with Marxism and the use of evolutionary theories in the social sciences. The emphasis on the biological constancy and functional necessity of the family came about in part as reaction against nineteenth-century theories about how the family evolved through the stages of human evolution. One of the leading theorists of cultural evolution was an American, Lewis Henry Morgan, a Republican lawyer who practiced anthropology as a hobby.

The prevailing verdict on Morgan in works on the family is negative; he is generally assumed to have been thoroughly

discredited, along with other fanciful nineteenth-century thinkers on the family. Perhaps the most important reason for Morgan's rejection was that his theory of family evolution became the basis for the Marxian theory of the family. Marx and Engels saw in Morgan's scheme a confirmation of the Marxian theory of history which originally had been applied only to Western societies. Engels' *The Origin of Private Property, the Family and the State* is based largely on Morgan's work. Morgan's ideas, as interpreted by Engels, became the official anthropological dogma of the Communist Party of the Soviet Union.

The fate of Morgan's reputation on the two sides of the Cold War is an interesting example of how far political considerations can intrude into scholarly matters. In the Soviet Union Morgan was revered, whereas in the West he was considered wildly and totally wrong. Harris (1968) argues that the attack on Morgan had profound consequences for anthropology for the first forty years of the twentieth century; for this period of time anthropologists no longer used the comparative method, and did not try to generalize about the processes of historical and cultural change.

Morgan and Engels were neither as historically correct as their supporters claimed, nor as wrong as Western social science insisted. Certainly Marxist ideas on the family deserved discussion for general intellectual reasons, but also on more contemporary grounds—they have been rediscovered in the new feminist movement. One often encounters in the literature on women's liberation references to Morgan's and Engels' notions, which are treated as gospel, about the evolution of the family.

Morgan's Scheme   As an anthropological hobbyist, Morgan became fascinated with the kinship terminology of American Indian tribes and decided to investigate the number of different types of kinship systems. He was intrigued to learn that, among the Iroquois, a person used the same term for his mother and his mother's sister. Some of a person's cousins—the children of father's sister and mother's brother—were called cousins, but the children of mother's sister and father's brother were called brothers and sisters rather than cousins. On the basis of questionnaires sent to government officials and missionaries, Morgan learned that the kinship systems of groups all around the world fell into a rather small number of types.

Eventually, Morgan came to believe that kinship terms reflected marriage rules and family patterns, which in turn reflected stages of economic development. He constructed an elaborate scheme correlating technological development, social and political structure, and the family (1870, 1877). Morgan divided human history into three broad stages: savagery, barbarism, and civilization. Further subdivisions were as follows:

Savagery
Lower: fruit and nut subsistence
Middle: fish subsistence and fire
Upper: bow and arrow

Barbarism
Lower: invention of pottery
Middle: domestication of animals in the Old World, irrigation and cultivation of maize in the New World
Upper: iron tools

Civilization: invention of phonetic alphabet and writing

Morgan believed that each of these periods had its own style of life and culture. Thus he assumed that knowing one aspect of a society's culture would make it possible to predict all the rest. Further, he held that the sequence represented a series of necessary evolutionary stages; any existing society could be placed in one of the categories.

In the same way, Morgan believed that family institutions have also gone through successive stages of development. He postulated five such forms, each with its own type of marriage:

1 *Consanguine:* group marriage between actual brothers and sisters

2 *Punaluan:*   a form of group marriage in which a group of brothers marries a group of sisters; brother-sister incest is taboo

3 *Pairing family:* a transitional form between group marriage and monogamy: single pairs of men and women would marry but either could end the marriage at any time, as well as cohabit with others at any time

4 *Patriarchal family:* marriage of one man with several wives

5 *Monogamian:* based on monogamy and an increase in female equality

Morgan's Errors   The errors in Morgan's scheme are many and serious. For example, he wrongly assumed that kinship terminology reflects actual marriage patterns. Thus, because the Hawaiians call all their aunts and uncles "mother" and "father," and all their cousins "brother" and sister," Morgan believed that a group of brothers and sisters must be intermarried. But group marriage probably never existed as an institutionalized form. Pairing arrangements with incest prohibitions within the nuclear family, however, appear to be universal in every known society (Harris, 1968, p. 186).

Morgan made other mistakes (Harris, 1968). First, he failed to relate the kinship or other aspects of social structure to the stages of technology in any sort of systematic way—that is, he did not explain why a particular form of subsistence should lead to a particular form of the family Second, his technological sequences contain drastic errors; the earliest stage of human society, Morgan's period of "savagery," was based on hunting as well as gathering. The invention of agriculture—*not* the invention of pottery—was the revolutionary development that ushered in the next great stage of human history. Third, iron and writing systems are not the correct criteria for defining civilizations. Finally, Morgan erred in insisting that, historically, matrilineal descent preceded patrilineal descent. Morgan and others had argued that, because of group marriage as well as ignorance of the father's role in reproduction, the earliest stages of human culture recognized only descent from the mother, since a child's mother was always certain.

Bachofen, Engels, and others extended this notion into the theory of matriarchy and mother-right. According to this theory there was an historical stage of matriarchy when women ruled human society and female deities were worshipped. This was followed by a universal defeat of the female sex by patriarchy, accompanied by the rise of private property.

Since the matriarchy notion has recently been revived as part of the women's movement, it will be useful to quote Marvin Harris's review of the controversy (Harris, it should be noted, is a defender of Morgan's work). About the controversy between the matriarchy theory and its opponents, he has this to say:

. . . Here Morgan was a participant in one of the most heated and useless discussions in the history of the social sciences. He and his supporters were opposed by an equally numerous group, who argued for the reverse priority. Both groups were wrong, constituting one of those rare cases of diametrically opposed positions about which it is impossible to say that either contained a grain of truth. (Harris, 1968, p. 187)

Descent rules—the question of whether a child belongs to its mother's or its father's line—seem to reflect residence patterns, whether a married couple lives with the wife's or the husband's people. Residence patterns in turn reflect local economic, technological, and environmental conditions. Groups at the same general level of economic development, however, can have varying descent rules. Besides, how descent is reckoned has little to do with either the status of women or knowledge of paternity:

The occurrence of matrilineal descent has no bearing on the status of women, since mother's brother rather than mother is generally head of the descent group. Furthermore, the idea that matrilineality is a result of confusion concerning paternity is wholly confounded by the numerous cases of primitive peoples who deny that the male is necessary for conception, but who regard themselves as descended from a line of males, and by the universal recognition of some degree of kinship with both maternal and paternal relatives, regardless of the nature of the unilineal rule. (Harris, 1968, p. 187)

Modern Evolutionism, Technology, and Family Life   In spite of Morgan's errors, he was right in believing that family and other aspects of social organization are tied to economic pursuits and technological development. Contemporary anthropologists are also concerned about the relation between social organization and technology, economic activities, and such environmental features as population density, disease, and food supply (see Alland, 1967).

Broadly speaking, Morgan's threefold division of societal development is still used by today's comparative anthropologists, although their terms differ somewhat: the divisions are "hunting and gathering societies," "agricultural societies," and "industrial societies." Again, these types represent a set of historical changes and also a set of categories into which any society can be placed.

As in Morgan's scheme, societal development or complexity influences family life. Modern theorists, however, do not leave the connections between society and family as vague and unspecified as Morgan did. Nor, incidentally, do they assume a mechanical sort of economic determinism; instead, they realize that how a society provides for basic needs, and the abundance it can produce, sets off a chain of influential consequences. For example, the sheer amount of food a society is able to produce determines how many and how densely people can live together. Further, more surplus frees people from agriculture and permits specialization in crafts and other occupations.

Modern scholars also agree with Morgan and Engels on the significance of the agricultural revolution as a major turning point in human history. The transition from hunting and gathering to the invention of agriculture made possible a settled way of life, the birth of individual and family property in land, herds, houses, and other objects, the rise of unequal social classes and the state. Although the nuclear family tends to be the major family unit in hunting societies, the extended kin group characterizes agricultural societies.

A second major transition is the shift from agrarian to industrial society. In industrial societies the nuclear family once again emerges as the dominant household form. Blumberg and Winch (1972) have documented this pattern for more than nine hundred societies. Not only does the structure of the family vary, but also the psychological quality of life. In general there are marked contrasts in the relations between men and women and parents and children over the range of societal development. Let us consider the family more closely under these major shifts in technology.

Hunting and Gathering Societies

For 99 percent of human history, hunting and gathering constituted the major means of subsistence.

. . . Of the estimated 80,000,000,000 men who ever lived out a life span on earth, over 90% have lived as hunters and gatherers, about 6% have lived by agriculture and the remaining few percent lived in industrial societies.

To date, the hunting way of life has been the most successful and persistent adaptation man has ever achieved. . . . It is still an open question whether man will be able to survive the exceedingly complex and unstable ecological conditions he has created for himself. If he fails in this task, interplanetary archeologists of the future will classify our planet as one in which a very long and stable period of small-scale hunting and gathering was followed by an apparently instantaneous efflorescence of technology and society rapidly leading to extinction. . . . The origin of agriculture and thermonuclear destruction will appear as essentially simultaneous. (Lee and DeVore, 1968, p. 3)

About 175 contemporary hunting and gathering cultures have been studied in detail, including Eskimos, Bushmen of the Kalahari Desert in southern Africa, forest Pygmies, and many Canadian and South American Indian groups (Gough, 1971). These living groups of hunters cannot be regarded as fossils—precise replicas of human society as it existed ten to fifteen thousand years ago—but they do offer clues to earlier family and social organization.

Although the technology of hunters is rudimentary, and they lack "social complexity," they are not primitive in mentality. Nor do hunting societies live up to the image of "bloodthirsty savages." Nineteenth-century anthropologists, including Morgan, erroneously concluded that people in simpler societies were less intelligent than people in "civilized" societies. Eighteenth-century philosophers erroneously thought hunters epitomized a simple "state of nature." But in religion, morality, art, and etiquette their culture is at least as elaborate as ours, and in one respect it is more elaborate. Some hunting groups possess enormously complex kinship systems. Moreover, there is no primitive language; the languages associated with primitive technologies may be more elaborated than the languages of some advanced societies. Still, the underlying structure of all human languages is identical, and any human infant placed in any group at birth will grow up a native speaker of whatever language he hears around him.

Although hunters live in many different environments with varying cultures, anthropologists consider it useful to analyze hunting societies as a major societal type:

In spite of their varied environments, hunters share certain features of social life. They live in bands of about 20 to 200 people, the majority of bands having fewer than 50. Bands are divided into families, which may forage alone in some seasons. Hunters have simple but ingenious technologies. Bows and arrows, spears, skin clothing, and temporary leaf or wood shelters are common. Most hunters do some fishing. The band forages and hunts in a large territory and usually moves camp often.

Social life is egalitarian. There is of course no state, no organized government. Apart from religious shamans or magicians, the division of labor is based only on sex and age. Resources are owned communally; tools and personal possessions are freely exchanged. Everyone works who can. Band leadership goes to whichever man has the intelligence, courage, and foresight to command the respect of his fellows. Intelligent older women are also looked up to. (Gough, 1971, p. 765)

Marriage and sex practices in hunting societies in some ways resemble those in modern societies more than those in the agrarian states at the middle range of societal complexity. Hunting societies tend to be relaxed sexually; there is premarital sexual freedom, special times of sexual license for people not married to each other, and a "pragmatic" approach to adultery. The best-known example of the relaxed sexual customs that tend to prevail among hunters is the Eskimo custom of the wife sleeping with male guests as part of normal hospitality.

Kathleen Gough (1971) notes that group marriage does not exist among hunters, but mating has more of a group character than in agrarian or industrial societies. There is less differentiation between the band and the nuclear family than in our society—the band is as much part of everyone's daily environment as the family.

Although elders arrange marriages, couples usually know each other and have some choice. "Both sexual and companionate love between individual men and women are known and deeply experienced. With comparative freedom of mating, love is less often separated from or opposed to marriage than in archaic states or even than in some modern nations" (Gough, 1971).

Relations between parents and children also appear to be more relaxed in hunting societies than in more complex ones. Stephens (1963) suggests that this may result from the greater authoritarianism of stratified states with central political leadership. When society is organized as a pyramid, with a king or chief at the top and social groups arranged in layers beneath him, children and women are likely to be at the bottom. Furthermore, children may be better treated in hunting societies because hunters seem to enjoy their work and life more than farmers or workers in industrial societies. Although the productivity of hunters is low, they do not work at hunting endlessly. They are not harried; indeed, many hunting peoples are extremely leisured. One anthropologist calls hunting society "the original affluent society" (Sahlins, 1968). Children in hunting societies, as part of their socialization, do the kinds of things that are intrinsically enjoyable for small children in any culture. Turnbull (1961) describes the way children's play in one hunting society imperceptibly changes into adult work:

> Like children everywhere, Pygmy children love to imitate their adult idols. This is the beginning of their schooling, for the adults will always encourage and help them. What else is there for them to learn except to grow into good adults? So a fond father will make a tiny bow for his son, and arrows of soft wood with blunt points. He may also give him a strip of hunting net. A mother will delight herself and her daughter by weaving a miniature carrying basket. At an early age, boys and girls are "playing house."
>
> They will also play at hunting, the boys stretching out their little bits of net while the girls beat the ground with bunches of leaves and drive some poor tired old frog in toward the boys. . . . One day they find that the games they have been playing are not games any longer, but the real things, for they have become adults. Their hunting is now real hunting; their tree climbing is in earnest search of inaccessible honey, in the pursuit of elusive game, or in avoiding malicious forest buffalo. It happens so gradually that they hardly notice the change at first, for even when they are proud and famous hunters their life is still full of fun and laughter. (Turnbull, 1961, pp. 128–129)

Finally, obedience is not a major value among hunters and gatherers. A study by Barry, Child, and Bacon (1959) compared child-training practices and child behavior in societies having different types of subsistence economy. They found that hunting and fishing societies emphasized achievement, independence, and self-reliance, whereas agricultural societies stressed compliance and obedience. If crops and animals must be tended regularly, disobedience or even innovation can endanger the food supply for months. Thus farmers and herders must be cautious and responsible. Since hunters cannot store food, cautiousness and responsibility are not so crucial.

In recent years hunting and gathering societies are coming to be viewed in a new light. In the nineteenth century peoples with low levels of technological development were considered savages, living fossils with mental capacities between civilized people and apes. Civilization was regarded as progress up the ladder of human perfection. If, as nineteenth-century "false Darwinism" had it, evolution was the survival of the fittest, then simple societies obviously were unfit. Now, however, assessing the alienation of modern society and the environmental crises, anthropologists and others are coming to reevaluate the "advantages" of civilization. Hunting and gathering societies are coming to be judged as models of environmental balance and of human interaction, and possibly as models for human societies in the postindustrial future:

> The Mbuti pygmies have apparently lived for many millennia in remarkable balance with their environment. . . . Mbuti society is permissive, egalitarian, supportive, fun-loving, and sharing. . . . We moderns may now have a similar possibility, as predicted by . . . curves of the evolutionary process. After twenty millennia of blood, sweat, and tears, we have a technology that can reduce environmental pressures to a minimum if it is administered properly. Man might again, like his remote African ancestors, live in balance with his environment, with all his needs provided for in a genuinely egalitarian, sharing society. (Lomax and Berkowitz, 1972, p. 238)

Societies of the Middle Range

The agricultural revolution represented a major step in the advance of civilization or, to use a less value-loaded term, societal complexity. Hunting and gathering societies depend wholly on what nature provides for food, clothing, and shelter. Since they are always on the move, possessions are a burden, and even infants, the very old, and the very sick may have to be abandoned in times of short supply.

Agriculture made it possible for people to settle in one place, and enormous consequences followed. The ownership of property and its hereditary transmission appeared on the scene. Surplus wealth led to the growth of population, increased population density, and a greater division of labor: people could specialize in crafts and trade. With the increase in population, larger social units began to appear, resulting in the rise of cities and the emergence of the centralized state ruled by kings or other hereditary monarchs, about 4000 B.C. (Gough, 1971). Military conquests of one people by another became possible, and they contributed to the increasing stratification of society into different social classes.

The characteristic form of the family in agrarian societies is the large kin group, whether the unilineal descent groups of preliterate peoples or the extended families of European peasants (see Blumberg and Winch, 1972; Winch and Blumberg, 1968). These kin groups are also hierarchically organized along patriarchal principles.

The agricultural revolution ushered in a way of life with its own social and psychological characteristics. The first farmers had more in common with modern peasants than with the prehistoric hunters who preceded them. "It might be said that for the individual, the revolutionary psychological change was the substitution of routine and hard work for excitement and uncertainty, while the social counterpart was a new stability demanding greater discipline and more government" (Hawkes, 1963, p. 354). The other important contrast between agrarian societies and those at either end of the scale of societal complexity is the importance in them of the extended patriarchal family.

The Traditional Family Observed   Traditional family systems, although differing among themselves, contrast sharply with the Western industrial family. In each, the role of the individual is defined by heredity and long tradition: the extended-family group is an economic unit tied to durable property of some kind; and deviation from community norms is severely sanctioned.

Societies at the middle of the scale of societal complexity—that is, traditional societies—tend to exhibit the most extreme patterns of age and sex subordination within the family. Indeed, William Stephens calls them "deference societies" (1963, p. 324), characterized by ritualized expressions of respect, submissiveness, and obedience. Deference customs between sons and fathers involve such behavior as the following:

1   Not addressing father by his first name
2   Using verbal restraint when speaking to father; speaking in a low voice, not arguing
3   Kneeling or bowing when greeting father
4   Not touching father
5   Not being permitted to eat with father
6   Father has a seat of honor
7   Father and son not supposed to laugh and joke together
8   Strict obedience rules for children

Deference behavior demanded of wives is similar to that demanded for sons. Wives may also be excluded from gatherings attended by husbands.

In studying deference customs cross-culturally, Stephens discovered an all-or-none effect: if there is one deference relationship, there tend to be others. The hub of it all is the child-to-father relationship. If the children must defer to father, there are usually deference rules for elder male relatives, as well as wife-to-husband deferences.

Patterns of subordination are illustrated in a classic study of the Irish peasant family system, first published in 1940 by Arensberg and Kimball (1968). Children in these families begin their work lives very early and attain sociological adulthood very late. A man remains a "boy" verbally and socially until his father dies or retires, and he inherits the family farm or his share of it.

. . . Parental dominance continues as long as the father lives. Even though the major work of the farm devolves upon the sons, they have no control of the direction of farm activities nor of the dispersal of farm income. Thus, the . . . farmer and his sons are often seen at fairs and markets together, but it is the farmer father who does the bargaining. Once when one of the authors asked a countryman about this at a potato market, he explained that he could not leave his post for long because his full-grown son "isn't well-known yet and isn't a good hand at selling."

. . . Even at forty-five and fifty, if the old couple have not made over their farm, the countryman remains a boy in respect to farm work and in the rural vocabulary. . . . The division of labor in the masculine sphere between father and sons, then, is more than an economic arrangement. It is very directly part of the systems of controls, duties and sentiments which make up the whole family life. . . . (Arensberg and Kimball, 1968, pp. 53–55)

Along with a subordination of the young, a sharp differentiation exists between sex roles and derogation of women.
Farm duties are divided into men's and women's work. Some
tasks are divided according to heaviness of the labor, but
many divisions are arbitrary, although those involved do not
consider them so. They assume that the distribution of tasks
corresponds to the natural propensities of the sexes. Thus
selling eggs and milking cows are "natural" for women, and
plowing is "naturally" a male activity. "There is . . . an
entire body of popular belief and superstition surrounding
the dichotomy in farm labor" (Arensberg and Kimball, 1968,
p. 48).

Cernea provides a similar description of the Rumanian
peasant family. About the position of the woman in the
family he writes:

> The inequality between husband and wife in the traditional
> Rumanian peasant family was enormous. Both societal and family
> values and rules reinforced that inequality. As several sociological
> investigations found, unwritten but very powerful village norms
> required that the woman should bow to the man and greet him first.
> A wife should not walk beside her husband but follow behind him;
> when he stopped to chat with another villager, she should stop at
> a definite distance behind him, not interfere with the conversation,
> wait, and start again only after her husband starts walking. At
> home she was "the humble servant of her husband, for all his needs,
> under the penalty of being beaten" (Negrea, 1936, p. 45). Out in the
> agricultural field, she had to perform a considerable share of the
> hardest activities, side by side with her husband. Advanced preg-
> nancy was not a reason to discontinue work, and giving birth to a
> child in the field was reported as a common occurrence. (Cernea,
> 1970, p. 55)

In cultures where deference roles apply in the family,
they appear to generate an emotional climate of reserve,
lacking in spontaneity. Not only is the behavior of the def-
erent person inhibited, but so is the behavior of the person
in the superior position. Extreme power inequality seems to
generate stiff, formal behavior from everyone in the family,
and may even result in family members avoiding each other;
indeed, some societies prescribe patterns of apartness and
estrangement (see LeVine, 1965, pp. 200–204). In the most
patriarchal societies, where the father is most all-powerful
over his children, he is often quite inhibited in his dealings

with them. He may order them around, but he doesn't play or laugh with them or let them sit on his lap. Here is an example of such a family climate from a study of Tepoztlan, Mexico:

> The husband avoids intimacy with members of his family [in order] to be respected by them. He expects them to demonstrate their respect by maintaining a proper social distance. His contacts with the children are brief and reserved. The Tepoztlan husband expects his wife to see that the children are quiet when he is at home, and it is her obligation to teach them to fear him. Men are generally not talkative at home and contribute little to family conversation, nor do they seek or expect their children to confide in them. When the husband is at home during the day, he sits apart from the rest of the family; at night, he eats alone or with his grown sons and goes out, or retires soon after. . . .
>
> Regardless of age or marital state, a son is under his father's authority as long as he lives or works with his father. The son receives no recompense other than his support and care and what spending money he can get from his mother or father . . . (Lewis, 1951, pp. 322–338)

What accounts for such family patterns? Scholars have offered political explanations based on the structure of authority in the larger society, as well as economic explanations based on the control over resources within the family. Stephens attributes the authoritarianism of traditional family life to the autocratic state. He examined family customs in fifty-one societies; those with extremely high deference patterns were parts of kingdoms, while tribal groups tended to be low in deference. Stephens describes the difference between tribes and kingdoms as follows:

> These are the defining attributes of the kingdom: a state, nobles and commoners, an agrarian economic base, exploitation of commoners by nobles, and a state religion.
>
> The other type of society—the tribe—is a society without a state. It is not subject to "a centralized organ of political control, with coercive power over the populace," with an army and tax collectors. Although the tribe may evince some rudimentary form of social stratification, it does not have "nobles" who have the power to economically exploit "commoners." . . . The tribe's subsistence may come from one or several of three sources: agriculture, animal husbandry, hunting (and/or fishing), and gathering.
>
> A tribe never embraces cities. A kingdom may . . . . Some kingdoms are also characterized by a group of culture traits that

are commonly termed "civilization"—large public works and esoteric arts and sciences (written languages, mathematics, astronomy, and so forth). Tribes never have "civilization," thus defined.

The tribe was the first political form to appear. During the earliest periods of human history, people managed to get along without any sort of state government whatsoever. . . . (Stephens, 1963, p. 329)

Between the time the centralized state developed—about 4000 B.C.—and about two hundred years ago, the history of the world was made by kingdoms. (Tribes may have histories too, but these are unrecorded.) Traditional European societies that preceded the modern democratic state belong to this same general cross-cultural type—that is, kingdoms.

Others explain the family patterns of traditional societies differently. Cernea (1970) suggests that the economic infrastructure of the peasant family accounts for the extreme subordination of women and children. The father not only exercises power as head of the household, but also owns and manages the economic unit of the family. Further, agriculture, unlike industrialism, encourages caution and conservation rather than innovation. When slow social change is valued and traditional ways are rewarded, the elders are thought to possess superior wisdom, heightening still further their position vis-à-vis the young.

The Traditional Family Idealized   In this book so far we have dealt at length with the familiar idealizations of the nuclear family in our contemporary culture. We have seen in the previous chapter how the nuclear family, in the writings of some students of the family, is presumed to be a harmoniously balanced social system providing for the satisfaction of human needs and societal stability But the other family systems have also been justified in exactly the same terms. Since the nineteenth century, critiques of the nuclear family have been made from the right and from the left, contrasting the nuclear family with an idealized version of a different family system.

The conservative defense of the traditional family was developed by scholars who mourned the passing of the old monarchial regimes based on hereditary status, religion, tradition, and blood ties. They combined a Utopian vision of feudal society with an acute insight into the strains of modern industrial ones. In traditional society everyone knew his duty and his place, and life was stable and cohesive. To these scholars the traditional family seemed to symbolize the principle of "authority without resentment."

For the scholars in this tradition the modern nuclear family is a disastrous social form. In fact, the popular cliché that the decline of family life leads to the downfall of civilization originated with this group of scholars. People who state the cliché today believe they are talking about the nuclear family, but it was the decline of the traditional family that was lamented in the original formulation of the idea. Thus Zimmerman (1947) wrote that the decline of patriarchal authority in the Roman family led to the demoralization of society and ultimately the downfall of Rome. Zimmerman argued that familistic values, which dictated that people subordinate their own needs to those of the family, gave way to individualism, leading to the breakdown of morality, authority, and social cohesiveness. Zimmerman thought the same process might be happening in the United States during the twentieth century.

Zimmerman's work was influenced by that of Frederic Le Play, a nineteenth-century French scholar. Like a number of other French scholars of the family and the old regime in France—that is, of France before the French Revolution—Le Play contrasted two extreme forms of the family, the patriarchal and the "unstable" or nuclear family, with an intermediate form, the stem family, which Le Play thought of as ideal. In the patriarchal family, sons and sometimes daughters remain in their parent's home after marriage. When the household grows too large some members leave to create a new patriarchal unit. Le Play saw the patriarchal family as a more primitive form, and emphasized that most of these families would be found in agriculture.

In the stem family only one heir inherits and lives in the ancestral home and lands. The others are given "dowries" and can become independent, although the ancestral home remains a permanent center for all the members of the family. The direct heir usually inherits the same profession as the father. Le Play thought the stem family "answered all the legitimate instincts of humanity. This is why public order prevails everywhere it exists in strength" (1935; originally 1866). The patriarchal system was too limiting, since all the sons were confined to the father's household and occupation, but Le Play saw it as a sound system nevertheless. But for the "unstable" family he had not a single good word to say.

Le Play saw the unstable family prevailing among factory workers as well as among the wealthy classes of France. He noted that the individual under the new family regime could rapidly reach a high social position, because he could dispose freely of his inheritance and his income. He need no longer provide for the needs of relatives. But for Le Play, mobility and achievement were not particularly attractive values. The detachment from the larger family that made mobility possible also made the "unstable" family very vulnerable to disorganization as a result of illness, death, and financial need. People not only could rise but also could rapidly fall into misery and pauperism. Le Play believed that happiness in private life was guaranteed in the stem family, because it balances tradition and novelty, liberty and restraint, individualism and association. As for the individualism of the new family system, Le Play had this to say:

The advantages which certain people derive from the unlimited extension of individual desires appear greater than they
are in reality Where individualism becomes dominant in social
relations men rapidly move towards barbarism. (Le Play, 1866, p. 14)

Because his values are so contrary to contemporary
American ones, it is easier to see how they influence Le Play's
analysis than a piece of work whose assumptions come closer
to our own. His work serves as a useful model of how ideological biases intertwine with valid description and astute
analysis.

Le Play disregarded the strains within the traditional
society and family, but his analysis of the weaknesses of the
modern family is still valid: its vulnerability to crisis, and
its replacement of duty and obligation by individual freedom. Le Play has traditionally been regarded by sociologists
as a mere propagandist for reactionary political positions.
Yet actually Le Play engaged in field work and made careful
observations of families in a large number of European
societies. Many of his insights were stated in the form of
testable hypotheses about the social conditions associated
with each form of the family (Parish and Schwartz, 1972).

Another idealization of traditional society may be found
in Philippe Aries' *Centuries of Childhood* (1962). Aries describes medieval society as a big, happy, sociable mixture of
young and old, rich and poor, from which the middle classes
came to withdraw over the centuries of their rise to social
power. Aries' glossing over of the social inequalities of the
medieval society places him in the conservative tradition;
class distinctions were sharply marked by dress and manner,
but people of different ranks were physically and emotionally
close to each other:

The valet never left his master, whose friend and accomplice
he was, in accordance with an emotional code to which we have lost
the key today. . . . The haughtiness of the master matched the
insolence of the servant and restored, for better or worse, a hierarchy which excessive familiarity was perpetually calling into
question.

People lived in a state of high contrast; high birth or great
wealth rubbed shoulders with poverty, vice with virtue, scandal
with devotion. Despite its shrill contrasts, this medley of colors
caused no surprise. A man or woman of quality felt no embarrassment at visiting in rich clothes the poor wretches in the prisons,
the hospitals or the streets, nearly naked beneath their rags. The

juxtaposition of these extremes no more embarrassed the rich than it humiliated the poor. (Aries, 1962, p. 414)

Although Aries' praise of medieval times and his rejection of modern society and the whole modernizing process — mass education, industrialism, achievement motivation — places him in a conservative camp, the value he places in individualism puts him on the opposite side from such writers as Le Play.

The conservative historians denounced individualism because it opposed the hereditary duties and customs of the traditional family. Aries argues that individualism has triumphed over the family. In Aries' view the increasing power of the intense, tightly knit nuclear family has flourished at the expense of the individual and also has destroyed the richly textured communal society of medieval times.

Strains in the Traditional Family   Considerable evidence indicates that the traditional family system was never as harmonious as its defenders would have us believe. It is interesting to contrast the idealized versions of traditional family life in Le Play and others with actual studies of peasant families showing the household and inheritance patterns of the patriarchal and stem family. Wherever studies of peasant families have been carried out, one finds the same picture of individual subordination to the demands of the land and to a patriarchal authority structure (Maspetiol, in Cernea, 1970). As Berkner points out:

The peasant's entire household may have looked like a big happy family, but it was held together by legal restrictions imposed in the peasant community and by the limited opportunities offered by the rural economy. (1972, p. 418)

Among peasants the father's parental authority is enhanced by his economic roles as manager, owner, and decision maker. The demands of the peasant father for obedience and discipline are strengthened to the extent that the children have no choice as to what they will be or where they will live: they would be farmers or farmers' wives. In short, the traditional peasant family imposes a life of toil and obedience and raises "virtually insurmountable barriers to possible attempts at escape" (Cernea, 1970).

The chief source of strain appears to have been in the father-son relationship. For the son the hardest time was when full grown, when he had to wait to inherit the farm in order to marry and achieve a man's status. For the father the hardest time was the retirement period, when the farm was transferred to the son during the father's lifetime. Such strains could be deduced from the prevalence of separate living quarters for the retired couple, and of detailed legal contracts setting forth the specific right the father retained after relinquishing the farm to the heir:

> When, for example, Joseph and Anna Maria Pichler decided to retire in October 1784, they drew up a contract with their son Johann and his bride Gertraud, selling them their house and fields for 100 florings. Joseph deducted 20 florings from the price as a wedding gift . . . and asked that the rest be paid in installments of 20 florings every . . . September 29. . . . They reserved the right to live in *Stubl* [retirement room] rent-free for the rest of their lives, the use of a small piece of meadow and a section of garden to grow cabbage and potatoes, and a yearly supply of seven bushels of wheat, thirty-two batches of hay, and two piles of wood. (Berkner, 1972, p. 401)

The prolongation of the lifespan in relatively modern times obviously increased this source of strain:

> The dutiful son mourned the day when his parents passed promptly to their reward . . . . That was as it should be and he inherited their place. But there were no attitudes proper for the situation in which the old people lived on and on while their successor waited impatiently. (Handlin and Handlin, 1971, p. 8)

Marriage in this system was part of the family business rather than an individual affair of the heart. We tend to forget that there was a time when marrying for love rather than to advance the fortunes of groups seemed as radical an act as living together unmarried, or joining a commune, is today. Stone (1960) describes the bitter family struggles in the English nobility that led to the acceptance of the woman's right to a veto over marriages arranged by parents. During the early part of the period marriages among the nobility were arranged as important business transactions without regard to the wishes of the marrying couple. It was common, for example, for small children to be bartered in advance by their families. Stone argues that these practices were supported by an ideology of strict parental control over children. These beliefs in the natural subjugation of children paralleled the political doctrine of the divine right of kings.

In addition, noble sons as well as daughters were totally dependent economically on their parents—another instance of similarity between the extreme ends of the social scale. In trying to account for the modification of parent-child relations that resulted in the right of a child to say "no" to the parent's choice of a spouse, Stone refers to the several ideological currents at the time that favored individualism in religion, economics, and politics: the rise of the Protestant Ethic, the growth of capitalism, and the growing challenge to the institution of absolute monarchy.

Besides the influence of new ideas, however, transportation affected the social lives of young people. The opening of roads and of a coach service between London and countryside led to the development of a "social season" in London. The nobility from all over England would come together every year for the balls and other events of the season. The increased social contacts resulting from the festivities may have made the old obligation to marry someone picked out by one's parents more objectionable. It was one thing to marry a stranger chosen by Father when you didn't know any other young men and women; it was something else to have to do so after having met the entire field of eligible young people during the season.

We also tend to forget that the freedom from having to inherit the occupation of one's father was part of the same liberating trend. Today, wherever the process of breaking away from traditional kinship patterns occurs, it goes along with the same sense of personal liberation. When a shift toward modernization takes place in underdeveloped countries, the resentments generated by traditional-family systems play an important role in enhancing change. Both modernization and the nuclear family, Goode notes, appeal to intellectuals, to the young, to women, and to the disadvantaged in general:

. . . The ideology of the conjugal family is a radical one, destructive of the older traditions in almost every society. . . . . Its appeal is almost as universal as that of "redistribution of the land." It asserts the equality of individuals, as against class, caste, or sex barriers. (1963, p. 19)

This does not mean, however, that in traditional-family systems people constantly chafe under their restrictions. In spite of their built-in strains traditional-family structures can remain stable for centuries, sustained by duty, law, and lack of other opportunities. Like most revolutions the revolution in family patterns requires that some alternative vision, some other way of doing things, becomes available or necessary to large numbers of people. Such change can be facilitated by a number of factors—literacy, improved transportation, access to market towns and outside jobs, or a poor harvest or too many sons for the land to support. All these factors promote migration of sons and brothers from the family farm, while illiteracy and isolation perpetuate traditional-family structures (Parish and Schwartz, 1972).

Modern Society, Modern Family

We realize that the world we live in and the lives we lead differ from those of the past. Modern Western societies of Europe and America seem to contrast with their own historic past, and with non-Western societies. Social scientists, including economists and historians as well as sociologists and anthropologists, have been much concerned with describing and analyzing such changes. Societies are often divided into two contrasting types: industrial/preindustrial, modern/traditional, advanced/underdeveloped, complex/simple, urban/folk, literate/preliterate. Each term accents a different aspect of the contrast between two types of society. None of the terms is completely satisfactory to the scholars involved.

Although social science disagrees about how to define the essential difference between modern and premodern societies, it generally recognizes that family life is deeply implicated in the change. The transition to modern society seems to involve changes in both the way people relate to each other within families, and the way family life fits into the rest of society. Scholars disagree, however, about how to define the difference, what causes it, and how pervasive it is.

The accompanying table (Table 1) summarizes some of the major contrasts the scholars have drawn between the modern and the traditional family. It should be noted that different scholars have emphasized different contrasts. Further, on several of the items they disagree as to whether traditional and modern families do differ from each other.

TABLE 1   TRADITIONALISM VS. MODERNISM IN FAMILY FORM, FUNCTION, AND IDEOLOGY

Traditional	Modern
1 Kinship is organizing principle of society; almost everything a person does he does as a member of a kinship group.	1 Kinship is differentiated from economic, political, and social life; recruitment to jobs is independent of one's relatives.
2 The extended or complex family may be basic unit of residence and domestic functions — e.g., meals, child care.	2 Conjugal or nuclear family is basic unit of residence and domestic functions.
3 Most adults work at home; the home is workshop as well as school, hospital, old-age home.	3 Separation of home and work; household consumes rather than produces.
4 Low geographic and social mobility; sons inherit father's status and occupation.	4 High geographic and social mobility; individual mobility based on merit.
5 Dominance of parents over children, men over women.	5 Relatively egalitarian relations within nuclear family in ideals and practice.
6 High fertility and high death rates, especially in infancy; rapid population turnover — death a constant presence in families.	6 Low, controlled fertility and low death rates, especially low in infancy; death a phenomenon of old age — four generations alive at the same time in many families.
7 Kinship bonds override economic efficiency and maximization of individual gain.	7 Advancement and economic gain of individuals prevails over kin obligations.
8 Ideology of duty, tradition, individual submission to authority and to fate.	8 Ideology of individual rights, equality, freedom, self-realization.
9 Little emphasis on emotional involvement within nuclear family; marriage not based on love; predominant loyalty of individual is to blood kin, rather than spouse; children are economic rather than emotional assets, but subordination and dependency of children on parents may continue as long as parent lives — in Europe parent-child bonds may be reduced further by practice of apprenticing children to other families at an early age.	9 Intense involvement of spouses, parents, and children with each other; ideologies of marital happiness and adjustment; great concern with child's development, current adjustment and future potential, but sharp break with parental authority upon attaining adulthood.
10 Little or no psychological separation between home and community; broad communal sociability; no large-scale institutions.	10 Sharp line of demarcation between home and outside world; home is a private retreat and outside world is impersonal, competitive, threatening.

The categories in the table represent ideal types—broad patterns rather than firm and certain distinctions. Ideal types suggest patterns of family change characteristic of many societies experiencing modernization. In any particular country, historical period, or social class, however, everything does not change all at once. In general the "modern" family pattern is found more completely and is more widespread in the middle class. Even today some aspects of the traditional pattern occur in families at the extreme ends of the socioeconomic class scale. Kinship, for example, is more important among American families in the Social Register, and among the poor, than it is in middle-class groups. And Japanese society has combined an advanced economy with a traditional patriarchal-family system.

Industrialism and the Family   Despite the possibility of citing major contrasts between the modern and traditional families, scholars still disagree on the essential difference between modern and traditional social organization as well as the family. Is it the presence of large factories, the growth of cities, widespread literacy, the spread of democratic ideas, the separation of kinship from other aspects of life? Or is it all of these taken together? It is similarly difficult to offer definitive answers to questions about the relation between social change and family life: does family life really change drastically in the transition to modern society? In what aspects is there an underlying stability and continuity? Finally, what aspects of family life do change—household living arrangements, who lives with whom, the quality of emotional relationships, the economic functions of the family, the ideas people have about marriage and family?

One source of confusion in discussions about the family and industrialization is the assumption that in modern societies all families are nuclear, whereas in the past all families were large, extended kin groups. Goode describes as a myth the "classical family of Western nostalgia": the stereotype of a happy life down on the farm, where lots of kinfolk and their children live in a big rambling house (Goode, 1963, p. 6). Recent work by historians has shown that the nuclear-family form predominated in Western Europe and America long before the coming of industrialism.

Another misleading assumption, found not only among laymen but also among family scholars, is the belief that the coming of factories destroyed the large kin group down on the farm. The correlation between industrial society and the nuclear family is often interpreted, in an overly literal and simplistic way, to mean that the nuclear family comes about *only* in an industrial society, and that the presence of factories leads in some inexorable way to the breakup of large kin groups. Often studies use literal models of industrialism to attack the idea that technological change leads to family change: thus, for example, a study might be done in country X to show that large industry moved in and did not at once destroy all existing kin ties. Or a study might attempt to show that working in factories did not destroy the kin ties of a group of nineteenth-century immigrants to America who came with extended-family structures. Or a study might argue that the nuclear family existed in Europe and America before industrialization, therefore technology does not cause family change.

The problem with such studies is that they attack straw men: simplistic and mechanical versions of the relation between economic and family change. The presence of large factories is only one of a number of factors that set off a modern or advanced society from a more traditional one. "Industrialism" is a convenient metaphor, a shorthand reference to a host of social changes that occur when a society modernizes: cities grow in size and importance; population size and density increase; demands arise for literacy and other trained skills; communication and transportation systems improve; and the rate of social change increases. Each of these changes by itself could have profound effects on family life. Yet the term may be misleading in its emphasis on factories as the essential ingredient of modern life, and the most important factor in family change. Indeed, some scholars have argued that industrialization is not even an essential part of modernization. The historian E. A. Wrigley (1972), for example, argues that a society might become modernized before becoming industrialized, and that this in fact occurred in Europe beginning in the sixteenth century. The essence of modernization in this view is the existence of commerce and trade, a money economy, and the values of economic self-interest and rationality—rationality being defined in a narrow sense as "that which maximizes economic returns either to the individual, the nuclear family, or the state," as opposed to the larger kin group (Wrigley, 1972, p. 229). Such rationality also implies that people are recruited to jobs on the basis of ability rather than hereditary status. Once kinship is no longer the basis of economic life, social, occupational and geographic mobility tend to increase. All these changes together weaken bonds based on kinship by making them less necessary and less enforceable.

Individualism and the Nuclear Family   The separation of individuals and the nuclear family from the larger kin group can occur in preindustrial or primitive societies as well as modern and industrial ones. Thus, in a survey of 250 societies, Murdock notes that the development of the nuclear (neolocal) family is favored by any influence that emphasizes the individual:

> Individualism in its various manifestations, e.g., private property, individual enterprise in the economic sphere, or personal freedom in the choice of marital partners, facilitates the establishment of independent households by married couples. A similar effect may be produced by individual migration, or by pioneer life in the occupation of new territory, or by the expansion of trade and industry, or by developing urbanization. . . . Even a change in architecture might exert an influence, e.g., the supplanting of a large communal house by a form of dwelling suited to the occupancy of a single family. (Murdock, 1949, pp. 203–204)

Another seemingly paradoxical finding about the nuclear family is that it appears in the most advanced, modern countries as well as in the most technologically simple. That is, the nuclear family appears as the dominant form in hunting societies such as the Eskimo, the extended family predominates in agricultural societies, then the nuclear family reappears in modern conditions. In other words, if all known societies were listed in the order of their complexity along the horizontal part of a graph and family type plotted on the vertical part of the scale, the relationship between societal development or complexity and family form would be curvilinear, as indicated in the accompanying graph. Why should this be so?

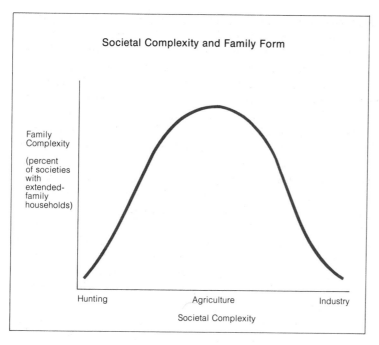

Societal Complexity and Family Form

Family
Complexity

(percent
of societies
with
extended-
family
households)

Hunting   Agriculture   Industry

Societal Complexity

This chart indicates that the percent of societies with extended-family households reaches highest in agricultural societies. (After Blumberg and Winch,
1972)

To answer this question, Nimkoff and Middleton examined more than five hundred societies for which detailed
ethnographic information existed. They concluded that
modern industrial societies in some important ways resemble
simpler hunting and gathering societies. Both hunting and
modern societies tend to individualize the worker.

The modern industrial society, with its small independent
family, is then like the simpler hunting and gathering society . . .
for some of the same reasons, namely limited need for family labor
and physical mobility. The hunter is mobile because he pursues
the game, the industrial worker, the job. (Nimkoff and Middleton,
1960, p. 225)

The variables associated with the appearance of the extended family were the reverse of the foregoing ones: an
ample and stable food supply, the use of the family as the
unit of labor, geographic immobility, and family-owned
property, especially in the form of land. Payment in money

also has individualizing effects. In peasant societies labor tends to be unpaid family labor. Property in the form of money rather than family-owned land or durable goods also favors the nuclear family over the extended family.

Winch and Blumberg (1968) found some striking parallels between Nimkoff and Middleton's variables and the correlates of extended families in American society today. That is, geographic mobility, family property, and the family as a unit of labor also account for variations in the extent to which American families are involved with extended kin. Winch and Blumberg also found that certain ethnic groups in American society, particularly Jews and Italians, tended to have stronger extended-family ties than others; they account for these differences in terms of length of time since immigration, social class, and occupational traditions. Thus the closer a group is to its immigrant roots, the stronger the extended-family ties. Also certain occupations such as storekeeping tend to encourage the maintenance of extended-family ties. In short, family patterns vary within industrial societies, and this variation can be explained in much the same terms as variation in family form among different kinds of societies.

The work of Winch and Blumberg also sheds light on the relationship between industrialism and the nuclear family. When they arranged 933 industrial societies in order of their complexity, they found that the nuclear family began to emerge *before* industrialism. In other words, the curve of extended familism took a downward turn in societies that were still mainly agricultural but complex, as indicated by their having irrigation, towns with more than five thousand people, and three or more levels of political hierarchy. These are indicators of societal complexity because they are complicated kinds of social organization, requiring specialized skills. They also show that the society is producing enough food to release some people from agriculture. These cross-cultural findings parallel the historical findings that the nuclear family emerged in Europe before the industrial revolution.

Ideology and Economic Change   In discussions of family change, the issue is sometimes posed in an either/or fashion, either technological change "causes" family change independent of people's wishes and feelings, or family values and ideologies are completely independent of economic factors. It is more useful to think of family and social change as a complex interplay of both sets of factors.

Scholars have pointed above all to individualism and a certain kind of individualistic rationality when trying to define the essential difference between modern and traditional societies. As Wrigley (1972) puts it, it is not that traditional societies are irrational, but they define rationality differently. Traditional rationality may mean working only enough to supply one's minimal wants or it may mean staying together in large kin groups even though the family lands can scarcely support everyone. In modern Western terms, however, rationality has come to mean maximizing economic gain. Wrigley argues that, once begun, modernization sets off a chain reaction of psychological effects that further increase the momentum of change; rationality and individualism "eat like acid" into the fabric of traditional society, destroying the web of rights and obligations as well as the structure of traditional authority.

Some scholars have suggested that the spread of literacy is the most meaningful feature of modernization, antedating industrial development (Goody and Watt, 1962; Parsons, 1965). For example, Parsons considers the invention of writing the dividing line between primitive and intermediate societies, and the extension of literacy from elite groups to the whole population a major distinguishing feature of modern societies. The growth of commerce and industry would be almost unthinkable without the existence of written records, bookkeeping, and accounting systems.

Though literacy spreads because of economic need, it has profound psychological consequences. Literacy fosters the same tendencies toward rationality and individualism that are encouraged by the economic aspects of modernization. Preliterate people are not unsophisticated, simple, or at a lower stage of intellect; rather, they are skilled in a different medium of communication—the oral tradition. Using human memory capacities that remain undeveloped where literacy prevails, people who live entirely in the oral tradition can store enormous amounts of information, experience, and entertainment and can reproduce this information with astonishing accuracy.

Literacy is a decisive dividing line in individual development also. There is by now an impressive body of research evidence showing that many psychological changes once thought to represent the unfolding of the innate capacities of the human mind may actually be the result of literacy (LeVine, 1970, p. 585). Such skills as the capacity for abstract thought, the ability to make logical inferences, for example, now appear to develop from the outside in rather than the inside out. Or, as Jerome Bruner (1964) puts it, cognitive development may be to a large degree the internalization of technology. David Riesman (1960) has summarized some of the consequences of the transition from the oral tradition to literacy. Writing tends to foster hierarchies of skill rather than age. In the oral tradition the status of the old is enhanced by their role as storehouses of experience and lore.

Another effect of literacy is individualizing the person, separating him from the primary group of family and kinsmen and his world of immediate experience. Books permit detachment and a critical attitude. Just as the ability to write improves the conversation one carries on with oneself, so the ability to read makes it possible to "converse" with people in distant times and places. Reading a book in the presence of others is an isolating act. We noted earlier the finding that geographic and social mobility is associated with the breakdown of extended kinship relations. Riesman has emphasized that reading is the mental equivalent of mobility—you can leave home in your imagination:

> Thus the book helps liberate the reader from his group and its emotions, and allows the contemplation of alternative responses and the trying on of new emotions. Weber has stressed the importance of the merchant's account book in rationalizing the merchant and his commerce; other historians have made familiar the role of the printed Bible in challenging the authority of the Roman Church. Luther, and especially Calvin, increasing by their doctrine the growing isolation of men, invited each pilgrim to progress by himself, book in hand, while at the same time trying to institute a new authority in the place of the old. But as the dissident sects of Protestantism illustrate, the book tends to be a solvent of authority: just as there are still blank pages in the merchant's account book, waiting to be filled, so there is always the question when one has challenged traditional authority "What next?"

At the same time, while the book helped people break away from family and parish, it linked them into noncontiguous associations of true believers. The Polish peasant who learned to read and write became identified with the urban world of progress and enlightenment, of ideology and Utopia, even while still in the peasant world. (Riesman, 1960, p. 113)

If literacy is used as an indicator of modernity, Western Europe began to change centuries before the first factories appeared on the scene. The growth of cities, trade, and perhaps above all the growth of empire during the age of exploration accelerated demand for people who could read and write. A recent study by the economic historian Carlo M. Cipolla (1969) traces the beginnings of the literacy revolution in Western Europe to the eleventh century.

The spread of literacy was accompanied by three different interpretations of its significance. Some saw it merely as a skill necessary to run the economy. Others saw it as a means of opening many minds to the benefits of civilization. Still others saw the spread of literacy as a subversive threat to the stability of the social order. Two arguments were used against the extension of literacy to the poor: the first was that it would make people despise the place in life that they had been born to, and the second that they would read seditious books and pamphlets that would "render them insolent to their superiors; and in a few years the result would be that the legislature would find it necessary to direct the strong arm of power towards them" (Cipolla, 1969, pp. 65–66). All these predictions came true. Education did encourage peasants to leave the fields, seditious books and pamphlets were written and read, and played a role in the French and American revolutions. In general, literacy fostered the same tendencies toward rationality and individualism that are also promoted by the economic and political aspects of modernization.

Psychological Quality of the Intimate Environment   What is it that sets the modern family off from its historical counterparts? We have seen that the classical family of Western nostalgia—the large household bursting with kin—is largely a myth. In America and Western Europe the nuclear family was the prevailing unit, although peasant families were extended during part of the life cycle, and the household often contained nonkinsmen in the form of peasants and servants. Is there then any basis for the assumption that family life was different in the past?

The answer, emerging now from historical studies, seems

to be "yes." Modern family life is different, but the size of the household is not what has changed. What seems to have changed is the psychological quality of the intimate environments of family life, and the relation between the family and the larger community. Within the home the family has become more intense emotionally, while the ties between home and the outside community have become more tenuous.

In the past the line of demarcation between the family and the outside world was not as marked as in our time. The historian John Demos has described the sense of continuity between the family and community in the Plymouth colony:

. . . While the family is now less important from a social standpoint, it may well be *more* important from a psychological one. The crucial factor here is a certain feeling of connectedness, or isolation, with regard to the community at large—the degree to which individual persons sense that their life in a family makes a natural whole with other aspects of their experience. At Plymouth, we have seen, the family was joined to other institutions and other purposes in an intricate web of interconnections. It did not stand out in any special way from adjacent parts of the social backdrop; it acquired no distinctive aura of emotional or ideological significance. Its importance, while impossible to doubt, was more assumed than understood—was, indeed, so basic and so automatic as to be almost invisible. Family and community, private and public life, formed part of the same moral equation. The one supported the other, and they became in a sense indistinguishable. (Demos, 1970, p. 186)

This continuity stemmed not only from the fact that people were unified through a set of common religious beliefs, but also from two facts that represent different aspects of the same circumstance: that families and households, not individuals, were the units of work, and that large-scale organizations outside the home were absent. Thus Peter Laslett describes the difference between preindustrial and contemporary England:

. . . In spite of all the subordination, the exploitation and the obliteration of those who were young, feminine, or in service, everyone belonged in a group, a family group . . . .

. . . [The relative absence] of large-scale institutions makes the contrast with our own world more telling than ever. We have only to think of the hundreds of children sitting everyday . . . in their classrooms, the hundreds and thousands together in the factories, the offices, the shops to recognize the difference. (P. Laslett, 1965, pp. 4–11)

In these preindustrial households people of both sexes and different ages were mixed together; some of the children might go to school, but adults did not usually go out to work. During the early stages of the industrial revolution, manufacturing was also carried on in homes. Thus English farm families might engage in the making of textiles during slow times on the farm. Actually, this cottage industry, or "putting-out system" as it was known, persisted in some industries into the twentieth century.

The coming of factories did not, then, create the nuclear-family structure in Europe, but it did change the quality of family life. It destroyed, as Laslett puts it, the "familial texture" of society; the removal of economic functions from the patriarchal family created the mass society. The transformation of the world outside the home from a small community into a place of impersonal, large-scale institutions transformed the home itself and the family. There began to be a sense of a gulf between the home and the society at large; each came to be perceived as a separate sphere of life. The home came to be idealized as an "Edenic retreat" from the harsh realities of nineteenth-century industrial society, a place of perfect love, companionship, and moral regeneration (Jeffrey, 1972). Demos describes the kind of gulf that separates the modern American family from society, in contrast to continuity between family and community in colonial times:

The family, in particular, stands quite apart from most other aspects of life. We have come to assume that whenever a man leaves his home "to go out into the world" he crosses a very critical boundary. Different rules, different values, different feelings apply on either side, and any failure to appreciate this brings, inevitably, the most painful kind of personal distress. The contrast has, of course, a pejorative character. The family becomes a kind of shrine for upholding and exemplifying all of the softer virtues — love, generosity, tenderness, altruism, harmony, repose. The world at large presents a much more sinister aspect. Impersonal, chaotic, unpredictable, often characterized by strife and sometimes by outright malignity, it requires of a man that he be constantly "on his guard." It goads and challenges him at every point, and occasionally provokes responses of a truly creative sort; but it also exhausts him. So it is that he must retreat periodically within the family circle. (Demos, 1970, p. 186)

In the next chapter we explore some of the issues scholars have raised concerning the paradoxical place of the family in modern society: as it has lost its economic functions, it has come to loom larger psychologically.

Summary

In recent years scholars have become increasingly interested in family change. Rather than considering the family as essentially "the same" everywhere, they have been looking at how broader aspects of society affect family life. The relationship between the family, technological change in general, and industrialism in particular has been the subject of much confusion and debate. Rather than being a product solely of industrial society, however, the nuclear family emerges whenever the individual is set off from the large family group. Thus hunting societies also have the nuclear family. Furthermore, in Western societies the nuclear-family structure appeared before the industrial revolution of the nineteenth century. It emerged in early modern times when towns grew in size and number, trade and handicrafts increased in importance, a monetary economy replaced barter, and literacy spread, along with other indicators of societal complexity. In short, the nuclear-family structure in Europe seems to have emerged in the context of mercantile, rather than industrial, capitalism. Industrial capitalism, however, altered the quality of family life by separating the workshop from the hearth, the family from society, leading to the enhancement of the psychological over the social and economic functions of the family.

KIN, COUPLES, AND COMMUNES: FAMILIES IN MODERN SOCIETY

Chapter 4

The word alienation is part of the cant of the mid-twentieth century and it began as an attempt to describe the separation of the worker from his world of work. We need not accept all that this expression has come to convey in order to recognize that it does point to something vital to us all in relation to our past. Time was when the whole of life went forward in the family, in a circle of loved, familiar faces, known and fondled objects, all to human size That time has gone forever. It makes us very different from our ancestors.

Peter Laslett, The World We Have Lost

Chapter Four   Around the turn of the century it was a sociological truism that the coming of the urban industrial society was causing the family to lose its functions and wither away. Not just the extended group but the nuclear family as well was included in predictions of decline.

The ideas of such scholars were paralleled in the arguments of feminists of the period, but with a different emphasis. Whereas the scholars regretted or had mixed feelings about the passing home and family, the feminists applauded it:

> The family, they thought, once the most important unit of production, had gradually surrendered its functions to institutions outside the home—manufacturing to the factory, control over property to the state, the education of children to the public schools. . . . The tasks formerly performed by the housewife and the family in general were now performed elsewhere, and the function of the housewife in consequence was reduced to the passive role of consumption. The feminists did not regret the passing of the family; on the contrary, as staunch evolutionists, they regarded it as highly desirable. . . . (Lasch, 1965, p. 47)

In 1903 Charlotte Perkins Gilman saw in the kindergarten and the day nursery the liberation of both women and children:

> There is no more brilliant hope on earth today than this new thought about the child . . . children as citizens with rights guaranteed by the state; instead of our previous attitude towards them of absolute personal ownership—the unchecked tyranny, or as unchecked indulgence, of the private home. (Gilman, 1903, p. 335)

During the period under discussion the issues raised by the feminists preoccupied the leading intellectuals as well as the pages of the women's magazines, just as today. Yet during the fifty-year eclipse of the feminist movement, the idea that the demise of the family was a mark of progress passed from popular consciousness, remaining alive only on the fringes of society in bohemian and socialist groups.

Assessing the Family in Modern Society

It is impossible to understand recent social-science literature on the role of the family in modern society without recognizing that much of it was written as an attack on scholars who had predicted the death of the family as a concomitant of urban industrialism.

Unlike the feminists the social scientists who believed the family would wither away were not happy about the prospect of a world without a strong family life. Some of these writers, most notably Le Play and Zimmerman, argued that "civilization" itself was threatened by the breakup of traditional kin bonds. They felt that the nuclear family, which Le Play called "the unstable family" and Zimmerman called "atomistic," was only a way station on the road to the total collapse of family life and civilization. They reasoned that once individualism replaced tradition and filial duty as the ruling principle of life, people would ultimately reject the burdens of family responsibility. Another group of writers—notably Louis Wirth and Ralph Linton—agreed that urban industrial society presaged the demise of the family, but they did not go along with the idea that the quality of civilization would also decline. Wirth acknowledged that city life was accompanied by a more impersonal and superficial level of human relations, but he also credited the city with the production of cosmopolitan tastes and sophisticated ideas.

All these writers recognized that modernization and urbanization introduced profound transformations in the culture and personality of individuals. In the traditional or folk society individual attitudes and behavior were shaped by norms governing familial obligations. Persons of a particular age, sex, and family status were supposed to behave in prescribed ways toward others occupying particular sex, age, and kinship categories. But a modern urban society stresses personal freedom. One is supposed to act in terms of individual need and preference, not in terms of preordained familial obligations. These pressures of urban life, as well as the loss of family economic function, were presumed to lead to the demise of the family in modern, urban, industrial society.

The Normal Parsonian Family

Talcott Parsons and his associates also recognized these psychological changes but have presented major arguments as to why the nuclear family remains as important as ever in modern society. The Parsonians agreed that the traditional family, linked by economic and residential rights and obligations as well as kinship bonds, was undone by industrial society. But, in contrast to earlier writers, Parsons argued that an industrial society still requires a stable family system to socialize children and to maintain the psychological balance of the men who face the pressures of competition in their work life.

As evidence for the separation of the nuclear family from kinship groups, Parsons pointed to the rise in jobs not based on kinship and the decline in family-operated economic units such as farms, small retail shops, and the like. Further, he pointed out that households were increasingly limited to nuclear-family members. In 1960, for example, 82.7 percent of the total population of the United States lived in nuclear-family households (husband, wife, and children), while the proportion of household members who were other kinds of relatives declined to 5.5 percent (Parsons, 1965, p. 32). Parsons also noted the strong preference for the single-family house as a family residence in America.

He found further support for the importance of the nuclear family in the high rates of marriage and remarriage after divorce, the drop in the average age of marriage, and the increase in the birth rate during the postwar era—the time of Parsons' major statements on the nuclear family. Thus, Parsons argues, rather than having lost its importance, the nuclear family under industrialism is more vital than ever, in both senses of the word. It has become specialized, as part of the general process of social change.

As Smelser, one of Parsons' leading students, explains, as a society develops, its social structure becomes more complex. This happens not only in the economy, in the increasing division of labor, but in other institutions:

. . . Rapid social development involves the same increasing complexity of structure in other institutions as well—in education, religion, politics, the family, and so on. For example, in the preindustrial family of a craftsman, the parents themselves are responsible for teaching the child minimal occupational skills, as well as for his emotional molding during his early years. When a growing economy places demands for greater literacy and more technical skills, the pressure is for this multifunctional family to give way to a new, more complex set of social arrangements. Structurally distinct educational institutions appear, and the family begins to surrender some of its previous training functions to these new institutions; having lost these functions, accordingly, the family becomes more specialized, focusing relatively more on emotional conditioning in the early childhood years and relatively less on its former economic and educational functions. This process of increasing specialization is called *structural differentiation*. (Smelser, 1968, pp. 78–79)

Parsons and his followers argued that the relative isolation of the nuclear family from the kinship group, and its loss of functions, made the family more rather than less important:

. . . The family has become a *more specialized agency* than before, probably more specialized than in any previously known society. This represents a decline of *certain* features which have traditionally been associated with families, but whether it represents a "decline of the family" in a more general sense is another matter. . . . The family is more specialized than before, but not in any general sense less important, because the society is dependent *more* exclusively on it for the performance of *certain* of its vital functions. (Parsons and Bales, 1955, pp. 3–9)

Parsons emphasizes the home as a place to escape from the pressures of work. It is the only place in urban industrial society where a person can find true solidarity and basic trust—the only place, that is, where a person can find affection and acceptance for himself, apart from particular achievements and accomplishments. The family remains the only dependable primary group in modern society—that is, a group involving regular, face-to-face contact over a long period of time in a mood of intimacy and informality. Parsons notes that in traditional societies the extended family is a primary group.

Parsons' Critics   Many criticisms can and have been made of Parsons' analysis, and some have been mentioned earlier in this book. He tends to disregard the diversity of family life and concentrate on the "normal American family" as a middle-class urban couple with young children and reduced kin ties; the husband plays an "instrumental" role as the breadwinner, and the wife follows an "expressive" domestic role. Deviation from these patterns implies social disorganization, or personal psychopathology, rather than an alternative life style.

Parsons also confounds the meaning of the term "function"; for example, he asserts that the two functions of the nuclear family — the socialization of children and the psychological security of adults — are more important than ever, because now the nuclear family is the only place where such nurturing can be found. In this statement Parsons uses the term "function" to refer to both a need and the fulfillment of the need. He assumes that if a social need exists, it must be satisfied. This assumption flows from the general concept of Parsons and many other sociologists that societies are neatly organized and balanced social systems.

As noted in the previous chapter, however, not all sociologists hold to such a Utopian model of social systems. For example, Gideon Sjoberg (1965) has suggested that industrial societies and cities — or any society for that matter — can give rise to contradictory functional requirements. Thus Parsons has offered a convincing explanation of why in modern society the family is desperately needed, but he is overly optimistic about the ease with which the "psychological gold" of warmth and affection can be created, stored, and circulated in an industrial urban society. (Parsons actually uses money as a metaphor for solidarity.) Parsons overlooks the possibility that the same social changes generating the need for a stable and secure family life may also undermine society's capacity to fulfill the need.

Parsons' writing on the nuclear family gave rise to a wave of critical articles, but few of Parsons' critics made the foregoing points. They focused their attack on the assumed dominance of the isolated nuclear family. The critics opposed both Parsons and the earlier writers who had predicted the decline and fall of the extended family, and they asserted that kinship groups remained alive and well in urban and industrial settings. Thus, the argument went, people are not isolated from their kin groups: people visit their relatives, speak to them on the telephone, write letters, exchange Christmas cards, celebrate happy occasions, and help in emergencies. What's more, the argument goes, parents often help their married children, and children help support their aged parents.

The debate between Parsons and his critics has passed into the literature as a victory for the critics. For example, many reviews in textbooks agree with the verdict of Sussman, one of the leading critics of Parsons:

The isolated nuclear family is a myth. This has already been conclusively demonstrated. It does not merit any further attention of the field, and I for one refuse to waste any more time even discussing it. (Sussman, in Rosow, 1965, p. 341)

Instead of the isolated nuclear family as the typical family structure of modern societies, the critics offered such concepts as the "modified extended family" and the kin network.

Criticizing Parsons' Critics   An understanding of the debate between Parsons and his critics on the issue of the isolated nuclear family is basic to any analysis of the role of the family in contemporary society. If the critics are correct that the isolated nuclear family is a myth, it is obviously foolish to ascribe contemporary family problems to a nonexistent family structure. Still, despite widespread agreement that the critics won the debate with Parsons, their own arguments are riddled with conceptual and methodological flaws. A fairly mild critique of the nuclear-family critics was offered by B. N. Adams (1968) and a more devastating critique has recently been published by Gibson (1972).

First, the critics create a straw man by making Parsons appear more extreme than he actually was. Parsons did not insist that the isolated nuclear family never saw any of its relatives. Indeed, as Parsons himself pointed out, his emphasis on the psychological importance of parent-child relations would suggest that people would not be likely to break off completely from their parents when they marry. It is worthwhile to look at Parsons' original statement about the isolation of the contemporary nuclear family:

This "isolation" is manifested in the fact that the members of the nuclear family, consisting of the parents and their still dependent children, ordinarily occupy a separate dwelling not shared with members of the family of orientation (parents) of either spouse, and this household is in the typical case economically independent, subsisting in the first instance from the occupational earnings of the husband-father. It is of course not uncommon to find a surviving parent of one or the other spouse, or even a sibling or cousin of one of them, residing with the family, but this is both statistically secondary, and it is clearly not felt to be the "normal" arrangement.

Of course, with the independence, particularly the marriage, of children, relations to the family of orientation are by no means broken. But a separate residence, very often in a different geo-

graphical community, and separate economic support, attenuate
these relations . . . .
. . . A particularly significant aspect of the isolation of the
nuclear family in our society is again the sharp discrimination . . .
which it emphasizes between family members and nonmembers
. . . . (Parsons, 1955, pp. 3–21)

Obviously, then, Parsons was not talking about "isolation" in the sense of no interaction whatever, but rather
about such issues as living in separate households in a different community from one's parents, about being economically independent, and about being emotionally as well as
ideologically more focused on one's spouse and children than
on one's parents and blood relatives. One problem of Parsons' analysis, however, is that the isolated nuclear family is
presented as a type, an either/or matter, rather than as a
continuum along which different families can be arranged.

Yet the problem of many of his critics is similar: they
also approached the issue in an either/or fashion. Asserting
that Parsons had said there was no kin interaction at all
among married couples, the critics point to family visiting
and helping in times of need as evidence that the typical
city dweller in modern society lives in close-knit kin networks. Gibson, however, points out that these critics often
use "absurdly low levels" of interaction between members of
different households to show that the nuclear family isn't
isolated (p. 14), and have overestimated their own statistics.
Their assertions that kin networks play a major role in urban
society show more enthusiasm than accuracy. For example,
data showing that people turn *more* to banks than to relatives
in time of financial need, *more* to clergymen and doctors in
times of trouble, and get *more* from friends and neighbors
during illness, and so on, are interpreted as showing the
strength of kinship ties in contemporary society!

Some writers, such as Litwak (1965) and Sussman (1959,
1965), argue that the basic family system of the United States
is "the modified extended family," consisting of coalitions
of nuclear families; yet they never specify precisely what it
takes for a group of families to become such a coalition. How
much interaction or exchange of services is needed? What
are the boundaries of such systems? Such questions are not
answered by the proponents of the "modified extended
family" notion. As Gibson states:

Unlike the classical extended structure, or the isolated nuclear family, for which clear identifying characteristics may be developed (i.e., household compositions), the modified extended family is not clearly defined for either conceptual or research purposes. If the case is to be made for the primacy of kin relations over non-kin relations, much clearer definitions need to be provided. . . . It is hard to avoid the conclusion that the concept of the modified extended family is intended more as an ideological device to refute Parsons than as a meaningful research tool to describe reality. (Gibson, 1972, p. 17)

In a previous chapter we noted the confusions about the universality of the nuclear family that resulted from failing to distinguish between kinship, living together, and domestic functions such as child care. A number of anthropologists have suggested that we ought to separate the issue of who lives with whom from concepts of kinship and family. Households do not always consist of family members, and family members do not always live together. Stephens (1963), for example, notes that one of the problems with the idea of the universal nuclear family is that in many societies, husbands and wives do not live together, and it is also common for children to live with someone other than their own parents.

The advocates of the "modified extended family" also fail to make crucial distinctions between degrees of interaction. They do not distinguish exchanging cards and telephone calls from face-to-face interaction, nor do they consider the significance of different amounts of interaction — daily, weekly, monthly. Above all they fail to take into account the differences between domestic functions and visiting. This is also the reason why it is important to know about who lives with whom — households are intimacy-producing environments.

Households as Intimate Environments   Household structures are important in two senses: first, knowing about the typical household structure in a society tells us something about the kinds of relationships and experiences that a society encourages. For example, Bohannan argues that the kind of houses people build, or would like to build, is an excellent indicator of the particular relationship emphasized in a kinship system. Mother-daughter, father-son, and husband-wife are the three relationships around which households most often are built:

> In short, the most telling characteristic of marriage and parenting, of divorce and failure of parenting, are characteristics of the household structure. The kind of houses people build reflects their social training and inclinations—and in turn also forms and restricts the social relationships they engage in and the experiences they undergo. Ultimately therefore, practice reaffirms training and values underscore values. (Bohannan, 1971, p. 56)

In the second sense, the household is the basic intimate environment in every society, and the process of living together, rather than the facts of kinship or marriage bonds, produces intimacy. Recently Parsons has observed that there is a

> central complex of privacy that seems to exist everywhere which consists of the sharing of "residence" in the sense of premises of daily living, perhaps above all sleeping, and . . . the privilege of eating in company with others. . . . Similarly, lines are drawn between clothing appropriate for public contexts and dress appropriate only to intimate occasions and company. (Parsons, 1971, p. 428)

An element of eroticism always exists in intimate environments, but the eroticism is not the central feature nor is it the basis of intimacy. We tend to exaggerate the erotic aspects of intimacy because our own household structures are most often based on sexual relationships. When the household is built around the husband-wife bond, however, the eroticism of that relationship seems to intensify the intimacy already generated in any household through the mere fact of living together. Slater (1963) has analyzed the tendencies to "dyadic" withdrawal when two people are deeply attached to each other; he includes mother-child relationships as also subject to dyadic withdrawal. Thus the nuclear-family household is more likely to withdraw from other relationships than any other kind of household structure. Gibson (1972) reports data showing that nuclear-family households are more isolated from kin in comparison with other types of households—for example, those with single people and/or extended families.

It is a mistake to think that the intimacy of the household results only from deep emotional or sexual attachment. Much of the emotional atmosphere of households arises from the fact that they are what Goffman (1959) has called a "backstage area." Goffman uses the terms "backstage" and "backstage behavior" to describe the way people act when they are relaxed, informal, and just being themselves rather than acting a role such as worker, teacher, host or hostess, and so on. Goffman gives the example of waiters who switch back and forth from scowling to smiling as they pass through the door from the kitchen to the dining room. Another example is the scene from a domestic comedy on television or in the movies in which a husband and wife smilingly say good-bye to the last guest, close the door, scowl at each other, and resume the argument they were having before the guests arrived.

Family secrets are not unique to families; all backstage regimes have them. Restaurant kitchens again serve as a prime example. The household also shares with other such backstage regions a kind of informality that permits a regression to "childish" ways. Goffman notes that backstage behavior has a certain uniformity whether it takes place in a worker's locker room, the backroom of a store, or in a home. "Polite" or public behavior requires certain styles of speech and posture indicating self-control and an appropriate distance from the other person. Backstage areas have their own codes of behavior:

> Throughout Western society, there tends to be one informal or backstage language of behavior, and another language of behavior for occasions when a performance is being presented. The backstage language consists of reciprocal first naming, cooperative decision making, profanity, open sexual remarks, elaborate griping, smoking, rough informal dress, "sloppy" sitting or standing posture, use of dialect or sub-standard speech, mumbling and shouting, playful aggressivity and "kidding," inconsiderateness for the other in minor . . . acts, minor physical self involvements such as humming, whistling, chewing, nibbling, belching, and flatulence. The frontstage behavior can be taken as the absence . . . of this. In general, then, backstage conduct is one which allows minor acts which might easily be taken as symbolic of intimacy and disrespect for others. . . . It may be noted here that backstage behavior has what psychologists might call a "regressive" character. (Goffman, 1959, p. 128)

Goffman warns against concluding that backstage is full of the pleasant things in life such as warmth and generosity:

Often, it seems that whatever enthusiasm and lively interest we have at our disposal we reserve for those before whom we are putting on a show and that the surest sign of backstage solidarity is to feel that it is safe to lapse into an asociable mood of sullen, silent irritability. (Goffman, 1959, p. 132)

Because family behavior is a backstage kind of interaction, it is of course extremely hard to observe. As Goffman notes, people in backstage regions know about their own unsavory secrets, but they are not in a position to know about other peoples'. Thus families may think of themselves in terms of their backroom knowledge, but judge other families by their onstage performances. This may be why the discoveries of the new family studies (Boszormenyi-Nagy and Framo, 1965) are at one and the same time so shocking and so familiar. By observing backstage family behavior, they have opened up for public discussion aspects of family life that could never be reached by means of questionnaires and formal interviews.

Rise of the Private Family   Although a distinction between public and private contexts may exist everywhere, the degree of family privacy in modern societies vastly exceeds that available elsewhere. Thus although, as Parsons notes, the places where people sleep and eat together seem always to be defined as intimate, private places, in most cultures and in our own historical past, households have been more open and accessible to outsiders. Furthermore, as we noted in the last chapter, the sense of a gulf between the home and the outside society seems to exist only in advanced industrial societies.

Indeed, there is reason to believe that the concept of the home as a sanctuary and retreat is a relatively recent cultural feature of the United States and, to a lesser degree, of England. In these countries we find not only the ideology but also the practice of family privacy. Sebastian de Grazia (1962) contrasts the "at-homeness" of Americans with the more extensive out-of-the-house leisure life that exists in Europe. Citing a 1954 survey showing that at 6:00 P.M. of any workday three-quarters of the American male population from age 20 to 59 had arrived home from work, to stay for the rest of the evening, he writes:

In part, this nesting activity goes back to an earlier evolution. The . . . separation of home and work . . . and the growth of cities into sprawling, black, transportation maps are two factors that help make the home a refuge against the impersonality outside. The trend seems to have begun in the reign of Victoria. Massive, comfortable chairs and sofas appeared in solidly appointed houses. By now the home as a sanctuary has legal and constitutional support in both England and the United States. (Grazia, 1962, p. 184)

On the Continent, however, Grazia notes, the concept of home as distinct from house is lacking. Particularly for men, the cafe and the bistro provide an out-of-the-house environment where they can "eat, drink, write letters or poetry, discuss women, and argue about politics and literature" (1962, p. 184).

The separation of the home from public life reflects not only a set of values, but also the technological self-sufficiency of the modern American home. The telephone, television, refrigerator, freezer, washer-dryer, air conditioner, backyard, swimming pool—all increase the privacy and isolation of the household by reducing the need to go out for the necessities of life or for entertainment.

The less the household is a self-contained unit, the more family life goes on in the presence of nonfamily members. For example, the Mexico City *vecindad* described by Oscar Lewis (1965, p. 501) arranges individual dwellings around a central patio. People do most of their work in the patio, and share a common toilet and washstand. This type of housing brings individuals from different and not necessarily blood-related households into intense daily interaction, and enables people to maintain in an urban setting the extended-family pattern of the rural village. On the other hand, Lewis notes, such intense interaction also leads to problems of privacy and quarrels among children and parents.

To an American the unappealing aspects of the lack of family privacy in the *vecindad* do not need to be spelled out. The drawbacks of too much family self-sufficiency and privacy are only recently beginning to be realized. The sociologist Barbara Laslett recently (1973) argued that only in contemporary America has the ideology of the private nuclear family actually been put into practice, and hence only in America are its problematic aspects becoming apparent. The chief difference between the traditional family and its modern counterpart, according to this analysis, is the public-private dimension. The family of the past was a much more public institution:

> The argument being made here is that an attempt to understand changes in the American family may fruitfully be pursued by attention to variations in family publicness and privateness. When it is common practice for family life to occur elsewhere than within the confines of the [home], such as in parks or front stoops, when it is common for non-domestic activities — such as political and economic — to be pursued within the domestic context, when it is common for non-family members — such as servants, apprentices, and boarders — to constitute part of the household, then the family can be described as having a public character. (B. Laslett, 1973, p. 70)

By contrast, family privacy increases when most of family life goes on within the home, and when family activities are purely domestic rather than economic. Laslett sees the significance of the public-private distinction in the social-psychological effects of being observed while acting out family roles. Following Goffman's concept of backstage interaction, she argues that the increase in family privacy in recent years may result in less social control over what goes on in families, as well as less social support for family roles — hence the increases in family strains that have recently led to dissatisfaction with the nuclear family and the search for alternatives such as communes.

Households as Units   The significance of the household in the American middle-class family system especially is that it is a unit, not only residentially but psychologically and economically as well. None of the anti-Parsonian critics has challenged the isolated household as the major form of the household for married couples. Nearly 98 percent of all married couples in the 1960 census had their own household, and only 10 percent contained relatives other than their own children (Winch, 1968). Nor have the critics challenged or even dealt with Parsons' argument that the income, occupation, and social status of the nuclear-family group depend on the husband's occupation, which is usually independent of kinsmen. Even when nuclear-family members interact with parents and siblings of the spouses, the boundaries around each nuclear unit do not disappear. There may be tension over the issue of which family unit has greater claim over the husband or wife at any particular moment, but parents and their adult children do not form a unit as they do in other cultures—for example, in the traditional Chinese extended family, the couple was absorbed into the husband's family. Francis L. K. Hsu contrasts the two family systems by pointing out that in America in-laws are "guests" in their children's homes; even when households have the same "structure," the content of family life in the two systems may differ:

> The difference between the two types of content may be made clearer if we scrutinize the matter of discipline more closely. The average American woman is a guest in the house of her daughter-in-law. . . . Even if she comes into the younger woman's home during an emergency to take over the temporary care of her grand-children, she is still supposed to follow her daughter-in-law's wishes. Not infrequently the younger woman will leave a memo indicating what her children can do, when they should go to bed, and so on. Interference is an accusation that most American mothers-in-law hope to avoid, even if in reality they do succeed in interfering to some degree. . . . Conversely, before the impact of the West, the average Chinese woman in her daughter-in-law's house was a mistress over the younger woman. . . . Whether or not the mother-in-law lived under the same roof with her son and his family, she was not only accustomed to oversee the welfare of her grandchildren, but thought nothing of overruling her daughter-in-law in such matters if she preferred to. The younger woman might resent this, but no one would criticize the mother-in-law for it. (Hsu, 1972, p. 7)

Finally, the American nuclear family constitutes a financial unit as well as a residential and a psychological one: it is an economic unit whose members "as a matter of course pool a common basis of economic support" (Parsons, 1949, p. 237). Just as it is necessary to distinguish between telephone calls, participation in the backstage of family life, and visiting relationships from membership in one psychological unit, it is also necessary to distinguish between "gift giving" and "helping out" from the actual pooling of income. The economic isolation of the modern nuclear family is one of its distinguishing features. Parsons notes:

> The isolation of the conjugal unit in this country is in strong contrast to much of the historic structure of European society where a much larger and more important element have inherited home, source of economic support, and specific occupational status (es-

pecially a farm or family enterprise) from their fathers. . . .
(Parsons, 1949, p. 237)

Parsons and the earlier writers who saw a withering away
of the family were not discussing family interaction such as
visits so much as the role of kinship in the larger society. In
comparison to other societies, relations between adult relatives in industrial society is peripheral to the functioning of
the total society. That relations with all relatives, even close
ones, are largely optional and voluntary places kin relations
in industrial society on an entirely different plane from the
obligatory roles found in traditional society.

Unlike kin relations in traditional societies, those in
industrial society are not clearly prescribed. No strict rules
dictate how often you should see your mother's brother or
your father's sister's son, how you should act in his presence,
or what precisely your mutual obligations are to each other.
Rather, kinship in America and other industrial societies
is much like friendship—people often interact with their
relatives according to how they feel about them. Goode (1963)
calls such kin relations "ascriptive friendship."

The Isolated Nuclear Family Is Alive But Not Well

The questions raised by the decline-of-the-family school
have never been dealt with in a detailed and serious way by
students of the family. Le Play, Zimmerman, Wirth, and Linton had seen in urban industrial society forces inimical to all
family ties, both of marriage and of blood. Parsons turned
the issue aside by declaring the nuclear family the basic unit.
He separated its fate from that of the traditional family by
arguing that while modern society was undermining extended-family ties, it rendered the nuclear family more
necessary than ever. The nuclear-family critics confused
the issue still further by arguing that the traditional family
never died.

By assuming that the nuclear family was either the norm
or nonexistent, both the Parsonians and the anti-Parsonians
failed to come to grips with the structural problems of modern family life. They did not consider the possibility that
modern social conditions unglue family ties and at the same
time make them more needed. What happens to family life
when the household stops being a workplace, and father and

older children leave for most of the day? What happens to women when they are freed from working on the family farm or trade under the supervision of the elders, and are left alone in isolated households with young children? What happens to the quality of family relationships when home becomes a refuge from the rest of society, and the family is the main place for people to enjoy intimate sociability?

Both Parsons and his critics share an optimistic view of family functioning in contemporary society. The structural-differentiation model assumes that changes are adaptive: "When a social organization becomes archaic under changing historical circumstances . . . it differentiates . . . into two or more roles or organizations which function more *effectively* in the new historical circumstances" (Smelser, 1963, p. 2; italics added).

But why make the assumption that the changes are adaptive? Goode (1963) suggests that the fit between industrialism and the nuclear family may be one-sided: the nuclear family may suit the needs of the industrial economy, but urban industrial society may not serve the needs of the nuclear family. Further, the nuclear family may not be as ideally suited to a complex industrial society as is usually thought. Like the early generation of writers, Goode asks whether the ultimate thrust of advanced societies is to do away with the family altogether, and make the basic unit of society the individual.

Goode and Parsons do recognize the strains placed on family members living in an advanced industrial society. But both Parsons and, to a lesser extent, Goode suffer from the sociologist's bias in favor of seeing societies as balanced and stable, or else changing in a controlled fashion — in a state of dynamic equilibrium. They also tend to see people as being integrated into their societies and social roles, and the family as the basis of this integration. In short, using the methods of sociological analysis, Parsons and Goode come close to seeing the nuclear family as caught in a tragic contradiction, but their functionalist framework prevents their going very far with it.

The Family as a Social (Structural) Problem   Kenneth Keniston (1971b, p. 6) has pointed to the remarkable fact that the emergence of dissenting youth in the late 1960's was predicted by no one in the 1950's. In the fifties and early sixties, he notes, most social scientists took the relative stability of Western democracies during that period as a natural state of affairs, rather than as a particular historical moment abnormal in its tranquility. The theories of society that prevailed at the time — such as the theory of the balanced social system — "effectively prevented us from understanding the increasingly wide-scale dissent among a growing minority of the young during the 1960's" (Keniston, 1971b, p. 8).

The same might be said for the theories of family adaptation and stability during the same period. As noted earlier, American society during the 1940's and '50's seemed to be living evidence for the validity of the nuclear-family ideology. The teachings of psychoanalysis about the necessity of a normal family life for both children and adults were embraced at different levels of society, with differing emphasis and accuracy. In general, Freud's ideas were received more enthusiastically in America than anywhere else, a matter which recent historians have been trying to explain (Hale, 1971). For people who thought of themselves as intellectuals, or merely up-to-date, psychoanalysis was *the* psychology. On the popular level, Freudian ideas were disseminated in the form of plays and movies on psychological themes, the togetherness celebration in the women's magazines, and the child-rearing advice of Dr. Spock and government pamphlets.

Very few voices argued that the family itself contained built-in flaws. C. Wright Mills was one such critical voice. He used marriage as an example of how the sociological imagination could transform personal troubles into social issues. Mills wrote that though a man and woman could have personal troubles inside a marriage, when 250 out of every 1000 marriages ended in divorce (the rates are now approaching 500 out of 1000 in some places), there had to be a "structural issue having to do with the institutions of marriage and the family and other institutions that bear upon them." He suggested, as some of these structural strains, a "crisis of ambition" for men in a corporate economy, and the stultifying role prescribed for women within the family:

> Insofar as the family as an institution turns women into darling little slaves and men into their chief providers and unweaned dependents, the problem of a satisfactory marriage remains incapable of purely private solution. (Mills, 1959, p. 10)

Another antiadjustment critic writing during the family togetherness celebration of the fifties was Barrington Moore (1958). At a time when it was axiomatic among social scientists that the family is a universally necessary institution in all societies, past, present, and future, Moore asked: ". . . to what extent may we regard the family as a repressive survival under the conditions of an advanced technology?"

With a frank cynicism Moore struck out at the "barbaric nature" of the duty of family affection:

> One of the most obviously obsolete features of the family is the obligation to give affection to a particular set of persons on account of the accident of birth. This is a true relic of barbarism. . . . In earlier times it was expedient to organize the division of labor and affection in human society through real or imagined kinship bonds. As civilization became technically more advanced, there has been less and less of a tendency to allocate both labor and affection according to slots in a kinship system, and in increasing tendency to award them on the basis of actual qualities and capacities that the individual possesses. (1958, p. 409)

Parent-child relations were included in Moore's dim view of all kin bonds. He wrote that if people were to talk to each other about the "sufferings brought on by raising a family today, the birth rate would drop to zero" (1958, p. 410).

Moore argued that the home of today is less effective than it was in earlier times as a place to rear children. The family was once an economic unit in which all members worked together, but the separation of home and work, brought on by industrialization, removed fathers from the household during the day. This meant that the child could have no direct experience of father's work, but even if he did, it was no longer an automatic model for his own career. Also the father would spend part of the day in a separate world of social interaction. More recently, mass media and peer groups have come to compete with parents in shaping children. The loss of work ties between family members, involvement in outside interests, and the intrusion of the media into the home all make it harder for family members to form genuine emotional ties with each other.

> The mass media have succeeded in battering down the social cell the family once constituted in the larger structure of society. . . . Newspapers, radios and television have largely destroyed the flow of private communications within the family that were once

the basis of socialization. Even meals are now much less of a family affair. . . . (Moore, 1958, p. 411)

Like Mills, Moore saw through the popular myths that the woman's place in the contemporary family was one of privilege and dominance as well as instinctual fulfillment:

> Is she, perhaps, the happy person whose face smiles at us from every advertisement, and whose arts justify the sociologists' case? A more accurate assessment might be that the wife suffers most in the modern middle class family, because the demands our culture puts upon her are impossible to meet. (Moore, 1958, p. 411)

Moore took his argument to its logical conclusion: the family is already a part-time thing for most people; in the future it would become more so. The trend toward more efficient technology and a greater division of labor would be extended to the home and its tasks. The child-rearing function would be carried on by specialized agencies, developing from today's play schools, boarding schools, and so on. Moore recognized that infants have a special problem: they need affection, fondling, and the "illusion of being the center of the universe." But, he reasoned, mechanized and bureaucratized child-rearing could be made warm and supporting, often more so than a family ridden by problems and conflict.

This analysis of the future of the family sounds even more chilling to many people now than it did during the togetherness era. Our sense of values has changed. Moore makes a criticism of the family of the fifties in terms of the values of the fifties: technology, efficiency, rationality. These are, of course, the very values against which there is so much protest. As we noted earlier, however, no social scientist predicted anything like the student revolts, the rise of the counterculture, the rebirth of feminism, and so on. So Moore could hardly have foreseen that the direction of family change would be opposite to the one he predicted: rather than technology and bureaucratic efficiency taking over home tasks, the family-togetherness principle moved out beyond the family into the commune movement, encounter groups, political-protest groups, the reawakening of religion, and so forth.

Nevertheless, Moore had pointed to strains in the mid-century American family that would shortly reach crisis proportions: the fact that, despite the ideology of "together-ness," mother, father, and children lived in different worlds of experience, values, and information. Moore also recognized the paradoxical quality of the emotional ties between family members—the obligation to love when the day-to-day relationship may not generate any feelings of warmth. Yet Moore also reiterated the concern of Le Play, Zimmerman, and other traditionalists: would not reduction of family burdens in the interests of individualism result in a world of "shallow and fleeting erotic intrigues"? He acknowledged that Hollywood might be the "ugly prototype" of such a world:

> The most that might be claimed by any future apologist for such institutions . . . is that they give greater scope to the development of the creative aspects of the personality than did the family. . . . (Moore, 1958, p. 417)

At the conclusion of his article, Moore notes that he is merely pointing to changes which seem to be happening already:

> It would appear that the burden of proof is on those who maintain that the family is a social institution whose fate will differ in its essential form than that which has befallen all the others. (Moore, 1958, p. 417)

Moore in effect presented the dark side of "structural differentiation." Parsons and his students saw the nuclear family stripped down to its basic psychological functions as an effective supplier of security for family members as well as the producer of new recruits to industrial society. The nuclear family was now the only source of the pure gold of solidarity. Moore, on the other hand, argued that the stripping away of work, education, and other functions from the nuclear family had left the members with little or nothing on which to base their relationships. The specialized function of the nuclear family amounts to a heightened emotionality, a pure togetherness paradoxically harder to achieve as a goal in itself than as a by-product of working together on some task.

Actually, despite the fact Mills and Moore are critics of "establishment" sociology while Parsons, and Goode to a lesser extent, are the establishment, the analysis of the family made by the four writers does not differ very much. The differences lie in the implications drawn from the analysis.

Parsons and Goode see tensions, points of strain, in an otherwise stable and functioning social system; for critics such as Mills and Moore, the same tensions represent fatal flaws, contradictions that call into question the viability of modern family arrangements and the social system that supports them.

Yet the built-in strains noted by Goode and Parsons are fundamental ones; they exist for the old and the young, for men and women, at work and at home. In Goode's analysis of the human costs of both industrialism and the conjugal family, the first and most obvious "cost" of the conjugal as opposed to the extended-family system is to the elders. Viewed as a power struggle, the rise of the conjugal system represents a victory of youth over age. Years of experience make one obsolescent rather than wise (Goode, 1963, p. 379).

Parsons sees the plight of older people not so much in terms of power but as a by-product of modern kinship, residential patterns, and occupational structures. In contrast to family systems emphasizing one line of descent—for example, from father to son—the modern family, particularly in America, is bilateral. That is, there is no structural bias built into the system favoring the husband's side of the family over the wife's, or vice versa. This is another aspect of the structural isolation of the conjugal family. Thus in modern family systems there is no "place" for the parental couple, typically, in the household of grown children, and no rule stating that such a "place" should be claimed more by one set of parents than the other. (Obviously, three-generation households do exist in America, but these are relatively rare and, as indicated by surveys of both the older generation and their married children, not the preferred pattern.)

The other reason for the isolated situation of the aged in modern societies is the occupational structure:

> In such fields as farming and the maintenance of small independent enterprises there is frequently no such thing as abrupt "retirement," rather a gradual relinquishment of the main responsibilities . . . with advancing age. So far, however, as an individual's occupational status centers in a specific "job," he either holds the job or does not, and the tendency is to maintain the full level of functioning up to a given point and then abruptly to retire. In view of the very great significance of the occupational status and its psychological correlates, retirement leaves the older man in a peculiarly functionless situation, cut off from participation

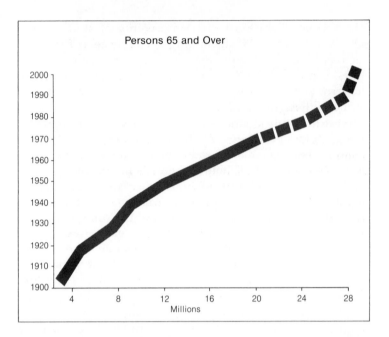

For the remainder of this century the number of persons of age sixty-five and over will be unaffected by our rate of growth. Their proportion of the population, however, will be affected by how fast the population grows. In the year 2000, for example, they would constitute 8.9 percent of the total population under the three-children-per-family average, and 10.6 percent of the population under the two-children-per-family average. (From *Population and the American Future*, Washington: U.S. Government Printing Office, 1972; based on data from the U.S. Bureau of the Census)

in the most important interests and activities of the society. (Parsons, 1949, p. 231)

Yet work in industrial society also has strains built in. But Goode, like Parsons, believes that the industrial system, based on competition and achievement, creates great psychological tension. Security and satisfaction in work are almost impossible, no matter whether one is janitor of the building or president of the corporation:

The modern technological system is psychologically burdensome on the individual because it demands an unremitting discipline. . . . Lower-level jobs give little pleasure to most people.

However, in higher-level professional, managerial and creative positions, the standards of performance are not only high but are often without clearly stated limits. The individual is under considerable pressure to perform better than he is able. (Goode, 1963, p. 14)

This recognition of strains built into male roles does not diminish Goode's and Parsons' estimates of the strains in women's roles in modern society. Goode emphasizes the contrast between the ideological values embodied in the conjugal system — freedom, individualism, sexual equality — and the daily realities of the housewife in a modern society. Ironically, the woman is liberated from the extended family only to find that her domestic burdens are increased rather than lightened:

The modern woman is given little relief from child care, which is typically handed over to one person, the wife, rather than to several women, some of them elders, who are part of the family unit in the more extended systems. . . . Even the substantial development of labor-saving devices and technology has not lightened labor in the modern United States home, contrary to both advertising in women's magazines and the stereotyped notions of Europeans. Most of these devices merely raise the standards for cleanliness and repairs, and allow the housewife to turn out more "domestic production" each day. Every study of the time allocation of mothers shows that housewives work extremely long hours. (Goode, 1963, p. 15)

Parsons' analysis of the strains in women's roles focuses not so much on the contrast between *family* structures — extended versus conjugal — but rather on the effects of the modern occupational structure on the family. The principal source of strain in women's roles, he notes, derives from the fact that the wife is no longer a partner in a common economic enterprise (Parsons, 1949, p. 223). When the home was also a workplace, economic roles were not differentiated from family roles. Women could combine child care and reproduction with economic activities. Industrialization, however, moves work, and the father along with it, out of the home. Men acquire the status that once was attached to the family as a group. The husband's occupation, more than any other factor, determines the status of the family in terms of prestige as well as its standard of living.

The common enterprise is reduced to the life of the family itself and to the informal social activities in which husband and wife participate together. (Parsons, 1949, p. 223)

In a society with a strong emphasis on individual achievement, the woman is left with the unstable, "pseudo-" occupation of housewife (p. 224) and no claim to status in her own right. The instability of the housewife role, especially in the middle class, Parsons notes, is indicated by the prevalence of women's varying strategies for escaping it—by hiring maids, by dissociating their personality from the role of domestic drudge and emphasizing glamor or cultural activities, and so forth. But because none of these is clearly defined, there tends to be a rather "unstable oscillation" between them, along with a considerable degree of neuroses in women.

The child does not escape built-in strains either, in Parsons' view. In the small modern conjugal family, the emotional intensity of family bonds is increased at the same time that a greater necessity to become emancipated from them is imposed. Thus adolescence is a particularly difficult time in advanced societies. Neither Goode nor Parsons, however, deals with the problematic aspects of modern family life for the very young child. Yet the isolation of the nuclear-family household and the strains of the modern female role probably have the most impact on the relationship between the mother and young child. It is widely recognized in both the popular and social-science literature that the years of infancy, toddlerhood, and preschool are a time of great strain on women (Pohlman, 1969). Usually, however, when such things are mentioned, the writer assumes that the strains are offset by the mutual, normal love between mother and child. As we shall see in the chapters on childhood and parenthood, however, very little is guaranteed in parent-child relations. Contrary to popular opinion, there are no maternal instincts, or at least none strong enough to prevent widespread physical and psychological abuse of children, or just plain incompetence.

The point is not that mothers—or fathers—are mean, irrational, and incompetent, but rather that the isolation of the nuclear-family household does nothing to prevent people who are that way from doing as they please with their children. Anthropologists who study child-rearing in other cultures are struck by the isolation of American children and their mothers (Minturn and Lambert, 1964; Stephens, 1963) and the strains this creates for both.

Anthropologists have also been struck by the extreme fragility of the conjugal household. Paul Bohannan (1971, p. 54) has noted that divorce is so disruptive in America because it strikes at the heart of the family system — the marital relationship. Where the married couple do not live together in the same household — as in the Tiv, an African people studied by Bohannan — the effects of divorce are less disruptive. He writes:

> "Broken homes" are necessarily a result of "breakable homes." . . . There are, on the other hand, some societies that have households that are not breakable on divorce. . . . It is obviously true that they may be breakable in some context or another — among the Tiv it is father-son conflict — and it will be *that* condition rather than husband-wife conflict that is dreaded by those people. (Bohannan, 1971, p. 54)

The disadvantages are not only one-sided, Bohannan notes. The American nuclear-family household offers privacy and individualism; the Tiv do not provide much scope for individualism, but they assure membership and support.

Communes: Solution or Part of the Problem?

The communes of the 1960's and 1970's are often regarded as a novel attempt to create a protective environment against the harsher and more materialistic pressures of contemporary social and economic life. In large part communes can be understood as a protest against modern industrial society and in particular against the tense and constraining role assigned to the isolated nuclear family. The contemporary communal movement seeks to combine the presumably warm and supportive group life of the extended family with a greater degree of personal freedom than is afforded by conventional middle-class family life.

During the 1950's a future of family-life experimentation would probably have seemed more far-fetched than a new wave of political activism. Political dissent had occurred within the twentieth century, but changes in family organization had not. Yet the flowering of communal-living experiments in America during the late 1960's was not something new under the sun, but rather the revival of an old American tradition. As Rosabeth M. Kanter writes:

> About a hundred utopian communities were born and died in nineteenth-century America, most founded before 1850. Some of these lasted as long as 180 years (the Shaker Villages), while others were in existence only six months (Yellow Springs, Ohio). Some were more or less sectarian, some primarily secular; some were celibate, others favored free love. Some utopias derived from immigrant groups and spoke a foreign language. There was a Catholic community, Owenite communes, Fourierite phalanxes (phalansteries), and even one community derived from a literary utopia (Icaria, after Etienne Cabot's *Voyage en Icarie*). While many of the nineteenth-century American utopian communities shared general values, they often implemented them in different ways. (Kanter, 1968, p. 499)

Hawthorne, Emerson, Thoreau, and other prominent Americans of the last century supported the communal tradition.

The Inevitability of the Nuclear Family   To the social scientists of the 1940's and 1950's who concerned themselves with such matters, the rise and fall of the communes of the last century only proved the inevitability of the nuclear family. The same verdict was rendered about the Soviet attempt to abolish the family during the 1920's and about the Israeli communes, the kibbutzim. No matter how one tried, the prevailing opinion went, the experimental form of the family would not be "viable," and the nuclear family would emerge like a phoenix from the ruins. There were few, if any, challenges to this verdict at the time. Until the rebirth of radical politics in the 1960's, no one questioned the definitions of viability, or pointed out that the critics of family "experiments" had, in their haste to affirm the natural inevitability of the nuclear family, overlooked the social and cultural factors accompanying the breakup of the various experiments.

Accordingly, although Utopian forms of the family have often been labeled "experimental," the designation is misleading. True, they are experimental in the sense that they are innovative. But they are not scientifically experimental because they usually involve at least two innovations at once: first, the introduction of new family and child-rearing patterns; and second, the founding of a new society from the ground up. In scientific terms the assessment of these two "variables" is confounded; as a result it is impossible to assess the effects of a particular feature. The problem resembles that of trying to interpret the effects of a new fertilizer on plant growth while also introducing more sunlight and less water. So, since Utopian communities do not "control" for the effects of variables that may significantly influence the outcome of the "experiment," they are not scientifically experimental.

The Soviet experience is often cited to illustrate the necessity of the nuclear family. Yet the Leninist attempt to equalize the woman's role failed for reasons irrelevant to a communistic ideology: the condition of the Soviet economy in that period did not permit such "luxuries" as day-care facilities and communal kitchens; few men, regardless of ideological commitment, believed in female equality; even those men, such as party leaders, who professed such beliefs did not always practice them; the government did not provide sufficient retraining to qualify women for skilled positions within the economy; and finally, the Soviet economy required a high birth rate. To meet economic needs Stalin revoked the previous laws and restored traditional norms. Accordingly, the Soviet experience does not offer conclusive evidence for the necessity of traditional nuclear-family organization.

The Israeli kibbutz presents a bit more complicated example of a Utopian family experiment. M. E. Spiro (1956) has described the kibbutz as a social organization consciously trying to emancipate women as a major goal, but tragically failing to alter the division of labor by sex. This conclusion has filtered through the social-science literature to become a definitive statement on the impossibility of altering the sexual division of labor. Closer examination of Spiro's own work, however, plus other data as well, casts doubt that the kibbutz was actually an experiment in sexual equality—or that it failed miserably.

When the first settlers began to work on the land, there was no sexual division of labor; women worked in the fields and men in the kitchen and laundry. Gradually, however, it emerged that women were not truly the equals of men in doing the hard work of the fields; furthermore, pregnancy and childbirth restricted them still more, in spite of the communal nurseries.

Hence, as the kibbutz grew older and the birth rate increased, more and more women were forced to leave the "productive" branches of the economy and enter its "service" branches. . . . The result was that women found themselves in the same jobs from which they were supposed to have been emancipated—*cooking, cleaning, laundering, teaching, caring for children, etc.*

. . . Instead of cooking and sewing and baking and cleaning and laundering and caring for children, the woman in Keryat Yedidim cooks, sews *or* launders *or* takes care of children for eight hours. . . . This new housekeeping is more boring and less rewarding than the traditional type. It is small wonder, then, given this combination of low prestige, difficult working conditions, and monotony, that the chavera (kibbutz woman) has found little happiness in her domestic activities. (Spiro, 1956, p. 229) (Italics in the original)

It may well be true that women may never achieve economic equality when heavy agricultural labor is the major means of subsistence, even if there is an ideological commitment to such equality. The first generation of kibbutz women, however, could provide no test of this because they had been brought up in cities by parents who held to traditional notions of woman's place. There is evidence also that the commitment of kibbutz men to female equality was less than their devotion to other radical kibbutz ideals such as achieving socialism, establishing a Jewish homeland, and overcoming ghetto stereotypes of Jews as weak, pale, bookish types incapable of hard farm work. (Women in the civil-rights movement have also been disappointed by the values and behavior of radical men toward women.) It is true that female equality, in communes and elsewhere, demands a set of conditions that are hard to meet. From that, it is erroneous to conclude that such equality is impossible to achieve or is against nature.

In the United States perhaps the most radical attempt to alter family relations was in the Oneida Community in New York, where the community practiced total economic communism and group sexual access—that is, any man and woman in the community might have relations together if mutually agreeable. The Oneida case highlights several interesting issues pertaining to communes: Is there a human need for "coupling"? How do we define communal stability? And how does a generation of rebels replace itself?

On coupling, Spiro suggests, basing his observations on the Israeli kibbutz where sex relations are free, that people seem to have need for psychological intimacy beyond sex alone. Still, the cultural background of kibbutzim hardly represents mankind in general. Indeed, Rosabeth Kanter concluded, on the basis of her research on nineteenth-century Utopian communities, that communes which forbade pairing, either to implement rules of celibacy or free love, lasted the longest. The commitments involved in coupling may undermine commitments to the larger community, but not necessarily, as witness the Israeli case. But in Israel, of course, the kibbutzim play a central role in defense of the national community, certainly creating special conditions.

There is also a question of the parameters of communal stability. Should we compare an experimental form of the family to the duration of the ordinary marriage or to the duration of a society? There is no obvious answer to that question, but it would certainly seem to be as appropriate to think of the experimental form of the family in the same terms as ordinary marriage. Furthermore, there is some question about the whole issue of durability. The commune represents a form of human experience and variation regarding sexual activity, work, reproduction, and socialization. That such a community could exist over a period of years may suggest more about the possibilities of variation than that it did not endure for centuries.

Further, every Utopian community has to face a genuine dilemma regarding its second generation. Can such a society actually duplicate itself? Communal organization begins with a first generation that has made a sharp break with its parents. In the second generation the community of rebels must raise a generation of conformists — children who accept the values and practices of their parents even though these may be and often are highly restrictive.

Margaret Mead once chided a group of kibbutz leaders for making greater demands on their children to stay put than would any other group of farm villagers. She pointed out that young people raised on farms often yearn to see the world. For kibbutz parents, of course, there is not just the issue of holding onto children, but of seeing lifelong ideals maintained. This dilemma offers an example of how the inevitable conflict of interest between generations translates itself into new terms in Utopian communities. Some communards have concluded that it is better for the children to "do their own thing" rather than maintain the community. Others have wondered whether a commune should not plan

for its own dissolution right from the start, so that its maintenance will not oppress members when the community no longer seems meaningful.

The New American Communes   The American communes of the 1970's are extremely varied. They can be urban or rural, political or apolitical, religious or nonreligious. Communes vary enormously in size, stability, family living styles, economic base, and in the demands they make on members. Some are relatively closed groups, others are open and enjoy a changing membership. Communes also vary in social and political organization—all the way from authoritarianism to egalitarianism. Researchers who have studied communes find it useful to distinguish between religious communes and those not organized around religion, and between urban and rural communes.

Carl Rogers (1972, pp. 128–131) has attempted to describe the variety and diversity of communal groups by citing:

1   A rural commune of eleven adults and six children functioning pretty much as an extended family but with freer sex relationships outside paired couples

2 An urban commune of a dozen professional men and women (and one child) who are paired off, engage in sexual experimentation, and employ encounter-group procedures to achieve harmony

3 A semirural commune, open to anyone, and eventually closed as a public-health menace

4 A coed house near a college, inhabited mostly by students, with great turnover but an eight-year record of stability; work is shared, relationships consist of the brother-sister type, and sexual companionship is found outside the house

5 An urban house containing three men and three women practicing group marriage; far from harmonious, the group finally developed a chart designating who was to sleep with whom on a given night

6 A group of agricultural communes, unified by religion, going back over four hundred years

7 A highly organized commune of thirty men and women (only two children) stressing work, cleanliness, and sexual freedom

8 A relationship of urban communes bound together by charismatic leadership, highly structured and emotional group sessions, and a history of drug addiction among members

9 A rural commune, bound together by Eastern mystical beliefs, and limited to twenty-five members

Zablocki (1972) has noted that communes can vary in size from five people to several hundred, but they seem to cluster around certain sizes. The most common, successful, and least-studied communes are those involving two to four couples who decide to live together in the same household, or to create close ties while living in separate households. These are the least observable kinds of communes because they are formed quietly by close friends who decide to merge households. The next most frequent size, according to Zablocki, is the group of twenty to thirty, the size of the typical hippie commune. It usually involves somewhat more formality and aloofness between members than the smaller, "couple" type of commune. The third most frequent size ranges from 50 to 150 people. Here organizational principles emerge as an important concern.

A good deal of variety also occurs in family ideology and style. Some communes do not define themselves as families at all; in urban areas, for example, it is hard to distinguish communes from the kinds of loose, group-living arrangements that have prevailed for years around universities and in bohemian districts of large cities. A commune may constitute nothing more than a rented house or apartment with fluid membership. Bennett Berger (1972) observes that rural communes represent a purer or more advanced form than urban ones, because they involve a greater degree of commitment. Rural communes are more likely to define themselves as families.

Familistic communes, urban or rural, also vary among themselves. Some center around nuclear families as the basic units. Thus a number of families may build houses on a piece of land, rent apartments in the same building, or live in separate rooms of a single house. Arrangements for sharing meals, child care, and sex also function as in extended families, with a reduced emphasis on the nuclear units; the nuclear families sleep together, but cooking, child care, and other domestic tasks may be communal. Some communes have no nuclear-family units at all; here we find a loose, "tribal" arrangement, where individuals claim their own rooms or private sleeping places. People may pair off as they wish, but couples do not live together and are not considered permanent. Some communes are based on group marriage, with all adults engaging in sexual relations with all others.

Child-rearing arrangements vary. Children may live with their own parents or in separate children's quarters. Children may be defined as belonging mainly to their own parents or to the group as a whole. The commune may have its own educational arrangements or it may send the children to outside schools.

Having discussed some of the major ways communes vary, we can turn to what they have in common—namely, the communal ideology. Although the researchers who have studied communes emphasize the great diversity of living styles, they find remarkable unity in the beliefs of communards—excepting again those who believe in systematic religions. Zablocki, for example, notes three motivations leading people to enter communal life: (1) to enjoy more freedom, (2) to recreate the extended family on the basis of fellowship rather than kinship, and (3) to escape from the city (1971, p. 305). There seems to be a strong antiurban trend even in urban communes; Berger notes that urban communes often talk about whether to get some land and move to the country, but rural communes almost never talk about moving back to the city.

The communal movement represents part of the counter-cultural revolt against the prevailing ethos of middle-class American society. The middle-class life style is perceived as sexually and sensually dulled, cold and manipulative, exploitive rather than generous, devoid of community and brotherhood, and finally, endowed with a perversely destructive rationality. Communal ideology rebels against all of this. Its contrasts with conventional middle-class beliefs have been summarized by Berger as follows:

People in the hip counter-culture prefer candid, total, effusive, and unrestrained expression of feeling, joy and sensuality, as well as anger and hostility, to the careful, guarded, modulated, balanced, and instrumental (or manipulative) modes of personal relatedness; "upfrontness" is for them a term of high praise. They want to possess and consume as little as they need rather than as much as they can be induced to want. They affirm the present, the immediate, the NOW, over careful future planning and anticipated future gratification. They value the "natural" (for nature is benign— particularly for rural communards), for example in nudity, organic foods, organic architecture, etc., over the civilized, the synthetic, the contrived. They prefer the colorful and the romantic to the classical, the sober and the orderly. Their sensibility is given to impulse and spontaneity rather than calculation and structure. Although they have and recognize leaders, their modes of relationship to each other affirm brotherhood and egalitarianism rather than hierarchy. They prefer the primitive to the sophisticated, transcendent ecstasy to order and security. They prefer invoking mystical and magical forces to scientific ones. Their impulse is to share as much of their lives as they can with the community of their brothers and sisters, sometimes even beyond the point where it threatens those areas of privacy and reserve to which many communards are still at least partially attached. They want to share a mutually dependent communal fate without the obligatory constraints of social bonds; indeed, they depend upon the affirmation by their brothers and sisters of the value of personal expressiveness to enable each of them to exercise an unbounded freedom to do his thing; to engage, above all, in a spiritual search for personal meaning, for health and happiness, for self and selflessness, for transcendence and godhood. (Berger et al., 1972, pp. 4–5)

Problems of Communes   Although family systems are best judged not by professed ideals but by daily reality, it is worth noting that the ideals of the conjugal or nuclear family parallel those of the communal one. The nuclear-family ideology similarly stresses love, freedom, equality, and withdrawal from the larger imperfect society to the more loving environment of the nuclear home. Indeed, some observers of the communal movement interpret it as a mirror and fulfillment of middle-class family life rather than as a radical departure from it. They see in the rural communal flight from the city a resemblance to the urban American emigration to the suburbs. Berger (1972), for example, detects a consistency between the communal ideology of brotherly love and the post-World War II ideology of family "togetherness." Philip Slater (1970) observes an unsavory resemblance between the age grading and attitudinal homogeneity that prevails in both suburb and commune; and both suburbanites and communards praise their style of life as being "good for the children."

Kirk Jeffrey (1972) has recently argued that the modern American idealization of the home can be traced to the same nineteenth-century sources as the communes of that era. The home was seen, in fact, as a kind of Utopian community; writings on the family were pervaded by the Utopian themes of retreat from urban society, conscious design, and perfectionism:

. . . Whether they [nineteenth-century writers on the family] regarded home as an utter and permanent retreat from life in a shocking and incomprehensible social order, or as a nursery and school for preparing regenerate individuals who would . . . remake American society, they agreed that domestic life ought to be perfect and could be made so. Through careful design of the home as a physical entity, and equally painstaking attention to the human relationships which would develop within it, the family could actually become a heaven on earth. Many of the significant features and patterns of middle-class family life in the nineteenth century, as well as significant points of strain, tension and guilt, arose directly from these extravagant expectations. (Jeffrey, 1972, p. 22)

The new communes and the conventional nuclear family are alike in their fragility and instability—and for similar reasons. The American household—and all households where the conjugal family prevails—are "breakable." This fragility stems not so much from conflict between husband and wife as from inflated expectations. Marriages ought to be both voluntary and emotionally satisfying. As Goode emphasizes, the conjugal-family ideology offers each spouse a "right" to family happiness, and in turn a high probability of disappointment leading to divorce.

Although the communes try to recreate the extended-family household organization, they typically do not insist upon lifelong, unbreakable, kinlike bonds. Instead, the contemporary commune emphasizes the freedom of members to come and go as they please, to enter and leave personal relationships at will. "Nobody would think of asking anybody else to make a permanent commitment to the life," Zablocki observes (1971, p. 306).

The hang-loose value extends to work as well: "Commune members generally work hard, but the choice of hours and tasks is strictly voluntary, as is the pooling of money and resources" (1971, p. 306). The predominant philosophy is repelled by appointed hours and administrative rationality.

To comprehend communal life and its tendencies toward dissolution, it is important to distinguish between couple relationships and the organization of the commune. Couples may remain stable while the commune dissolves, or the communal household may continue as a more-or-less stable unit while couples form and break up. Couple relationships are usually even more fragile than communes, most of which last less than a year (Zablocki, 1972).

Berger notes that fragility is the single most important feature of hip-couple relationships. There is nothing in the communal ideology or in its household organization to encourage a couple to stay together when tensions or dissatisfactions arise. There is instead a desire to remain unencumbered, uncommitted, and with all options open. On the other hand, Berger observes, in spite of this fragility, many people, particularly women, still hold to the ideal of a permanent mate, although they have little expectation of fulfillment. Another "traditional" aspect of hip-couple relationships is that, while they last, they are usually monogamous (except, of course, in group-marriage communes).

The commune itself is undermined by similar problems of retaining commitment. Observers of communes detect a number of logical contradictions in communal ideology: the contradiction between the ideal of individual freedom and the ideal of group solidarity; the conflict between the ideals of openness and spontaneity and the ideal of brotherly love; and the conflict between the principle of egalitarianism and impulsive individuality with the need for decisiveness and stability of expectations if the commune is to survive.

These paradoxes emerge in daily life in the form of disputes over privacy, private property, who is to do what tasks when, and who is to decide who does what:

> Like any other value system, the hip communal one is replete with logical contradictions and discontinuities between theory and practice. Freedom and communal solidarity can and do cause conflicts, and the balance between privacy and communal sharing is a recurrently thorny problem in several of the communes we have observed. Despite the emphasis on spontaneity and impulse, the apples have got to be picked when ripe, the goats have got to be milked regularly, the meals have to get cooked and the dishes washed. Despite the benignity of nature, something's got to be done about the flies in the kitchen and the mice in the cupboard. Despite egalitarianism, some communards are deferred to more than others; despite the emphasis on the present and the immediate, wood's got to be laid in for the winter, and crops put in for the growing season, and money set aside for the rent or the mortgage and the taxes; despite transcendent ecstasy, the communards have got to be discreet about acid or peyote freak-outs in town. And they'll wear clothes when alien eyes will be offended by their nudity. (Berger et al., 1972, p. 6)

Zablocki too observes that most communes are eventually stumped by the basic conflict between freedom and community, but he admires the brief golden age—a honeymoon period—that many communes experience at their outset, when do-your-own-thing coexists with gentleness, love, and a sense of family:

> Ephemeral as it is, the brief golden age of complete anarchism on a commune is inspiring to experience. To me it seems a brief foretaste of how the human race may someday be able to live. Visiting a commune early in its history, one often feels that a new age has already dawned for mankind. Superhuman labors are accomplished with no apparent strain. Money is simply kept in a pot to which anyone can go and take what he needs. Mothers, fathers,

and childless people cooperate in taking care of children, resulting in liberation for both parent and child. Portents of later conflicts are visible, but usually are not disturbing. One can sense a mild tension between parents and non-parents, and between those who are thinking of the commune as a long range home and those who are living there from moment to moment. (Zablocki, 1971, p. 309)

Zablocki remarks that the first cracks in communal tranquility often arise over the issue of the sense of family. The founders sense the group as a family; believing in anarchy and openness, they welcome newcomers who may not "fit in," but nobody can bring themselves to ask them to leave. So many newcomers may join that original members feel "their" commune no longer exists. Power struggles and disputes over property may arise. Resources pooled during the golden age may be claimed as private property. Zablocki offers a vivid example:

One evening, the members of Dawn commune were just finishing dinner. They took their meals seated on two long benches at either side of a long table. A couple who had formerly been in the commune suddenly came into the house and politely asked those seated at one side of the table to stand up. Then they calmly picked up one of the benches and, before the unbelieving eyes of the commune members, carried it out of the house, loaded it onto their truck, and drove away. These two people had constructed the bench and therefore felt entitled to it. At the time the bench was built, everyone had been working on the principle of "from each according to his ability, to each according to his need." But since this had never been made explicit, there was nothing the commune could do. (Zablocki, 1971, p. 311)

As the golden age recedes further into the past, communal life can turn ugly. Zablocki notes that anarchism can be transformed from freedom to inefficiency to tyranny—of the strong over the weak, of the least committed over the most. There is also a tendency to exploit women in communes, without even an initial golden age of equality. The Manson commune presents a most extreme example of how strong males can dominate and exploit weaker males and women. Most communal observers agree that the status of women may be no better and often worse than in conventional American society. Although women are included in the general ideology of egalitarianism, they tend in practice to perform traditional women's work and are treated as sex objects to an even more extreme degree than in outside society. One highly sympathetic study of communes (Speck et al., 1972, p. 89) noted that only males were considered full-fledged members of the communes, while the status of women ranked somewhere between objects and pets. Still, the problem of women's status is not intrinsic to the communal ideology. Unlike the conflict between freedom and community, it does not rest on a logical contradiction and may be interpreted as a hang-up inherited from the larger culture.

One final problem that may or may not be intrinsic pervades communal life. This is the problem of emotional turmoil and freaking out. Use of drugs, emphasis on deep inner feelings, and a general lack of structure often unveil deeply repressed emotions and fantasies. Getting close to a group of people may lead to a frightening sensation of losing one's identity and dissolving into the group. Tense interpersonal relations, panic, and feelings of great vulnerability sometimes result. Zablocki attributes surprising communal changes from anarchism to extreme authoritarianism to such emotional turmoil: the guru leader may make sense of mystical experience and provide an escape from what becomes a fearful and burdensome freedom.

Analysis of how the communal dream can turn into a nightmare does not necessarily invalidate communal ideology. Communes need not inevitably dissolve, or degenerate into exploitation or psychedelic fascism. But just as the nuclear family cannot be judged by its best examples and stated ideals, neither can the commune be judged only by its successes. The communal scene can provide a fulfilling and attractive environment for children. The "best" communes may be more supportive and secure than the "best" nuclear families; children can develop a strong sense of belonging to others besides their parents, and they have many role models who provide mothering and fathering. The integration of work and household affords children the experience of contributing to the economy of the family while very young, working alongside adults and other children. Their sexual learning can be more open and relaxed, without the secrecy and the heightening and repressing of sexuality characteristic of the nuclear-family household. Nevertheless, the costs and dangers of communal life have turned out to be greater in practice than planners and theorists had anticipated at the outset.

Summary

The turn-of-the-century feminists and social analysts who predicted the end of family life as the inevitable result of social evolution were both right and wrong. They were right in predicting the death of "the family"—a single pattern to be followed by everyone in society. But they underestimated how much people even in urban industrial societies would want the intimate environments and enduring solidarity symbolized if not practiced by kin groups.

The advocates of the nuclear family and the modified extended family saw these needs but they too easily assumed that the prevailing forms of family life could accommodate them. The commune movement similarly underestimated the ease of resolving the strain between individualism and community. The commune movement also erred in advocating the commune as the only way of organizing family life. Its lasting significance may be found in its break with the ideological monopoly held by the nuclear family.

There has always been great variation in actual family life. Still, such variation has usually been considered as deviance or a sign of social disorganization. In part, this was because people who lived in such structures—for example, single parents with children, strong extended families—did not make an argument for them on principle. The commune movement has helped to move family preferences out of the realm of pathology and deviance and into the realm of value and choice. If the shift from the traditional kin group to the conjugal family legitimated the right to happiness as a norm in family life, the commune movement, along with the counterculture in general, helped to bring about a recognition of the possibility of diversity in family life and to legitimate experimentation in family forms.

SEXUAL DESTINY, SEXUAL KNOWLEDGE, AND SOCIAL CHANGE

Chapter 5

The domestic career is no more natural to most women than the military career is natural to all men; although it may be necessary that every able-bodied woman be called upon to risk her life in child-bed just as it may be necessary that every man should be called upon to risk his life in the battlefield . . . . If we have come to think that the nursery and the kitchen are the natural sphere of a woman, we have done so exactly as English children come to think that a cage is the natural sphere of a parrot—because they have never seen one anywhere else.

George Bernard Shaw, *The Womanly Woman*

Chapter Five   People have been theorizing about sexuality for thousands of years, yet the scientific study and public discussion of sexual matters is barely seventy years old. Many of the questions that earlier generations have puzzled over remain unanswered, the experts in disagreement. The study of sexuality illustrates in an extreme way many of the problems that beset the social sciences in general and the family in particular.

In speculating why the social sciences have "lagged behind" the natural sciences like physics and chemistry, some writers have argued that the social sciences are too new; they are only now at the point that physics was when Galileo was dropping balls off the Leaning Tower of Pisa. Others who have thought about the matter come to the opposite conclusion: the social sciences have lagged because they are too old. People have always had theories about what social life is all about, and these folk psychologies and folk sociologies get in the way of, and even get mixed up with, the more scientific models (Murphy, 1971). Still others have argued a third position: that the social sciences can never attain the precision and predictability of the natural sciences for the simple reason that the subject matter is so different; the physicist, watching a ball roll down an inclined plane, does not have to worry about the ball's reactions to being observed—that it might be too embarrassed to roll at all or, just to be contrary, might decide to roll uphill.

Prudery and Patriarchalism

Besides sharing in the general difficulties that beset the study of human behavior, the study of sexuality has been hampered by cultural attitudes surrounding sexuality with anxiety, making it a taboo topic for private or public discussion, and by patriarchal traditions defining women as the natural subordinates of men because of biological and intellectual inferiority.

As John Stuart Mill and later feminists have argued, the history of relations between the sexes is analogous to those between different races, classes, and castes. All such relationships have involved the domination of one group, defined by birth, by members of another group, also defined by birth. Thus patriarchy—the rule of men over women—must be placed alongside feudalism, despotism, slavery, aristocracy, and racism. When in practice, however, such power arrangements appear natural and inevitable, and alternatives to them unthinkable. When religion is given as the major justification for behavior, subordination of one group by another is explained in religious terms. More recently, domination is usually justified in terms of biological necessity, irrevocable instincts, and inherent inferiority. Thus, in approaching the study of either the physical or the social relations between the sexes, it is important to understand how male dominance may have influenced both popular and professional conceptions of sexuality and sex differences.

Albert Memmi's analysis of racism applies well to the issue of sex differences. He notes that the essence of racism or anti-Semitism or any prejudice is the way it emphasizes differences that may be either real or imaginary. Memmi writes:

. . . Revealing a characteristic differentiating two individuals or two groups does not in itself constitute a racist attitude. After all, this is part of what any student of the human sciences does. The assertion that there is a difference takes on a special *significance* in the racist context: by emphasizing the difference, the racist aims to intensify or cause the *exclusion*, the *separation* by which the victim is placed outside the community or even outside humanity. (Memmi, 1968, p. 187) (Italics in the original)

Thus, Memmi goes on, colonialists argue that the natives are too culturally inferior to be included in the community, anti-Semites argue that Jews are too strange and clannish to live and work near non-Jews, and so forth. Extending this analysis to women, alleged sex differences are used to justify keeping women in their place — preferably at home. Memmi continues:

Making use of the difference is an essential step in the racist process: *but it is not the difference which always entails racism, it is racism which makes use of the difference.* (Memmi, 1968, p. 187) (Italics in the original)

There are several other aspects to the racist mode of thought. The "difference" is generalized to encompass all of the victim's personality and all the members of his group. Every manifestation of the person's being is marked by his membership in it. In terms of sex difference, a women is "all woman" in whatever she does, and all women are presumed to be alike. The new feminism has made us aware how deeply entrenched sexist attitudes are in men and women, even our language and habits of expression. It is difficult for students of sexual biology and behavior to escape the patriarchal image of the passive egg, waiting for the purposeful, active sperm to impregnate it, or of female animals during their periods of sexual interest as being "receptive," when in fact their behavior shows them to be the initiator of the sex act (see Herschberger, 1948). There is also some question whether sex differences would even be a topic of scientific interest if it weren't that sex differences lead to important social consequences. Jessie Bernard (1972) has raised the question of whether such research is a "copout" to avoid dealing with problems of sexual inequality and discrimination.

Science and Sexuality

In spite of the new morality and more open communication about sex, we have not escaped from the shadow of Victorian morality, the so-called "civilized" morality that prevailed all over Europe, not just in England in the nineteenth century. At the moment sexual morality is in something of a time warp. In the space of two generations one of the most repressive sexual ideologies that ever existed anywhere has given way, in significant numbers of people at any rate, to one of the most liberal.

Actually, social-science models of sexuality have remained on the whole remarkably similar to folk or popular models of sexuality. Sexuality is said to represent the instinctive "animal" side of human nature, separate from, and opposed to, the higher forms of human behavior which are learned and cultural.

The prevailing ideas about sex and sex differences argue that sex is a powerful natural drive, necessary for reproduction, but one that must be socially controlled. Learning and culture enter into the process only as controls, not as influences on the patterning or development of sexuality.

Sexuality in the folk model includes more than the urgency of lust. It accounts for masculine and feminine behavior, the choice of sex partners, and the differences between the father's and mother's role in child rearing. Thus the natural model of sexuality implies that the person intuitively knows whether he or she is male or female. His or her behavior follows naturally the patterns laid down by the body's biological gender. And, in the same way, a person will naturally be sexually attracted to and fall in love with members of the opposite sex.

Sex is used to mark off humanity into two separate species. At birth children are divided into males and females, with the assumption that everything else about them is secondary to, or flows from, that basic distinction. If the child is a boy, he will be active, assertive, aggressive; he will go out into the world and seek his fortune. If the child is a girl, she will be gentle, passive, dependent, intuitive; her place will be at home. The notion that maleness or femaleness necessarily determines social role and behavior runs deep in many cultural traditions. Ancient Chinese sages divided the world into male and female qualities: yang is bright, hot, active, and positive; yin is dark, moist, cold, and passive. The essential feature of the folk beliefs about sex differences is duality, with gender being a matter of either/or rather than both/and or more/less. Social-science theorists similarly hold that the biological division of labor between the sexes, and a sharp differentiation between men and women, is necessary to the functioning of any society. The prevailing tendency takes the present relations between men and women for granted, and looks for biological "reasons" to explain these relations.

Sex Roles and Biology

Biological determinism often seems more compelling to both laymen and scholars than the notion that sexual destiny is basically a matter of culture and learning. For the laymen it is relatively easy to believe that innate biological forces transform boy babies into men and girl babies into women, since most men and women until very recently have lived up to the prescribed sex roles. Such exceptions as obviously "gay" homosexuals could also be accounted for on biological grounds.

Scholars, however, should find it harder to ascribe to biological determinism of adult sex roles, since evidence clearly reveals cultural variation. In American culture, for example, it is considered "feminine" to be artistic and emotional, but in other cultures men are supposed to be more emotionally expressive and artistic than women. Margaret Mead's classic study of sex and temperament in three cultures (1935) is the best example of the variability of sex-role patterning. In one of the New Guinea tribes, the Arapesh, both men and women were found to be cooperative, unaggressive, and gentle. In contrast, the Mundugumor tribe prescribed what would be a masculine temperament in our culture for both sexes—ruthlessness, aggressiveness, and severity. Neither the Arapesh nor the Mundugumor emphasized a contrast between the sexes. In a third New Guinea tribe, however, the Tchambuli, there was such a contrast, but it was the reverse of sex-role temperament in our culture. Tchambuli women tended to be aggressive, domineering, and managerial, whereas the men tended to be dependent, artistic, and sensitive. In short, the study concludes that sex differences are arbitrary and do not reflect any underlying predisposition.

Further, the realities of everyday social life in modern societies do not support the notion that biological differences automatically assign certain activities to men and others to women. Evelyne Sullerot (1971) has pointed to a time-lag in sex-role differentiation in modern societies: social changes seem more rapid for men. For example, when cars were scarce and driving was prestigeful, few women drove. Driving

seemed a "masculine" activity. Now driving a car is a commonplace necessity of everyday life in many places. But piloting airplanes still seems more a masculine activity than driving cars. Nor does simply looking around at people support the notion that every male is bigger, stronger, and more aggressive as well as more logical than every female.

In trying to reconcile social reality with the notion of innate biological differences between the sexes, scholars have come up with a variety of compromise positions. They all share a belief in some degree of biological determinism, but they allow room for culture and learning to influence the patterning of sexual attitudes. These modified or partial determinism theories differ, however, in the way they conceive of the "natural" forces and the "cultural" forces working together.

Roger Brown (1965, p. 171), for example, puts forth what could be called an "overlap" theory. He argues that although there is a natural biological tendency for males to be rougher and tougher and more active than most females, there is also considerable overlap between the sexes: some women are bigger and stronger and rougher and tougher than some men. Most cultures, moreover, subscribe to sex-role stereotypes that force people into predetermined molds regardless of their individual inclinations. Thus a tough, dominant woman is regarded as a deviant female in our culture, but among Tchambuli she would be considered a normal female. In Mundugumor society she would be regarded as merely a normal person, but in Arapesh society she would be regarded as a deviant human being, not merely a deviant from a sex role. In similar fashion the fate of a temperamentally gentle, sensitive male would vary from culture to culture. Brown concludes that the sex difference is an inadequate method of assigning people to roles.

The essential difficulty is this: temperaments and tastes and attitudes are usually prescribed on the basis of biological sex when they actually reveal an imperfect natural linkage with sex. Men aren't always big, tough, and logical; women aren't necessarily small, gentle, and flighty. If you want your furniture moved, you would be better off with a heavyweight woman than a bantamweight male. Or, to use one of Brown's examples, if you want to hire a door-to-door salesperson, you'd be wiser to hire a determined, aggressive woman than a shy, retiring male.

A similar difficulty often arises when roles are assigned on the basis of other inherited attributes:

. . . not all brahmans have a religious "vocation"; not all elderly men are wise, not all sons of kings are equipped to lead a nation. . . .
The answer must be to detach leadership, aggressiveness, aestheticism, wisdom and the like, from irrelevant ascribed attributes and incorporate them in pure achievement roles. . . . (R. Brown, 1965, p. 171)

Another modified biological-determinism position, that of Diamond, comes somewhat closer to the anatomy-is-destiny notion. It posits innate masculinity and femininity, but leaves some room for the influence of culture and learning. Thus Diamond writes:

. . . Human beings are definitely predisposed at birth to a male or female gender orientation. Sexual behavior of an individual, and thus gender role, are not neutral and without initial direction at birth. Nevertheless sexual predisposition is only a potentiality setting limits to a pattern that is greatly modifiable by . . . experiences. (1965, p. 187)

In a certain sense all theories about sex and sex roles agree that there is some interaction between biological determinants and social factors. But they disagree over the source of the patterning of sexuality. Are sex roles biologically determined, is biology tempered by social learning, or are the learned factors the means by which undirected biological capacities are shaped? In this sense the modified theories of biological determinism are like the stricter ones because they see the basic patterns as innate.

Freudian Biological Determinism   Freud was a stoic biological determinist. He believed in one prototype for humanity — the male. This "sexual monism," as one writer described it (Shainess, 1971, p. 14), is not unique to Freud. Indeed, it is built into the English language. Thus "man" or "mankind" is used to describe the human race, and "he" is the generalized term for person. But Freud went further: he presented an elaborate psychological theory based on the idea that the female constitutes a defective or incomplete male. For Freud there were not really two sexes, but only one. Freud believed that the little girl thinks of herself as a little man until she discovers, to her horror, that she is castrated. This discovery

represents the crucial point in her development, according to
Freud and his followers. She can either accept her biological
destiny, transform the wish for a penis into the wish for a
child, and become a passive female as nature intended her to
be, or she can persist in the misguided belief she is really a
man and can do things men can do.

   In the perspective of the 1970's it seems remarkable that
psychoanalytic writers of the forties and fifties — even women
— could confidently interpret departures from wifely and
maternal roles as abnormal. Helene Deutsch, a leading psychoanalytic authority on the psychology of women, believed
that an "overgrowth" of a girl's intellect was a form of mas-
culinization; it could only impoverish her own emotional
life, wreck her marriage, and ruin her children. She believed
that a healthy woman would renounce her own claims to
accomplishment and originality, and realize herself through
identification with her husband and sons:

   They are the loveliest and the most unaggressive of helpmates
   and they want to remain in that role; they do not insist on their
   rights, quite the contrary. They are easy to handle in every way — if
   only one loves them. (Deutsch, 1944, p. 192)

   The belief that the anatomical distinction between the
sexes has the most fateful influence on a person's destiny
persists among many writers in the psychoanalytic tradition.
Anatomy is destiny, not only for Freud at the turn of the
century but also for many psychologists, sociologists, and
biologists down to the present time. Even Erik Erikson, who
has changed Freud's libido theory in major ways, persists
in the belief that anatomy is destiny; men are directed by
their bodies to an interest in "outer space," whereas women
will be forever focused on "inner space." (Erikson, 1964)

The New Biological Determinism: Man as Ape   In the past ten
years in the writing of such men as Lorenz, Ardry, Morris,
and Tiger, a new version of biological determinism has
arisen. These writers have put forth a number of books arguing that human behavior can be understood as the result of
powerful instinct or rigid patterns genetically programmed
during the course of evolution. They offer a version of what
is supposedly "natural" human nature by using primate
societies as models of the earlier stages of human evolution.
They argue that man evolved as a killer ape. He is genetically

programmed, they assert, with implacable instincts to make war on his fellow man, to seize and defend territory, and to exclude and dominate females. Females, in this theory, are obviously programmed to attract males and to bear and nurture the young.

Although the books of Ardry, Morris, and the others have proved extremely popular, they are for the most part not taken seriously as contributions by other scholars. Recently, because of the popularity of the man-is-an-ape school, a number of detailed rebuttals have appeared (e.g., Alland, 1972; Pilbeam, 1972). As the article by Pilbeam states: "The fashionable view of man as naked ape is: . . . an insult to apes . . . simplistic . . . male-oriented . . . rubbish." The basic flaw consists of exaggerating the similarities between man and other primates (as well as the similarities among the primates themselves) and ignoring the crucial differences between human beings and apes.

Still, the naked-ape school represents in exaggerated form a kind of biological reductionism which has been stated somewhat more respectably by others. For example, Harlow, a psychologist, reports on some of his findings on the play behavior of infant macaque monkeys and generalizes his observations to humans:

> . . . As soon as the sexual responses can be observed and measured, male and female sexual responses differ in form. Furthermore, there are many other behaviors which differ between males and females as soon as they can be observed and measured. . . . Males threaten other males and females but females are innately blessed with better manners; in particular, little girl monkeys do not threaten little boy monkeys. . . . Play behavior in the playroom is typically initiated by males, seldom by females. However, let us not belittle the female, for they also serve who only stand and wait. Contact play is far more frequent among the males than the females and is almost invariably initiated by the males. Playpen data show that real rough-and-tumble play is strictly for the boys.
>
> I am convinced that these data have almost total generality to man. Several months ago I was present at a school picnic attended by twenty-five second graders and their parents. While the parents sat and the girls stood around or skipped about hand in hand, thirteen boys tackled and wrestled, chased and retreated. No little girl chased any boy, but some little boys chased some little girls. . . . (Harlow, 1962, pp. 3–6)

A curious paradox appears in Harlow's insistence on innate biological determinism. His most notable contribution to psychology is to have shown that certain kinds of behavior that had always been believed to be instinctive have large learned components. In the same article from which the preceding quotation is taken, Harlow reports on the sexual and maternal behavior of rhesus monkeys who have been raised in total isolation. These isolated monkeys did not know how to have sex relations when they grew up. When, after many attempts to teach them, some of the isolation-reared females became pregnant, they did not know how to "mother" the infants born to them, and even attacked them.

In any event, Harlow, the experimental psychologist working with monkeys, should be distinguished from Harlow, the maker of coy remarks comparing monkey and human behavior. The range of sex-role behavior among primates is actually much more diverse than is generally recognized. In some, for example, females are more aggressive than males, and, in some, males participate in child care more than females (Mitchell, 1969).

Regardless of whether monkey sex-role behavior is varied or rigid, its relevance to human beings is highly dubious. What does it mean to say that monkey behavior shows what human behavior "naturally" is? Does it mean that humans are biologically incapable of acting in any other way? If that were the case, "unnatural" sex or sex-role behavior would never occur, and there would be no need for writers to argue against women violating their natural sex roles. For example, a single instance of a little girl chasing a little boy would be enough to disprove Harlow's generalization that children's playground behavior is determined by innate biological differences.

Another way "natural" is used in talking about sex differences is to point to the way things ought to be, not the way they necessarily are (Pierce, 1971). Thus, Harlow might argue that it is "unnatural" for little girls to chase little boys, and therefore they shouldn't. But in that case the burden would be on him to explain why it is "better" for human beings to act like certain species of monkeys. As another psychologist, Naomi Weisstein, puts it:

. . . There are no grounds to assume that anything primates do is necessary, natural, or desirable in humans, for the simple reason that humans are not non-humans. For instance it is found that male chimpanzees placed alone with infants will not "mother" them.

Jumping from hard data to ideological speculation, researchers conclude from this information that *human* females are necessary for the safe growth of human infants. Following this logic, it would be as reasonable to conclude that it is quite useless to teach human infants to speak, since it has been tried with chimpanzees and it does not work. (Weisstein, 1971, p. 218)

Sex Roles in Cross-cultural Research   Cross-cultural research demonstrates that a division of labor by sex occurs in all cultures; women's work centers around preparing food and caring for children; men's work varies according to the economy of a particular culture, but it is more likely to involve being away from home—as in hunting, herding, traveling, and fighting—and is more often strenuous (D'Andrade, 1966).

The conclusion often drawn from such findings is that sex roles and the division of labor by sex are innate and biologically necessary. The critical question is: What is "biological necessity"? Do the "biological necessities" similarly prevail in advanced industrial societies? The cultures in the cross-cultural surveys differ in three crucial ways from modern ones: they lack the technology of contraception and bottle feeding; they have high infant-mortality rates; and they highly value children's labor. Given these circumstances the lives of women in preindustrial societies are often dominated by an endless cycle of pregnancy, nursing for one to three years, then another pregnancy, and so on, until the end of fertility, which often coincides with the end of the woman's life itself. It makes sense then that while women are thus preoccupied, the tasks of hunting, herding, and so forth are carried out by the men.

Given the necessity for women to bear and nurse children, women's "nature" can be explained as part of the requirements of women's work. Their working role requires them to be giving, nurturant, responsible, unaggressive. Men's work may or may not require the opposite of such traits. In some cultures, as Margaret Mead pointed out, both sexes have "feminine" personalities, whereas in others both sexes are "masculine."

These differences in cultural emphasis, however, seem to depend to some extent at least on the type of work that is done in the economy. Where agriculture or herding represents the means of subsistence, both boys and girls are socialized to be compliant; but in hunting societies children

are socialized to be independent and assertive (Barry, Child, and Bacon, 1959).

Hormonal Determinism   The primate analogy represents one form of the argument that sex behavior is biologically determined. Another version of the biological theory of sexual behavior is based on hormones. Females and males differ in the kinds and amounts of hormones their bodies produce. Hormones shape the bodies of men and women and cause the secondary sex characteristics to take their characteristic form — body and facial hair, voice depth, fat and muscle distribution. Hormones also enter the brain. Therefore, the theory goes, hormones explain everything there is to know about sex, the rise and fall of sexual desire, sex-role differences in interests and temperament, and choice of sex object.

Actually, however, as Ford and Beach (1951) point out, the dominant fact with regard to human sexuality is the evolutionary trend away from hormonal control over sexual behavior and toward control by the higher centers of the brain — in other words, control by learning and by symbolic social meaning. Studies of the actual effects of hormones reveal that no simple relation exists between the amount of sex hormones in a person's blood and erotic arousal; that is, high arousal is possible at low levels of the hormones, and high levels need not necessarily lead to arousal. Furthermore, attempts to cure sexual problems such as impotence or frigidity with hormones generally have been unsuccessful (Hardy, 1964). In short, the research emphasizes the importance of social and psychological factors in erotic arousal. People are turned on by other people, situations, emotions, and imagination; hormones play a relatively minor role.

Sexuality: "Life Force" or Appetite? The alternative to the "life force" or hormonal view of sexuality emphasizes the role of learning and the social context in the shaping and patterning of sexual experience and behavior. This concept of sexuality has been put forth by a number of social psychologists, sociologists, and anthropologists. Basically it conceives of sexuality, or any human biological motive for that matter, as a two-step process at least, involving a biological capacity that is shaped, directed, and amplified by social learning as well as individual cognitive processes. In other words, sex is in the head and in the social environment, as well as in the genitals.

Udry sums up the social-learning view of sexuality:

> The basic statement of the social-psychological explanation of human sexuality is this: sexual behavior is learned behavior. "Sex drive" is learned, sex interest is learned. If the requisite learning experiences occur, the individual becomes sexually interested and active; if they are absent, he does not. . . . (Udry, 1971, p. 98)

Sexuality can begin in infancy. Hardy (1964) has noted that there are two distinct constitutional bases around which sexual "appetites" can form: mild local stimulation of the genital area, and the more intense excitement-relaxation of orgasm. Although some children are capable of genital climax, cross-cultural evidence shows that sexual interest and behavior does not depend on the maturation of the sex glands or the ability to experience orgasms. Hardy (1964) notes that mild stimulation of the genital regions is pleasurable from infancy, and even in the preschool years may lead to orgasm. The cultural shaping of sexual appetites and sexual behavior, he argues, is built upon this constitutional basis. Thus some cultures encourage young children to masturbate and play at having intercourse. In such societies sexual behavior is continuous from childhood to adulthood.

Stephens (1963) reports on a number of societies around the world where sexual stimulation is used as a pacifier for infants, and as an aid in weaning older babies from the breast. In a number of cultures children play at intercourse all during childhood, and "real" intercourse may begin at the age of eight or ten. Some societies believe that children will not mature properly or be able to produce babies when they are adults unless they have regular sexual practice early in life (Ford and Beach, 1951).

American parents typically discourage masturbation and any other form of sexual behavior in children, and try to keep them from observing sexual behavior. Most American children, therefore, do not develop a sex interest until their teens, at which time it is expected of them. The male peer group encourages boys to have sexual interests in girls, but the girls' peer group, as well as parents, inclines girls toward a more social interest in boys.

Learning thus plays a role in the development of a general appetite for sex, as well as specific tastes. As with food, everyone needs to eat in order to stay alive, but beyond the minimal caloric requirements a great deal of individual variation is possible in what people like to eat, which is often what they have learned to like as children. As there are different cuisines in different cultures, with different tastes and styles of food preparation, there are varying symbols of sexual attractiveness and types of sexual behavior among cultures.

Even within one culture, such as ours, some people think about food often even when they are not hungry; other people express particular tastes in food, and will refuse to eat certain dishes even when very hungry. Both obesity and an interest in gourmet cooking represent in different ways psychological approaches to food irrelevant to tissue needs.

Ultimately, however, the analogy between sex and food breaks down because there is little evidence that sex fulfills any tissue need. There is no sexual counterpart to starvation. As Beach puts it:

No genuine tissue or biological needs are generated by sexual abstinence. It used to be believed that prolonged sexual inactivity in adulthood resulted in the progressive accumulation of secretions within the accessory sex glands, and that nerve impulses from these distended receptacles gave rise to sexual urges. Modern evidence negates this hypothesis. . . . What is commonly confused with a primary drive associated with sexual deprivation is in actuality sexual appetite, and this has little or no relation to biological or physiological needs. (Beach, 1956, p. 4)

Physiological states alone are never enough to produce emotional arousal and behavior. As Silvan Tomkins has put it, the "oomph" of biological drives is an illusion. The "oomph" comes not from physiology but from the person's response to a physiological state. Tomkins offers the example of oxygen deprivation. What motive could be more urgent than that of a drowning or choking person for air? Yet, Tomkins notes, the tissue need for oxygen, by itself, does not create a psychological need for air. In fact, when oxygen deprivation is gradual, people become euphoric. Some pilots in World War II refused to wear their oxygen masks at high altitudes, and died with smiles on their lips. In the same way, argues Tomkins, sexual arousal is a state of conscious excitement, which amplifies the physiological arousal. No one, he writes, "has ever observed an excited penis. . . ."

One is excited and breathes hard, not in the penis, but in the chest, the esophagus, the face, and the nose and nostrils. Both the sexual urge and the sexual pleasure of intercourse are ordinarily amplified by excitement as anoxia is amplified by panic. . . . To be fully sexually aroused and satisfied, one must be capable of excitement as well as tumescence. (Tomkins, 1965, pp. 118–119)

Tomkins notes that the concept of amplification helps explain how couples can report that they have orgasms and yet complain of the lack of sexual satisfaction:

Sexual intercourse repeated with the same partner is vulnerable to such attenuation of satisfaction whenever the decline in novelty of the interpersonal relationship is such that excitement can no longer be sustained. Those who are generally bored with each other may also be unable to become sexually excited even when they are capable . . . of orgasm. (p. 119)

Not only sex is subject to amplification effects. It is possible to manipulate a person's physiological state with drugs and yet not produce an emotional response. For example, Schacter (1964) has shown that a person injected with adrenalin will show the symptoms of emotional arousal — palpitation, tremor, accelerated breathing, and yet he will not experience an emotion. He will say, "I feel as if I were afraid." In a classic experiment, Schacter showed that a person under the influence of adrenalin could be more easily made angry or very happy than somebody not given adrenalin, or somebody given a shot of adrenalin but told of its effects. In short, body chemistry does not lead to an emotional experience until it has been amplified or interpreted.

New Views of Sexual Development

Challenges to the innate-determinism view of sexuality and sex-role development have also been emerging in recent years from research on the sexual development of normal children, as well as on people with sexual anomalies of various kinds. Some of the most dramatic findings have emerged from studies of "sex errors of the body": people born with physical characteristics of both sexes. Studies of such people, generally referred to as hermaphrodites or intersexed individuals, have provided new insights into the development and patterning of sexuality. They have revealed that these processes are more complex than anyone had thought. These studies have also shown that popular discussions tend to use sexual terms in a confused and imprecise way, and some scholarly writing does so also. Thus Brown and Lynn (1966) point out that the following terms are often used as synonyms:

male and masculine

female and feminine

homosexuality, sexual transvestism, inversion, and trans-sexualism

Actually, most contemporary sex researchers agree that it is important to distinguish between the biological aspects of sexuality and the psychological aspects. "Male" and "female" are the terms used to refer to biological aspects of sex, but "masculinity" and "femininity" are psychological and behavioral characteristics. We are so accustomed to thinking of all the aspects of sexuality as hanging together that it is difficult to get used to the idea that anatomy may be independent of the sense of gender identity ("I am a boy" or "I am a girl"). Table 2 presents the physiological and psychological aspects of sex differences.

TABLE 2   MALE/FEMALE CHARACTERISTICS

Characteristic	Male	Female	Explanation
Physiological:			
1 Chromosomal composition	XY	XX	At the moment of conception the unborn child's sex is determined by whether the father's sperm cell contains an X or a Y chromosome; if it is a Y chromosome, child will be a boy
2 Gonads	Testicles	Ovaries	
3 Hormonal composition	Androgen, etc.	Estrogen, progesterone, etc.	These hormones operate before birth to differentiate male and female fetuses and again at adolescence to produce secondary sex characteristics— e.g., deep voices, beards, and body hair in men, breasts and menstruation in women
4 Internal accessory organs	Seminal vesicles and prostate gland	Vagina, uterus, and fallopian tubes	
5 External genitalia	Penis and testicles	Vulva	
Psychological:			
1 Gender identity	I am a male	I am a female	The basic sense of one's social identity
2 Masculinity-feminity	I am a masculine or effeminate male	I am a feminine or mannish woman	This refers to the person's conformity to the sex-role standards of the particular culture; it involves certain interests, attitudes, fantasies, ways of moving and speaking.[a]
3 Sex-object preference			Whether one is aroused by members of one's own sex or the opposite one

[a]Roger Brown caricatures American sex typing as follows: "In the United States a real boy climbs trees, disdains girls, dirties his knees, plays with soldiers, and takes blue for his favorite color. A real girl dresses dolls, jumps rope, plays hopscotch, and takes pink for her favorite color. When they go to school, real girls like English and music and 'auditorium'; real boys prefer manual training, gym, and arithmetic." . . . (R. Brown, 1965, p. 161)

Masculinity and femininity are not to be confused with gender identity. Thus a tomboy is a girl with boyish interests in, say, sports, tree climbing, and playing with soldiers, but there is no doubt about what gender she belongs to. A boy may have an interest in the things the culture places in the feminine world but he is still a boy. People may worry about their femininity and masculinity but, with rare exceptions, they have no doubts about their gender identity. Furthermore, there appears to be very little relationship between being worried about one's masculinity or femininity and the actual degree of discrepancy between one's behavior and the cultural standards. Thus a male who seems very "masculine" to other people may go through a crisis of doubt about his masculinity during adolescence, whereas an "effeminate" male may go through life without any such worries at all (Kohlberg, 1966, p. 91).

Gender identity and masculinity-femininity are also to be distinguished from the third aspect of psychological sexuality, sex-object preference. Whether a person is sexually aroused by a member of his own or the opposite sex is independent of gender identity and masculinity-femininity. Homosexuals are not confused about their gender identity. Nor do homosexual men and women necessarily differ from their "straight" counterparts in masculinity and femininity. Some homosexual men view themselves as masculine and take the masculine role in sexual encounters. Others view themselves as feminine and take the feminine role, whereas still others see their masculinity as independent of homosexual roles (Hooker, 1965).

The argument that the psychological aspects of sexuality —gender identity, masculinity and femininity, or sex-object choice—are learned rather than innate comes in two versions. The first is a social-learning model of sex development.

The Social-Learning Model   According to this approach the child learns sex-typed behavior the same way he or she learns any other type of behavior, through a combination of reward, punishment, and observation of what other people are doing. Proponents of this view include psychologists, such as Mischel, Bandura, and Walters, and anthropologists, such as Margaret Mead in her early writings. In essence, proponents argue that it is unnecessary to invoke innate biological

drives or tendencies to account for sexual behavior, particularly sex-role behavior, since learning can and does account for whatever behavioral differences are found between the sexes. Bandura, for example, describes sex-role learning as a process of indoctrination that begins at birth:

> Sex-role differentiation usually commences immediately after birth, when the baby is named and both the infant and the nursery are given the blue or pink treatment depending upon the sex of the child. Thereafter, indoctrination into masculinity and femininity is diligently promulgated by adorning children with distinctive clothes and hair styles, selecting sex-appropriate play materials and recreational activities, promoting associations with same-sex playmates, and through non-permissive parental reactions to deviant sex-role behavior. (Bandura, 1969, p. 215)

Besides direct indoctrination, the view of sexual development includes modeling as a way of learning: the boy will be rewarded for imitating his father, and discouraged from using his mother as a model for his own behavior; the girl will be rewarded for the reverse. Eventually the child will find imitating the appropriate models rewarding in itself.

The Cognitive-Development Model   Unlike the social-learning model of sex-role development, which reflects a general approach held by a number of psychologists, sociologists, and anthropologists, the cognitive-development model of sexuality is mainly the work of one scholar, Lawrence Kohlberg. Kohlberg's approach is largely an elaboration of the theories of Piaget, applied to the area of sexual development.

Like the social-learning theorists, Kohlberg argues against the notion that sexuality is instinctually patterned. Nevertheless, he does not believe that sexuality and sex-role learning are based on learned conformity to cultural patterns. Rather, he argues, the child's concepts of sexuality arise in the same way as all his other concepts about the world and the things in it. Sexual ideas and sex-role concepts result from the child's *active structuring of his own experience*, rather than from something directly taught by other people.

The key cognitive event is the categorization of one's self as male or female. Once this recognition of self is acquired, between the ages of one and a half to three, it organizes the way the child perceives and categorizes the rest of the world and his or her place in it. For example, other people are defined as belonging to one category or the other, male or female. The child places himself or herself in one of these categories, and begins the process of "cognitive rehearsal" — the lifelong accumulation of memories and fantasies in which he/she acts out the appropriate sex roles. A little boy will dream of being a fireman or a policeman or an astronaut when he grows up, and when he thinks of his future family life he will imagine himself as a daddy with a wife and children. A little girl will dream of having breasts and wearing grown-up clothes and lipstick and attracting men, and her fantasies of family life will feature her in the role of mother. The learning is *very* gradual, and changes with the child's stage of thinking — that is, young children may think that one's sexual identity is something that can change, like one's age.

Kohlberg also shows that genital anatomy plays a surprisingly small part in young children's thinking about sex differences. Clothing styles and social-role differences, such as the fact that males are policemen and firemen, are more impressive to childish minds. In short, learning to be male or female seems to be a process of understanding and interpreting the rules, both explicit and implicit, defining sex roles.

Kohlberg cites evidence showing that bright children tend to be ahead of their age mates of average intelligence in the maturity of their sexual attitudes. For example, between the ages of four and eight, all boys tend to show a number of changes in preference for masculine toys, and toward affiliation with male figures rather than female. Bright boys show these shifts earlier than average boys.

Kohlberg cites the work of Money and his associates as further evidence for the theory. These were studies of hermaphrodites, children born with genital abnormalities which make it hard to tell whether the child is a boy or a girl (Money, 1961; Money, Hampson, and Hampson, 1957). Certain tests now make it possible to tell whether the child is "really" male or female—that is, whether its chromosomes are male or female in pattern. But in previous years the doctor merely had to guess. Sometimes the doctor would find out later that he had assigned the child to the wrong sex. In such a case the child might be reassigned to the approriate gender.

Body, Mind, and Gender   Money and his associates undertook a series of studies of children and adults with sexual abnormalities of one kind or another. The most striking discovery of this research was the finding that children with the same anatomical structures could be assigned to either sex, and grow up to be a psychologically "normal" member of that sex. These researchers argued that the biological aspects of sexuality are independent of the psychological aspects—that is, the sex category to which one is assigned at birth and reared in, one's own sense of gender identity, and one's preference in sex objects. Thus, not only can intersexed or hermaphroditic children be raised successfully in either sex, but children erroneously assigned to the wrong category can grow up to be psychologically normal members of the sex to which they were assigned.

Money ultimately concludes that every child is "psychosexually neutral" at birth.* Because it is so extremely rare for a child to be assigned to the wrong sex, we assume that masculinity or feminity is a natural unfolding of innate biological inclinations. The psychosexual-neutrality concept argues that we *assign* children to one sex or the other on

---

*In his more recent research, Money has moved away from the concept of complete psychosexual neutrality at birth. Although he acknowledges that prenatal hormone levels may influence behavior to some degree, he does not subscribe to the notion that sex-role differences are determined in a simple and direct way by biological forces. Money (1972) argues that gender identity, despite hormonal influences, arises mainly from learning and social interaction.

the basis of their anatomy and then believe that the psychological aspects of sexuality are caused by anatomy and physiology.

The child does not, however, remain psychosexually neutral for very long; once the child has established a gender identity (during the period of language mastery from one and a half to three) it seems to be irreversible. Before that age a child can be reassigned to the other sex; after that age it becomes much more difficult. Money compares the process to "imprinting" in birds. In certain species of birds there is a critical period during which a young bird will follow any moving object it sees, and later will try to mate only with something that resembles the "imprinted" object. Usually the baby bird will see its mother and so become imprinted with appropriate responses. Experiments carried out by Lorenz and others, however, show that the baby birds can become imprinted on humans or vacuum cleaners or any moving object. Money suggests that sexual imprinting is something like that in humans. Kohlberg warns, however, that the notion of imprinting is only a metaphor in human sexuality. He argues that early sexual identities are difficult to reverse later because they are basic to other learning. They constitute the cognitive categories around which experience and memory have been organized, and any such categories learned early in life are hard to reverse.

Sex-Role Learning in Infancy Regardless of whether one uses a social-learning or a cognitive model to explain the development of sex-role identity, the observational facts are that sex-role learning begins at birth. Lois Hoffman, in the review of the literature on early sex typing, writes:

. . . One thing appears certain from this body of research on early mother-infant interaction, there are sex differences in both maternal and infant behavior in the first year of life. That sex role learning is begun so early should not be surprising. Sex is a primary status — the first one announced at birth. The mother is very much aware of it. Her early behaviors towards the infant are not deliberate efforts to teach the child his proper sex role but she has internalized society's view and acts accordingly. She acts towards her son as though he were sturdy and active and she is more likely to show pleasure when his behavior fits this image. Her daughter is her doll — sweet and delicate and pink. . . . If the child exhibits behavior consistent with the female stereotype, such as dependency, she is not as likely to discourage it as she would with a son. (Hoffman, 1972, p. 141)

As the infant grows the parent's behavior continues to be guided by traditional sex-role conception. Hoffman's review of the literature reveals that girls are protected more than boys, and given less encouragement for independent, adventurous, exploratory behavior. As a result little girls do not develop skills in coping with the environment, but remain dependent on adults, particularly their mothers. As David McClelland (1953) has put it, males tend to be interested in things, and females tend to be interested in people. Hoffman argues that these early childhood experiences help to explain how girls are turned away from the kinds of experiences that lead to achievement striving in later life, and develop an overemphasis on emotional relationships. In boys the emphasis is reversed. She suggests that a better balance of love and achievement would be desirable for both.

Sex in History

So far we have been discussing sex and sex roles from an analytic perspective. In this section we focus on the subjective aspects of sexuality, especially the question of how sexual experience is modified by the social and historical context.

Although we are still far from being free of anxiety about sexual matters today, our current hangups must seem trivial when we think of what it must have been like living in Victorian times. If you were a woman the leading medical authorities and their popularizers would have assured you that it was normal to have no sexual feelings at all—to have any would have marked you as a degenerate or a whore. It would have been wrong, however, for you to refuse your husband his "marital rights" since this would harm his health. Although men were acknowledged to have sexual desires, sex was dirty and dangerous for them also. Doctors of the Victorian era warned against "excess" and its dire consequences to mental and physical health. One of the leading authorities warned married men that they should have intercourse no oftener than every seven to ten days, and that often only if they were very strong and healthy (Comfort, 1967, p. 58).

The rise and fall of sexual morality is an uncharted part of history, only now beginning to receive the serious attention of scholars. Although Victorian morality was a more

stringent form of the "civilized morality" that prevailed in
Europe during the nineteenth century, American morality
in turn may have been more severe than that of England:

American morality bore the stamp of Anglo-Saxon culture, evan-
gelical Protestantism, the absence of aristocratic or popular traditions of hedonism. The American code formally required mental
chastity of both men and women, placed a special emphasis on
female purity, and installed the mother as the guardian of morals.
The sexual secretions, it was taught, must be conserved, lest
character and intellect be weakened or destroyed. (Hale, 1971,
p. 465)

Obviously, these ideas have not disappeared today.

The most bizarre example of the tendency of Victorian
doctors to mix morality with medicine is the concept of
"masturbation insanity." A number of medical writers have
described the rise and fall of this concept. Alex Comfort
(1967) shows how the promotion of sexual anxiety came to be
practiced by the medical profession. Comfort argues that sex
anxiety is an *iatrogenic* malady—a disorder produced as a
result of medical intervention. He compares the history of
masturbation insanity with the outbursts of witch hunting
that occurred in earlier periods of European and American
history. Although masturbation had always been considered
a sin by the Church, it was not regarded as a worse sin than
any other form of disapproved sex; and medical authorities
showed no particular concern with the subject. Some writers
before the eighteenth century regarded masturbation as a
useful form of sexual relief. The notion that masturbation not
only is sinful but the leading cause of insanity, blindness,
and epilepsy was put forth in the eighteenth century and
reached its peak in the middle of the nineteenth. The preoccupation led to numerous devices for controlling masturbation, such as chastity belts and even surgical intervention.

Perhaps the most widespread and pernicious effect of
the concern about the practice was its effect on child rearing.
From the mid-nineteenth century to the first half of the
twentieth, mothers were warned by child-rearing manuals to
be ever watchful lest their children touch their genitals.
Comfort quotes some advice given by Dr. Emma Drake
in 1901:

Mothers need to be Argus-eyed, to guard their babies from all
the evils that beset them. . . . While very young . . . they can be

taught that handling [the genitals] will hurt them and make them sick. Tell them that little children, when they do not know this, form the habit of handling themselves and as a result they become listless and sick, and many times idiotic and insane, or develop epileptic fits. . . . (Drake, 1901, p. 87)

As late as 1928 an English child-rearing manual was still recommending "untiring zeal" on the part of the mother to prevent masturbation, and suggesting that it might be necessary to put the child to bed with its legs in splints (Comfort, p. 111). Comfort writes that the outbreak of masturbation-insanity nonsense did not really end until the Kinsey reports of the late 1940's, showing that masturbation was practically universal for both sexes.

Ironically, the very prevalence of masturbation made it possible for the proponents of masturbation as the cause of insanity to give the appearance of proving their point: they found if they were to interrogate any mental patient, he would confess to being a masturbator.

Legacy of "Civilized" Morality   The current sexual climate in many ways appears to have been shaped by the previous era of repression. For one thing our very preoccupation with sexuality may be a backlash phenomenon, a sudden outpouring of all the questions that couldn't be asked, all the words that couldn't be said, all the sights that couldn't be seen. But the present sexual atmosphere is more than an outpouring of blocked impulses. The assumptions of "civilized" morality provide much of the framework for today's liberal morality, as well as for research into sex. For example the view of sexuality as a powerful, natural force that civilized society holds in check was and is the prevailing model of sexuality for the Victorians, for Freud, as well as for *Playboy* magazine and the liberal morality it represents. The Victorians believed in taming sexuality and banishing it even from thoughts; Freud believed that people should control their sexuality consciously, and direct sexual "energy" into useful work. *Playboy* and other advocates of "liberal morality" believe it is healthy and natural to follow the dictates of nature, and act on one's sexual impulses. All agree with the "life force" model of sexuality.

Freud was an outspoken critic of the excesses of "civilized" morality, particularly the silence and secrecy that prevented even doctors and patients from discussing sexual problems. Yet he shared many of the assumptions of the most extreme representatives of sexual conservatism. The historian Nathan Hale has recently pointed out the parallels between Freud and Anthony Comstock, the guardian of American purity who campaigned for censorship and obscenity laws:

> Despite enormous differences . . . they agreed on certain fundamentals. They believed that civilization and progress depended directly on the control of sexuality and on the stable monogamous family. They believed in different ways that "mind" should govern the "sensual nature." Even Freud displayed some of the reticence Comstock would enforce by public censorship. It was only after great inner resistance that Freud brought himself to publish the sexual histories of his patients. These broad similarities between men so unlike testify to the strength of the common elements in European and American versions of "civilized" morality. (Hale, 1971, p. 25)

Freud, too, in his earlier years, believed in a version of masturbational insanity. "Neurasthenia," a common psychiatric complaint of Victorian times—involving weakness and weariness and lassitude—was attributed by Freud to masturbation. At the same time, however, Freud believed that the guilt and anxiety caused by the taboos on masturbation might cause more harm than the practice itself.

The Social Context of Sexuality

Not only the past theories about sexuality and sex differences influence present theories; in addition, the social context surrounding sexuality may influence sexual experience and behavior itself. Thus the common notion that the sexual drive is pretty much the same everywhere, only the openness of talking about it varies, is probably wrong. Whether or not one can talk about sex or think about it, who can talk to each other about it, and how one learns about sex—all of this may have an enormous influence on the experience itself.

Most discussions of sexuality focus on sexual behavior itself, or the content of people's information and beliefs, or their attitudes, rather than on the context in which sex is learned and acted out. A number of researchers have suggested that it is also useful to look not only at what people say and do but also at the context of the interaction. For example, Lennard and Bernstein (1969) suggest that when a patient goes to see a psychotherapist, the patient may be helped as much by the form of the interaction as anything the therapist may say. In this perspective therapy is a process of going to a place one or several times a week where you speak your innermost thoughts in confidentiality with the complete interest and attention of another person, and with the assurance that you will not be criticized or scolded.

Lennard and Bernstein use television as another example of the contrast between content and context. They note, for example, that people tend to worry a great deal about the effect of the content of television programs on their children — whether watching violent programs will make children act aggressive. But few people worry about the effects of television as a medium or context — the fact that television turns experiences on and off arbitrarily, that reports of serious real-life events such as wars, disasters, and human tragedies are interrupted by cheery advertisements.

What is the medium or context in which information about sex, and sexuality itself, is exchanged? The most important of such features are secrecy, the aura of shame and anxiety, the transmission of information via childhood peer groups rather than by adults, the preoccupation with health, morality, and normality, the taboos about discussing sexuality, the fact that "any statement by an individual is presumed to be related to the sexual preferences and desires of that individual" (Gagnon, 1965, p. 215), and, as a corollary of the latter, the assumption that talking about sex is an act of seduction.

Until very recently sexual knowledge in America was in a state sociologists call "pluralistic ignorance" — everybody knew about his own sexual behavior, but nobody knew what anyone else was doing or feeling. Thus everyone had a "backstage" or undressed view of his own sexuality, and a frontstage, dressed-up view of other people's. The Freudian revolution had made sexual feelings more acceptable than previously, but this loosening up was accompanied by rather strict notions of normality. For many people the old concern with the sinfulness of sex was replaced by a concern with normality. For women the change from Victorian sexuality to Freudian was like jumping from the frying pan into the fire — or, more aptly, from the freezer into the refrigerator. The Freudian revolution discovered women have sexual feelings after all, but it created the myth of two orgasms: the notion that the clitoris transfers its sensitivity to the vagina in "mature," nonneurotic women. Actually, as Kinsey and later Masters and Johnson have shown, all orgasms center on the clitoris, although the stimulation that leads to orgasm can come from any erogenous zone or from the imagination.

From the perspective of the 1970's it appears that the truly revolutionary event in the social context of sexuality was the publication of the Kinsey reports from 1948 to 1953. Kinsey's statistics not only broke through the curtain of pluralistic ignorance, but they made it permissible to discuss sexuality in conventional social situations. They revealed widespread deviance from conventional moral standards, and upset previously held notions of rigid distinctions between normality and deviance in sexual matters. For example, Kinsey found considerable evidence of childhood sexual activity, homosexual experiences in the sex histories of "normal" heterosexual men, premarital and extramarital sexuality, as well as deviations from presumably "normal" patterns of intercourse in marriage.

The Effects of Secrecy   The secrecy previously surrounding sexuality has had profound effects. For one thing it sets the stage for guilt and anxiety. Masturbation is the classic instance of a practice that is practically universal, yet so taboo that countless millions of people have been tortured by the thought that "I must be the only one to have done this." One of the reasons the notion of masturbational insanity seemed plausible was that people were indeed "driven crazy" by guilt and worry over having ruined themselves physically and mentally.

Another effect of secrecy is to call attention to whatever the secret is about. Georg Simmel, one of the classic sociologists of the nineteenth century, described the secret as a sociological form. Any secret, he noted, creates a great atmosphere of tension. Does the other person know my secret? What would happen if I told?

. . . The secret is surrounded by the possibility and temptation of betrayal; and the external danger of being discovered is interwoven with the internal danger, which is like the fascination of the abyss, of giving oneself away. The secret creates a barrier between men but, at the same time, it creates the tempting challenge to break through it, by gossip or confession—and this challenge accompanies its psychology like a constant overtone. (Simmel, 1950, p. 334)

Adding sexual guilt and anxiety to the general tensions of any kind of secrecy results in a very potent mix. The context of prudery and repression may well have had the effect of heightening the excitement and "oomph" of sexuality. Laing has pointed out that the repression has paradoxical effects. He notes that if you try very hard to have only clean thoughts, it is difficult to avoid thinking "dirty" ones. It is like being told "Do not think of a white monkey." To be constantly on guard against sexual thoughts is to live in a highly erotic atmosphere; the Victorians found piano legs guilty of indecent exposure. Further, as Laing also notes, warnings and injunctions against doing things also may incline people to do those very things. A classic instance is the little boy who was playing with a bean. His mother told him "Don't put that bean in your ear." The end of the story, of course, is that the boy puts the bean in his ear. Why? Because the warning may have put an idea into his head that wasn't there in the first place, and also because telling someone not to do something suggests that they really are inclined to do it, if it weren't forbidden. Of repressive morality Laing writes:

It must constitute one of the biggest knots in which man has ever tied himself. One of its many peculiar features is that the more tied in the knot, the less aware we are that we are tied in it.

Anyone caught in the full anticalculus of this kind cannot possibly avoid being bad in order to be good. In order to comply with the rules, rules have to be broken. Even if one could wash out one's brain three times a day, part of oneself must be aware of what one is not supposed to know. (Laing, 1969a, p. 116)

Freud and Secrecy Breaking through the knots of secrecy that surrounded sex was one of the major achievements of the Freudian revolution. Part of the "miracle" cures of the early analysts—severe symptoms clearing up after only a session—may have been due to the fact that the early analysts were able to attack the social context surrounding sex.

The discoveries of Freud have transformed emotional life itself. There is a vast difference between a psychoanalytic patient in 1899 learning of his romantic attachment to his mother, and one in the 1960's. Mary McCarthy once wrote about the banality of the insights she had gained from her psychoanalyst. She was disappointed to learn how un-original her neurosis was; she suffered from the same con-flicts as everybody else.

For several decades now sophisticated parents have been watching their offspring for the first stirrings of sexual attachments to mother, Oedipal hostility to father, and sibling rivalry for the little sister, with the same parental interest as other milestones of development, such as the first tooth, the first word, the first step. In short, the Freudian revolution transformed what had been a private, unthink-able torment — what kind of monster must I be to have such thoughts and feelings — into a problem common to everyone. As the mama in the joke put it, "Oedipus, shmedipus, as long as he loves his mother."

Another aspect of the Freudian revolution was to legit-imize thinking previously forbidden thoughts. Freud drew a sharp line between having a fantasy and acting it out. Victorian morality did not make this distinction. It was almost as much a sin to have unclean thoughts as to do un-clean things. Much of the torment of Freud's patients as well as of their contemporaries must have come about through struggles with their own thoughts as well as reactions to them — the knots of Western conscience, as Laing has de-scribed them.

When Freud began his psychiatric career, it was un-heard of for patients to discuss their sex lives with physi-cians. Patients tried hard to conceal any information about the subject, and doctors were as "prudish" and "lascivious" as any other "civilized" people of that time (Hale, 1971, p. 10).

Freud argued that every nervous illness could be traced to a sexual origin. As Freud freely admitted, this idea did not originate with him. But Freud's method of treatment, "the talking cure," was original, and it required that the doctor and the patient communicate with complete open-ness. In one of his early papers (1898) he pleaded that it should be possible to discuss sexual matters "without being stamped as a disturber of the peace or as a person whose aim is to arouse the lower instincts." He summarized the arguments against doctors' inquiring into their patients' sexuality:

I hear it said that a physician has no right to intrude upon his patients' privacy in sexual matters, or to wound their modesty (especially that of his women patients) so grossly as such an interrogation would do. His clumsy hand would only ruin family happiness, and with youthful patients destroy innocence and undermine the authority of parents; with adults he would become the uncomfortable possessor of disquieting knowledge and his relations with his patients would suffer in consequence. It is therefore his ethical duty to hold himself aloof from the whole question of their sexual life. (1898, p. 221)

Sexuality in Early Modern Europe   Before the nineteenth century, European culture was not nearly so repressive as it was to become. Before the Protestant reformation of the sixteenth century, it was even less so. It is instructive to look at this pattern of sexuality because it contrasts both with the "civilized" morality of Victorian times and with our own. Anyone who has read Chaucer, or Boccaccio, or Rabelais is aware of the bawdiness of early modern literature. The evidence is that people's everyday behavior was more openly sexual than even today, in the sense that there were fewer taboos on sexual talk, and sexual horseplay was a usual part of adult interactions. Even more surprising than the ribaldries of adult life was the fact that adults felt no need to shield children from these goings-on. Aries writes:

> One of the unwritten laws of contemporary morality requires adults to avoid any reference, above all, any humorous reference, to sexual matters in the presence of children. This notion was entirely foreign to the society of old. The modern reader of the diary in which Henry IV's physician, Heroard, recorded the details of the young Louis XIII's life is astonished by the liberties which people took with children, by the coarseness of the jokes they made, and by the indecency of gestures made in public which shocked nobody and were regarded as perfectly natural. . . .
>
> There is no reason to believe that the moral climate was any different in other families, whether nobles or commoners; the practice of associating children with the sexual ribaldries of adults formed part of contemporary manners. . . . (Aries, 1962, pp. 100–103)

In the fifteenth and sixteenth centuries there began to be a new concern with protecting childhood innocence, but the new attitude was slow in separating children from adult sexuality. "Broad talk," writes Aries, "was so natural that even later on, the strictest reformers would introduce into their sermons to children and students comparisons which would seem shocking today" (Aries, 1962, p. 109). He also points out that sixteenth-century textbooks for schoolboys often included sex jokes and riddles as well as conversations about sexual matters in order to illustrate points of grammar and so forth. "The coarsest jokes, as well as topics of anything but educational value, are to be found in these dialogues" (Aries, 1962, p. 109).

The campaign to desexualize childhood eventually succeeded in building the taboos we are familiar with today, taboos so firmly entrenched as to have been practically untouched by the sexual revolution. Even the educational discussion of sex in schools is extremely controversial today, in spite of, or perhaps because of, the fact that parents find it extremely hard to teach their children "the facts of life."

The campaign for childhood innocence did not succeed, of course, in eradicating children's sexual interests; it only succeeded in driving it underground. On their side of the sexual generation gap, children created their own cultural traditions of sexual lore and misinformation. Such works as the Opies' *Lore and Language of Schoolchildren* (1959) and Martha Wolfenstein's study of children's jokes (1954) document the pervasiveness of sexual interest in children, as part of a "subversive" (i.e., antiadult) culture passed on through generations of children.

The result of the taboos between adult-child sexual communication has resulted in a system of sex education where the vast majority of people learn about sex from their peers. It is a system of negative teaching and nonteaching from parents and positive learning from peers. As the students of human communication point out, not communicating about sex is one form of communicating about it. This context of sexual learning has profound consequences for individual experience and for the relations between men and women.

Sexual Learning and Nonlearning in the Family   The sexual attitudes and feelings learned in early childhood have a way of persisting even in people who have reevaluated or rejected their parents' attitudes and values in politics, religion, and other matters. Thus changes in adult behavior and the liberalization of public attitudes may obscure the persistence of traditional patterns of parent-child communication — and noncommunication — about sexual matters. One rather dramatic bit of evidence on this point is the study of Leah Shaefer (1964) of a group of middle-class women in their twenties and thirties when she interviewed them in the early 1960's. These women had all rebelled against the sexual Victorianism with which they had been brought up. Yet many or most of them seemed to be raising their daughters in the same way they had been raised. They were able to overcome the feeling of shame and guilt as far as their own sexual feelings were concerned, but found it difficult to think of their children as having sexual feelings. Particularly as far as their daughters were concerned, they were afraid that if they expressed approval of sexuality, this would lead to promiscuity.

John Gagnon (1965) provides a cogent analysis of why early sexual learning tends to be so heavily negative and so persistent. First, he notes that American parents tend to respond to the children's sexual behavior—handling the genitals, sex play, etc.—in one of two ways. One way is to tell the child not to do that—that the behavior is wrong or bad. This type of response from the parent will not surprise the child because he has heard many don'ts before—don't touch the stove or knife, don't step into the street. The other way is to avoid saying anything to the child, but to try to distract him by pointing to something more "enjoyable" to do, or by pointing out some other reason than the sexual one to stop the behavior—"it's too cold to have your pants down," or "kissing can spread germs." Both the negative injunction—"it's wrong"—and the distraction technique—nonlabeling or mislabeling—may have much the same effect. The child learns there is something vaguely wrong with sexuality. Further, as a result of the parents' reluctance to label sexual parts and activities and acts of excretion, he is left with an infantile vocabulary that will later be filled in by terms learned from other children.

Parent-child relations are influenced by the lack of a vocabulary for matter-of-fact discussions of sexuality: the four-letter words have been tainted by their long use as curse words. Adults are beginning to use them more easily, but they are not felt to be a proper medium of instruction for children. Medical terms are too forbidding and polysyllabic.

In any event nonlabeling or mislabeling may result in profound consequences. First, early sexual negative learning is never corrected. Gagnon points out that the parents modify their early no's and don'ts about many things as the child grows older—thus the child later learns how to cross the street and how to use knives and manage stoves. But the primitive early learning about sexuality is rarely, if ever, corrected in the same way.

Further, the child's lack of a vocabulary to describe what he sees and feels, plus difficulties of communication with parents, permits fantasies to flourish for long periods of time without correction.

The mysterious penis that must exist behind the female pubic hair, the feeling that females have been castrated, and other childhood fantasies are common because there has been no system of naming which will adequately control the child's nascent interest in his own or others' bodies. The second consequence of the lack of a controlling set of symbols is probably related to the tendency for children to identify their sexual organs with excretory functions. . . . This may also be related to some of the sexual differences between girls and boys; since boys may get dirty—therefore dirt is not so bad—and girls may not, the association may be more firmly entrenched among the latter. (Gagnon, 1965, p. 222)

To point out the problems in early sexual education of children in this culture is not, however, the same as suggesting a solution. The sexual instruction or noninstruction of children in families is part of a complex cultural pattern that includes family structure as well as adult sexuality. The concept of childhood innocence is deeply rooted in our culture, even though we can trace its beginnings in relatively recent historical times. It may well have arisen as an intensified form of the incest taboo, made necessary by the intimate emotional climate of the nuclear family.

Sex and Sex-Role Socialization in Peer Groups   Because parents and other adults provide little in the way of sex education for children, the information gap is filled by the growing child's friends and acquaintances—his peer group. After a child becomes of school age, both sex education and sex-role learning are carried out in large part by sex-segregated groups of children of comparable ages. Evidence indicates that elementary-school children are no longer as rigidly separated into same-sex groups as they once were (Udry, 1971, p. 86), but for many generations the existence of separate male and female subcultures among school children has had profound effects on definitions of masculinity and femininity, as well as relations between the sexes.

As far as sexuality is concerned, the exchange of sex information by children is guilty and clandestine. It generally tends to reinforce the negative attitudes the child has acquired at home, as a result of the parents' direct teaching or silence. Actually, Gagnon points to studies showing that about half to three-quarters of American parents fail to provide any sex information at all to their children. Interestingly, the mother rather than the father appears to be the source of whatever information the child of either sex receives. Gagnon notes that "the myth of the good heart-to-heart talk between father and son seems to be just that."

Although communication about sex is much more open in child and adolescent peer groups than in the family, much of what is said is not very informative. Male sociologists report that the sexual emphasis in the male subculture is both pornographic and achievement-oriented. Gagnon writes:

The exchange of information between males in American culture is not sexually informative except in an indirect sense. The information comes as part of tales of sexual prowess or of humor in which emphasis is placed on heterosexual expertise or exploits. What evolves from this male-to-male interaction is an image of the sexual self rather than knowledge of sexuality. (Gagnon, 1965, p. 214)

And Udry writes:

Since status results from convincing other boys of one's heterosexual escapades, most early adolescent heterosexual activity is discussed in male groups. There is considerable fabrication and elaboration of experience, and boys learn to discount one another's tales of prowess. The emphasis in the descriptions is on anatomical and manipulatory detail and erotic responses. . . . Sex emerges as something which boys "do to" girls. . . . Accounts of boys' early coital experience with girls show the boys to have been unconcerned with and largely unaware of the girls' own behavior. Among unattached adolescent boys, sex is sex, and it is divorced from emotional involvement, love or romance. (Udry, 1971, pp. 77–78)

Udry notes that the male orientation to sex acquired in child and adolescent groups persists into adulthood, and does not disappear at marriage. He suggests it accounts for the man's greater interest in and participation in extramarital affairs and pornography, and is the cause of much misunderstanding between husbands and wives.

In the girls' subculture the order of priorities is reversed. If boys like sex more than they like girls, little girls like boys much more than they like sex. Typically, the girl does not arrive at an image of a sexual self. There is often a huge gap between the images of love and romance and thoughts of direct sexual activity. The girl has no role models for sexual behavior such as those provided by male pornography or even male-oriented literature. In adolescence the girl tends to be caught in a bind between the wish and need to be "popular" with boys and the fear of losing her "reputation" or being taken "advantage of" by "giving in" to male sexual demands. Parents often contribute to the bind by pressures on the girl to be popular and have lots of dates, but not to be "cheap" or to let boys go "too far." The anthropologist Jules Henry, in a perceptive analysis of teen-age culture in the 1950's and '60's, saw the American girl as living on a "razor edge of sexual competition."

Because boys are united in "flocks" by the requirements of their games, they are held together more tightly than girls, and hence the competition among girls for friends is more intense than among boys. . . . As courtship becomes more important to the girls, competition and gossip increase in intensity. What makes the courtship experience particularly intense for girls is that it is the only activity through which they can validate their femininity. Since boys can validate their masculinity in a greater variety of ways, the chase does not have the same self-validating importance for them. Behind the girls' courtship drive, of course, looms the parental—usually the maternal—image, tirelessly keeping tally of each date. . . .

. . . It is not exaggeration to say that the teen-age American girl lives on a razor edge of sexual competition. Thus, beneath the gaiety of any teen-age party throbs the anxiety of being left out next time, of losing a boy tomorrow that one has today or not getting the right one; of not getting the one you really want, of not getting the popular one, and so on. (Henry, 1963, p. 181)

Since Jules Henry wrote, the teen-age world in America has been exposed to extraordinary changes in sex attitudes, culture, generation conflict, women's and gay liberation, as well as by countermovements to all of these. The whole pattern of dating, going steady, and early marriage seems to have altered—to what extent we don't yet know. It appears, however, that teen-agers today are in the process of being liberated from the rigid rating and dating codes of the last two decades, and all the tensions they entailed, and are beginning to face the problems involved in making personal choices without the guidance of strict rules.

Sexual Changes across Time and Space

A few scholars have tried to place the rise and fall of sexual moralities in broader historical and cross-cultural contexts. Taylor (1954) has shown that European sex history has followed an uneven course, with periods of sexual freedom alternating with periods of greater strictness. Also, at any one time, there was great variation in sexual mores according to social class; the classes at either extreme of the social scale have traditionally been freer than the middle classes.

Taylor and other scholars have also noted that sexual mores seem to alternate with changes in family structure and the political order. Strict sex seems to go along with strict or authoritarian methods of child rearing in all areas—not just sex—and with nondemocratic political orders. William Stephens finds this general pattern across cultures as well. He writes, as we noted earlier, that primitive tribes tend to have relatively relaxed child-rearing methods, liberal sexual norms, and democratic political structures. At the middle range of social development, in patriarchal agrarian societies, there is a move toward strictness, while liberal patterns seem to reemerge in industrial democracies. Stephens writes:

> The development of the kingdom seems to bring with it certain basic changes in the family; among these are an elaboration of deference customs between family members and a tightening of sex restrictions. When the kingdom, the autocratic agrarian state, evolves into a democratic state, these family customs seem to gradually liberalize: family relationships become less deferential and more democratic, and sex restrictions loosen. (1963, p. 258)

The job of untangling the complex connections between sexual moralities and political, economic, and religious change remains to be done. In Europe sexual morality has been heavily influenced by religious factors. Christianity has always been a relatively ascetic religion, and the Protestant reformation marked a greater tendency toward strictness. The peak of repressive morality in Europe, however, occurred during the nineteenth century, at a time when political regimes were becoming less autocratic.

On Sexual Revolutions   The sexual revolution of the past decade represents the continuation of a trend that began around the turn of the century. The decisive break with Victorian morality was the Freudian revolution.

To those scholars who have studied the rise and fall of sexual moralities, the Freudian contribution was only part of a larger revolution in attitudes toward sexuality and toward the family. These social attitudes in turn seem to have been part of still wider changes in the society, especially in the economic and religious order. These changes accompanied the beginning of the economy of affluence and the decline of the Protestant Ethic with its emphasis on work and its distrust of idleness and pleasure. Thus Hale notes that the sexual revolution of the twentieth century coincided with the decline of

exactly those factors that caused the nineteenth century addictions to "civilized" morality. The decline of religious controls over sexuality has been noted. By 1900 American observers had become aware of decisive changes in the economic system. The American sociologist Simon Pattern argued in 1908 that America was moving from an economy of deficit and saving to one of surplus and abundance. A new kind of character had to emerge, no longer dedicated to austerity and sacrifice but to leisure and rational enjoyment. Repression would give way to release. The new economy was giving a new place to women outside the home and family. (Hale, 1971, p. 476)

The first half of the twentieth century also witnessed three advances with profound implications for sexuality, the family, and the roles of women—the demographic revolution, the contraceptive revolution, and the technological revolution.

The demographic revolution resulted from medical advances that reduced infant mortality and extended the lifespan. Before the nineteenth century a married woman could expect to devote the greater portion of her adult years to reproduction. In the United States, for example, the average number of births per woman around 1800 was seven (see accompanying chart). Infant-mortality rates varied over time and place, but until the twentieth century many and at times most infants could be expected to die. Thus high fertility rates were "needed" to offset the high death rates.

The reduction of infant mortality, as well as the invention of contraception, made it possible to separate sexuality from reproduction. The invention, development, and widespread acceptance of contraception—and, increasingly, of abortion—will probably prove to be the decisive advance in women's liberation. At least some of what we take to be

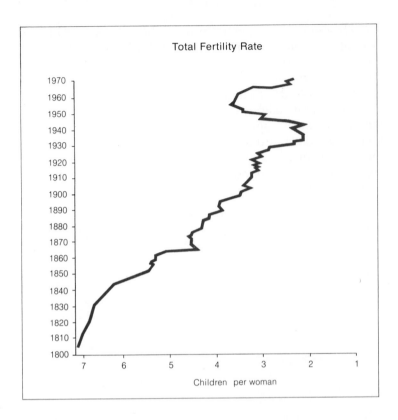

Annual births, expressed in terms of implied completed-family size, declined until the 1930's, rose until the mid-1950's, and then fell again. (From *Population and the American Future,* Washington: U.S. Government Printing Office, 1972)

sexist thinking today reflects the realities of women's lives in the past. The idea that "all women are mothers" was not quite so much of a distortion during the centuries when women could exercise slight control over their own reproductive capacities. In those days women were not only mothers, they were mothers many times over.

Finally, the technological revolution—that is, the move from an agrarian to an industrial to a postindustrial economy —will enhance the freedom of women and encourage the development of their mental capacities and talents. A postindustrial society emphasizes intellectual ability, educational specialization, and interpersonal skills in employment. Whether women can match men in brute strength has sometimes been an issue, but in a technologically advanced society it is irrelevant.

The demographic revolution, the contraceptive revolution, and the technological revolution have radically altered the potential role, status, and the very destiny of women in society. The current ferment over sex, sex roles, and family life may accordingly be interpreted as a form of "cultural lag"—a method of bringing social practices into cohesion with already existing biological and technological realities.

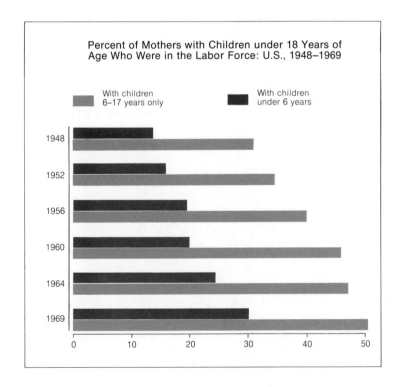

During the past two decades employment has become increasingly prevalent among mothers of school and preschool children. By 1969 more than half the mothers of children aged six to seventeen were in the labor force. (From *Profiles of Children*, White House Conference on Children 1970, Washington: U.S. Government Printing Office)

Summary

In both popular thought and many social-scientific writings, thinking about sexuality and sex differences has been dominated by biological imagery. Sexuality has been defined as a life force pressing for release, and sex-role differences are assumed to reflect innate temperamental inclinations. Obviously, males and females differ in anatomy, physiology, and perhaps even in temperament to some degree. Neither sexuality nor sex differences, however, can be understood as being independent of learning, culture, and the historical context.

Anatomy is destiny largely because children are assigned at birth to two different worlds of experience and self-definition on the basis of the genital difference. Further, the biological capacity of women to bear children is much more fateful in societies without contraception and with high rates of infant mortality.

As a human motive, sexuality fits the model of an appetite or craving rather than a "life force." In general, then, our sexual selves are not simple reflections of the animal side of human nature; in our sexual lives as elsewhere we are shaped by our time, place, and situation.

MARRIAGE:
IMAGE AND INSTITUTION

Chapter 6

Whatever marriage is, it is always and everywhere more than sexual intercourse. However divergent the directions may be in which marriage transcends sexual intercourse, the fact that it transcends it at all makes marriage what it is.

Georg Simmel

Chapter Six   A feminist writer recently complained that "just as God has been pronounced dead quite often, but has this sneaky way of resurrecting himself, so everyone debunks marriage, yet ends up married" (Firestone, 1970, p. 251). Current statistics (see accompanying chart) do show a decline in the proportion of young people getting married from the historic high proportions of recent years. But in spite of all the ferment surrounding marriage today, it is far from dead. True, there are communes, group marriages, couples of any combination of sexes, and individuals leading a variety of single life styles, but marriage still persists. Nor is marriage confined to the politically conservative and culturally straight. So, whether one laments the fact or celebrates it, marriage promises to be part of the social landscape for some time to come.

In this chapter we are going to look at marriage in rather broad and abstract terms. Marriage has always had a dual aspect which has puzzled students of marriage as well as ordinary folk; marriage is a relationship between two people, but it is more than a couple relationship—it is an institution. Marriage is an intensely private affair, but it is public as well. "Marriage" seems to lead its own separate existence, quite apart from particular married couples. Indeed, many people today experience "marriage" as an alien presence, an unwelcome third party, intruding itself into what may be an otherwise delightful relationship. In this chapter we are going to look at marriage in this abstract sense—as image, idea, and institution.

The Two Faces of Marriage

Attacks on marriage as an institution are not a novelty brought on by the current wave of family and sexual unrest. Although some of these criticisms are new, hostility toward marriage has deep roots in Western culture. Usually, however, antimarriage attitudes have coexisted with respect for the institution and a sense of its inevitability. What is novel in the contemporary scene is that the positive side of the ambivalence has diminished, emphasizing the hostility.

This ambivalence toward marriage takes many forms, beginning perhaps with the statement of St. Paul that it is better to marry than to burn. Not marrying and not burning

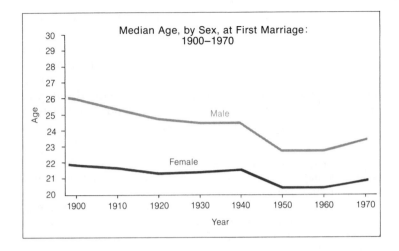

Since 1960 the median age at first marriage has increased for both sexes. (Based on data in *Population Characteristics*, U.S. Department of Commerce, Bureau of the Census, Series P-20, No. 225, Washington: U.S. Government Printing Office, 1971)

was better still but conceded to be beyond the capacities of most. Besides Christian ambivalence, the models of marriage put forth by the professionals in the field also have two faces. We shall look at the professional work on marriage later, but let us look first at what could be called the classical ambivalence of popular culture:

. . . Two myths describe the popular image of marriage: one is cynical, the other, idealistic. Both are held simultaneously by many people. The first myth says, "and they lived happily ever after." This is the myth which holds marriage to be a continuous courtship. The second myth is the picture of the domestic grind: the husband sits behind the paper, the wife moves about the morning disarray; the husband leaves for work, the wife spends the day among dishes, diapers, and dirty little children. Although, as with most myths, no one *really* believes either one of them, they continue to affect the behavior of most people. Perhaps most people faintly hope to live happily ever after, but rather fear dreary domesticity will be their lot. (Udry, 1971, p. 270)

This popular ambivalence about marriage forms the basis of much of the humor on television and in the comics and cartoons, as exemplified in such fare as "Maggie and Jinks," "I Love Lucy," "Dagwood and Blondie," mother-in-law jokes, and ball-and-chain jokes. George Orwell once took a long look at this kind of humor, in the particular form of obscene penny postcards. Orwell was writing of the English scene around the early 1940's, but the kind of humor he describes persists; it is, as he says, "something as traditional as Greek tragedy, a sort of sub-world of smacked bottoms and scrawny mothers-in-law which is a part of Western European consciousness." He lists the conventions of the sex joke:

. . . Marriage only benefits the woman. Every man is plotting seduction and every woman is plotting marriage. No woman ever remains unmarried voluntarily.

. . . Sex-appeal vanishes at about the age of 25. Well-preserved and good-looking people beyond their first youth are never represented. The amorous honeymooning couple reappear as the grim-visaged wife and shapeless, mustachioed, red-nosed husband, no intermediate stage being allowed for.

. . . Next to sex, the henpecked husband is the favorite joke. Typical caption: "Did they get an X-ray of your wife's jaw at the hospital?"—"No, they got a moving picture instead."

CONVENTIONS:

(i)   There is no such thing as a happy marriage.

(ii)   No man ever gets the better of a woman in an argument. (Orwell, 1946, p. 107)

Orwell explains this humor in much the same way as some sociologists have explained the persistence of prostitution and pornography, as a sort of safety valve, a harmless rebellion against virtue, which protects a stable family life by giving some expression to otherwise disrupting impulses. This humor, says Orwell, implies that

Marriage is something profoundly exciting and important, the biggest event in the average human being's life. . . . Jokes about nagging wives and tyrannous mothers-in-law . . . imply a stable society in which marriage is indissoluble and family loyalty taken for granted. . . . The working-class outlook . . . takes it almost as a matter of course that youth and adventure—almost indeed, individual life—end with marriage. (1946, p. 109)

Orwell overlooks something else about such jokes; they are practically all based on the point of view of men, and express male resentment of women. There are no male counterparts to the stock figures of the wife in curlers wielding a rolling pin, the nagging mother-in-law, the crotchety old maid. Males appear only as victims of female domination—

Dagwood Bumstead, Jinks, Fred Flintstone, and others. There is no positive image of women other than the sweet young thing. Antifemale humor was encouraged during the Middle Ages when people who deviated from marital norms were publicly taunted. The historian Natalie Davis (1971) has described communal festivals where all sorts of people were mocked, in something like the spirit of a school play making fun of the teachers. A prominent part of these festivities, or *charivari,* was the public humiliation of husbands who had allowed themselves to be henpecked or deceived, of widows and widowers who had remarried younger spouses, and newlyweds who had failed to produce a child in the first year of marriage. These customs were obviously an attempt to control family behavior, particularly women's. Davis notes, however, that they may have unintentionally encouraged the kind of rebellious behavior they mocked.

Sophisticated Ambivalence Another brand of humorous ambivalence toward marriage occurs in the sophisticated tradition. This includes the French bedroom farce and the humor of such magazines as *Esquire* and *Playboy.* Here the main source of humor is adultery, and the complications arising from deception and discovery.

This brand of humor reflects the moral order of the Continental upper middle class, where separation of love and marriage is assumed, love affairs are expected of both spouses, but especially the husband, and conjugal love, particularly of long standing, is perverse.

> I've been married 18 years
> And still adore my wife
> I have no hunger for other women,
> I am content to be faithful
> I am resigned to decency.
> I actually think I have found love
>   and Life.
> What's the matter with me?
>   —John Haynes Holmes

This poem was recently printed in the *San Francisco Chronicle* (Klemesrud, 1971, p. 23) in an article which noted, "Even back in 1922, when those lines were written, people were asking themselves, albeit ironically, whether they were some kind of freaks because their marriages were happy." Although this view of marriage has long been traditional in certain sectors of European society, only recently has it come to be publicly expressed in America. It now seems, however, to be the prevailing Hollywood image of marriage.

Cross-cultural Ambivalence   It would be a mistake to conclude that marital conflict and ambivalence toward marriage are peculiar to Western European culture. William Stephens (1963), in his worldwide survey of family practices, has shown that divorce is as universal a custom as is marriage. No known society forbids divorce—with the exception of Christian countries. Even here, however, escape can be found in the form of annulments and informal separations, as well as approved ways of not marrying at all, such as joining religious orders. In spite of the widespread belief that marital disharmony is unique to modern industrial society, no culture has found the formula for perfect marriage, although marital disharmony does seem to vary from society to society.

Sexual Politics and the Power Struggle   Two separate sources of marital strain are often inextricably bound up in real life, but should be kept separate for purposes of analysis. The first results as the inevitable by-product of any prolonged intimate association between two people without regard to their gender: difficulties may arise from basic temperamental incompatibilities and differences in tastes and opinions or from changes in these. There are also momentary disharmonies of mood—one partner may feel tired while the other feels lively. Further there is always the issue of whose wishes will prevail at a given moment, and how to decide whose wishes will prevail. Such problems of rule making and communication will be discussed in a later section.

The other leading source of marital tension arises from the sexual politics implicit in a union between a man and a woman. Until sexual equality prevails, we will never know how much the sex difference in itself adds to the general strain of dyadic interaction. But until sex differences no longer imply differences in status and power, the stage will be set for the classic battle of the sexes: the struggle on the part of most men to keep women in their place, and the maneuvering of women to evade or exploit that place.

The balance of power in society is linked, in complex ways not yet understood, to various characteristics of face-to-face interaction.

We have such propositions as the following: the subordinate is more "oriented" toward the superordinate. Just as the student "psyches out" the professor, and the child works his or her way around parental mood, so too, the woman may be more oriented toward her husband than he is to her. (Hochschild, 1973, p. 1020)

To the extent that sex roles are sharply marked off, and the sexes differ in status and resources, marriage will continue to be a somewhat different institution for men and women; or, as Jessie Bernard puts it, every marital union contains two marriages, his and hers (1972, p. 15).

The Husband's Marriage versus the Wife's   Marital humor usually reflects prevailing cultural definitions of the husband's marriage. These define marriage as a trap set for men by women, and encourage a myth of happy bachelorhood — if only women would let him alone a man could lead a happy and free existence. This myth is part of the "masculine protest" aspect of male socialization: to be masculine in this culture is to be free of responsibility to females, particularly maternal females.

The cultural notion that men don't really need or want strong attachments to women may make them uncomfortable when they do wish such attachments. But the myth encourages them to a grudging resentment of wife and children. Simone de Beauvoir comments on how oppression by men paradoxically results in feelings of being oppressed:

. . . In oppressing, one becomes oppressed. Men are enchained by reason of their very sovereignty; it is because they alone earn money that wives demand checks; it is because they alone engage

in a business or profession that their wives require them to be successful. . . .

. . . Man and wife together undergo the oppression of an institution they did not create. If it is asserted that *men* oppress *women* the husband is indignant; he feels that he is the one who is oppressed—and he is; but the fact is that it is the masculine code, it is the society developed by the males and in their interest, that has established woman's situation in a form that is at present a source of torment for both sexes. (Beauvoir, 1949, p. 454)

I recently interviewed a moderately successful business-man, in his forties, as part of a longitudinal study of a normal population. As he thought over his life thus far he said that though he liked his wife and loved his children, he probably wouldn't marry if he could live his life over. He liked freedom—the idea of always being able to come and go as he pleased, to take off for a fishing trip or a distant city whenever he felt like it, and not to be committed to eating his wife's cooking all his life. He also felt that, though his family was always struggling to get by on his salary, he would have been almost rich if he had it all to himself. On the other hand, his wife had wanted to take up a career when the children were all in school, but he had discouraged her from doing so. It was better for the children, he thought, if their mother were home all the time and not distracted by outside interests.

The attitudes and assumptions expressed by this man illustrate why feminists believe marriage is not very good for women. This man feels short of money, but he won't let his wife work; he can't stand her cooking, but it doesn't occur to him that he could help prepare the family meals himself.

Legal Images of Marriage: Institutionalized Sexism

The feminist critique of marriage starts from the initial assumption that the feminine half of the human race is as fully human as the masculine. Traditionally, however, marriage has never been defined as a partnership of two equal persons. In popular thought, in learned writing on the family, and, most significantly, in terms of the law, marriage is a hierarchical institution defining the wife as the dependent and subordinate of the husband.

We mentioned earlier that marriage always involves something more than just the relationship between people. The legal aspects of marriage are one of the important ways the institution goes beyond the interpersonal relationship. For most people the legal side of marriage is experienced only at the time of marriage or divorce, or when inheritance of property becomes an issue. Yet there is more to marriage as a legal institution than a series of procedures one has to go through to get married or divorced.

Laws indicate status: who is counted as a citizen, who can vote, who can own property — all these show who is considered a full person under the law, and who is not. The historical traditions of Western law, from Roman times on, have defined women as inferior beings who must be under the protection of a man. The wedding custom of a father "giving" his daughter to the groom reflects this legal notion. Further, whatever women's status in general, they usually

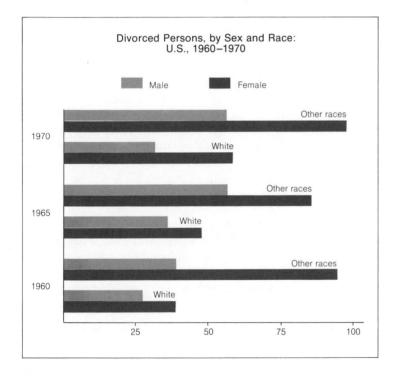

Number of divorced persons per 1,000 married, by sex and race. During the last ten years there has been a rise in the ratio of divorced persons to those persons who are partners in intact marriages, and the increase has been more pronounced among women than men. (Based on data in *Population Characteristics*, U.S. Department of Commerce, Bureau of the Census, Series P-20, No. 212, Washington: U.S. Government Printing Office, 1971)

lose legal rights by marrying. In most countries there are two legal statuses for women: one for spinsters and one for married women.

The married woman's loss of legal rights can be traced to the feudal doctrine of coverture, the notion that the husband and wife are a unity.

> Based in part upon biblical notions of the unity of flesh of husband and wife, the doctrine was described by Blackstone as follows: "By marriage, the husband and wife are one person in law; that is, the very being or legal existence of the woman is suspended during the marriage, or at least is incorporated and consolidated." . . . The doctrine . . . has worked out in reality to mean . . . the one is the husband. (Kanowitz, 1969, p. 35)

Even in the United States today, married women lose some of their rights to control property, and they cannot enter into contracts on the same basis as men or single women. In some states the husband controls the wife's earnings and property, and can dispose of it without her consent. The wife, on the other hand, has no right to a share of her husband's earnings beyond that necessary to run the household (Freeman, 1970, p. 8; Sullerot, 1971, pp. 207–211). She is not entitled to direct compensation for doing domestic work—her husband is merely obliged to "maintain" her. This distribution of obligations has been described by one observer as the economic relationship between an owner and his property, rather than between two free individuals (Crozier, 1935). Other disabilities of marriage for women include the obligation to follow the husband if he moves, to use his address as her legal address, and to change her name.

Discussions of family law can sound abstract and irrelevant for most people's lives, but family law is a part of an invisible web of forces maintaining family structures in the traditional forms. Family structures are backed in many ways that are not easily observable. As William Goode has pointed out, most people take family structures they live in for granted, and do not challenge them:

> They know in advance they would fail. In most families the structure is not overthrown, because it is viewed as inalterable or at best the only alternative. Thus, force plays a role even when no deviant act is actually committed. The rebellious child or wife knows that the father or husband is stronger, and can call upon outsiders who will support that force with more force. (Goode, 1971, p. 625)

We do not see the application of force to maintain family patterns, but its threat creates and maintains an imbalance of power:

For example, if in a patrilineal polygamous society an older woman were to announce that she is henceforth to be treated as the leader of her patriline, tried to sell its cattle, started to give orders, set dates for rituals, or chose a chief, very likely she would be beaten or treated as insane. Similarly, if a child in our society were to claim the headship of the family, give orders to his parents or siblings, try to write checks on his father's account, or trade in the automobile for a new one, the same result would occur. (Goode, 1971, p. 625)

The legal restrictions and obligations enter in subtle ways into the social exchange between marriage partners. Even if both spouses try to have a more egalitarian arrangement than the law allows, they may run into legal difficulties. Thus a couple may agree that the wife should keep her maiden name, or maintain a residence in another state, or buy a house on her own, or open her own charge account, but legal traditions and business practices may prevent them from carrying out these wishes or cost the wife or the couple certain privileges (Kanowitz, 1969). Or a couple may wish to challenge the legal precedent that a wife owes her husband household services and is not to be directly paid for them. The courts, however, may not grant a husband the right to pay for something he is entitled to free:

The wife's services and society are so essential a part of what the law considers the husband is entitled to as part of the marriage that it will not recognize any agreement between spouses which provides that the husband is to pay for such services or society.

In a Texas case, David promised his wife, Fannie, that he would give her $5000 if she would stay with him while he lived and continue taking care of the house and farm accounts, selling his butter and doing all the other tasks which she had done since their marriage. After David's death, Fannie sued his estate for the money which had been promised her. The court held the contract was unenforceable since Fannie had agreed to do nothing which she was not already legally and morally bound to do as David's wife. (Pilpel and Zavin, 1964, p. 65)

The Housewife Problem   The feminists quarrel with family law not only because the low status and impaired rights of

women are unjust, but also because this injustice is reflected all too well in daily realities. Thus the assumptions of the law on the subject of domestic work are fairly descriptive of the realities of the division of labor in most marriages.

The concept of the housewife role is central to understanding the feminist complaint about marriage. Their argument has several facets. First, domestic work remains the last occupation to which a person is fated at birth. As Daryl and Sandra Bem (1970) have pointed out, when a boy is born it is hard to predict what he will be doing in twenty-five years—his future is open. If the newborn child is a girl, however, how she will be spending her time in twenty-five years can be predicted with almost complete statistical certainty. Looking at the two newborns, we can tell with even more certainty who will be washing socks and who will have them washed for him. It doesn't matter that the girl baby is nominally free to choose a career or not to marry. Until very recently socialization pressures have worked effectively to prevent all but a small minority of women from acting on the options presumably available. If they do try to enter the world of work, they will find not only lower pay and discrimination in a variety of forms, but they will never entirely escape the long shadow of domesticity. As one feminist writer put it, "We are all housewives."

Studies of working women indicate that the egalitarian family which supposedly prevails in America is largely a myth. Although husbands of working wives do more housework than husbands of nonemployed ones, they do not do as much as the wives. Thus Blood and Hamblin (1958) estimated that nonworking wives in their sample did 85 percent of the housework and working wives did 75 percent. A more recent study of fifty-three couples where both partners were professionals also revealed a marked inequality in the allocation of domestic tasks (Poloma and Garland, 1971). The research shows that married women can follow what Jessie Bernard (1971) has called the "one-role option," either career as a single woman or the full-time housewife and mother role; or the "two-role option"—career woman plus mother and housewife. The "shared-role option"—both husband and wife working and sharing all domestic work—has rarely been tried, although many couples who are now marrying are attempting to follow this pattern.

Another feminist objection to the housewife role, apart

from its castelike aspects, is that it is highly burdensome in terms of time and monotony and yet is devalued. Thus studies show that housewives spend an enormous amount of time at their occupation—99.5 hours a week according to a Chase Manhattan Bank study—yet it is not counted as real work. The housewife is considered by economists, the dictionary, and most people, as a person who does not work. In terms of prestige it is an occupation near the bottom of the scale.

Finally, feminists argue that the occupation of housewife does not even deliver the security it promises. The housewife has no guarantee that, after she has given her "best years" to marriage, she will not be traded in for a newer model. As Germaine Greer has noted:

> The housewife is an unpaid worker in her husband's house in return for the security of being a permanent employee: hers is the *reductio ad absurdum* of the case of the employee who accepts a lower wage in return for permanence in his employment. But the lowest-paid employees can be and are laid off, and so are wives. They have no savings, no skills which they can bargain with elsewhere, and they must bear the stigma of having been sacked. (Greer, 1971, p. 239)

Furthermore, evidence suggests that the housewife role is debilitating to morale and well-being. Jessie Bernard has compiled a body of research findings showing that more married than single women are bothered by depression, worries and phobias of various kinds, severe neurotic symptoms, and physical pains and ailments (Bernard, 1972). A study of middle-aged women by Pauline Bart (1970) revealed that the women who had made the deepest commitments to motherhood and domesticity were most likely to experience depression at the time of menopause. In a study comparing recent mental-illness rates among men and women, as indicated by community surveys, admissions to mental hospitals, and so on, Gove and Tudor (1973) found women to have higher rates of "mental illness."

These higher rates of "mental illness" for women, however, are found mainly when married women are compared to married men. In studies of unmarried, widowed, and divorced people, the sex difference either does not appear or men may turn out to have higher rates. There is also evidence that higher rates of "mental illness" for women developed after World War II, and vary from community to community — small, traditional, culturally isolated communities showing lower rates for women than for men. Gove and Tudor conclude that women's roles in modern industrial societies have certain stresses built into them:

> . . . First, most women are restricted to a single societal role — housewife, whereas most men occupy two such roles, household head and worker. . . . If a male finds one of his roles unsatisfactory, he can frequently focus his interest and concern on the other role. In contrast, if a woman finds her family role unsatisfactory, she typically has no major alternative source of gratification.
>
> Second, it seems reasonable to assume that a large number of women find their major instrumental activities — raising children and keeping house — frustrating. . . . The occupancy of such a static, technically undemanding position is not consonant with the educational and intellectual attainment of a large number of women in our society. . . .
>
> Third, the role of housewife is relatively unstructured and invisible. It is possible for the housewife to put things off, to let things slide . . . to brood over her troubles. In contrast the job holder must meet demands that constantly force him to be involved with his environment. Having to meet these structured demands should draw his attention from his troubles, and help prevent him from becoming obsessed with his worries.
>
> Fourth, even when a married woman works, she is typically in a less satisfactory position than the married male. There has been a persistent decline in the relative status of women since 1940 as measured by occupation, income, and even education. . . .
>
> Fifth, several observers have noted that the expectations confronting women are unclear and diffuse. . . . (Gove and Tudor, 1973, pp. 814–816) (References deleted)

Yet in spite of the various shortcomings of marriage as an institution in its present and past forms, only a minority of feminists hold to the view that marriage must inevitably oppress women. Most would argue that marriage can be saved through genuine equality of opportunity in work, widely available child-care facilities, and a greater willingness on the part of men to undertake a more even share of the domestic workload. Many couples are trying to work out egalitarian marriages, as part of the general spirit of experimentation that prevails in the family today. Even if marriage roles were to be equalized, however, the likelihood is small that the institution would qualify as a Utopia.

Models of Marriage: Paradise and Paradox

The omission thus far of detailed attention to the literature of marital satisfaction and adjustment is not, as the saying goes, an accident. Any social science dealing with the experience of daily life should consider popular or folk conceptions of the subject before proceeding to the ideas of "experts." In this field in particular there is cause to wonder whether the insights of the nonexperts are less valid than those of the marital-adjustment experts. Many studies on marriage have failed to recognize that, even under the most stable social conditions, marriage is a complex and ambivalent form of human interaction. Orwell recognized this when he described sex and marriage jokes as a kind of collective jeer, a protest against marriage on the part of people who take it very seriously.

In modern urban societies marriage becomes even more problematic as tolerance for divorce and adultery rises, individuals change, and the need for intimacy and personal realization increases. Marriage studies typically overlook the large social forces altering marital relations, marriage, and the people in them. They perpetuate a romantic mystique of marriage.

There are actually two romantic models of marriage: one occurs mainly in the family sociological studies of marital satisfaction and adjustment; the other, in writings in the psychoanalytic tradition. As we shall see later, there are also two different models defining marriage in terms of conflict.

Utopian Marriage: The Adjustment Model   Probably the most famous single statement about family life is Tolstoy's opening words to *Anna Karenina*: "Happy families are all alike; unhappy families are unhappy each in its own way." It states a surprising yet obvious truth in a pithy way. And the prevailing images of family life in family sociology and marriage counseling coincide with it; there are normal families, all more or less alike in their normality, and there are sick and disturbed or unhappy families, each with its own particular tale to be told. We are going to suggest in this section, however, that Tolstoy's words tell us less about the realities of family life, in particular marriage, than they do about the kinds of imagery of marriage that people hold.

A dilemma lies at the heart of the attempt to study marital success scientifically: it is impossible to define a successful marriage in an objective way. To see the problem, perhaps the reader should take a moment to determine his or her own definition of a good, successful marriage. Then consider whether the definition contains a value judgment—that is, a notion of what a "good" marriage *should be*. It has proved to be impossible to find a purely descriptive definition of marital success—one that does not include value judgments. People with different values will inevitably define success in marriage differently. In contrast, a group of doctors can agree, except in rare cases, on the health of a person, no matter what their personal values and opinions may be. As Ryder puts it:

> There is no descriptively defined entity that can reasonably be called a successful marriage because there is no general agreement as to what marriages should be. Yet study after study has contrasted "good" marriages with "bad" marriages as if there were such an entity. A successful marriage is clearly one of which we approve. The concept is a value judgment dressed up to look like a matter of objective descriptive fact. (Ryder, 1967, p. 807)

What are the value judgments that we "dress up" to look like facts in marriage? By and large these include contentment with middle-class values, conservative definitions of sex roles, and a stress on harmony and absence of conflict.

The following definition of successful marriage, taken from a recent textbook, coincides with the leading scales of marital adjustment:

1 Both husband and wife are happy and satisfied with their marriage.
2 There is a quality of permanence to the relationship.
3 There is good adjustment (including sexual adjustment).
4 The attitudes and acts of the husband and wife are in agreement on the chief issues of the marriage.
5 . . . the personalities of the husband and wife interact in such a way as [to] complement each other for the mutual satisfaction and achievement of common objectives. (Lantz and Snyder, 1969, p. 220)

If there is any conflict at all, it is confined to the "period of adjustment," that stage between the bliss of the honeymoon and the mellow years of pure conjugal love. Udry has summarized this vision of the ups and downs of marriage that prevails in the family literature:

> Couples marry at the height of their romantic love for one another. The honeymoon period is one of continued courtship . . . . After the honeymoon . . . the couple enter the "period of adjustment." Gradually, or sometimes suddenly, they are presented with the realities of marital life. Their idealized pictures of one another from courtship crumble under the impact of sharing the same bathroom and listening to one another snore. Their "true selves" are revealed to one another in the harsh glare of marital reality. . . . Their sexual life is troublesome because of their (or the wife's) lack of experience and (the husband's) clumsiness. Money problems arise for the first time. The first year or two is rough. However, they are in love, and love helps them solve some of their problems. . . . Those people who did not select their mates properly are not able to solve the problems of the adjustment period, and the marriage eventually breaks up. . . .
>
> . . . the good marriages, where sensible mate selection prevailed and where the partners are "mature," come through the adjustment period changed, however, from what they were. Romantic love has been transmuted into "mature" conjugal love which continues to be the basis of permanent marriages. (Udry, 1971, pp. 270–271)

The concept of marital adjustment used in the major studies, and in particular the prediction-of-success type of study, has been severely criticized on several grounds. One complaint charges that the studies rely too heavily on self-reports—that is, the person himself rates how happy his marriage is and how happy his childhood was, so the correlations may reflect nothing more than the tendency of some people to describe themselves and their families in favorable terms. This point has been documented in a series of studies by Edmonds (1967, 1972). He put together a series of statements about marriage that would be too good to be true for anyone—for example, "If my mate has any faults, I am not aware of them"; "Every new thing I have learned about my mate has pleased me" (1967, p. 286). Agreeing with such statements is an indicator of what Edmonds calls marital "conventionalization." He finds that conventionalization is widespread and that marital adjustment scales are heavily influenced by the tendency. Further, Edmonds' data show that, contrary to the prevailing views in the marriage literature, there is no connection between being conventional and conservative and having a happy marriage. He finds that when the distorting tendency of conventionalism is controlled statistically, people who hold traditional moral attitudes, who go to church regularly, and who abstain from premarital sex do not have a greater degree of marital adjustment than those who do not.

Edmonds' argument is with the measurement of adjustment in marriage rather than with the concept itself. Other critics have argued with the assumption that happiness is the criteria for a good relationship:

> On the happiness schedule of Burgess and Wallin any person who gets very high scores may not be happy but slap-happy, indeed even schizophrenic to the point of living in a world of fantasy and self-delusion. . . . Their general satisfaction schedule is no less unsatisfactory from the standpoint of depth psychology. . . . Here we find the question: Do you ever regret your marriage? Answers and scores are as follows: frequently, 0; occasionally, 1; rarely, 3; never, 5. But a mature answer is: of course, but the very regret is the ambivalent aspect of my joy in it. All human satisfaction is tinged with dissatisfaction; by taking up one option, we surrender others. The human psyche is not structured in such a way that answers to such questions give any indication of fundamental personality traits or make possible understanding of an individual's capacity for being interrelated with another. (Simpson, 1960, p. 216)

Similar problems arise if happiness is defined as an absence of conflict and quarreling. One reason a couple may not have any arguments is that they do not talk to each other very much in the first place. Simpson contends:

> On the Burgess-Wallin Schedule of Consensus we find the question: How many serious quarrels or arguments have you had with your mate in the past twelve months? Possible answers are 4 or more, 3, 2, 1, 0. The respective scores are 0, 1, 2, 3, 4. But quarrels and arguments are inherent in the marital situation. . . . Twelve months without a quarrel may be twelve months without love. (Simpson, 1960, p. 217)

In a more poetic way, Laing has described "the happy family" as a collusive game, an agreement, usually unspoken, among family members to put on a good front and to deny conflicts, even among themselves, but especially in front of the neighbors.

So we are a happy family and we have no secrets from one another.
If we are unhappy/ we have to keep it a secret.
And we are unhappy that we have to keep it a secret.
And unhappy that we *have* to keep secret/ the fact/ that we
Have to keep it a secret
And that we *are* keeping all that secret.
But since we are a happy family you can see
This difficulty does not arise.

(Laing, 1969, p. 100)

A Psychoanalytic Utopia: The Intimacy Model   Critics of the
conventional adjustment notion argue that it is based on
the wrong values, that it is superficial and does not deal
with the quality of the couple's relationship and the kind of
life they lead. Really "good" marriages, they say, focus on
the qualities of openness, intimacy, trust, and personal
growth. The classic statement on this ideal of marriage is
provided by Erik Erikson (1963).

In this model of marriage the focus of marital success or
failure rests squarely in the psyche of each spouse—more
specifically, in his ego capacities. Marriage is seen as a
critical developmental stage in the life of each individual, a
sort of "maturity test" that a person must pass if he or she
is to be a healthy, well-adjusted person. Erikson divides the
lifespan into eight stages, each with its own point of conflict
or encounter between the individual and the environment,
and with its own distinctive outcome of personality "success" or "failure." Thus the first stage centers around how
well the infant's need for "love" in the form of food and
tender care are fulfilled, and the outcome is a basic sense
of trust or mistrust. The most well-known of Erikson's stages,
the adolescent period, focuses on the "identity crisis"—the
problem of finding one's own identity.

The next stage of life after adolescence is called the stage
of "intimacy versus isolation," and one passes it, in part, by
having a successful marriage. Erikson describes this stage
as follows:

. . . The young adult, emerging from the search for an insistence
on identity, is eager and willing to fuse his identity with that of
another. He is ready for intimacy, that is, the capacity to commit
himself to concrete affiliations and partnerships and to develop
the ethical strength to abide by such commitments, even though

they may call for significant sacrifices and compromises. . . . (1963, p. 263)

Only during this period can "true genitality" develop, adolescent sexuality being dominated by searching for one's own identity or for a competitive kind of sexual combat. True genitality involves, to quote Erikson again:

1   Mutuality of orgasm
2   With a loved partner
3   Of the other sex
4   With whom one is able and willing to share a mutual trust
5   And with whom one is able and willing to regulate the cycles of:
    (a)   Work
    (b)   Procreation
    (c)   Recreation
6   So as to secure to the offspring, too, all the stages of a satisfactory development (Erikson, 1963, p. 260)

Erikson did not originate the intimacy concept. The idea that marriage makes a unit of two people is, of course, an ancient one. "A man shall leave father and mother and shall cleave to his wife and they twain shall be one flesh," says the Bible. Within social science the idea of marriage as mutual identification also goes back a long time, relatively speaking. Burgess (1926) wrote of marriage as a unity of interacting personalities. Burgess and Locke argued that the intimacy or companionship model has become *the* contemporary pattern of marriage, replacing the "institutional" type of marriage of earlier times. Parsons and Bales' analysis of the isolated nuclear family also describes marriage as a meshing of two personalities.

More recently a new version of the intimacy model of marriage has been suggested by people connected with the "human potential" movement, or humanistic psychology, or the encounter-group movement. For example, Herbert Otto writes:

. . . Marriage can be envisioned as a framework for actualizing personal potential.
. . . the New Marriage offers an ongoing adventure of self-discovery, personal growth, unfoldment and fulfillment. Growth by its very nature is not smooth or easy, for growth involves change and the emergence of the new. But growth and the actualizing of personal potential is also a joyous and deeply satisfying process

which can bring the marriage a new quality of zest for living, of joie de vivre, and of excitement. (Otto, 1970, p. 113)

Yet in most instances the intimacy model confounds description with evaluation and reality with an idealized image of what life should be like. When someone offers such a model of marriage, he implies one of the following alternatives: that most marriages fit the model, except for the minority of immature or neurotic individuals who need psychoanalytic therapy to repair their personality defects; or that most marriages do not fit the intimacy model, in which case one can either be pessimistic about the human condition or assert that radical change is needed to make the ideal real.

Probably most psychoanalysts and marriage counselors belong in the first category; they believe in the reality of the model as a description of the way normal people live, although they know that the people they see in their offices differ from it. What they are not aware of is the extent of the falling away from the ideal model, as documented in the findings of empirical research on American marriage as well as in the experience of daily life. The psychoanalytic view of marriage as a developmental task, or a stage on which deep psychological wishes and conflicts are acted out, ignores the texture of everyday household life, the horde of seemingly irrelevant trivia—missing buttons, lost keys, dental appointments, PTA meetings, broken washing machines, etc., etc.— that impinge on family members and determine the time, energy, and moods that family members bring to their interactions with each other. It also ignores the ways marriage as an institution is caught between contradictory norms and practices of modern societies. As John Shaffer writes, in reviewing a well-written, sophisticated book elaborating Erikson's idea of marriage as a developmental task:

. . . [The book] omits large segments of the realities and ambivalences of everyday conjugal life in today's America, which leave many—if not most—marriages only partially successful, neither sick nor well. It is as if all problems encountered in marriage result from the unresolved neurotic difficulties of each spouse rather than being partly inherent in the institution itself, as well as in the complex social fabric of adult life. One finds no reference to the social, technological, and sexual upheavals that have transformed the urban scene and increased the pressures within marriage. For example, the increasing acceptability of adultery and divorce tends to increase people's sensitivity to potential sources of dissatisfaction in their marriage. . . . The nuclear family as the prime locus of intimacy doubtlessly places additional strain on the marriage relationship in that it reduces the opportunity to satisfy needs for closeness and support within the larger community. It is ironic that a book characterized by sophisticated psychoanalytic theorizing tends to perpetuate the romantic mystique that Americans have always attached to marriage; nowhere is one able to find the vaguest hint of the ennui, the struggle over the minute details of existence, the hostility, and the sense of confinement that *at times* characterize the very best of marriages. (Shaffer, 1970, p. 173)

The romanticization of marriage contained in the intimacy model joins with the idealization of family life in popular culture and gets in the way of personal experience. It provides an image by which to measure our lives and find them wanting.

A somewhat similar criticism has been made by Thomas Szasz, who has taken the profession of psychiatry to task for turning notions of psychological health and normality into something akin to religious virtue. He suggests that psychiatry has made it seem as sinful, as much an indication of personal failure, to be worried or anxious or sad as it once was to be lazy or gluttonous or covetous of one's neighbor's wife.

In understanding particular marriages the intimacy model serves more as an impediment than as a useful analytic tool. Consider, for example, the marriage described by Simpson of a psychopathic man and a highly dependent woman. People labeled as psychopathic have traits opposite to those that usually are said to define a good marriage partner: "Individuals with psychopathic traits are . . . lacking in such feelings as shame and tenderness, lack responsiveness to the social demands of honesty, truthfulness or decency, and are self-centered and show little consideration for others. . . ." Yet, Simpson goes on:

. . . Even this criterion of unadaptability can turn out to be a poor indicator of marital conflict. Stewart gives the example of a man who came to the clinic not because of marital unhappiness, but because the man despite great ability had been unable to hold a job for any length of time. The man's psychopathic score was high. But the marriage was very successful because of the wife's attitude toward him. "Her attitude, in effect, proved to be 'I am happy to do what my husband wants. I accept my husband's desires and wishes as pre-eminent in our marriage. He is the more intelligent, he is the leader, the decisions are his. What he wishes, I shall agree to gladly.'" This woman was basically anaclitic [dependent like an infant]. Her marriage to a man with highly psychopathic tendencies made for success—indeed, unconsciously they have chosen each precisely because of this underlying compatibility between her anaclitism and his psychopathic tendencies. One might indeed generalize by asserting that unless there were anaclitic women available for men with psychopathic tendencies we would be in something of a mess. (1960, pp. 224–225)

This couple illustrates the point that the same marriage can be considered a great success or an awful failure, depending on one's point of view. For Simpson, who recognizes that psychoanalysis defines most people as "sick" in one way or another but takes that to be a fact of life to be lived with, the critical question is whether the neuroses of the two spouses fit together well in jigsaw fashion. In terms of the intimacy model, with its criterion of two healthy people in healthily intimate interaction that fosters their development, this marriage is a bad one indeed, as it is from the viewpoint of women's liberation also. From the point of view of the typical marital-adjustment study, the couple would probably rate high because the two spouses seem to be satisfied with each other.

It is not only in dealing with extreme cases—if the couple above is indeed extreme—that the intimacy model proves less than useful. Cuber and Harroff looked at the marriages of a number of affluent, successful, middle-class, middle-aged people. They separated out of this group couples who had been married for more than fifteen years, who seemed reasonably content with their marriages, and who had never considered separating or getting divorced. Only a few of these couples had marriages that would fit the intimacy model—or the traditional "adjustment" model for that matter. For example, one group of couples consisted of people who did not think of marriage as an intense, emotional experience, but rather as a practical, friendly, but businesslike way of arranging their lives. These people had other demanding involvements, such as their work, that left little room for great personal involvement at home. Again one might argue that marriage *should* be more intimate than that, but to do so is to make a moral judgment rather than to state a scientific fact. If one does hold the intimacy model as a norm, one is forced to define American marriage as a social problem.

Love's Labor and Intimacy Lost: Marriage over Time   The troubles afflicting marriage are well if depressingly documented in many studies of the developmental course of marriage over time. The leading studies use as their key terms disenchantment, disengagement, and corrosion. An important study is the one Blood and Wolfe (1960) made in the Detroit area. They conducted extensive interviews in the middle 1950's with 731 urban and suburban wives and with 178 farm wives. In contrast to many studies of marriage, the sample was not limited to middle-class people, but it did not include the husband's point of view. The authors summarize their findings on the course of marriage over time as follows:

> The first few years of marriage are a honeymoon period which continues the romance of courtship. With the birth of the first baby, satisfaction with the standard of living and companionship decline. In subsequent years, love and understanding lag. If children do not come, their absence is an alternative source of dissatisfaction.
>
> These trends do not involve all couples, but affect a very large proportion of the total. In the first two years of marriage, 52 percent of the wives are very satisfied with their marriages, and none notably dissatisfied. Twenty years later, only 6 percent are still very satisfied, while 21 percent are conspicuously dissatisfied. These figures suggest that a majority of wives become significantly less satisfied in later marriage than they were at the beginning.
>
> Some of this decline involves the calming of enthusiasm into satisfaction as a result of getting used to the partner, no matter how fine he may be. . . . However, much of the decline in satisfaction reflects observable decreases in the number of things husbands and wives do with and for each other. Hence, corrosion is not too harsh a term for what happens to the average marriage over the course of time. . . . (1960, pp. 87–88)

This study was a cross-sectional—that is, at one point in time it looked at couples of different ages who had been married differing lengths of time. A number of other studies done in the same cross-sectional way found similar declines in marital satisfaction with length of marriage.

Studies, however, of the same couples over time—longitudinal studies—yield essentially similar conclusions. In the best-known of these longitudinal studies, researchers interviewed couples during their engagement period, again after three to five years of marriage, and a third time after they had been married eighteen to twenty years. They found a decline over time in the following areas: companionship, demonstration of affection including both kissing and inter-course, common interests, common beliefs and values, belief in permanence of the marriage, and marital adjustment. Feelings of loneliness increased. On the other hand, marital happiness, sex adjustments, and ratings of the spouse did not decline.

Using the term "disengagement" to describe these changes, one writer, Pineo (1961), sees them as the inevitable result of mate selection based on choice. Since the couple begins marriage at a high point of love and "fit" between their personalities, they have nowhere to go but down. He compares the disengagement process in marriage to the phenomenon known as statistical regression: a group of people who score extremely high or extremely low on some test, such as an I.Q. test, are likely to come out more average on any retesting. This happens because no test is perfect, and some of those who attained very high or very low scores got them through some sort of chance fluctuation, such as guessing correctly or not feeling well that day. Thus people marry at the maximal point of liking and fit, and any unfore-seen changes must result in less satisfaction. Rather than resulting from individual neurotic conflict, this view sees marital unhappiness as a normal operating feature of the institution. The description is rather far from the genital Utopia that psychoanalysis offers as a model for marriage.

Marriage as Conflict: Exchange and Strategy Models   Although the prevailing models of marriage in the family literature have stressed adjustment, intimacy, and mutuality of in-terests between spouses, there has always tended to be a minority view stressing the competitive and conflictful aspects of marriage. Jessie Bernard has traced the history of this view of marriage:

Popular wisdom has long recognized that marital adjustments are a matter of give and take. The conception of the relation between the sexes as a bargaining situation is very old. Quite aside from the patent form of bride purchase of the dowry, the psychological give and take between men and women has long been viewed as essentially a duel of wits for advantage. The courts of love in the twelfth century dealt with the nature of such bargains: who owed what to whom and why. A knight might perform certain feats in order to obligate his lady to become his love: ". . . there was never a joy which was not purchased at the expense of a hundred griefs." . . .

It was Waller who formulated most elaborately and insightfully the bargaining model of the relations between the sexes. His application was primarily to the premarital period, but the fundamental processes are the same, although the specific "goods" involved in the exchange may vary greatly—love, mink coats, sex relations, approval, "freedom," etc. (Bernard, 1964, p. 705)

In recent years the old insight that the daily events of social life could be compared to economic transactions or the dealings between hostile countries has been greatly systematized. Game theory, social-exchange theory, and strategic-bargaining theory all represent attempts to offer precise analyses or models of various types of competitive— and cooperative—behavior.

Classical game theory—based on pure competition and the assumption that any loss incurred by one side is matched by pure gain on the other—is not regarded as an appropriate model for international relations, much less marriage, so it need not concern us here.

The kind of model that is applied to marriage, one called a "mixed-motive" or "cooperative" model, was developed by Luce and Raiffa and Schelling. It is based, among other things, on a situation in which both sides can win and both can lose. Here is a rather simple situation: John and Mary, a married couple, have had a fight. They have said some harsh things to each other. Each would like to make up, but each is afraid of being the first to act friendly, and being rebuffed by the other person. A similar situation: a young man and woman, strangers to each other, are deciding whether to act friendly or to ignore the other. Each party's preferred outcome is to smile and to receive a smile in return, but since each fears a frown, neither smiles! (Those who know something about the literature on mixed-motive models will recognize the outline of the Prisoner's Dilemma game.)

All exchange approaches share a cost-benefit-analysis way of looking at personal relations, but they differ among

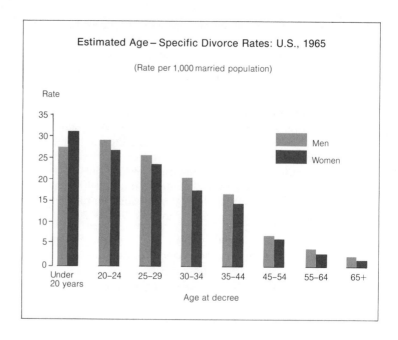

This chart indicates that divorce rates are highest for teen-age marriages in the United States. (From *Profiles of Children*, White House Conference on Children 1970, Washington: U.S. Government Printing Office)

themselves in assumptions and detail. Here are tests of social-exchange theory from Peter Blau's observations on love:

The more an individual is in love with another, the more anxious he or she is likely to be to please the other. The individual who is less deeply involved in a love relationship, therefore, is in an advantageous position, since the other's greater concern with continuing the relationship makes him or her dependent and gives the less involved individual power. Waller called this "the principle of least interest." This power can be used to exploit the other; the woman who exploits a man's affection for economic gain and the boy who sexually exploits a girl who is in love with him are obvious examples. . . .

How valuable a woman is as a love object to a man depends to a considerable extent on her apparent popularity with other men. . . .

. . . A woman who readily gives proof of her affection to a man, therefore, provides presumptive evidence of her lack of popularity and thus tends to depreciate the value of her affection for him. . . .

To safeguard the value of her affection, a woman must be un-generous in expressing it and make any evidence of her growing love a cherished prize that cannot easily be won. . . .

. . . The aim of both sexes in courtship is to furnish sufficient rewards to seduce the other, but not enough to deflate their value, yet the line defined by these two conditions is often imperceptible. (Blau, 1964, pp. 78–80)

Blau's notions of social exchange involve subtleties not explicitly discussed by the partners in an interaction, and which they may be aware of only dimly if at all. By contrast, Bernard, applying Thomas Schelling's notions of international relations to marriage, envisions marital strategic bargaining as an explicit process:

. . . Three basic strategic moves are: "first move," strategic threat or "second move," and strategic promises. All depend on commitments. . . .

"*First move.*" If one party can commit himself irrevocably to a certain position . . . and convince the other party that his position is indeed irrevocable no matter what, he has won. . . .

The *fait accompli* is a form of first move. "I've already bought the tickets to the concert, we'll have to go," says the spouse who did not want to go to the prizefight. . . .

Strategic threats. Strategic threats, like "first move," depend on commitments, but they are characteristic of situations where the opponent has first move. They are, in fact, an attempt to gain the advantage of "first move."

. . . A strategic threat places on the threatened person the responsibility of the dire consequences to the threatener himself. It shifts blame. "If you continue to run home to your mother, I'll go back to drinking," says the husband as he brings home a fifth of whiskey. In order to be more convincing, he tells her he has told his cronies what he will do. Neither he nor she wants him to go back to drinking; the strategic threat now puts her in the position of having to save him from doing something he doesn't want to do anyway in order to save his face vis-à-vis his friends and her-self. . . . "If you don't stop running around with other women, I'll divorce you," says a wife, "and I have told mother so." Neither wants a divorce. She has given herself an incentive (again, face saving vis-à-vis her mother) to do something she prefers not to do. She is putting him in the position of being to blame for the divorce, for ruining the marriage, which neither wants to end. The threatened person must, in effect, protect the threatener in order to protect himself. (Bernard, 1964, pp. 707–708)

Social scientists have questioned whether game theory and similar models actually apply to the real-life situations, such as international relations, they are intended to describe. Their applicability to family life is even more questionable. Such models seem to rule out situations where simple self-interest is mixed with concern for the other person, or where the person changes his preferences in light of the other person's feelings. Nor do these models deal very well with ambivalence—where an individual is in conflict about what he wants. Consider the following instance, which arises out of the problem of defining the marital relationship as voluntary or compulsory:

> . . . A young couple began having trouble a few years after marriage. . . . They separated, but continued to associate. When they entered therapy, the husband wanted to go back together again, but was uncertain about it. The wife, having taken up with another man, did not want to live with her husband, but wanted to associate with him and consider possible future reconciliation. At one moment, the husband insisted on immediate divorce, at the next he asked for a reconciliation. Each time he spoke more firmly about his plans for divorce, the wife began to discuss the great potential of their marriage and how fond she was of him. When the husband began talking about going back together, the wife discussed how miserable their marriage had been. After several sessions of trying to clarify the situation, the issue was forced by a suggestion that if the couple continue treatment they do so in a trial period of living together. . . . The wife refused. The husband managed to arrange a divorce, although when he was no longer compulsively involved with her, the wife was finding him attractive again. (Haley, 1963, p. 122)

A similar instance of ambivalence is that of a young mother who worked out an agreement with her graduate-student husband to divide child care between them equally; if he failed to live up to what seemed a full share of the burden, particularly if he forgot to be responsible for figuring out what needed to be done, she was angry. But the better he performed, the more useless and displaced she felt; after all he had another identity in his work, but being a mother was what she *was*.

At best, such models offer an incomplete view of human relations.

Marriage as Paradox: Communications Model   The objection
to game-theory models is not their portrayal of marriage as
a conflict-prone institution but rather the qualities they
ascribe to marital conflict. In these models conflict consists
of the coldly rational sparring of two opponents simply trying to maximize their own gains.

Seemingly scientific descriptions of human behavior,
in fact such models are probably quite limited hypotheses
about behavior. To assume, as Blau does, that lovers are
always tallying the market value of each other or, as Schelling
does, that the value of saving face exceeds that of self-
preservation is to overgeneralize the responses of particular
people in a particular milieu into a universal law.

A model that seems to fit better the daily facts of marital
and other family conflict is based on what has been called
a "communicational" or "systems approach" to the family.
It was originally developed by a group of psychiatrists and
psychologists who studied the interaction in families with
a schizophrenic member (Bateson et al., 1956; Haley, 1963;
Ruesch and Bateson, 1968; Watzlawick, Beavin, and Jackson,
1967). As we noted earlier, the insights developed by this
research have been extended to normal family life.

The basic tenets of communication theory may be contained in a short set of statements. These statements are more
like assumptions of theorems in mathematics than hypotheses that can be tested and possibly rejected. That is, within
the perspective of the theory, they are self-evidently true.

The most basic principle is that it is impossible not to
communicate—just as it is impossible not to behave. When
two people meet, therefore, they have to decide how they
are going to behave toward each other, and what kinds of
messages they are going to exchange. They also must decide what sorts of things they will not say and do. This process is referred to as "defining the relationship."

Whenever one person speaks to another, his message
either reinforces the ongoing definition or suggests a shift.
For example, one of the issues they can't avoid dealing with
is that of dominance versus equality: will they deal with each
other as equals, or will they assume complementary positions
in which one will show respect for the other? These decisions
will determine how they will address one another—whether

they will use each other's first names, call each other "mis-ter," or whether one will use "mister" and the other the first name. The other basic dimension of social life is what Roger Brown (1965, p. 57) has called solidarity or affection. This will also determine the content of messages as well as such things as how far the two people will stand from each other when speaking and whether one may put an arm around the other.

Another basic concept of communications analysis is that human communication always takes place at several levels. People not only say something, but they qualify what they say by their tone of voice, their facial expressions and body movements, and the context. For example, a person can say "yes" to a request in almost an infinite number of ways, expressing anything from eagerness to extreme reluc-tance. Incongruity often occurs among these levels. Teasing and sarcasm are familiar ways of qualifying statements; in each instance the main message is disqualified by the speaker: "Don't take this statement seriously."

Finally, communications theory sees in any statement a person makes to another an attempt to control or define that relationship. This does not mean that one tries neces-sarily to be the boss or to advance one's self-interest in an obvious way. Consider the example of a person who acts helpless; such behavior is an invitation for the other person to take care of the helpless one. But the helpless person may control the relationship since he has been able to exert in-fluence over the behavior of the other person. The more extreme the helplessness of the dependent one, as for exam-ple a baby or a very sick person, the more the dependency may seem to be a form of domination.

One cannot avoid communicating, or qualifying one's communication, or controlling the definition of the relationship:

It must be emphasized that no one can avoid being involved in a struggle over the definition of his relationship with someone else. Everyone is constantly involved in defining his relationship or countering the other person's definition. If a person speaks, he is inevitably indicating what type of relationship he has with the other person. By whatever he says, he is indicating "This is the sort of relationship where this is said." If a person remains mute he is also inevitably indicating by not speaking that he is qualifying the other person's behavior. Just as one cannot *fail* to qualify a message, he also cannot *fail* to indicate what behavior is to take place in the relationship. If a person wishes to avoid defining his relationship with another and therefore talks only about the weather, he is inevitably indicating that the kind of communication which should take place between them should be neutral, and this defines the relationship. (Haley, 1963, p. 9)

How does the communication perspective apply to marriage? Marriage in these terms is seen as a situation where two people must define their relationship to each other. That is, they must work out rules for living together, and rules for making the rules. The couple need not necessarily be aware of the rules they are following, but they cannot, accordingly, avoid having them:

. . . Whenever they complete a transaction, a rule is being established. Even if they should set out to behave entirely spontaneously, they would be establishing the rule that they are to behave in that way. (Haley, 1963, p. 123)

For example, couples must make rules about what kind of work the husband will do, whether the wife will work, how much say each one will have in the other's work, whose responsibility the various household chores will be, whether or not each can criticize the other, whether when one person makes a mistake the other is to comfort or criticize him or her, what topics are open for discussion and what topics are too sensitive to bring up, what roles outsiders are to play in the marriage, whether in-laws are outsiders, and so on.

Conflicts arise over the rules themselves, over who sets the rules, and over incompatible rules. One almost inevitable source of conflict results from the fact that the two spouses come from two different families. Each family would have impressed its child with its own set of implicit and explicit rules for dealing with people, for managing household finances and routines, and even for the proper distance one should stand from another person while talking to him. Disagreements over the rules themselves can often be settled by compromise. The really emotional battles occur over who is to make the rules. These have to do with the control aspects of the marriage.

For example, a wife could insist that her husband hang up his clothes so that she does not have to pick up after him like a servant. The husband might agree with his wife that she should not be his servant, and so agree to the definition of the relationship, but he still might not agree that *she* should be the one to give him orders on what to do about his clothes. (Haley, 1963, p. 226)

The communications approach helps to explain why talking things out doesn't always lead to a resolution of the problem and why heated arguments can arise over trivial matters. The proponents of this view do not argue that improved communication leads to improved relationships, or that interpersonal conflicts result only from "failures of communication." Rather they point out that talking things over and expressing feelings openly may make things worse between a wife and husband, or a parent and child, as often as it clears the air (see Levenson, 1972).

The communications perspective shows how anyone can become involved in irritating and disappointing hang-ups in the nitty-gritty struggles of daily life. It reveals how the interaction between two people has properties of its own, independent of their particular personalities. Consider, for example, the concept of paradoxical communication. This is a snare that no family can entirely escape; in extreme degrees it is often found in families in which one member is a schizophrenic. A simple example of a paradoxical communication is the statement, "I command you to disobey me." The situation of the wife telling the husband to pick up his clothes also contains a paradox, but a more subtle one:

The communication of bids for two incompatible types of relationships can occur whenever there is an incompatibility between (a) the rule defining a relationship, and (b) the type of relationship implicit in *who* is defining the relationship. For example, if a wife tells her husband to pick up his own clothes. However, *when she tells him to do this* she is defining the relationship as complementary—she orders and he is to follow the orders. The husband is then faced with two different definitions of the relationship so that whichever way he responds, he cannot satisfy both requests. If he picks up his clothes, accepting the symmetrical definition, he is following her directions and so accepting a complementary definition. He cannot accept one definition without the other unless he comments on the situation in a way that redefines it. More likely he will erupt in indignation while uncertain what he is indignant about and his wife will similarly be indignant because he erupts over this simple request. (Haley, 1963, pp. 127–128)

A similar kind of paradox occurs when one spouse tells another to be more independent, or expressive, or assertive.

"I command you to be spontaneous," or "I command you to love me."

Sexual relationships are full of such paradoxical messages, providing further examples of the problems of communication. Not only are there taboos about talking about sex matters in the first place, but there are taboos against talking about the taboos. Laing has pointed out there are rules that one cannot talk about without breaking the rule that one should not talk about them:

A family has a rule that little Johnny should not think filthy thoughts. Little Johnny is a good boy: he does not have to be told not to think filthy thoughts. They never have *taught* him *not* to think filthy thoughts. He never has.

So, according to the family, and even little Johnny, there is no rule against filthy thoughts, because there is no need to have a rule against what never happens. Moreover, we do not talk in the family about a rule against filthy thoughts, because since there are no filthy thoughts, and no rule against them, there is no need to talk about this dreary, abstract, irrelevant, or even vaguely filthy subject. . . .

Perhaps no one outside such a family rule-system could knowingly embrace it—Rule A: Don't. Rule A-1: Rule A does not exist. Rule A-2: Rule A-1 does not exist. (Laing, 1969, p. 113)

Furthermore, even if a couple does talk to each other about sex, talking may often lead to conflicts that are difficult to resolve:

For example, if a wife turns her back on her husband in bed, assuming that if he is interested in sexual relations he will turn her over, the husband might assume from her behavior that she is not interested in sexual relations and so he does not turn her over. Both spouses can then feel that the other is disinterested, and both can then feel righteously indignant. If this conflict is at the level of what kind of relationship to have, it can be resolved as a misunderstanding. Discussion and correction of the signals involved will lead to more amiable relations. However, if the couple is in a struggle over who is to define the type of relationship, discussion of the situation will not necessarily relieve the problem. After discussion, the wife may still feel that it is a law of life that only the man initiates sex relations, and she will not let him impose a different relationship upon her. The husband may continue to feel that he will not impose himself upon his wife until she has expressed some interest, and she is not going to tell him how to conduct himself. In this struggle, he might label her as frigid, and she might label him as unmanly. (Haley, 1963, p. 130)

Similar problems can arise over specific practices; one partner might define a satisfactory sex relationship as one that includes oral sex, whereas the other partner might define oral sex as unnecessary or even disgusting.

There are still other paradoxes in sexual interaction. For example, sex is supposed to be the ultimate refuge from the rat race, but achievement pressures exist as much in the bedroom as elsewhere. On the one hand, sex is supposed to be a free surrender to basic impulses and instincts; on the other hand, what you do and when you do it are supposed to be in tune with the needs of the other person. Each partner is supposed to let the other know what he or she wants. If a person doesn't communicate this information, he/she may be frustrated, and this frustration may spoil the partner's pleasure directly or indirectly. But the other horn of the dilemma is this: if one person communicates his/her own needs too clearly or too insistently, then the partner is likely to resent being *told* what to do; he/she may feel like a masturbatory tool of the other person, rather than a free sexual being.

Sexual hangups between couples probably result as much from communicational knots as from purely sexual problems. One of the attractions of affairs may be escape from the old knots, and the exploration of a new set of rules and metarules for talking about sex.

It is interesting that the Masters-Johnson (1970) therapy for couples having troubles in their sex lives is largely an attack on the couples' old communication or noncommunication patterns. This occurs at two levels. On the level of specifics, each partner is taught the preferences of the other by means of a hand-on-hand technique that eliminates the need for verbal communication. This technique and whole-therapy situation nearly disposes of the communications problem at the initial level. Now the therapists are telling the couple what to do and what not to do, thus extricating them from their impasse and presumably freeing them from their sex hangups by controlling their behavior and commanding that they be spontaneous.

Still another kind of communicational paradox occurs in the demand to be told what to do. Haley cites the example of a rebellious child who says to his parents, "All right, tell me what to do from now on and I'll do it." If they tell him what to do, they are doing what the child tells them. The parents are likely to react to his statement of compliance with the same angry helplessness as they do to his demands. A similar situation is the following: a couple are trying to decide what movie to see or where to go on their vacation. After each one has suggested several alternatives and had them rejected by the other, one—say the husband—may say, "OK, *you* decide where we are going. Whatever you say, that's what we'll do." The recipient of such a message is likely to feel perplexed without knowing why. What has happened is that a symmetrical or equal relationship, deciding together what to do, has been changed to a complementary or unequal relationship in a paradoxical way. By demanding that the wife tell him what to do, the husband is in fact controlling her behavior, at the same time absolving himself of any blame if the movie or vacation spot turns out to be a dud.

In sum then, the communication analysis of conflict, with its emphasis on ambivalence, paradox, and shifting emotional preferences, seems to do more justice to the complexities of marriage than the rational, cost-benefit analysis of game and exchange theory, or the face-saving of strategic-bargaining theory. One question that remains to be answered is whether paradoxical communication occurs in all human interaction or only in Western culture, and particularly in contemporary family life.

The Social Contexts of Marriage

Some writings that present the communcational or systems approach to marriage and the family portray the family as a closed world of interaction. Paradoxically, the same theorists who argued that a person's psychological problems could not be understood apart from the context of his or her family sometimes treat the family group as if it existed in a social and cultural vacuum. Lennard and Bernstein (1969, p. 210) note that some family therapists fail to recognize the "family's vulnerability to prescriptions, demands, and values originating from outside its boundaries." Thus family interaction may reflect and be sensitive to the values of the children's peer group, the husband's coworkers, the wife's friends and neighbors, the images of family roles in the mass media, and a variety of conflicting norms in the community.

Family definitions and roles, as we noted earlier, are backed by legal and economic sanctions. There are limits beyond which family roles cannot be changed, no matter what the outcome of open communication, without major changes in the larger social structure:

> For all their efforts at openness and communication, father and son are bound to each other . . . by the social requirements of their respective roles (being a son the father can be proud of) and the social institutions within which they have to exist. This last is vitally important. There are inevitable hegemonies built in the present family structure. For example, the child is quite simply financially dependent on the parent. The parent has legal control and responsibility. The father is compelled by a society that holds *him* responsible morally and psychiatrically for his son's troubles. If the son of a prominent jurist has legal difficulties, we know he is getting even with his father, or at least that's what our present systems lead us to believe — that it is the father's fault. (Levenson, 1972, pp. 128–129)

A similar analysis may be made of husband-wife interaction. Marriages are surrounded by a complex network of social pressures and rewards and sanctions that pull the partners apart, push them together, and limit their options. Proposals for "open" or "liberated" marriage often overlook these realities. They suggest that couples can turn their marriages into unions of two free and independent beings merely by resolving to respect each other's individuality and by dividing economic and domestic responsibilities. Open marriage, like open communication, is an attractive-sounding goal that is difficult to achieve for most people. Apart from the fact that "openness" does not guarantee harmony but may increase conflict, advocates of open marriage overlook the harsh realities of the marketplace, both economic and sexual, in which couples find themselves:

> . . . The average working man does not have an easy life; being king of his castle is at least some compensation for job tensions.
>
> The average woman learns early that she had better catch a man if she wants to avoid a future of low-paying dead-end jobs and the social stigma of being unmarried. . . . Every housewife knows that there are lots of younger, prettier women around and that her residual secretarial skills from 20 years ago are worth zilch on the job market.

Is it surprising if she is possessive and jealous?

There is no way for a married couple to escape the pervasive effects of the sex-role system. For one thing, our entire economy is based on the premise that men should work and women should stay home.

A husband and wife may decide that they would really like to exchange roles—that she loves holding down a job, while he would rather take care of the children and garden. But if his job pays twice as much as any she could get, chances are they can't afford to switch.

. . . Most part-time jobs pay next to nothing and offer no fringe benefits, security, or opportunity for promotion. . . .

. . . Until there is genuine equality between the sexes, "open marriage" can be nothing but a cotton-candy slogan. (Willis, 1972, p. 16)

The pushes and pulls generated by contemporary social life strain the best of marriages and, at the same time, hold together couples whose marriages are only "empty shells."

There is a growing realization in the professional literature that contrary to what used to be assumed, marital stability does not necessarily indicate marital happiness or satisfaction (Hicks and Platt, 1970). There appear to be many couples who stay together even though there is a lack of affection and companionship. It is possible that such marriages could be improved if the partners became more open with each other, but it is also possible that open communication would only reveal that each partner perceived the other as the least unattractive of all available alternatives. It might be revealed, for example, that she puts up with him because she likes her home and children, and besides, what kind of job or man could she get at her age; he puts up with her because she takes decent care of the house and children and doesn't interfere with his work or sexual adventures, and besides, it's cheaper and more convenient to be married than to have to pay alimony. This sort of marriage, which Cuber and Harroff have characterized as "utilitarian," seems to be something of a hybrid, midway between the "institutional" marriage of former times, which was based on social and economic necessity, and the companionship or love marriage, which is the marital ideal if not the reality of modern industrial societies. To the extent that marriage in the future ceases to be defined as the only valid life style, there should be fewer of these marriages.

The Future of Marriage

Some see marriage as an obsolete, ridiculous institution, doomed to pass into extinction in a few years. Others believe it to be so fundamentally rooted in man's nature, either biologically or psychologically or both, that marriage is bound to be the main form of man-woman relations for years to come.

For the immediate future, say the next twenty-five years, reality is likely to be somewhere between the two extremes. We seem to be entering a period in which pluralistic forms of the family will be more of a reality in that more people will be involved in them, and also there will be a greater acceptance of them.

It is remarkable how quickly things are changing. Although the women's movement has revealed sexual biases as deep if not deeper than racism, it has at least made many people conscious of these biases and has punctured the myths surrounding marriage and motherhood. Recent census figures reveal declines in both the birth rates and marriage rates.

A couple marrying today can hardly do so with the sense of inevitability that was common only a few years ago. The lessened pressure to marry and remain married may revitalize marriage; people who feel reluctant to marry in their twenties or at all can follow their own feelings more easily than in the past, and there will be less and less justification for couples locked in "holy deadlock" to remain together.

More than the ideology of women's liberation is involved in the recent challenges to marriage. In fact, the ideology can be seen as much as an adaption to present and future realities as a revolt against the past. The population crisis makes it imperative that women no longer devote themselves to childbearing; recent polls reveal that the need to reduce the birth rate has been widely recognized by the American public—the two-child family necessary for population maintenance but zero growth is replacing the four-child family as the ideal size. With the reduced amount of time out of a woman's lifespan devoted to child rearing, the chief justification for the prevailing division of labor in marriage also disappears. The industrial revolution took work out of the home and created the exclusively domestic role of housewife-mother. As numerous observers have

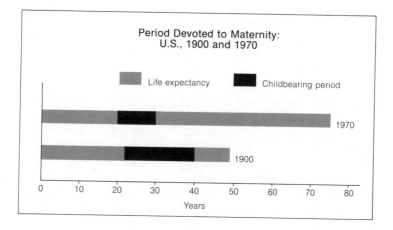

Period devoted to maternity in the average lifespan of the American woman, 1900 and 1970. The lifespan has increased but the childbearing period has decreased. (After Sullerot, 1971)

pointed out, this role increasingly has become unable to fill the lengthened lifespan of twentieth-century women (see accompanying chart). The decline in the motherhood function makes marriage still less of an answer than it ever was to the question of what women are going to do with their lives.

Summary

Although a marriage is a relationship between a man and woman, it involves more than the sum of these two personalities. It is a social institution, a legally defined status involving legal rights and obligations, and a social group — the dyad — with its own interactional properties. In addition, the partners have been socialized to be different and unequal in status.

A great deal of ambivalence about marriage occurs in our culture, but in no culture anywhere is marital harmony the general rule. In the marriage and family literature, four broad models of marriage may be discerned. Two of these stress the positive, harmonious side of marriage; the other two emphasize the conflictual aspects. The adjustment model sees happiness, harmony, and stability as the hallmarks of marital success. Psychoanalytic models reject the adjustment concept as superficial and emphasize the attainment of intimacy and personality growth. Both of these models tend to assume that conflict indicates marital difficulty or failure.

By contrast, the conflict models assume that all social interaction involves conflict. Game theory or exchange theory tends to see marriage as a battle of the sexes, a rational struggle of two parties to maximize their own positions. The systems or communications approach emphasizes ambivalence and the paradoxes of human communication as the source of conflict in marriage.

All four models tend to view marriage largely as an interpersonal relationship in a social vacuum. They tend to ignore the ways in which social, economic, and cultural factors influence marriages.

COUPLES:
IN AND OUT OF MARRIAGE

Chapter 7

Above all, it must not be thought that the couple relationship is a simple one: a man and woman bound by some obvious contract.

Albert Memmi, *Dominated Man*

Chapter Seven   In the last chapter we looked at the institution of marriage in more or less abstract, general terms. Marriage, the institution, transcends the relationship between two people. Marriage constitutes a public and legal status, a religious status, a link between groups of kin, a sociological form—the dyad—that has qualities of its own apart from the two personalities involved. In this chapter we will look at the couple relationship in terms of the two individuals. We will try to look at the various ways in which married couples and other couples relate to each other and the rest of the world. Rather than ask "What is marriage?" and "How has it been conceived?" we will ask "How does this couple differ from that couple?" How do different people define and arrange their lives as couples?

Still it should not be assumed that the relationship of a particular man and woman can be considered in total isolation from the more abstract questions. At what point do two individuals cease being two independent individuals and become a couple instead? In what ways does the state of couplehood differ from marriage?

Indeed, there is one theoretical position in the literature that questions the distinction between marriage and any other form of couple relationship. Noting that marriage no longer implies monogamy and permanence, and that couple relationships outside marriage no longer exclude sex and a sense of commitment, Farber (1964) has suggested that the American system of mate selection and marriage is best described as one based on the "permanent availability" of all adults as potential marriage partners, whether they are currently married or not. Thus marriage used to be the endpoint of a series of distinct stages—dating, keeping company, going steady, a private agreement to be married, announcement of the engagement, and finally marriage, presumably for life. Divorce was regarded as a tragic failure, perhaps a shameful event, certainly an oddity.

Farber argues that all this has changed, even the vocabulary. Divorce is no longer stigmatized, and remarriage is common. He notes that the term "keeping company" has dropped out of use—and since Farber wrote, "dating" also has begun to have an old-fashioned ring to it. Thus the whole system of courtship of the 1920's and '30's, with the ever-narrowing field of eligible spouses and stages of ever-increasing commitment, has given way to a series of so-called "involvements," one of which may result in marriage.

As McCall (1966) has pointed out, there is a paradox in the new pattern of couple relationships. Marriage has become less exclusive and permanent, but in what used to be the courtship stage there is an emphasis on deep personal intimacy, on some kind of commitment. Yet neither type of involvement is expected to last if it turns out to be dissatisfying. Couple relationships are both more intensely personal and less stable and enduring. The notion of the "one and only love" has faded.

Although couple relationships are becoming more and more diverse, there has always been a great deal more variation in marriage than was generally recognized in the literature. The social-science equivalent of Tolstoy's assertion — happy families are alike, but each unhappy family is unhappy in its own way — is the notion that widely shared social norms regulate family behavior. Thus the happy and/or adjusted families are seen as following the prescribed and expected norms for family behavior, whereas the unhappy ones are deviating from them in some way — are failing to perform in appropriate ways. Elizabeth Bott has characterized these assumptions as follows:

> It is often assumed that there is a large measure of agreement on familial norms in the society as a whole. . . . Such a view implies that given individuals will recognize that these agreed-upon external standards exist, and that they will be able to make the norms explicit without difficulty. (Bott, 1957, p. 194)

In her own research on marital roles in urban families, however, Bott found much more variation in the norms than is commonly assumed. Further, many of the people interviewed had a hard time generalizing about customary and proper behavior for husbands and wives. They were too much aware of variation among their acquaintances:

> From an intensive study of twenty urban families, I can report that there was considerable variation in the norms of familial roles. There were some points of agreement; most of these were very vague and general and did not give a precise blueprint for action. On many points there was considerable variation from one research couple to another. Furthermore, . . . several couples drew

attention to the fact that there was variation among the people they knew personally. (Bott, 1957, p. 195)

That couples vary a great deal from each other seems obvious once stated; it is only the assumption of normative consensus that makes the foregoing findings seem unexpected.

Types of Marriage

In recent years a number of other studies of marriage have also begun to explore some of the diversity in outwardly conventional marriages. Most previous marriage studies tended to assume that the most important feature of any marriage was a quality that could be referred to as adjustment, or satisfaction, or happiness. The notion was that all marriage could be lined up along a single dimension—with all the "good" marriages on one end of the scale and all the "bad" marriages on the other end.

The most well known of the recent descriptive studies is the one done by Cuber and Harroff (1965). These authors departed from the typical marriage study in several ways: they did not use the one-dimensional rationale of marital "adjustment"; they were more interested in collecting accounts of personal experience than in gathering statistics; they used no schedule of formal questions, but simply conversed with each person on the general subject of men and women for as many hours as the subjects felt like talking; and finally, they chose to study an elite group of subjects. Feeling that too many marriage studies had been done on families in crisis situations and too few on successful, "normal" upper middle-class people, they chose their subjects from the top end of the income and occupation distribution: business executives, lawyers, government officials, and the like. They interviewed 437 such men and women, between the ages of 35 and 55.

One of the most widely quoted findings of this study is its description of five types of enduring marriage. The authors discovered enormous variation within a group of stable marriages among people of similar class positions, thus destroying the myth that "happy families are all alike."

Conflict-Habituated Marriage　Cuber and Harroff describe the "conflict-habituated marriage" as the type that is furthest removed from the notion of the happy-stable-conflict-free adjusted couple as opposed to the unhappy-unstable-fighting maladjusted couple. This type of marriage, though not the most prevalent, was the most dramatic one in the sample. In such marriages the couples simply fight with each other often. Being together usually suffices to trigger an argument, and the couple has a reputation for battling among the rest of the family. They do not, however, define the fighting as grounds for dissolving the marriages — to use communication terms, the husband and wife define it as acceptable to talk to each other that way. Cuber and Harroff speculate that such spouses feel a lot of hostility that must be expressed, and the marital battles therefore bind them together.

Devitalized Marriage   In the second type, the "devitalized" marriage, the term applies to the couple relationship, not the individual wife or husband. Starting out their marriages romantically with love and closeness, these couples have drifted apart over the years but still get along with each other and want to stay married. The description of these couples sounds like the findings by Blood and Wolfe and by Pineo on the decline of marital morale over time.

Passive-Congenial Marriage   In the third type of marriage, called "passive-congenial," the couples differ from the devitalized couples in that they were never highly emotional about each other to begin with. Rather, they view being married as a convenient and comfortable way to live while directing one's true interests and creative energies elsewhere. Unlike the devitalized couples these people do not regret the failure of their marriages to attain romantic stereotypes. Such a marriage can free the individuals to become absorbed in their careers or other social commitments. In other words these couples define their lack of intense involvement in each other as the way marriage ought to be — at least for them.

Although such a utilitarian version of marriage does not go along with popular romantic attitudes toward marriage or with the psychoanalytic intimacy model, it coincides with the European approach to marriage mentioned earlier. Moreover, it is not just upper-class or upper middle-class circles where this type of marriage is found. Elizabeth Bott, in her study of English working-class and lower middle-class families (1957), found many marriages in which husband and wife led rather separate lives. Rather than having high-powered careers as did the Cuber and Harroff subjects, however, these people were involved in close-linked social networks of relatives, friends, and neighbors in relation to which the marriage tie was secondary.

Although all marriages must be understood in the context of their social and environmental surroundings, the dependency on outside forces is highlighted in the utilitarian type of marriage. If the strong involvement in career or community is missing, then such marriages can become drab cages of empty togetherness. Mirra Komarovsky, in a sensitive study of blue-collar marriages (1962), deals with a group of white, Protestant, native-born American workers and their wives in a town she calls "Glenton." These people do not hold romantic or psychological notions about marital companionship or intimacy, but—in contrast to Elizabeth Bott's Londoners and the Cuber and Harroff jet-setters—they also do not have many or strong outside associations and interests. Dr. Komarovsky argues that outside sources of stimulation, interest, and accomplishment may nourish a marriage while too much togetherness may overburden it, particularly for people who have not cultivated the skills of reflecting on and verbalizing their reactions to their experiences as daily life unfolds. She writes:

> Many couples in their late thirties, especially among the less educated, seem almost to have withdrawn from life. There they sit in front of the television set: "What's there to say? We both see it." "If you had two extra hours every day, how would you like to spend them?" asked the interviewer, and a man mused: "This would make the evening long and tiring if you're watching TV." (Komarovsky, 1962, p. 107)

The passive-congenial or utilitarian marriage, though failing to live up to the ideal of what marriage should be, nevertheless confirms a common belief that a person must choose between work involvement and family involvement, that a hard-driving professional or successful executive must inevitably have an atrophied family life, and conversely that a man or woman deeply involved with spouse and children must lose out in the work rat race. There are, of course, plenty of examples of this stereotype. Most of the people studied by Cuber and Harroff fell into this category. But other findings by them and by Komarovsky dispute the notion that the more a person invests in the family, the less time he has for work and outside friendships, and vice versa.

Komarovsky found that the people who were most involved in their work were the same ones who had more emotionally intense marriages. Similarly, the women who engaged in more leisure-time activities with their husbands also spent more time in club work and with women friends. The active, involved people had more education, which in this sample of blue-collar people meant having graduated from high school.

Vital Marriage   In the elite sample of Cuber and Harroff, there were also couples who belied the either/or stereotype about work involvement versus family involvement. The last two of their five types of marriage, the "vital" and the "total," conform more closely to the ideal image of what marriage is supposed to be. About one out of six of the marriages they studied fell into these two types. Again, the term "vital" refers to the relationship, not the personalities of the spouses. In the vital relationship the couple not only spends a lot of time together, but enjoys being together. The relationship itself is extremely important to each one, although the spouses do not lose their separate identities. Since the entire sample in this study was highly successful in work, there were of course no differences on that score between the vital couples and those with more utilitarian marriages.

Total Marriage   The last of the five Cuber and Harroff types, the "total" marriage, differs from the vital marriages in that there are more aspects of life in which the couple participates together. For example, the wife often is involved in various ways in the husband's work.

An interesting feature of these types of relationship, which the authors call "intrinsic," is the sense of being deviant among their friends and neighbors. Many of them felt that they had to hide their true feeling about their spouses for fear of being laughed at or doubted. That they were correct in judging how most people would react to them is shown by the comments of the Cuber and Harroff subjects in the more utilitarian types of marriage when the intrinsic types of marriage were discussed: some people doubted that there really were any such marriages, and some thought the people must be "oddballs" or immature. Others who knew people in such marriages disapproved of them—they felt that the spouses were so involved with each other that they weren't as devoted to their children as parents should be, or that they expressed too much affection in front of the children. The intrinsic couples, on the other hand, felt they did enough for their children, and that many couples not that interested in each other often compensated by becoming overinvolved in their children's lives.

Other Typologies   Cuber and Harroff do not claim that their typology is the last word on marriages, or that their study is as high on methodological rigor as it is on human interest. They have presented suggestive findings and pointed out how some of the supposedly more "scientific" studies of marriage fall short as descriptions of real-life marriages. Inevitably, however, their own study leaves many questions unanswered. Would different researchers, looking at the same sample of subjects, divide the subjects the same way and arrive at the same five types of marriages? Would another researcher perhaps have emphasized the sexual aspects less and considered other dimensions more—such as attitudes toward parenthood? Or, granting that the five types of marriage do have validity for the sample in the Cuber and Harroff study, would the same five types appear in a sample of people less affluent and of a different ethnic background?

Other researchers, looking at other families, have come up with different schemes for analyzing family life. For example, a study of families by Hess and Handel (1959) dealt with such matters as the images each family member has of the others, the ways each member establishes his separateness and connectedness, the way families deal with experience—how intensely they feel things, whether they evaluate their experiences and family themes. A family theme is a particular notion or motivation that determines how a particular family sees things, and all family members share it. For example, one family might be dominated by the theme of acquiring and displaying possessions, another by the theme of blaming and avoiding blame. One family might draw a tight boundary around itself in trying to maintain the home as a secure island in a threatening outside world; another family might see the world as its oyster, a place to explore and savor. Hess and Handel were dealing with whole families, but the same concepts could be applied to the study of married couples.

Still another way of looking at marriages is found in a study carried out by researchers at the National Institute of Mental Health. The original sample included 2162 young, recently married couples in the Washington, D.C., area. The particular study we are concerned with here is only a small part of a large and still ongoing research project. To arrive at a typology of couples, one of the researchers, Ryder (1970b), selected at random two hundred interview abstracts, read them, and grouped together the couples who seemed to belong together. The basis for the similarity of the couples grouped together and their differences from the other types was certain combinations of husband and wife characteristics. The husbands seemed to differ from each other in terms of their effectiveness in fulfilling middle-class male roles. Ryder calls these variables "potency" and "impulse control"; the former term is a bit misleading because it refers not to sexual performance but to some combination of occupational success, intelligence, and personal dynamism.

The women seemed to differ from each other in terms of their dependency, their attitudes toward sex, and their investment in marriage — the extent to which the wife's interests and satisfactions are bound up in the marriage. (It seems odd that the women differed from each other on this, but not the men.)

Let us look at some of the twenty-one types of marriages that emerged from this analysis. One recurrent pattern is called "competent husband/incompetent wife":

. . . The husband is said to be highly intelligent, capable, planful, ambitious, but not very colorful, who is married to a woman seen by both of them as inferior: less organized, less attractive, unintelligent, etc. The wife wants and gets frequent reassurances that she is not worthless or unloved; but even with these reassurances the wife may feel that if she were more worthwhile her husband would be more attentive. . . . (Ryder, 1970b, p. 389–390)

This pattern seems to have validity as a description of some marriages (I have encountered quite a few couples like this among the Institute of Human Development sample). It's surprising though that Ryder found this pattern among fairly young couples whom one might have expected to start out

their marriages more nearly equal to each other in competence. The IHD sample is in their forties and fifties, and the
competent husband/incompetent wife pattern seems to
occur more often in that group of couples where the husband
has been very successful in business and the wife has had
no career or major interest outside the roles of wife and
mother.

A variation of this pattern, called "stern husband,"
differs from the first in that the husband does not reassure
his wife:

. . . They are more ostentatiously "masculine," i.e., stern, hard,
unfeeling, and may find it desirable to be deliberately unkind or
unsympathetic to their wives' distress. The wife . . . cries more
and is more depressed than in the preceding pattern. . . . Further,
she may have some private sorrow about which she cannot speak
to her husband, since he would take it to be a sign of weakness. . . .
(Ryder, 1970b, p. 392)

Another type of marriage in which the husband rates
high on the "potency" dimension is called "husband negative about children." The husband is not really impulsive in
the sense that he can't or doesn't control his impulses and
feelings or isn't dependable, but he is not as tightly controlled—uptight, some would say—as the previous types:

These husbands . . . tend to be exciting and active in physical ways. They may swim, boat, engage in contact sports, enjoy
sports cars (and perhaps sell them). There is a fun emphasis, particularly on the part of the husband. He was not eager to acquire
the restrictions of being married, and is less eager to be further
restricted by having children. The wife may feel neglected, but
wants to participate in her husband's active life (Ryder, 1970b,
p. 393)

There turned out to be more types of marriages in which
the husband rated low on the "potency" dimension than
ones in which he was both occupationally ambitious or successful and had a strong personality:

[These] husbands may be hard-working and ambitious, but their
most salient characteristic is that they are, in a word, dull. . . .
(p. 394)

One such type is called "second-choice husband." In this
pattern the wife had lived an adventurous, sexually free life
while single. Then, for some reason, perhaps pregnancy or
an unhappy love affair,

she lowers her sights to select a sturdy, responsible, dependable husband, who is probably thought physically unattractive. The wife is pretty, impulsive, competitive with other women, and not very sexually interested in her husband. (p. 396)

Most of the types of marriages in which the husband rates low in "potency" differ from each other in terms of the wife's characteristics, her dependency, whether or not she enjoys sex, and how much her marriage is a consuming part of her life. One type of couple in which the wife has what Ryder calls a "non-marriage orientation" is named "easy wife":

A wife in this group likes the feeling of having men interested and attentive to her and is perfectly willing to go to bed with them. The husband may be considered unexciting or dull, but is valued as a secure home base. The other men involved are for that matter not thought to be unusually wonderful. In the clearest case of this pattern the wife consciously intended to move from one affair to another from time to time, for as many years as she could manage it. (pp. 397–398)

We shall not describe all of the twenty-one types; there are several types in which, as Ryder saw it, the wife "pushes the husband around in various ways"; in another group of marriages the husband is violent, or footloose and irresponsible. In one rather large group, called "lonely spouses," both husband and wife have tended to have had lonely, frustrating lives, including job failures, mental hospitalization, suicide attempts, and so on. Very little interaction occurs between the spouses, but what does occur is positive.

At the very least this catalog of couples makes interesting reading, and seems to resemble couples that one encounters in real life. There are other types of marriages that did not seem to get into this catalog—marriages in which the couples are more nearly equal in competence and dependency, or the "intrinsic" or "total" kinds of relationships found by Cuber and Harroff. All of the twenty-one types of couples seem to be described in terms of some weakness or inadequacy, as if in trying to avoid the "happy marriage" concept Ryder leaned over backward and considered all marriages as bizarre in one way or another. Actually, Ryder found he couldn't classify about one-third of the couples because they seemed to be "unique."

The task of making sense, scientifically, out of marriage as a phenomenon is an elusive one. It is difficult to point to a piece of marriage research that has the theoretical elegance or predictive value of some of the best studies in individual psychology, or the other branches of sociology. The foregoing typological studies are certainly inelegant and difficult to use for predicting anything, but at least they describe couples, rather than fitting marriages into an abstract, unidimensional scheme.

New Styles of Marriage

As we noted in the introduction to this chapter, the downgrading of marriage has a long history. Furthermore, there has always been deviance from the prevailing ideal norms of marital life. What is novel about the present discontent about marriage is that it questions the institution itself. Previously, no matter how much people griped about the problems of married life, or how much their own behavior departed from the prescribed norms, they tended to take marriage for granted as an ideal and as a fact of life. Today, however, respectable professionals in family counseling, clinical psychology, and other fields are seriously proposing as valid forms of marriage such arrangements as group marriage, polygamy, polyandry, voluntary nonlegal unions, marriages based on the mutual freedom of spouses to have extramarital sex, temporary marriage, and so forth (see Otto, 1970).

Before we proceed to examine some of these proposals for alternative forms of marriage, two points should be kept in mind. The first is that most if not all of these forms already exist and have done so for some time. The aim of the people who argue for them is that these alternative life styles should be rationalized, and made responsible and respectable. That is, both society and the concerned people themselves should see their ways of living as valid rather than abnormal or illegal (laws should be changed), and should be aware that each variant form of marriage involves rights, costs and benefits, and obligations, just as regular marriage does. Thus the proposals we shall be discussing were for the most part put forth in the name of morality and ethics, rather than being primarily amoral or hedonistic.

The second point to remember is that the current ferment with regard to marriage comes directly after a period in which marriage was more a universal norm in society than it had ever been previously. During the 1950's and 1960's only a few people out of every hundred never married. This was not true of earlier generations of Americans. David Riesman once compared his mother's generation to that of his daughter (his mother had graduated from Bryn Mawr in 1903):

> In my mother's generation, the nun who chose a vocation or the school teacher or librarian who, whether by choice or not, remained a spinster, was not made to feel that there was something monstrous and unnatural about her life; such women were often extremely spirited and lacking in any feeling of deprivation. Today, even a bachelor, let alone a spinster, is made to feel that there is something wrong with him, and it is a rare person who does not internalize this feeling and who does not become defensive about it. Partly, this reflects the sheer demographic fact that 94% of all women will be married before age 40—an incomparably higher proportion than ever before; a very different situation from earlier America or a country like Ireland, where even today marriage is still often late and not a near-unanimous choice. (Riesman, 1964, p. 722)

Riesman was writing in the early sixties; since then the single life has once again begun to seem a viable alternative to married life, especially when lived episodically—i.e., between marriages. Although several years ago singleness meant only the negative condition of not being married, today the unmarried person has two positive images of his status—that of the fun-loving swinger or the political rebel.

But the intense pressures toward marriage that lasted for at least two decades, resulting in the marriages of many people who might otherwise have preferred to be single, or who might have married more wisely if they hadn't felt pressed, combined with the belief that the purpose of marriage was to make the spouses happy, resulted in strains in the institution of marriage. The proposals for alternative forms of marriage are one response to these strains.

Conventional marriage is based on the model of a life-long, monogamous union. The alternative marital forms change either the temporal or the monogamous aspect of the conventional pattern, or both. Perhaps the oldest proposal for revising marriage, and the closest to current marital realities, is Bertrand Russell's model presented in *Marriage and Morals* in 1929. Although his ideas seem rather tame in the light of today's freedom of expression and behavior in such matters, Russell's book caused a major scandal—the notoriety cost him a teaching position at the City College of New York. Russell had suggested that husbands and wives, over the course of married life, would tend to develop strong ties of affection and companionship, but that their sexual interest in each other might wane, only to be rekindled by others. Russell believed that in most cases marriage should be for a lifetime, but he did not think it should exclude sex relations with others.

A rather different variation from the conventional pattern is the idea of the temporary marriage, which may or may not be monogamous while it lasts. A version of this type of union is Margaret Mead's notion of two-step marriage (1966). She argues that there ought to be two types of marriage contract—individual marriage and parental marriage. The first type corresponds to what others have called companionate or trial marriage; it aims to give the two partners a chance to really get to know each other in order to find out whether they want to go on to the more serious and hopefully more permanent commitment of having a child together. Mead sees students and young people in general as the prime participants in individual marriage, but people of any age could have that type of marriage if they couldn't or didn't want to have children. But she emphasizes individual marriage for young people. She argues that young people on the one hand need the opportunity to experience intimacy, both sexually and personally. On the other hand, their inexperience makes it unlikely that they will be able to choose a partner for a lifetime commitment. Thus the main purpose of the individual marriage is for two people to get to know each other; it would not include having children.

If the friendship between the couple did not work out, they could part with no great trauma or stamp of failure. If the individual marriage did work, then the partners might decide they wanted to go on to the parental marriage and have children. Divorce would not be ruled out in the parental marriage, but it would be much harder and slower than in the individual marriage. The expectation would be, however, for parental marriage to be a lifetime commitment.

Something resembling this scheme has come to be a familiar pattern in middle-class circles, without the legal paraphernalia of formal marriage contracts. Many young people in their twenties, particularly those who have gone or could have gone to "the best" colleges, are in "living together" arrangements. Many of the new styles of wedding ceremony represent the legal certification of a couple that is already married in every other sense; the decision to get married on the part of a couple already living together is something like the parental marriage just described.

An alternative marriage system of even greater freedom and fewer specific prescriptions for behavior has been presented by the sociologist John Cuber. The basic features of this system include:

Pairings of the socially and physically mature . . . would be permitted at any time at the mutual consent of the partners. . . . Whenever such pairs should desire to make public acknowledgement of their relationship, probably called "marriage," they would be free to do so with any kind of religious or civil ceremonies they might desire.

Prior to marriage or in the absence of it, couples would be expected to practice contraception and would be expected to limit their childbearing to the married stage. . . . No suppositions are made regarding the permanence of marriage, but the pair having children would be presumed to be responsible for the maintenance of their children. . . . Termination of marriage would be by mutual consent . . . whenever *either* wished dissolution.

Married pairs could maintain any of a variety of domicile arrangements. Something resembling the present nuclear family would, of course, be permitted but not regulated. The pair might live separately from one another or together and separately from their children. Whatever course chosen, however, would necessarily impose responsibilities and could be changed if and when so desired. Since the responsibility for rearing and socializing children would be shared by parents and state, there would need to be provisions for more institutional and state participation in the socializing process. (Cuber, 1970, pp 19–20)

A still more unusual alternative to marriage is presented by Shulamith Firestone (1970, pp. 332–337), the feminist writer we discussed earlier. In her scenario, set in a future time when automation will have produced abundance and leisure for all, and reproduction will be via test tube, there is no place for the conventional marriage or nuclear family. The living-together arrangement is the standard unit in which most people would live most of their lives. But there would also be special professions for single people—glamorous, all-consuming occupations such as astronaut, open to both sexes. (She points out that there have been male roles where there was no stigma attached to being single, but no comparable women's roles, except those defined by sexuality, such as nun or prostitute.)

The most radical feature of this scheme is the provision for child rearing. In the ultimate version of this system, natural reproduction would have been replaced by the artificial, test-tube method, but even before that children would be brought up in households of about ten to fifteen people who agree to stay together for about seven to ten years, or whatever was decided to be the minimum time needed to provide the children with a stable situation in which to grow up. The household, then, becomes the substitute for the parental family, although it may not include children. Another important feature of this scheme is the complete social equality of women and children, made possible by a guaranteed income for all individuals.

The Free Couple   The common denominator of most of the new forms of marriage is simply the couple who lives together without the legal certification and the set of obligations and responsibilities of conventional marriage. As we noted earlier, this form of relationship has long flourished outside the middle classes—among the poor and among bohemian artists and intellectuals.

Probably the most famous example of this type of couple is Simone de Beauvoir and Jean-Paul Sartre. We will approach the discussion of this type of arrangement by using what they and others have written of their experience. There are several reasons for doing so. The first, and least important reason, is that they are world-famous figures—he as philosopher, playwright, novelist, and political activist, and she primarily as a writer and intellectual. More important, Simone de Beauvoir has been concerned over her lifetime with the problems of women on three levels; her two-volume work, *The Second Sex,* on the history and cultural situation of women, is regarded as a classic of world literature. Furthermore, in her own life and particularly in her relation with Sartre, she has tried to provide a living example of a solution to the predicament of women in contemporary society.

Their relationship is like a two-person experimental community. Finally, she has written of her own experiences as a woman and as a French intellectual in the form of a running autobiography of her life, in such works as *Memoirs of a Dutiful Daughter, The Prime of Life, Force of Circumstance*, etc.

The Beauvoir-Sartre relationship has been discussed by European intellectuals with the same seriousness as have their written ideas. Such questions as "Have they made a success of their relationship?," "How well do they get on with each other?," and "What is their sex life like?" are not mere gossip—although there is of course a certain amount of titillation in discussing such items—but have a serious political content: Is this kind of relationship the solution to the problem of women's oppression? Would a failure in the Beauvoir-Sartre relationship, say in dealing with jealousy, have significance only for them, or would it mean that this form of relationship is basically flawed? There has been a tendency to seize on statements of one or the other member of the couple concerning some problem or other as an indication that the experiment has been a failure. This may reflect only the common bias in looking at variant forms of the family; when something goes wrong in an alternative type of family—this is especially true of communes—we tend to locate the source of trouble in that form of the family, rather than in the individuals. By contrast, when difficulty occurs in a marriage, our first reaction is to see the individual personalities as the source of the problem.

Nevertheless, valid questions can be asked about the Beauvoir-Sartre relationship in itself and as a model for other couples to follow. In a discussion of their relationship, particularly as a solution to the woman problem (which is of course really a man problem, just as the race issue is really a white problem), Albert Memmi (1968) raises the question: How much can you take away from the couple relationship and still have a couple? Or to put it another way: What is the essential bond between a man and a woman in the absence of the legal contract of marriage? How free can a couple be and still be a couple?

We have seen in the schemes cited earlier that the free couple may or may not decide to be monogamous, although some writers on the subject would feel that in a relationship based only on the desire of the two people to be together there would be no reason for the partners to have sex elsewhere. The Beauvoir-Sartre relationship was not committed to monogamy, nor to having children, nor to living together. Further, each has been financially well-off independent of the other, so that their relationship did not include an economic partnership. In their own eyes, nevertheless, they have always been a couple.

A dilemma implicit in any couple relationship—most obvious in legal marriage but not eliminated in a "free couple"—is the tension between commitment and freedom:

> When a man and a woman decide their association should be solemnized by a marriage ceremony, they pose themselves a problem which will continue through the marriage: Now that they are married, are they staying together because they wish to or because they must? The inevitable conflicts which arise in a marriage occur within a framework of a more or less voluntary relationship. It is not so much whether marriage *is* a compulsory or a voluntary relationship, but how the couple choose to define it. A woman may, for example, wish to stay with her husband but be unwilling to concede that her choice is voluntary and so say that they cannot separate for religious reasons. Another wife might insist that she could leave her husband at any time, defining the relationship as voluntary, although her history would indicate that she has a rather desperate need of him and could not leave him. (Haley, 1963, p. 119)

The free couple has the same problem without the religious and legal element. For example, are they staying together because they said they would, or for convenience, or do they still want to be together as much as they did in the first place? But the free couple has the opposite problem as well, which also arises out of the tension between commitment and freedom. That is, is my partner going off without me or sleeping with that other person because he or she is exercising the right to freedom I happily granted, or because he or she is tired of me and really wants to leave me or be a couple with that other person? If boredom and the feeling of compulsion are the occupational hazards of marriage, the corresponding hazards of the free couple are insecurity and jealousy.

A *New Yorker* short story (A. Adams, 1971) portrays the insecurity dilemma neatly. A young woman is living with a young man in San Francisco. He has moved into her apartment with some of his belongings. They have never made clear exactly what their commitment is to each other, except that they are both to be very cool and free. Usually he comes for supper, which she cooks and cleans up after, but if he doesn't come he usually calls to let her know that he won't. He has let it be known, however, that he doesn't want to be held to account if he just doesn't show up. One day she returns home from work and finds a fur rug, his most prized possession, missing. This is where the story begins. Not knowing whether he has taken the rug to the cleaners or moved out of her life, she becomes upset with uncertainty and sense of loss. Finally, after a long period of brooding, he calls and it turns out to her great relief that the rug has been "ripped off" — the title of the story — a possibility which hadn't occurred to her. The story ends with everything as it was before, except for the disturbing insight she got into the uncertainties of her relationship. The title seems to have two meanings.

The commitment problem among living-together couples has recently been documented in a study comparing eighteen such couples with thirty-one "going steady" couples in a college community (Lyness, Lipetz, and Davis, 1972). Among the going-together couples, commitments to marriage were equal in both partners; among the living-together couples, however, the women were almost as committed to marriage as the more conventional going-together women, but their male partners were not. Only three of the eighteen men voiced any marital commitment. On the other hand, couples in both groups were equally happy and emotionally involved in their relationships. Depending on one's assumption, these results can be interpreted as showing the immaturity and exploitiveness of the living-together men, the insecurity and unliberatedness of the living-together women, or a realistic assessment on the part of these women that marriage offers certain advantages in a sexist society.

The Green-Eyed Monster   Insecurity often takes the form of jealousy. Bertrand Russell writes of jealousy as something rather easily controlled if it is recognized as bad, rather than as the expression of a just moral indignation. Memmi writes that "The great minds of left and right agree that jealousy is an outmoded emotion" (1968, p. 148). Yet for many people it just isn't as easy as that. It is difficult to imagine a firmer intellectual commitment to the total liberty of each partner than that of Beauvoir and Sartre. Yet she suffered during his liaisons with others. For example:

I often wondered if he did not care more for M than for me . . . According to what he told me, M shared completely in his reactions, his emotions, his desires. . . . Was this perhaps the sign of a profound harmony between them—a harmony at the very well-spring of life, present in the rhythm of its ebb and flow—that Sartre did not sense with me, and which was more precious to him than our understanding? (Beauvoir, 1968, p. 147)

We do not know Sartre's feelings in these matters, since he has not chronicled the relationship as has Simone de Beauvoir, but Memmi writes that jealousy was not absent from his side either. The general cultural belief is that men are more prone to jealousy than women, and that it is harder for men to take their woman being with another man than vice versa. The reasons for this are usually thought to arise from the concept of the woman as the sexual property of her man, and the notion that woman should be sexually pure. But there are other instances of men without commitments to such reactionary notions who still suffer pangs of jealousy when their women enter liaisons with others. A fictional example is the revolutionary hero in Malraux's *Man's Fate,* who on the eve of the Shanghai uprising is devastated to learn from his wife of her fleeting affair with a colleague of hers. Jan Myrdal, the son of the famous Swedish sociologist, and a radical, writes in his autobiography of a fateful quarrel with the young woman he had been living with. He finds a letter in her coat pocket from a lover. He himself is also having an affair with someone else, but this does not prevent him from being overwhelmed by jealousy:

I read the letter. I find it strange that such a letter—I myself have also written them—has such a totally different effect when you yourself are neither sender nor receiver but only the third party. It would be sane and reasonable to put it back again in its envelope and stick the envelope back in the pocket. Reasonable and calm . . . But I don't do so. I know that I won't do it. Anyway, everything is unavoidable . . . I will stage a scene of jealousy. The consciousness of this disgusts me.

. . . I stand for a couple of seconds in the hall before I enter the room. Beforehand I experience all that is going to happen. Once more I think: if I were really rational I would shut off all emotions, take a deep breath and walk into the room and take a cup of coffee with her. But it is impossible, I am in a state of emotional tension. I observe my pulse, it is quickening, my mouth has become dry . . . I am *cocu*. Swindled, betrayed. (Myrdal, 1968, pp. 157–158)

In the scene that follows, he says to "A," the young woman,

I don't mind being swindled . . . But God damn me, I dislike being exploited. This office work, this home was a self-imposed bondage. A yoke I bore. But I am not giving up my freedom to support your lovers. (1968, p. 159)

He is referring to having taken a regular job and fixing up the apartment after A came to live with him. This is what arouses his sense of betrayal; his own infidelity is emotionally irrelevant. Myrdal and A separate at this point, and she later commits suicide in the apartment. He continues to be haunted by the scene of her suicide and the above quarrel, which he always saw as morally unjustified, even while it was going on.

A peculiarity about the psychology of jealousy and betrayal comes through clearly in the passage cited above. There is often a lack of parity in the perception of each member of a couple about the relations of each with another party. That is, consider any couple A and B (these could also be close friends of the same sex): A may feel that he can enter into a relationship with a third party X without taking away anything from his relationship with B; he may well even feel that he can love X without reducing his love for B. The relationship between A and X looks very different from B's point of view, however. No matter how uninvolved this relationship may be, it is likely to be magnified in B's perspective. And the same is true for a relationship between B and another person from A's viewpoint.

Carl Rogers presents a clinical case study showing these mechanisms in action. He describes how a sexually liberated couple returned to monogamy as a way of resolving conflicts over jealousy and openness. Both partners had love affairs with others, and each was willing to accept the other's outside relationships. But it turned out that this willingness was more intellectual than emotional:

Eric experiences a full measure of primitive jealousy when he knows she is having sexual relationships with another man. And Denise, though ashamed of her feeling, is hurt when he is sexually involved with another woman, a hurt she feels even though she has been similarly involved with other men. . . .

So they have come to a somewhat peculiar accommodation. If either feels such attraction to another person that he/she wants it to come to a climax in a sexual relationship, so be it. But they will keep these matters private from each other, simply because openness brings too much pain and hurt. But since they are accustomed to an astonishing degree of complete openness with each other, such deceit does not come easily and the result is to make them monogamous! (Rogers, 1972, pp. 195–196)

Oddly enough, sexual jealousy does not appear to have been studied systematically by any psychologist. In the indices of the five volumes of the *Handbook of Social Psychology* there are three references to jealousy, none of which refers to an empirical study (Lindzey and Aronson, 1968).

Anthropologists have had more to say about sexual jealousy than the psychologists. William Stephens (1963) observes that though there seems to be great variation in the jealousy potential of different societies and social arrangements, in no society is jealousy completely absent or incomprehensible. The peoples with the least amount of jealousy live in polyandrous societies — those very rare cultures in which a woman can have several husbands at the same time. Usually the cohusbands are brothers or other relatives. Polyandrous societies tend to be sexually free, the most extreme instance, according to Stephens, being the Marquesans of the South Pacific. There the children and adolescents had free access to sex, and adults were permitted to have extramarital liaisons, ritual orgies, and public intercourse. (The past tense is used because the Marquesans are no longer as they were due to Western influences.) Yet even in polyandrous societies, some husbands experience jealousy and some do not.

One reason for the absence of extreme jealousy in polyandrous groups, according to Stephens, is the fact that husbands are given some say in whether the wife will take a cohusband and, further, there is usually an economic benefit in bringing another man into the household. Although men's feelings in polyandrous societies are spared, women's feelings in polygynous societies are not. Stephens writes that in most cases where men can take several wives, at least some of the wives suffer intensely from jealousy, and many polygynous families are strife-torn. Again, there is a great deal of individual variation.

The final kind of situation Stephens discusses in relation to the jealousy issue is that of permitted adultery. In the most extreme instance, among the Lesu, another Pacific people, adultery is institutionalized. A woman's lover gives her gifts — *tsera* — which are to be passed along to the husband. Stephens writes:

> It is interesting that in some of these societies which allow adultery, the jealousy problem still exists; some people are still hurt when their spouses engage in perfectly proper and virtuous adultery. In Lesu, says Powdermaker, "Some men are jealous, and some are not. Some men gladly accept the *tsera* from their wives, who have received it from their lovers, and there is no rift in the family. However, others, who are the exceptions rather than the rule, instead of taking the *tsera* fight the wife's lover. There is the same difference in the woman's attitude towards her husband's mistresses." . . .
>
>   . . . Among the Kaingang, according to Henry, people are sexually promiscuous; yet they still wish — rather pathetically — for marital fidelity. . . . (Stephens, 1963, pp. 252–253)

The societies with the most extreme expression of jealousy are those Latin cultures where the ideals of machismo prevail. In Tepoztlan, Mexico, for example, husbands try to prove their virility by seducing other men's wives, but worry obsessively about other men seducing theirs (in Stephens, 1963, p. 253). And in the United States there has been something called "the unwritten law": if an irate spouse, especially a husband, were to shoot his wife's lover, a jury would be likely to let him off.

So the emotion of jealousy seems to be a human trait that transcends cultural differences. The culture seems to determine whether the feeling of jealousy should be amplified — that is, expressed in words or action — or suppressed, but the culture doesn't seem to put the idea of being jealous into people's heads in the first place. Thus the idea that jealousy stems from Western concepts of private property, or Christianity, or monogamy, seems not to be true.

It would certainly be interesting to know what personality and situational factors give rise to greater and lesser degrees of jealousy. There are reports in the literature of couples who are able to maintain a close relationship with each other and tolerate affairs on the part of each other. Cuber and Harroff, for example, write that the couples they put in the "vital" category — as couples, that is, not necessarily as individuals — are sometimes adulterous.

To some of them, sexual aggrandizement is a way of life. Frequently the infidelity is condoned by the partner and in some instances even provides an indirect (through empathy) kind of gratification. The act of infidelity in such cases is not construed as disloyalty or as a threat to continuity, but rather as a basic human right which the loved one ought to be permitted to have—and which the other perhaps wants also for himself. (Cuber and Harroff, 1965, p. 63)

But Cuber and Harroff state that adultery does not take place in the "total" type of relationship. It would be interesting to know why the belief in sexual freedom leads to an absence of or control over jealousy in some cases and fails to do so in others.

Another context in which jealousy appears to be controlled is in "swinging" groups, or mate-swappers. These couples are said to control their jealousy, however, by submitting their behavior to strict rules—for example, not engaging in certain sexual practices with others, not meeting sex partners outside the group setting, and so on. In effect, each spouse has veto power over the sexual behavior of the other.

Why should jealousy be such a deeply rooted—and hard to control—emotion? Two hypotheses suggest themselves; one is psychological, the other sociological. The psychological explanation would trace jealousy back to infancy and the nearly universal fact that infants are nurtured by, and form a primary attachment to, one person. An intimate attachment to someone later in life may bring back some of the earlier feelings—the sense of dependency and the wish to be the exclusive recipient of the loved one's love. Thus jealousy in adult life might be the equivalent of sibling rivalry in childhood. There is some recognition of this in the often-heard advice to parents about what to say when a new baby is brought home. The parent is told not to tell the older child "We love you so much we decided to have another baby." How would the parent feel if his or her spouse came home and said "I love you so much I decided to have another one just like you"?

The sociological explanation of jealousy is based not on individual emotions but on the structural properties of the two-person group. Georg Simmel (1950) pointed out that the dyad differs from groups of all other sizes from three on up in a fundamental way. In groups larger than two a sense of groupness exists apart from the individual members. Even in a triad, for example, one person can leave and there is still the sense of a group carried on by the other two people. But in a dyad there is no group independent of the two people. If one person leaves or dies, that is the end of the relationship:

. . . The difference between the dyad and larger groups consists in the fact that the dyad has a different relation to each of its two elements than have larger groups to *their* members. Although, for the outsider, the group consisting of two may function as an autonomous, super-individual unit, it usually does not do so for its participants. Rather, each of the two feels himself confronted only by the other, not by a collectivity above him. The social structure here rests immediately on the one and the other of the two, and the secession of either would destroy the whole. (Simmel, 1950, p. 123)

Thus, argues Simmel, the peculiar properties of the dyad make it the most intimate of groups, and hence the most vulnerable to jealousy. The addition of a third party to a two-person group results in a very different social structure and changes the relationship between the original two. Where there was a relationship only between person A and person B, now there are three dyads: A and B, B and C, and A and C. This complication results in a certain instability:

No matter how close a triad may be, there is always the occasion on which two of the three members regard the third as an intruder. The reason may be the mere fact he shares in certain moods that can unfold in all their intensity and tenderness only when two can meet without distraction: the sensitive union of two is always irritated by the spectator. It may also be noted how extraordinarily difficult and rare it is for three people to attain a really uniform mood—when visiting a museum, for instance, or looking at a landscape—and how much more easily such a mood emerges between two. (Simmel, 1950, pp. 135–136)

Simmel's analysis of dyads and triads does not apply only to face-to-face interaction: the third party, obviously, need not be present to disrupt the relations of a dyad. Nor, it should be emphasized, does the analysis apply only to heterosexual couples: Simmel applies it to parents and children, friends, and even political parties.

The Equal Couple   There is some danger that we have over-emphasized sexuality as a disruptive force. As we mentioned earlier, the increased sexual consciousness of the present moment in the United States and elsewhere may well be a product of the transition between a puritanical sexual ethic and a more relaxed one. Once we have all recovered from puritanism and the rebound from it, preoccupation with sexuality will likely recede. Some evidence for this can be found in the experience of the Scandinavian countries. Many people are not tempted to go beyond whatever commitments they have made, or find controlling temptation relatively easy. But controlling sexuality seems to be more difficult in actuality than in theory, and much of the instability of communal life can be attributed to hard feelings stirred up by sexual struggles of one kind or another.

Another leading cause of trouble in communes, and in nuclear-family households, is housework. There is often, in fact, a sort of trade-off or exchange between sexuality and housework. We saw in a preceding example how Jan Myrdal felt betrayed when he found out about his lover's affair partly because he had tried hard to fix up his apartment to please her. Recently, a lawyer described a sort of agreement common at the turn of the century between spouses who decide to go back again after a separation: he agrees to quit fooling around with other women; she agrees to keep the house clean.

In communes there is often a conflict between the hang-loose-everybody-do-his-own-thing ethic and the likelihood that housework will turn out to be nobody's thing. A novel method for dealing with one part of the problem, dirty dishes, is the everybody-do-his-own-plus-one-more principle. In San Francisco recently, plans for a new communal residence in the city were announced; the housework problem would be eliminated in the traditional middle-class way by hiring outside help.

The problem of housework is the sore point in women's liberation. The reform of women doing men's work and receiving equal pay for it is much more easily accomplished than the corresponding reform of men doing the jobs traditionally reserved for women. The clearest evidence of this is in the experience of the Soviet Union. In spite of great occupational equality, numerous studies have shown that Soviet women who work do as much housework as those who do not, regardless of whether they are professional or unskilled workers. There is no class of domestics and Soviet men do not share in the housework. The result is that Soviet women work extremely long hours. The same tends to be true of the United States as well, except that middle-class working women are able to "buy back" their time by hiring maids (Poloma and Garland, 1971).

Housework is a curious thing; it is at the same time vitally necessary, socially devalued, and invisible when done well. Simone de Beauvoir, commenting on the frustrations of the housewife's role, notes how a clean, well-ordered house looks normal and unexceptional. Most people do not see such a state of order as a product of good workmanship or hard effort. Disorder, such as dirty dishes in the sink or clothing on the floor, *is* noticeable, however. In the same way, shopping for and putting away of groceries is not noticed if the pantry and refrigerator are full of the family's needs. On the other hand, if something is missing when the husband or children look for it, then complaints are heard. The most dramatic evidence of the invisible work that goes into the running of a household occurs when the wife gets sick, particularly if there are children:

It is interesting to watch the differences in family behavior depending on which mate is sick. When the husband is sick, everything in the house can go on as usual except for his disrupting demands. . . . However, when the wife becomes sick, family life usually undergoes a shocking rearrangement. The proverb states, "Many a fallen woman has been forgiven, but never for falling ill." Husbands frequently discover this for the first time at the birth of the first child, but the strain is even greater when there are already young children. Suddenly the husband has to do everything. Child care has to be provided first. Meals have to be prepared. Groceries have to be bought, dishes done, beds made, pets fed, bills paid, and all this must be added to the husband's employment schedule. Many families will have a hard time, feeling "It was a dirty trick for mother to get sick and leave us all in the lurch." (Udry, 1971, p. 370)

One of the major complaints of the women's liberation movement is precisely this role of taken-for-granted family servant. Although some young women feel that the servility of the wife can never be overcome in marriage and therefore do not wish to marry, probably a larger proportion of young women affiliated with the movement feel that it is possible to work out an equal division of labor in marriage. Equality in marriage, however, seems to be as full of pitfalls on the way to achievement as racial equality, and for similar reasons. Cultural traditions and the allocation of rights, privileges, and obligations are not easily overcome. For one thing, the man's work must be redefined as a privilege that does not relieve him of household responsibilities, rather than as something that he does in exchange for the wife's shouldering the burden.

One such marital arrangement was described by Alix Shulman (1970). During the early days of the marriage, she writes, she and her husband both worked. They went out a lot and did the minimal household chores together, mostly on weekends. The arrival of two children drastically changed their roles. They moved to a larger apartment, and the amount of housework increased enormously. She had quit her job to stay home, and her husband had to work longer hours to support the family. When she revealed how dissatisfied she was, her husband agreed to participate in the child care and housework. They tried to recreate the equality that had prevailed during the first days of their marriage. But when the agreement was informal and verbal, she writes, they kept slipping back into their old division of labor. Ultimately, they resorted to a formal written agreement, including a detailed breakdown of the jobs that had to be done, and the periods for which each spouse had to be responsible, so that each would end up with 50 percent of the responsibility. Perhaps the most striking aspect of this contract, aside from its businesslike breakdown of the minutia of domestic life—e.g., "Item: Nighttime: getting children to take baths, brush their teeth, go to bed . . . reading with them, tucking them in and having night-talks . . ."—is the redefinition of the husband's career as a personal privilege, rather than family duty:

> We reject the notion that the work which brings in more money is more valuable. The ability to earn more money is already a privilege which must not be compounded by enabling the larger earner to buy out of his or her duties and put the burden on the one who earns less, or on someone hired from the outside.
>
> We believe that each member of the family has an equal right to his/her own time, work, values, choices. As long as all duties are performed, each person may use his or her extra time any way

he/she chooses. If he/she wants to use it making money, fine. If he/she wants to spend it with spouse, fine. If not, fine. (Shulman, 1970, p. 6)

Probably the idea of negotiated contracts between husbands and wives seems, to most readers, an intrusion of business practices into an intimate relationship. Yet it is not only women's liberationists who have argued for such explicit bargaining; some marriage counselors have advocated this approach to dealing with the nitty-gritty conflicts of daily life.

"Equal" marriage, however, does not escape the interactional pitfalls of marriage in general. Earlier we noted the problem of the young woman whose husband agreed to take over half the burden of child care — the better he carried out his promise, the more displaced she felt. Different problems arose in this marriage in connection with housework. On the one hand, due to cultural conditioning, an equal division of labor was impossible; this was especially so at the level of keeping track of what needed to be done. The wife could not help keeping a running record of such things as when the laundry needed to be done, and there was no way of getting her husband to do this, although he was quite willing to do his share of the tasks themselves. In spite of the lack of true equality from the wife's point of view, however, the outside world saw her husband as a paragon of husbandly helpfulness. Thus the whole concept of "helping" represents only a more liberal form of the old unequal division of labor.

Family Power and Decision Making

Most textbooks on the family and marriage have a chapter or section on family power. There are descriptions of many studies which have asked: Who is dominant in this family, husband or wife? Who makes the major decisions? These studies suffer from an overemphasis on interpersonal relations and too little attention to how family power relations are influenced by outside social factors.

The studies of family power suffer from another important limitation: they assume that power is a single dimension along which all families can be arranged, with husband-dominant families at one end, egalitarian families in the middle, and wife-dominant families on the opposite end.

They further assume that all family members are aware of the family power structure, and agree on their perception. Further, most such studies assume that where a family belongs on the line can be learned simply by asking one family member, usually the wife. All these assumptions are probably wrong. For example, if a group of Americans is asked who makes the decisions in their family, the husband, the wife, or both equally, most of them will say decisions are equal; the next largest group will say the husband is dominant; and very few are likely to accord the wife the dominant position. The best interpretation of these data is that they reflect more about values, either egalitarian or traditional, than the realities of family life.

The systems approach to the family suggests that the "official" boss in a family may not be the one who controls what goes on. Haley (1963) gives the case of a woman married to a tyrannical husband of the old-school German type. He insisted on having his own way promptly, and generally being the master of the house. His wife was thoroughly intimidated and unable to oppose him. She developed a psychiatric symptom, however, which enabled her to refuse to do anything her husband suggested. It was a severe handwashing compulsion that prevented her from doing housework or going anyplace with her husband that might be "contaminated." As Haley puts it, the husband was "dethroned by the simple washing of a pair of hands." Who should receive the rating of the most powerful or influential in that family?

In a review of studies of family power over the last decade, the reviewer came to the conclusion that the issue was much more complicated than most of the studies seemed to assume (Safilios-Rothschild, 1970). The concept of power has many facets to it, and one is not a purer measure of family power than any other. The tyrannical husband in the preceding anecdote had a certain kind of power and authority as the titular head of the family, but the wife's control over what actually went on in the household was also a kind of power. The spouse who has more sex appeal, the spouse who is more independent, the spouse who is more violent, all have a different kind of power that may or may not come into play in a particular decision. In some families power struggles may be an important theme that goes on from day to day.

In others the issue of power may simply be irrelevant. Ryder notes:

> Careful attention to actual conversations between husbands and wives quickly reveals the arbitrary nature of a dominance ranking. For example, does power reside in the person who wins in a disagreement, or in the person who decides who wins, or in the person who decides who decides? In dyadic (or higher order) interaction, power does not necessarily reside with anyone; the interactional system may just operate as a system. (Ryder, 1970a, p. 52)

A more basic problem with the studies of family power is that they tend to perpetuate the myth that the American family is egalitarian or even wife-dominated despite research evidence to the contrary:

> Neither decision-making nor the division of labor in the family (even among middle-class spouses) has been found to be equalitarian, nor has the conception of marital roles by married people been reported as companionate or equal in any sense. (Safilios-Rothschild, 1972, p. 64)

The same author notes a tendency on the part of researchers to conclude that the family is equal, when in fact their own data indicate a strong tendency toward husband dominance (1972, p. 68).

How is it, in view of the biases and discrimination against women that have been brought to light by the women's liberation movement, that the belief in female domination has been so persistent? The belief is found not only in the sociological studies of family power, but in antimarriage humor and in psychiatric and literary works dealing with the predations of "Mom" and castrating bitches such as the wife in *Who's Afraid of Virginia Woolf?* The literature of psychiatry often describes a family constellation consisting of an aggressive, domineering, seductive mother, who subtly or not so subtly disparages her weak, passive husband. This constellation has been reported in the families of college dropouts, schizophrenics, alienated youth, homosexuals, and alcoholics. As one psychiatrist puts it, it is "the ultimate psychoanalytic banality explaining everything from schizophrenia to ingrown toenails" (Levenson, 1972, p. 73).

The belief in the smothering yet rejecting mother and the castrating, domineering wife runs deep in our culture.

How can we reconcile the women's liberation view with this? There seem to be several answers: first of all, the beliefs in female power reflect the fact that in infancy women are universally the main caretakers of both boys and girls. This fundamental regularity is, as Margaret Mead notes, based on lactation and the division of labor which it leads to: because women breast-feed children, they have also been the ones to care for them (1949, p. 159). The belief in female power seems to be a mythical enlargement of the mother's extreme power over her child, which is greater the less the father or other caretakers are involved, and the more the mother's role is restricted to child care. The mother's enormous role in early childhood gives rise to what Karen Horney (1932) has described as a "dread of women," a fear that is deeper and more universal than the fear of the father. In the mind of the young child, as well as in folklore, the mother appears in two guises: one is the gentle queen or the fairy godmother, who heals, protects, and nurtures; the other is the witch or the evil stepmother, who poisons and eats little children.

Sex-role development is complicated in little boys by the pervasiveness of the mother's influence. The tendency of both little boys and little girls is to identify with the first provider. But boys have to learn to differentiate themselves from mother and from female things. Thus studies of sex-role socialization find that becoming a woman is, for a little girl, merely "growing up." For little boys, however, the process of achieving manhood is becoming not female (D. G. Brown, 1958; Emmerich, 1959). The need to dissociate oneself from femininity seems to lead to widespread tendencies on the part of males to disparage female roles and activities (Burton and Whiting, 1961; Slater and Slater, 1965). The child's struggle with female power does not disappear in adult life. Elizabeth Janeway describes the continuity:

> Having left his mother, a man takes a wife and a new duality begins. It would be odd if the fears and hopes of the old relationship did not have some part in the new, and specifically if the ancient dread of female power did not sometimes awaken. We should not suppose, either, that women have forgotten about these lines of force. Were they not also subject to all-powerful mothers? Did they not have to fight free of the first bond, just as their brothers did? Except that fighting, they knew they fought their own sex and would, in time or principle, become the very thing with which

they were struggling: daughters and heirs of the all-powerful mother, givers and witholders, healers and deniers. (Janeway, 1971, p. 194)

There is also a reality in the adult lives of men and women that reinforces the image of woman as all-powerful giver and withholder. To the extent that the household is the woman's exclusive domain, the husband is in certain ways in a dependent position—like the man in the last chapter who couldn't stand his wife's cooking. This is one of the paradoxes of power: the greater the prestige and power of a given individual, the more he can call on underlings to do things for him; but the more he delegates to others, the less control he has. This is the classic plight of kings and the very rich vis-à-vis their servants, a plight that has often been portrayed in literary works in the figure of the insolent or malevolent maid or butler. In the same way women in certain patriarchal cultures may have even more real power within the family than American women. For example, in Tepoztlan, the deference patterns are so strong that father becomes a remote and aloof figure, too dignified to be bothered by household trivia. As a result the respectful wife need not consult with her husband at all in making decisions about handling the children, managing the household, and so on (Lewis, 1951). Robert Lifton (1965) notes that in Japan the wife is usually given the husband's paycheck, which she then controls, giving the husband an allowance. When an American becomes intimate enough with Japanese life, Lifton writes, "It has been their turn to look with horror and fascination at the Japanese woman's way of treating her husband in public as uncontested lord and master, and in private as another child in need of maternal care" (Lifton, 1965, p. 44).

Finally, a good deal of confusion and disagreement concerning dominance comes about because perceptions of dominance may be influenced by the sex of both the observer and the observed. That is, a given act will seem more or less dominant depending on whether it is performed by a man or a woman. It will also be judged somewhat differently depending on whether the judge is a man or a woman (see Haan and Livson, 1972).

Often statements reporting sex equality or female dominance in a culture or in a relationship seem to be based on a standard of comparison heavily weighted in the direction of male dominance. Thus the belief in the equality of American marriages derives from an implicit use of the patriarchal family as a standard of comparison, the assumption that the dominance of the husband-father is the norm, and that any deviation from that standard represents family democracy. An example of this is found in Stephens' cross-cultural review of family practices (1963). He persistently refers to husband-wife relations in American society as democratic, and contrasts American norms and practices with the extreme patterns of female subordination found in traditional societies.

Within American culture there are also norms of male dominance, in two senses of the term "norm": first, it is regarded as natural that males lead and females follow; second, there is widespread agreement that men *should* be dominant. Goode notes that:

. . . There is a strong reservoir of attitude on the part of the American male generally, that he has a *right* to tell his wife what to do. This attitude is given more overt expression, and is more frequently backed by force, in the lower strata . . . . In our society, the husband who successfully asserts his dominance does enjoy some approval and even a modicum of envy from other males. Male dominance is to some extent actually approved. (Goode, 1956, p. 122)

In interpreting a given marriage or other male-female relationship, then, an observer must choose between two competing cultural norms—the more informal but probably more pervasive one of male dominance, and the more abstract and formal one of equality. Thus the situation of women in American society today is analogous to that of blacks: looking at the extremes of past inequities, both groups have come a long way; but judging by a standard of true equality, both still have a long way to go.

Consider the following example of a description of an "equal" marriage:

Both the husband and wife earned Ph.D. degrees in their respective disciplines. The husband turned down a superior academic post in Oregon and accepted a slightly less desirable position in Pennsylvania, where his wife could obtain a part-time teaching job and do research at one of the several other colleges in the area. Although the husband would have preferred to live in a suburb, they purchased a home near the wife's college so that she could have an office at home where she would be when the children came home from school. Because the wife earns a good salary, she can easily afford to pay a maid to do her major household chores. The husband and wife share all other tasks around the house equally. For example, she cooks the meals, but the husband does the laundry for her and helps with many of her other household tasks. (Bem and Bem, 1970, pp. 112–113)

Probably to most people this marriage sounds remarkably egalitarian. The authors of this description of a hypothetical but not uncommon academic marriage suggest the following test of interpersonal equality—reverse the roles and check the flavor of the description:

Both the wife and husband earned Ph.D. degrees in their respective disciplines. The wife turned down a superior academic post in Oregon and accepted a slightly less desirable position in Pennsylvania, where her husband could obtain a part-time teaching job and do research at one of the several other colleges in the area. Although the wife would have preferred to live in a suburb, they purchased a home near the husband's college so that he could have an office at home where he could be when the children came home from school. Because the husband earns a good salary, he can easily afford to pay a maid to do his major household chores. The wife and husband share all other tasks around the house equally. For example, he cooks the meals, but the wife does the laundry for him and helps with many of his household tasks. (Bem and Bem, 1970, p. 113)

I happen to have heard one of the authors of the foregoing descriptions read them aloud at a meeting of psychologists. The second description produced a lot of laughs at each role reversal. The authors acknowledge that the seeming oddness of the arrangements is a measure of the distance from real equality even in seemingly egalitarian marriages:

It is a mark of how well the woman has been kept in her place that the husband in such a marriage is often adulated by women, including his wife, for "permitting" her to squeeze a career into the interstices of their marriage as long as his own career is not unduly inconvenienced. Thus is the white man blessed for exercising his power benignly while his "natural" right to that power remains unquestioned. (1970, p. 114)

Summary

Every couple, married or not, differs from every other couple. Until recently, however, relatively little attention has been paid to variations among "normal" marriages. It was assumed, first, that marital behavior was governed by widely shared norms concerning proper roles of husbands and wives. Second, the prevailing approaches to marriage emphasized a single dimension of adjustment — satisfaction and happiness. Thus the particular marriage could be understood by how well it seemed to adhere to the norms, and how happy it was. Recently, however, a number of studies have looked into variations among marital relationships. They have discovered much variety in what couples want out of marriage, what they get, and how they behave. The idea that there are widely shared and explicit norms governing marriage in urban society was not found to be true in the last decade, and is probably less true today.

Recently, there has been a great deal of experimentation with new forms of marriage, particularly concerning the issues of commitment, permanence, and sexual relations with others. There is little evidence that the new forms escape the predicaments of the old. Some of the problems faced by couples arise out of certain structural issues built into any dyadic relationship — the degree of commitment of each partner to the other, relationships with other people including relatives and friends of either sex, the division of labor, and decision making. Further, any couple relationship between a man and a woman, whether or not they are married, is influenced in a variety of ways by factors outside the relationship, especially those having to do with the situation of women in the larger society.

THE PARENTAL MYSTIQUE

Chapter 8

It may well be believed that if procreation had not been put under the dominion of a great passion, it would have been caused to cease by the burdens it entails. Abortion and infanticide are especially interesting because they show how early in the history of civilization the burden of children became so heavy that parents began to shirk it. . . .

William Graham Sumner, *Folkways*

In some ways the romantic complex surrounding parenthood is even deeper and more unrealistic than that relating to marriage.

E. E. LeMasters, *Parents in Modern America*

Chapter Eight

Freud is said to have once remarked that nature had played a joke on the human race by linking the sexual apparatus to excretion. It can be argued that nature was also being mischievous, but with more tragic results, in linking sex to the production of tiny, weak infants. For thousands of years people have been trying to break this link.

Far from being a modern preoccupation, the search for some sure, safe way of preventing conception occurs in the oldest records and in the most primitive preliterate groups. The oldest written medical prescriptions for contraception are from ancient Egypt and date from 1850 B.C. They recommend the use of a paste made with crocodile dung to block the vagina (Himes, 1963). Unfortunately, such methods do not work very well in preventing conception, nor do the other ancient methods such as drinking potions, wearing magic amulets, jumping up and down after intercourse, or remaining passive during it. Since abortion until very recently has been a dangerous operation (the abortion laws were originally aimed at preventing the death of the pregnant woman), the leading method of birth control, historically and cross-culturally, has been infanticide.

TABLE 3   UNWANTED FERTILITY IN THE UNITED STATES, 1970

Race and Education	Most Likely No. of Births per Woman	% of Births Unwanted, 1966–70	% of Births Unplanned,[a] 1966–70	Theoretical Births without Unwanted Births
All women	3.0	15%	44%	2.7
College 4+	2.5	7	32	2.4
College 1–3	2.8	11	39	2.6
High school 4	2.8	14	44	2.6
High school 1–3	3.4	20	48	2.9
Less	3.9	31	56	3.0
White women	2.9	13	42	2.6
College 4+	2.5	7	32	2.4
College 1–3	2.8	10	39	2.6
High school 4	2.8	13	42	2.6
High school 1–3	3.2	18	44	2.8
Less	3.5	25	53	2.9
Black women	3.7	27	61	2.9
College 4+	2.3	3	21	2.2
College 1–3	2.6	21	46	2.3
High school 4	3.3	19	62	2.8
High school 1–3	4.2	31	66	3.2
Less	5.2	55	68	3.1

[a]Unplanned births include unwanted births.
Source: Population and the American Future, report of the Commission on Population Growth and the American Future (Washington: U.S. Government Printing Office, 1972), p. 97. Based on data from the National Fertility Study for currently married women under 45 years of age.

Of course, if sexual relations were painful rather than pleasurable, human beings would probably have become extinct long ago, as Sumner observed around the turn of the century. Sumner argues that the relation of parent to child is one of sacrifice; children add to the burdens of the parents in their own "struggle for existence." That there are compensations for the parents does not alter the fact that "the interests of parents and children are antagonistic."

In comparison with more recent social-science writings on parenthood, Sumner's views sound perverse and even cruel. These views tend to idealize parent-child relations, emphasizing the naturalness of parenthood and the harmony of interests between parents, children, and society. Disharmony enters only in the form of pathology, an alien growth on the sound body of the family. The pathology can be individual or social: the rejecting mother, the out-of-wedlock pregnancy, the fatherless family.

The prevailing view of parenthood in the family literature is curiously unidimensional. It is normal to want children, society needs children, nature has arranged it so that we have the appropriate instincts and enough food to take care of all the children we are capable of producing. The implications of the individual and social desire for birth control, in the absence of effective contraceptive methods, do not enter into hypotheses about the nature of parenthood.

"Natural" Interpretation of Parenthood

Much thinking about parent-child relationships in the social sciences assumes a natural fit between the needs of the infant for nurturance, the needs of the parents, particularly the mother, to nurture the child, and the need of society to support and encourage the parents. Thus psychoanalysts argue that every woman's deepest instinctual wish is to bear and nurture an infant; the child represents the substitute for the never-to-be-obtained penis, and being a mother represents the fulfillment of the girl's Oedipal wish to replace her own mother.

The more contemporary ego-psychology version of psychoanalysis defines parenthood in terms of the growth of skills and personality resources. For Erikson (1963), parenthood represents a stage of development in the course of

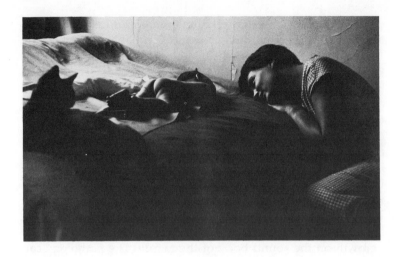

the life cycle. Erikson asserts that the desire to care for very young children is built into the human nature of both men and women. "Adult man is so constituted as to *need to be needed*, lest he suffer the mental deformation of self-absorption . . . . I have therefore postulated an instinctual and psychosocial stage of 'generativity' beyond that of genitality" (1963, p. 130).

Erikson and other writers in the psychoanalytic tradition argue that within each society institutions arise that take into account the needs of the very young. Parents provide physical care and teach the child what he needs to know to deal with his environment and society, and society supports the parents in their efforts because it "needs" stable adults (Levy, 1965). Sociological thinking about child rearing also tends to assume an intuitive fit between social patterns and the needs of children. The very term "socialization," or even "child rearing," implies that parental behavior toward children is usually dedicated to the child's education and welfare.

Functional sociology interprets reproduction and child rearing in terms of society's need for "social replacement," the production of a new generation to replace the parents. This interpretation tends to assume that every child comes into the world with a fixed, positive value. It does not allow for the possibility that a new mouth to feed may, at a particular time, be dysfunctional for the parent or the community, possibilities seen very clearly by Sumner and still earlier by Malthus and Darwin.

A recent fashionable interpretation sees human parenthood in the light of animal models. Detailed descriptions of parent-child relations among chimpanzees, monkeys, and other animals are offered with the implication that these relate directly to human parents and their children. The continuity across species is emphasized: parenthood is part of nature. The infant of a species provides the specific stimulus to release an appropriate response in the mother, which in turn will evoke a further response in the infant and so on in a chain of coordinated behavior. Thus the human child is said to be equipped with an innate tendency to attach itself to a mothering figure early in life. This tendency is said to be matched by a built-in responsiveness on the part of the mother (Bowlby, 1969). Or, the seeking, sucking infant is guided to the breast, relieving both his own hunger and his mother's fullness. As the introduction to a recent anthology put it, parenthood is part of "the process of evolutionary biology as it repeats itself in each human being and directs human behavior, under the aegis of the genetic code, toward procreation and parenthood. . . . Parenthood is a manifestation of 'natural man' and, as such, is governed by the laws of biologic processes that are universal" (Anthony and Benedek, 1970, p. xvii).

Or, "What is the most humanly significant biological denominator common to all human beings and to all human groups? It occurred to me that this might be the concern of parents for their young. This parental concern has a long biological heritage and is absolutely essential for the survival of most species" (Fremont-Smith, 1970, p. 3).

Misuses of Biology   The belief that "biology" guides and directs parental behavior pervades both popular and "expert" thinking, as the preceding quotations show. The older notion of "blind" instinct has given way to the more sophisticated view that mother and child are genetically "programmed" to be attracted to each other. Yet both the old and the newer versions of the idea that mothering is a "natural" biological process are seriously flawed. Like arguments about the biological determination of sexual behavior, they underestimate the role of culture and social context. Furthermore, the belief in innate nurturance is based on an oversimplified version of biology and evolution. First, the argument that maternal instincts in animals reveal the biological source of human mothering overestimates the similarities between humans and other species. Furthermore, it presents only one side of animal behavior. As Pohlman puts it:

> If research from comparative psychology and anecdotal observation of animal life are cited to try to show innate tendencies toward parenthood, in fairness we should note that some animals, including mammals, will kill and eat their own offspring. (Pohlman, 1969, p. 52)

Animal analogies can offer useful and interesting illustrations for understanding human behavior, but they certainly should not be used to define the human condition.

The innateness-of-parenthood argument also rests on a misunderstanding of evolutionary process. It assumes that evolution works on the principle of preserving every individual newborn animal or human. Rather, evolution works on the principle of species survival, and this may involve considerable waste of individual lives.

Margaret Mead (1957), for example, argues that breast-feeding seems to fit the model of a process designed to eliminate all but the strongest, "fittest" babies. She criticizes the ethnologist's model of nursing which pictures every mother as biologically able to nourish every infant she brings into the world, and nursing itself as a chain of mutually beneficial responses.

The War of the Breast   It is well known that women in contemporary society have a great deal of trouble breast-feeding their children. The very fact that there are organizations devoted to convincing women to breast-feed and to helping them do so indicates how far from automatic nursing is. Nursing difficulties usually are attributed to the hectic pace of modern life, or the fact that women are rejecting their children, or are just unwilling to do their motherly duties, or some combination of the three. Yet the irony of blaming somebody for failing to do something instinctive usually passes unnoticed. As far as the child is concerned, the prevailing assumption is that the availability of bottles represents a loss for the child.

In spite of the belief that breast-feeding has been a problem only in recent times, the historical records indicate otherwise. The nursing of children has been a matter of serious concern in Western civilization for the past two thousand years. William Kessen (1965), in a history of ideas about child development, writes about the "war of the breast." He notes that the most persistent theme in the history of the child is the reluctance of mothers to suckle their babies. "The running war between the mother, who does not want to nurse, and the philosopher-psychologists, who insist she must, stretches over 2000 years" (1965, p. 1).

Margaret Mead's analysis of mother-child relations in early infancy is more consistent with the historical picture than the alternative image of nursing as a mutually beneficial instinctive relationship. She writes that lactation and early maternal care may be biologically a life-*selecting* process as much as a life-*saving* one. In other words, "nature" is not a benevolent, child-saving force. Rather, the biological factors seem to be arranged to ensure that only the strongest, most vigorous babies will survive, and only if they are born to women with the right physical qualifications to feed them. Far from being a simple process by which any mother can feed any baby born to her if only she wants to, lactation seems to require a specific set of physical and constitutional capacities on the part of both mother and child. For example, Dr. Mead cites studies showing that many babies have individual quirks of temperament that make them hard to feed. Thus there are "rejecting" babies — babies who shortly after birth seem to fight the whole feeding process. There are also babies born with a seemingly innate disinterest in being fed, as well as babies with breathing difficulties and mouths too small to nurse.

Further complications arise from the shape of the mother's breast. One study found that the suckling response in human infants is elicited by the whole front of the mother's breast filling the entire oral cavity of the child. About one-quarter of mothers do not have breasts of the right shape or elasticity to fill the child's mouth.

Finally, the production of milk is based on a "letting down" reflex that is highly vulnerable to anxiety. When a child sucks well and thrives, a mother has little anxiety and much milk. But if there is some difficulty such as those just

suggested, a vicious circle starts. The child fails to suck well or thrive, the mother is made anxious, her milk supply fails, the infant receives still less food, and soon, if there are no other ways to feed the child, it will die.

This, argues Mead, is the "natural" biological fate of an "unfit" infant under survival conditions. She sees a parallel in the maternal behavior of herd animals such as reindeer, sheep, and goats. Immediately after giving birth such animals are highly attentive to their infants. The mother will nuzzle the infant, lick it, feed it, try to get it up on its feet. But she will only do this for a certain number of hours. If the baby does not stand up and walk well enough to follow the herd, the mother will no longer recognize it as hers. She will abandon it and go with the herd, because that is the only way she can survive. Mead suggests that the human situation is comparable. The very vulnerability of the mother's milk supply, the ease in which it can be turned off, may have been in evolutionary terms a selective device for ensuring that the mother's energy would not be wasted on trying to rear a child who did not have a vigorous grasp on life.

Thus it is not "nature" but culture that values human life and holds it as an ideal that every infant shall live, the weak as well as the strong, the premature as well as the full term. And it is not instinct but human inventiveness that found other ways to nurture infants than by the lactation of their biological mothers.

The Nurturance Gap

The invention of bottles to feed babies illustrates one of the paradoxes of the human condition. The same evolutionary pressures that created a brain able to conceive of inventing something to save infants' lives, and a pair of hands capable of actually making it, resulted in human infants' being born into a nurturance gap: the human infant comes into the world the most helpless of all the primates, and yet its care is less assured than that of any other.

The idea that evolution works by the principle of guaranteed nurturance is remarkably at odds with recent studies of human evolution. Mother Nature appears to be more of a trickster than a Lady Bountiful. The trick nature played on humans was to give them the most burdensome infants of all the primates, while removing the detailed genetic instructions that guide maternal behavior among other species. To say the same thing more correctly, without making nature into a person: the extreme helplessness of the human newborn, its existential plight, results from the same evolutionary pressures that created human intelligence.

Most people know how newborns look, but our imagery of babies comes mostly from photographs, paintings, and advertisements showing plump, smiling, rosy-cheeked little cherubs. Therefore some parents are disappointed and perhaps even shocked when they first see their scrawny, limp, unresponsive offspring. It takes about six months for the child to resemble its cherubic advertising image.

The human infant is, in primate terms, at least six months premature at birth, perhaps more. That is, if a human infant were born at a comparable point to other primate newborns, he would be like a six-month-old. The burdensomeness of the human infant is a by-product of the evolutionary process. Chimpanzee or baboon babies are much more developed at birth. They can, in part, determine their own relationship to the mother, and after weaning they gather their own food (Washburn and DeVore, 1961).

At one stage in human development, babies were born in such an advanced state. The large human brain developed rather late. Our earliest immediate ancestors—the Australopithecines, the so-called apemen of southern and eastern Africa—were tool-using bipeds with ape-sized brains. The Australopithecines lived two million years ago, but proto-humans did not look like today's people for about a million years. The tool-using, cooperative way of life of these hominids led to the enlargement of the human brain. This is a relatively new version of human evolution; it used to be thought that human beings first acquired the physical form that distinguished them from the apes, then developed culture. It now appears, however, that tool use and cultural life shaped the human body and brain by favoring the survival of those who could handle tools and symbols, and disfavoring those with small brains and big teeth.

Tools, language, and cultural life set human beings apart as a species. Man is an "incomplete" ape or, as Geertz puts it, humans are born into "an information gap":

As our central nervous system grew up in great part in inter-action with culture, it is incapable of directing our behavior or organizing our experience without the guidance provided by sys-tems or significant symbols. What happened in the Ice Age is that we were forced to abandon the regularity and precision of detailed genetic control over our conduct. . . . Beavers build dams, birds build nests, bees locate food, baboons organize social groups and mice mate on the basis of forms of learning that rest predominantly on instructions encoded in their genes and evoked by appropriate patterns of external stimuli: physical keys inserted into organic locks. But men build dams or shelters, locate food, organize their social groups, or find sexual partners under the guidance of in-structions encoded in flow charts and blueprints, hunting lore, moral systems, and esthetic judgments: conceptual structure molding formless talents. (Geertz, 1965, p. 112)

While the brain and head were growing larger during the course of evolution, the human pelvis was (and is) more limited in the size it could grow. Thus the same selection pressures that led to larger brains led to earlier births. The psychological effects of this change in the direction of pre-mature birth were momentous. As Washburn and DeVore describe it:

The psychological consequences of the change from the monkey pattern to the human are profound. . . . When the baby baboon is born, it has its own reflexes and motor development that enable it to help determine its own relationship to the mother. . . . The helpless human infant is exposed to maternal whim, custom, or vagary in a way that is true of no other primate. (1961, p. 39)

The relationship between the monkey or ape infant and its mother is not completely determined by the infant's reflexes and its mother's drives and physiology. Learning and even custom play a role in primal maternal behavior patterns. For example, one study (Harlow et al., 1963) has shown that female rhesus monkeys raised in isolation do not treat their infants in a "normal" way when they become mothers. They may ignore, reject, or even beat them. They evidently have to learn from living in a social group of other monkeys how to handle infants, although even when the isolation continues, the rhesus mother acts more "normally" when she has a second and third child.

But biological drives and reflexes play an even smaller role in human mothering:

Although female monkeys appear to learn part of their maternal behavior patterns, and older juvenile females hold and carry infants before they have any of their own, the role of learning, culture and custom in determining the care of the young is vastly greater in man than in any nonhuman primate. (Washburn and DeVore, 1961, p. 42)

In short, the human infant is born into a nurturance gap. Once the large brain had been built, people no longer lived in a world of things, of simple stimuli, but a world of meanings, concepts, and significant symbols. Furthermore, the human consciousness can negate the world, can imagine the hypothetical. A human parent is uniquely capable of imagining the nonexistence of his child. This capacity can lead to a cherishing of the child as an irreplaceable treasure, to resentment, or to a search for a means of birth control. No ape ever tried to invent a contraceptive device. Even supposing an ape had the capacity to think of doing such a thing, it would have no need to. The nonhuman primates are tropical creatures. Each one finds his own food in the rich vegetation. Man developed as a separate species in response to the food scarcities of the Ice Age. Therefore a human infant can never be considered a bundle of stimulus patterns that can call forth a predetermined response in the mother; each infant comes into the world carrying a very specific set of meanings for that particular mother, at that particular moment, in that particular set of circumstances, in that particular culture. This freedom may have tragic implications.

The analysis of the evolution of human mother-child relations offered by Washburn and DeVore makes it clear that nothing is guaranteed about the reception an infant will receive on being born. "The helpless human infant is exposed to maternal whim, custom, or vagary in a way that is true of no other primate" (1961, p. 39). Everything people do is mediated by language and culture. There is no such thing as "natural" childbirth and child rearing, in the sense of a process unmediated by learning and cultural rules.

For example, Margaret Mead (1957) has filmed a childbirth in a "primitive" tribe, the Iatmul of New Guinea. In an article she gives a detailed description of this film, which is called "First Five Days in the Life of a New Guinea Baby." The film begins immediately after the birth before the cord is cut and shows the mother-child relationship during the next four days. On first glance it seems to show a perfect model of "natural childbirth." The mother is overtaken by labor pains while on an errand and gives birth alone. There are no complications. Although people quickly come to her aid, she attends to the baby and herself with very little help and walks back to the village. She breast-feeds the child easily.

Mead points out how this seemingly natural child-birth is actually highly stylized—that is, governed by arbitrary cultural rules. The umbilical cord has to be tied in a certain way, and the placenta has to be placed in a coconut shell and ritually disposed of. A wet nurse is on hand to give the baby its first feeding. The wet nurse, a neighbor and also a new mother, qualifies for the job because she observes the same food taboos the new mother must observe. The mother has to toss the baby up and sideways in the air after birth, give him a patterned set of baths in clay and warm and cold water, and shape his nose with fingers warmed on a leaf laid on a glowing log. Thus even among the "simplest" people, technologically speaking, there is enormous cultural complexity in the practice of childbirth.

Infanticide

We have mentioned earlier the prevalence of infanticide as a leading means of population control in precontraceptive societies. Not only is the infant not guaranteed a warm welcome through natural mechanisms in the mother, but in many times and places a new infant would simply not be allowed to live. When we think of such practices at all, we think of them as barbaric customs existing only at primitive levels of culture, and as incompatible with "civilization." (There is a paradox here in the idea of the maternal instinct needing civilization in order to flourish.) Actually, however, infanticide has been much more widespread in Western civilization than is generally recognized (see Shorter, 1973; Trexler, 1973).

Further, one savage practice has flourished during most periods of European history, but has not been reported for other cultures: the maiming and crippling of children to use them as beggars. The fact that such practices now seem horrible beyond belief indicates that our feelings about maimed children, not to speak of adults, has changed drastically. In Roman times, however, sensibilities were very different:

In the "Controversy" of Seneca the question is whether those who mutilated exposed children have done a wrong toward the State. The debate is opened by Porcius Latro, who asks if after having suffered the misfortune of being exposed, it is not a piece of luck to have someone find them. Cassius Severus then expresses his opinion. "Look," he exclaims, "on the blind wandering about the streets leaning on their sticks, and on those with crushed feet, and still again look on those with broken limbs. This one is without arms, that one has had his shoulders pulled down out of shape in order that his grotesqueries may excite laughter. Let us view the entire miserable family shivering, trembling, blind, mutilated, perishing from hunger—in fact, already half dead. Let us go to the origin of all these ills—a laboratory for the manufacture of human wrecks—a cavern filled with the limbs torn from living children—each has a different profession, a different mutilation has given each a different occupation." The conclusion is that inasmuch as the exposed children are slaves, being the property of those who rear them, they have no cause for complaints against the State. "What wrong has been done to the Republic?" asks Gallio in reply to Severus. "On the contrary, have not these children been done a service inasmuch as their parents had cast them out?" (Payne, 1916, pp. 242–243)

The historian Langer (1972) has recently reviewed the history of infanticide as a means of population control in Europe and Britain. He notes that Plato, Aristotle, and other writers of the same period advocated infanticide as a means of regulating the size of the population as well as ridding society of deformed and diseased infants. During later times both the church and governments made infanticide a crime punishable by death. Yet, as late as the last century, infanticide was frequent as well as publicly noticeable. Langer concentrates on the period between 1750–1850 when the population of Europe nearly doubled. He argues that the two major brakes on population growth were celibacy and infanticide, and that without these controls the population of Europe would have outrun the food supply. He notes that:

In England as late as 1878 about 6 percent of all violent deaths could be classed as infanticides. . . . In the 18th century it was not an uncommon spectacle to see the corpses of infants lying in the streets or in the dunghills of London and other large cities. . . .

A thick volume of newspaper clippings can be found in the library of the Harvard Law School, most of them from the London press in the years 1861–1863. Together with the extensive report of the Select Committee on the Protection of Infant Life in 1871, the clippings provide appalling evidence of the frequency of infanticide in those times. . . . In 1862 one of the coroners for Middlesex county stated infanticide had become so commonplace "that the police seemed to think no more of finding a dead child than they did of finding a dead cat or a dead dog." The *Morning Star* (June 23, 1863) declared that infanticide "is possibly becoming a national institution"; the *Morning Post* (September 2, 1863) termed it "this commonest of crimes." (Langer, 1972, pp. 96–97)

Public attitudes toward infanticide were remarkably lenient, according to Langer. In contrast with the attitudes of most people today, and with religious and legal authorities then, public sympathy tended to be on the side of any woman who was charged with killing her child. Very few culprits were discovered anyhow, and very few of those ever reached the courts. One London coroner said he had never known a woman to be punished for killing her baby, "no matter how flagrant the circumstances." Usually the women involved in court cases were destitute workers or servants who had been abandoned by the men involved.

Before recent times it was difficult to draw a line between infanticide, child abandonment, and putting an infant in a foundling home. The mortality rates of the latter tended to be 80–90 percent. Foundling homes were started by reformers such as St. Vincent de Paul, Thomas Coram, and Napoleon, who were shocked at infanticide. Whenever one opened, however, it was swamped by more babies than it could handle. Conditions were so bad that foundling homes became, ironically, another form of the infanticide they were designed to prevent:

When Coram's London Foundling Hospital was finally opened in 1741, it immediately became evident that he had underestimated the need. The pressure of applicants was so great that women fought at the hospital gates. Eventually, in 1756, Parliament undertook to provide the Foundling Hospital with funds on the understanding that all children who were offered would be accepted. . . .

The policy of open admissions completely swamped the Foundling Hospital; in the first four years nearly 15,000 children were accepted. It was impossible to find enough wet nurses for such a number and thousands died in early infancy; only 4,400 of the foundlings lived to reach adolescence. The cost to Parliament was 500,000 pounds sterling, and in 1760 the policy was abandoned. Thenceforth only London children were accepted at the Foundling Hospital, and those in limited numbers. In the countryside, foundlings were again assigned to the parish workhouses, which Jonas

Hanway, a governor of the Foundling Hospital, called "slaughter-houses of infants" because the mortality was well nigh total. In order to save trouble and money parish officers assigned the infants to paid nurses, who were universally detested and nicknamed "killing nurses" and "she-butchers" because no child ever escaped their care alive. (Langer, 1972, p. 96)

Wherever foundling homes sprang up as a way of saving abandoned children, the same ironic process was repeated. At the height of his power Napoleon decreed that foundling homes be set up in every region of France and if possible in every arrondissement (neighborhood). Again the facilities were overburdened and the expenses staggering to local governments. Napoleon tried to make it possible for a baby to be left without anyone seeing the person who was leaving it. The method was so successful that one-fourth to one-third of the foundlings were thought to be *legitimate* children whose parents either could not or would not care for them. The mortality rates led one writer to suggest that the homes put up signs saying "Children killed at government expense" (Langer, 1972, p. 98).

Langer's article deals mainly with demographic issues: the factors that led to the population explosion in Europe between 1750 and 1850, and the checks on population growth. He does not deal with the many questions that might be asked about the psychological and social aspects of the situation. How did the factors to which Langer attributes the rise in population—the introduction of the potato and corn from the New World—actually get translated into the production of more children? How did the need for checks on population become translated into individual acts of infanticide? Why were mothers increasingly likely to abandon children until 1850, and why did the attitude toward children change thereafter?

Evidence now emerging from the work of Langer and other historians shatters easy notions of an intuitive fit between the needs of children, the inclinations of parents to nurture them, and the functional need of every society to care for infants. Langer's work also illustrates how technological changes enter into the parent-child relationship. For example, better sanitation and the introduction of smallpox vaccination seem in part to have been responsible for the rise in population. Malthus had described smallpox as one

of the major natural checks on population. Before the vaccination was invented, 96 percent of the population contracted
the disease, which was fatal in one-seventh of the cases
(Langer, 1972). The chief victims of this "hideous illness"
were children in the first year of life. The eradication of smallpox and the plague, another epidemic killer, must have
tremendously reduced infant mortality. Contraception, however, was not widely known or practiced. Hence the result
was a baby glut dealt with by the means just discussed.

Parenthood in Early Modern France

David Hunt's work (1970) on parenthood in seventeenth-
century France similarly raises questions about the intuitive
wisdom and benevolence of parents. Hunt's work deals not
with abandoned children, but with well-born infants. One
of his major sources is a journal of the infancy of the future
King Louis XIII, the most precious infant in France. Although
dealing mostly with the children of the nobility and upper
classes, Hunt nevertheless describes the situation he finds
as a "breakdown in parental care."

Hunt's aim in writing *Parents and Children in History* was
to combine the insights of Erikson and Aries in trying to
understand the psychology of family life in early modern
times. As we noted earlier, Aries had described infancy in
medieval times as a period of "benign indifference." Infants
did not count for much emotionally in the lives of their
parents, but they were treated kindly.

Hunt takes issue with Aries. He argues that parents of
the Old Regime were neither as benign nor as indifferent
to their infants as Aries says they were. Rather, parents
appear to have been destructive and irrational toward their
infants. Hunt argues that parents were deeply disturbed by
infants' physical needs—their hunger and messes—as well
as, later on, their assertive willfulness. Each one of Erikson's
three earliest stages was typically met with a failure to satisfy
the particular need involved; or, to put it even more strongly,
the child was met with attack at each stage in its area of
greatest vulnerability. Thus the oral stage was met by a
reluctance to nurse on the part of mothers, the stage of autonomy was met with beatings to break the child's will, and
infant sexuality was met with cruel and seductive teasing.

The Feeding Problem If anything symbolizes the instinctive naturalness of motherhood, it is the image of a nursing mother and her infant. Hunt presents evidence showing that even in families where the child was accepted and highly valued, there was a large-scale failure to nourish infants. He argues that infant feeding represented a major crisis and contributed to the huge infant-mortality rates.

Hunt's book as well as other evidence shows that the unwillingness of large numbers of women to nurse their infants preceded by several centuries the technology of bottles and prepared baby foods. In the absence of this technology the prevailing substitute for those who could afford it was a wet nurse, supplemented by various prepared concoctions. Hunt cites evidence showing that infants were seen as not quite human. He emphasizes the emotional quality of this view: people tended to see children as "gluttonous little animals . . . sucking away the mother's blood" (p. 121). This feeling stemmed from the belief of the medical experts of the time that mother's milk was actually whitened blood rather than a special secretion made to feed infants. Although the act of giving birth was regarded as a proud occasion, child rearing itself tended to be viewed as tedious and degrading. For any woman who could afford it, a wet nurse was the preferred way of feeding an infant.

Hunt is probably in error when he writes of wet-nursing and other practices in the seventeenth century as a "breakdown in parental care," implying a sudden decline from a level of better care. Rather, as we noted earlier in this chapter, a conflict between the needs of infants and the willingness of mothers to nurse them has been going on, at least in Western culture, for the past two thousand years (Kessen, 1965).

Unfortunately, we don't know the prevalence of the various forms of infant feeding in specific times and places, and the ups and downs of trends in the use of wet nurses. Kessen does present some evidence, however, as to distribution of various feeding practices at one particular time and place: Paris in the year 1780. Of 21,000 children born each year, 700 were wet-nursed by their own mothers, 700 were wet-nursed at home, 2000–3000 well-to-do were sent to the suburbs to be wet-nursed, and 17,000 or so went to the country. These baby farms were notorious for their high mortality rate. Sending an infant to one meant a two- or three-day journey without food. If a child managed to survive the trip, he would remain at the farm for two to three years.

Kessen uses the "war of the breast" as a model for the history of child development in general; the same themes and issues keep reappearing in each new generation. The problem of baby feeding exemplifies both the redundancy of the basic argument and the way new concepts are grafted onto old issues. Thus Plutarch argued against wet nurses because their affection was spurious, "they love for hire." A poet in 1584 warned mothers:

> The crying infant with a venal nurse;
> Whose foreign blood but ill supplies
> What the ungrateful mother now denies;
> What tenderness can e'er from her be known
> Who, for another's child, neglects her own?
> (Sainte-Marthe, in Kessen, 1965, p. 2)

Rousseau argued that if only mothers would nurse their own children, there would be a general reform of morals. In our times the prevailing arguments have been based on the child's physical and, in the teachings of the psychoanalysts, psychological welfare. In the literature of the past, when wet nurses rather than bottles were the "unnatural" means of feeding, the "natural mother" seems to be treated less harshly than the wet nurse, whose character, morals, and intelligence are regularly assailed. As Hunt notes, these women are the hated scapegoats of the literature on child rearing (1970, p. 101). The children who concern the philosopher-psychologists are more often the upper-class children who will imbibe the inferior qualities of the lower-class nurse along with her milk. An occasional voice was raised on the part of the wet nurse's own children; thus Montaigne wrote:

> . . . We tear . . . their own infants from their mothers' arms and make these mothers take charge of ours. We cause them to abandon their children to some wretched nurse, to whom we do not wish to commit our own, or to some goat. . . . And one sees, in the majority of cases . . . a greater solicitude for the borrowed infant than for their own. As for the goats, it is common around here to see women of the village, when they cannot feed the children at their breast, call the goats to their rescue. (D. Hunt, 1970, p. 104)

The voice of the wet nurse herself is not entirely missing from the record. It occurs in the form of a lullaby sung by American slave nurses to their white charges:

> Husha bye don't you cry
> Go to sleep, little baby
> When you wake, you'll have cake
> And all the pretty little horses . . .

> Over yonder in the meadow
> There's a poor little lambie
> Bees and butterflies
> Buzzin' round its eyes
> Hear the poor little thing cry mama

The "lambie" in the last stanza refers to the child of the nurse.

Parenthood and Power

If a generalization can be made about parenthood on the basis of the foregoing historical evidence, it is that no easy generalizations can be made. John Stuart Mill, writing about the Victorian family, argues that one should not judge a social institution by its best examples, nor by its worst. One must look at each institution as a system, considering not only the virtues of its best practitioners but also the abuses it allows and encourages. Thus absolute monarchy produced some enlightened kings and queens—truly benevolent despots. The problem with despotism, as Mill puts it, was not that most despots were bloodthirsty ogres, looking down with glee at the suffering of their subjects; rather, the problem was that nothing was built into the system to prevent the ogres from coming to power and carrying out their whims.

Mill finds the key to the problem of the family in the distribution and control of power. He argued that the Victorian family concentrated enormous power in the hands of the husband-father, made women and children powerless economically and legally, and yet did nothing to prevent the worst sort of brute from finding some poor woman to marry and doing with her whatever he liked.

Today the most flagrant abuses of the Victorian family have been reformed. Women are no longer legally defined as having a childlike status in relation to their husbands. The official version of child rearing no longer makes a virtue of beating children in the interests of breaking their will and shaping their character. Even parents who believe in strictness and obedience tend to think of spankings more as a last resort than as a good thing in themselves.

Yet the structural problems resulting from the power imbalances in the nuclear family remain. These are more subtle but no less real for women, although women are not typically in as much physical danger as in Victorian times. Children, however, in the isolated nuclear-family household face physical risk. This does not mean that all or most parents are ogres, but that the nuclear-family system is not structured to prevent child abuse, and may even encourage it. Babies and young children really are weak and dependent—that is, powerless—emotionally, physically, and intellectually. Notions such as permissiveness, the child-centered society, and others mislead in many ways, but especially when they obscure the basic inequality with which parent and child confront each other at the outset of the child's life. The basic imbalance is corrected in other societies by the presence of other people in or near the household.

Child Abuse   Researchers point to the difficulty of drawing a line between "normal" discipline and child abuse because the parent is legally empowered to use corporal punishment to enforce his rules, no matter how arbitrary they may appear to the child or to others. If the parent should kill his child in the course of administering a "deserved" beating, some states would consider the event an excusable homicide.

It is also difficult to state how abusing parents differ from normal parents. There is a strong tendency to interpret child abuse as the result of some gross psychological abnormality—what sort of parental monsters would abuse their children? Yet the literature on battered children reveals no clear line of demarcation between battering parents and "normal" ones. Nothing sets them off in terms of social class, occupation, I. Q., urban-rural residence, or psychopathology. Research has found nothing more striking than a pattern of child rearing merely exaggerating the usual one (Gil, 1971).

Most instances of physical abuse occur when the parent or caretaker gets carried away in anger and goes too far. Some battering parents expect strict obedience from very young

children; they possess a marked sense of righteousness, and feel they are encouraging their children to behave and be respectful. Or they may be under severe economic or other strains. For example, B. F. Steele and C. B. Pollock write:

> There seems to be an unbroken spectrum of parental action towards children ranging from the breaking of bones and the fracturing of skulls through severe bruising through severe spanking and on to mild "reminder" pats on the bottom. To be aware of this, one has only to look and listen to the parent/child interactions at the playground and the supermarket, or even to recall how one raised one's own children or how one was raised oneself. The amount of yelling, scolding, slapping, punching, hitting and yanking acted out by parents on very small children is almost shocking. Hence, we have felt that in dealing with the abused child we are not observing an isolated, unique phenomenon, but only the extreme form of what we would call a pattern or style of child rearing quite prevalent in our culture. (1968, p. 104)

It is impossible to determine accurately the number of instances of child abuse. About 10,000 cases of serious injury to children inflicted by parents or their caretakers are recorded annually by child-abuse registries. The rate is nine cases per 100,000 children per year. Researchers in the field assume this to be merely the tip of an iceberg; it is impossible to estimate the number of injuries passed off as accidents or never even reported. A recent English study of parents whose children were hospitalized for treatment of burns found many instances of what appeared to be willful negligence on the part of parents; for example, the parent was angry at the child, and somehow just didn't move fast enough to prevent the child from tipping a pot of boiling soup onto himself.

Accidents constitute the leading cause of death in young children, almost three times more frequent than the next leading cause. Assuming that many of these accidents actually represent cases of child abuse, or willful negligence shading into carelessness, some researchers have suggested that parental abuse and neglect may be the most frequent cause of death to children in the United States today (Fontana, 1964, p. ix). On the other hand David Gil, another child-abuse researcher, argues that physical abuse of children may not be the major killer and maimer that others have claimed. Gil argues that individual acts of violence against children within the family may be overshadowed by collective societal abuse through poverty and discrimination:

America has sometimes been described as child-centered; however, any unbiased observer of child life in this nation will find that many millions of children are living and growing up under circumstances of severe social and economic deprivation which tend to inhibit the fullest possible development of their innate capacities. . . . Many of these children lack adequate nutrition, medical and dental care, and educational vocational opportunities. Any serious student of child life in American society would have to conclude that, however high the prevalence of physical abuse of individual children within their families and homes may be, the abuse inflicted upon children collectively by society as a whole is far larger in scope and far more serious in its consequences. (Gil, 1970, pp. 15–16)

Gil does not interpret child abuse to overshadow the child problems caused by poverty and inequality, but he agrees with other researchers that the propensity toward child abuse is extremely widespread in the population.

In a national survey carried out by Gil, about 60 percent of all the adults interviewed thought that "almost anybody could at some time injure a child in his care" (Gil, 1970, p. 56). Gil suggests these results show that the infliction of physical injury on children is viewed as an "almost normal occurrence" in the course of caring for a child. His results are all the more striking in that the survey defined as physical abuse only those incidents resulting in actual injuries.

Gil notes that if the definition had included attacks that did not result in injury, an even higher proportion of people would have agreed that almost anyone could at times abuse a child in his care.

Thus child abuse must be seen as *potential* behavior in a majority of families, but actually may be relatively rare. The research on actual incidents of child abuse suggests that other factors have to be added to this general propensity in order for an attack on a child to occur. One of these extra factors appears to be the experience of the parents themselves as children. Many of the abusing parents who come to the attention of social agencies and researchers appear to have been—or felt—unloved or unlistened to as children. They expect their own children to supply the love they missed when they were children. Such a parent may take a baby's crying, or the failure of an eighteen-month-old to obey commands instantly, as a sign that the child really doesn't love him or her:

> In early life, the infant is most likely to be attacked during the normal care-taking, mothering functions of feedings, diapering, bathing, dressing and comforting, and in later months during training and "obedience" situations. If the infant responds with cooperation and pleasure, all goes well. Should the infant be uncooperative, however, continuing to cry, or persisting in wriggling . . . the parent may feel disappointed, disapproved of, unloved, and criticized, and will respond with attack in the form of yanking, slapping, hitting, and throwing about in an effort to make the baby behave. This leads to the bruises, lacerations, visceral injuries and fractures which we call the "battered child syndrome." (Steele, 1970, p. 452)

The child-abusing parent tends to find himself or herself entangled in a complicated web of emotions. He tends to see the child as both his own unloving parent and his bad, needy, childhood self. When the parent hits the child, he sometimes seems to be reenacting a scene from his own childhood. Often the parent reports he feels as if hitting the child is like hitting himself (Steele, 1970).

Such psychological mechanisms do not operate in a vacuum. Situational pressures and the social context also contribute to the chain of events leading to physical child abuse. Money worries, unemployment, and illness are some of the other factors that can tip the delicate balance of parental inclinations toward the child one way or the other. Despite our initial horror and indignation when we first learn of child abuse, many of the actual incidents reveal familiar feelings and understandable—if not forgivable—reponses to a difficult situation. The following case of child abuse, for instance, came to the writer's attention:

A school counselor in a California suburb said there were many instances where she and the teachers in the school suspected child abuse. Most often the children would not "tell" on their parents. There was one instance which was confirmed. An 11-year-old boy came to school with a broken arm. He said he had fallen out of a tree. The counselor was working with the boy on learning problems, and eventually he took her into his confidence and said his father had broken his arm, but made him swear not to tell anybody on pain of another beating. The circumstances were as follows: the boy's mother had died shortly before, leaving the husband with four children, of which this boy was the oldest. The father, who was a skilled worker in an aerospace industry, had been struggling to manage the housework and child care as well as keep up his job. One after another, a series of housekeepers had been hired, but they all quit. The incident of the broken arm occurred when the most recent housekeeper walked off. The father had done the wash and asked the boy to hang it on the line. Through carelessness or accident, the whole wash landed in the dirt in the back yard. That was the last straw for the father, and he hit the boy in the arm with a baseball bat.

Actually, reactions to incidents of child abuse are complicated: on the one hand we are horrified and cannot understand how a parent could harm a child; on the other hand, as Gil's statistics indicate, most people feel that almost anyone could abuse a child at one time or another. The following letter from a mother to a child psychologist illustrates both the accepting attitude toward child abuse and the ease with which a conscientious middle-class mother can find herself cast in the role of child abuser:

One Saturday morning, I was rushing to gather the children's clothes, bottles and diapers, preparing to leave for the weekend.
I was making some hot milk for the girls. While the baby was crying in the high chair and throwing his breakfast on the floor, the milk boiled over. June, my 5-year-old, was giving me her tenth excuse why she didn't want to put on her shoes, even though she was sick and the floor was cold. I blew up: "Do I have to start screaming before you'll listen to me?" (Thinking to myself at that moment—this isn't me—this is my mother yelling.)

June stood there holding her ground. I picked her up in a sweep of anger, dragged her to her room, and heaved her onto the floor yelling, "and don't come out until your shoes are on!" She landed on her stomach and chin and I immediately saw that she was hurt. I ran in, picked her up and laid her on her bed.

Under her chin was a gash so deep I couldn't see the end of it. I don't remember what I said to comfort her. All I remember is how I felt: I had taken a child who was whole and broken her.

I ran out into the front hall and rang my neighbor's doorbell. He is a doctor. When no one answered immediately, I rang another bell. Two neighbors came to the door at the same time. I told them what had happened and they came in to help. The doctor wasn't home but his wife knew what to do. She stopped the bleeding, and told me to get hold of myself. She phoned my pediatrician and told him that June had had an accident and described the wound. The doctor asked for me. I told him the truth. He laughed and said, "It happens in the best homes."

He told me to take her to the emergency room at the hospital and assured me that she would be all right. Both my neighbors told me to forget it, "It was an accident, it happens all the time." The doctor's wife said she had hurt her sons a few times by throwing them against the wall and the other neighbor, a minister's wife, told me that once she had thrown a shoe at her youngest daughter and cut her forehead open.

"Forget it. It was an accident," they all advised. It took six stitches to sew my daughter up. She was wrapped in a sheet like a mummy, and taped down to the table. She kept crying: she was afraid that I would be angry with her because her tights would be dirty from the tape.

I never understood how a parent could hurt a child. I learned that it was very easy, and that it's accepted by friends and neighbors as an accident, as something to forget.

When June got home from the hospital, I held her in my arms and told her that I never meant to hurt her, that I loved her and that we were going to have a new rule in our home: People are not for hurting. (Ginott, 1972)

Parenthood in Cross-cultural Perspective

As the preceding incidents illustrate, there is something peculiar about American child rearing which has been remarked upon by a number of anthropologists. This peculiarity apparently stems from the isolation and privacy of the nuclear family which leads to intensive parent-child interaction. Thus the isolated family may tend to produce child abuse along with overprotection and other forms of psychological engulfment.

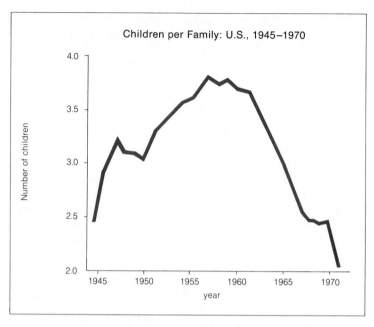

Number of children per family in the United States (total fertility rate) for 1945–1970. The chart reflects the postwar baby boom and the present continuing decline in births. (Based on data from the U.S. Bureau of the Census and prepared by the New York Times Service, *San Francisco Chronicle*, March 3, 1973, p. 4)

The issue has been stated most bluntly by Jules Henry:

> In our culture babies are a private enterprise—everybody is in the baby business as soon as he gets married. He produces his own babies; they are his; only he has a say-so in their management . . . . Pinched off alone in one's house, shielded from critical eyes, one can be as irrational as one pleases with one's children as long as severe damage does not attract the attention of the police. (Henry, 1963, pp. 331–332)

Henry contrasts this private-enterprise version of parenthood with the social regulation of parent-child relations in other cultures. In primitive cultures or large households many eyes watch what a mother does; she cannot do what she pleases with the child. Of course, this means a mother may have to carry out what she or a medical authority from another culture might consider harmful traditional practices, but the child is shielded from its mother's whims or gross incompetence. Often, as Henry points out, the child is thought of as belonging to the clan or whole family as much as it does to the parents.

The point is further documented by William Stephens (1963) in his cross-cultural survey of family life. Stephens writes how, in a number of ways, American child-rearing practices are "strikingly deviant" from those of other cultures; it seems, says Stephens, that practically the whole world does things one way, while we do it another way (p. 348).

One of the areas of great deviance concerns this matter of the isolated nuclear-family household. In every other society but one, the Copper Eskimo, Stephens finds the nuclear family living with or near the husband's or wife's kin. Regardless of the degree to which the nuclear family is thought of as a separate unit, ecologically it is part of a larger household or complex of households.

Americans appear to have an extreme form of the nuclear family, even with respect to other advanced industrial societies. Mobility, both social and geographical, became an early feature of American life because open land and an open occupational structure made it no longer the norm, as in the old country, for the son to follow in the occupational footsteps of his father (Demos, 1970; Slater, 1970). Since the country was settled by waves of immigrants, this meant that each first-generation American would know an experiential gap between the kin from the old country on the one hand and his Americanized children on the other.

In the traditional extended form of the family the child is surrounded by parental surrogates in the form of grandparents, aunts and uncles, and older cousins. The influence of the nuclear-family ideology has led to this situation being described at times as a deprivation for the child, as if the child can receive only a fixed amount of love—all of it from his mother, or the same amount divided in several ways. Actually, however, the presence of stand-ins and helpers for the mother may increase the amount of warmth and attention the mother can give to the child. For example, a six-culture study (Lambert, 1971; Minturn and Lambert, 1964; Whiting, 1963) found that the more mother substitutes were available, the warmer and more stable the mother was in interacting with the child. One of these authors, Lambert, writes of this as perhaps the most important finding of the study: "It

suggests that the mental health, or at least the style of
emotional life of both the mother and her child, are enhanced
by the availability of acceptable surrogates" (Lambert, 1971,
p. 55). Whiting (1961) reports that the attention and comfort-
ing a child receives is roughly proportional to the number of

adults living in the household. For example, the more adults there are in a house, the more time an infant is likely to spend in someone's arms, and the sooner he or she will be attended to after starting to cry.

Most of the world's children live in large households. In most societies, moreover, children are nursed for two or three years and they sleep with their mothers or both parents (Stephens, 1963; Whiting, Kluckhohn, and Anthony, 1958). By comparison the typical American child leads a rather lonely life.

Once the point has been made it seems rather obvious that the all-your-eggs-in-one-basket system of the isolated family imposes strains on both mother and child. As Stephens (1963) puts it, Mother's feelings become very important because she is the only mother you have. If she gets angry with you, there's no place else to go; nor is there anyplace for her to go to rest or to get out of an angry mood. This sets the stage for emotional outbursts, which at the extreme may result in child abuse, but more frequently result in scoldings and complaints, perhaps spankings, sometimes accidents. It's not a matter of villains, or bad parents, but rather an ecological one: great demands being placed on limited parental resources of time, energy, and money.

The lack of social regulation of parenthood by the clan or community has many disadvantages for the parent even as it increases his power over the child. The parent does not seek enormous power; power is gained through the family system which gives it with the birth of a child. Again we encounter one of the many paradoxes of freedom: in the tribal family or traditional kin group, the child not only does not belong to parents in the same way as he does to isolated nuclear parents, but also the parent deals with his child according to a script written by the larger culture. The culture's traditional beliefs and superstitions strengthen the parents' position in dealing with a child and, again paradoxically, can make the parent more relaxed, warm, and affectionate. In the old system the parent resembles an administrator in a large bureaucracy, carrying out policies made by higher authorities. The child may disobey or fail to carry out an assigned task, but he is unlikely to argue with very many of the rules themselves. Even if he does, however, the parent can argue back that it's beyond his power to change the rules.

What the parent loses in personal power he more than makes up for in institutional backing for his position. By contrast, the American parent is often uncertain about rules because no community tradition exists, and advice from experts may be contradictory and difficult to apply. Whether or not the parent is unsure, the child recognizes the parent as the source of the rules—the parent is the legislator as well as the executive and the judiciary. Thus the stage is set for submission or resentment or rebellion.

No matter what the outcome, it is a two-party conflict, a win-or-lose game between parent and child. Books of advice to parents often suggest that parents state rules impersonally, not in the form of orders. Thus they are advised not to say to their children "Go to bed" but "It's bedtime"; not to say "Pick those toys up off the floor" but "There are some toys on the floor that need to be put away." The parent can even say "I know you want to stay up, but it's bedtime," indicating even further separation of himself from the rules and a closeness to the child. This technique often does work since it avoids challenging, face-to-face confrontations between the parents and the children. But it hardly duplicates the situation of the parent in a traditional society. The child usually comprehends that the buck really does stop at the parent, and that there is only a remote authority, if any at all, supervising his parent's acts and his own.

The most extreme form of social support for parental authority is the supernatural. Consider the following incident, reported by a Hopi Indian man about his childhood:

I later saw some giantlike Katchinas (masked dancers who impersonate supernatural beings) stalking into the village with long black bills, and big sawlike teeth. One carried a rope to lasso disobedient children. He stopped at a certain house and called for a boy. "You have been naughty," he scolded. "You fight with other children. You kill chickens. You pay no attention to the old people. We have come to get you and eat you." The boy cried and promised to behave better. The giants became angrier and threatened to tie him up and take him away. But the boy's parents begged for his life and offered fresh meat in his place. The giant reached out his hand as if to grab the boy but took the meat instead. Placing it in his basket, he warned the boy that he would get one more chance to change his conduct. I was frightened and got out of sight. I heard that sometimes these giants captured boys and really ate them. (Stephens, 1963, p. 341)

Notice the role of the parents in the anecdote—from the child's point of view they are benevolent protectors saving him from a terrible fate. In the American family system, the frightening giant and kind protector are one person.

Experiencing Parenthood in Daily Life

In looking at parenthood as an institution, we have not yet focused on the parents themselves. What is the meaning of parenthood in the lives of parents? How are the strains and contradictions in the nuclear-family system translated into the day-to-day experiences of mothers and fathers?

In recent years there has been a growing tendency in both the professional and the popular literature to look at parenthood in less idyllic terms than once was common. From the late 1940's to the 1960's parenthood was defined as happy self-fulfillment. Psychoanalysis contributed to this prevailing mystique of parenthood. The older version of Freudian theory saw parenthood as the realization of infantile wishes. In the newer ego psychology, parenthood became a stage of normal personality development. For a woman especially, the coming of children represented the crowning achievement of her life, the justification of her own existence. For men, the father role, although it is peripheral in the sense that it does not include day-to-day responsibilities for child care, has traditionally been seen as proof of manhood. The masculinity-confirming aspects of fatherhood are emphasized in one way in the notion of machismo, and in another way in the psychoanalytic version of maturity that prevailed during the 1950's. Along with the notion of parenthood as inherently rewarding and fulfilling have gone some subsidiary ideas, such as the notion that children bring a couple close together, and thus can repair a bad marriage or improve a good one.

LeMasters has listed seventeen "folk beliefs" about parenthood that have been popular in American culture—a folk belief being an idea that is widely shared yet not supported by evidence. Some examples of these include:

> Rearing children is fun.
> Children are sweet and cute.
> Children will turn out well if they have "good" parents.

Children appreciate all the advantages their parents give them.

Two parents are always better than one.

Love is enough to sustain good parental performance.

All married couples should have children.

Childless married couples are frustrated and unhappy.

Children improve a marriage.

Child rearing is easier today because of modern medicine, modern appliances, child psychology, etc. (LeMasters, 1970, pp. 18–29)

On this last point LeMasters makes the paradoxical observation that increased knowledge of pediatrics and child psychology does not necessarily make child rearing any easier. Just as improvements in household appliances have failed to reduce the housewife's working hours, but merely have raised standards of housekeeping, so have child psychology and improved pediatrics raised the standards for child rearing.

Child-development experts — psychologists, psychiatrists, and doctors — have been "worshipped as the high-priests of child rearing" (Pohlman, 1969, p. 102). Yet the advice of the experts is often inconsistent, and usually difficult to apply to specific situations. One expert may write, for example, that hugging and kissing is good for babies and children, whereas another writes that physical affection is seductive and disturbing. Some experts favor "permissiveness"; others argue that children "need" firm rules and authoritative direction. In a classic article Martha Wolfenstein (1955) reviewed the changes in advice given in various editions of the pamphlet *Infant Care*, published by the United States government on consultation with the experts in the field. In the ten editions issued over the last forty years, there have been remarkable alterations in concepts of the child's psychological and physical needs, and the kind of parental behavior recommended:

In the earlier period, the mother's character was one of strong moral devotion. There were frequent references to her "self-control," "wisdom," "strength," "persistence" . . . . In the 1929–1938 period, parenthood became predominantly a matter of know-how. The parents had to use the right technique to impose routines and keep the child from dominating them.

In the most recent period, parenthood becomes a major source of enjoyment for both parents. . . . The parents are promised that having children will keep them together, keep them young, and give them fun and happiness. . . . Enjoyment, fun, and play now permeate all activities with the child. "Babies—and usually their mothers—enjoy breast feeding," nursing brings "joy and happiness" to the mother. At bath time, the baby "delights" his parents, and so on. (Wolfenstein, 1955, p. 173)

A review of child-rearing research by Bronfenbrenner (1958) revealed that middle-class parents seemed to reflect in their actual child-rearing practices the swings in expert opinion. During the first half of the twentieth century middle-class parents tended to be more strict with their children than working- and lower-class parents, but by the fifties they had crossed over and become more permissive. During the earlier period, for example, middle-class parents tended to wean and toilet train their infants earlier and to keep them on stricter schedules than did working-class parents; in more recent years, however, middle-class parents have swung over to later weaning and toilet training and to more flexible schedules. Bronfenbrenner, attributing these changes to the great sensitivity of middle-class parents to expert opinion, writes:

Taken as a whole, the correspondence between Wolfenstein's data and our own suggests a general hypothesis extending beyond the confines of social class as such: *child-rearing practices are likely to change most quickly in those segments of society which have closest access to and are most receptive to the agencies or agents of change (e.g., public media, clinics, physicians, and counselors).* (Bronfenbrenner, 1958, p. 411) (Italics in the original)

Ironically, attention to the experts among middle-class people seems to raise anxiety rather than reduce it. Research on middle-class mothers, such as that conducted by Sears and his associates (1957), suggests that the more awareness a mother has of the child-rearing literature, the more uncertain she feels that she is doing the right thing:

" . . . I spend most of my time thinking I am a perfectly lousy mother and I suppose all mothers feel that way. The thing of motherhood brings out my own inefficiencies, my own deficiencies, so terribly, that . . . the outstanding thought in my mind is that I should try to be a better mother each new day." (Sears et al., 1957, p. 43)

Problems such as bed wetting or stuttering tend to be interpreted by middle-class parents as a negative reflection of their parenting. But in former days, particularly in the working classes, parents more often blamed such problems on the child's character or on physical difficulties. Furthermore, working-class parents show relatively more concern for the child's outward behavior than his inner states (Kohn, 1963). A concern for the inner life of the child may make things harder for both parent and child.

The notion that parenthood is fun may lead paradoxically to greater strains for parents:

> The characterization of parenthood in terms of fun and enjoyment . . . may express a new imperative: You ought to enjoy your child. When a mother is told that most mothers enjoy nursing, she may wonder what is wrong with her in case she does not. Her self-evaluation can no longer be based entirely on whether she is doing the right and necessary things but becomes involved with nuances of feeling which are not under voluntary control. (Wolfenstein, 1955, pp. 174–175)

The Costs of Parenthood   In recent years there has begun to be a trend away from the notions of parenthood-as-fulfillment and of child rearing as part of the grand design of the social system. There is a growing awareness that even wanted and dearly loved children seem to bring heavy costs to parents. One of the landmarks of this new trend was a 1957 article by E. E. LeMasters entitled "Parenthood as Crisis." LeMasters argued that the romantic complex surrounding parenthood goes even deeper than the one surrounding marriage, and he especially challenged the notion that the coming of children improves marital relationships. He and other writers have documented some of the ways in which the coming of children disrupts marriage.

One study reported that following childbirth the amount of time the wife and husband converse with each other is cut in half (Feldman, 1962). The sexual relationship is disrupted and may even be discontinued for as long as four months— eight weeks before birth and eight weeks after birth while tissues heal. Some women remain indifferent toward sex even after their physical recovery from childbirth. The presence of the child looms large, and parental sex may be interrupted by its cries. The exhaustion of the new mother hovers

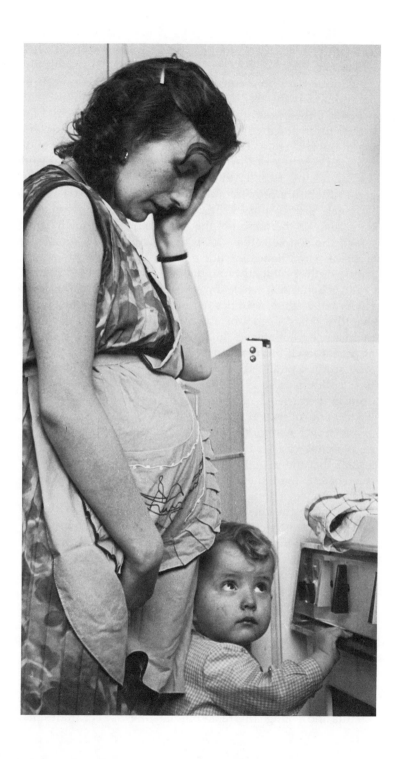

constantly in the background, and at times becomes over-whelming.

Another of the themes of this literature on the costs of parenthood is the feeling on the part of many parents, particularly fathers, that they are competing with the child for the attention and love of the spouse. In many homes the coming of the first child changes the household from a husband-centered one to a child-centered one for waking, eating, and use of leisure time (Waller and Hill, 1951). Some of the earlier literature on parenthood as crisis saw the crisis as a "normal" one. Just as in the conventional literature on marriage there is the notion of the "period of adjustment," after which the couple settles down to a mature marriage, so the crisis-of-parenthood literature emphasized the transitory nature of the problems brought on by the coming of children.

Alice Rossi's article on the transition to parenthood (1968) takes issue with the "normal" crisis idea. She argues that the crisis need not always have a positive outcome: people need not always "mature" in response to the strains of parenthood, but may suffer deterioration. This is particularly so for women, she notes, since the cultural pressure to bear children is so great that many women may have children in the absence of a genuine desire for them or the ability to perform well at the task.

A novel feature of this analysis is Rossi's comparison of parental roles with those of marriage and work. She argues that the parent role is much more difficult in American society than the other two roles. Marriage and work often involve a long period of preparation, with gradual transition to the role. The transition to parenthood, on the other hand, occurs abruptly and totally, as if a person shifted from being a graduate student to a full professor with little intervening apprenticeship experience of slowly increasing responsibility. The new mother starts out immediately on twenty-four-hour-a-day duty with full responsibilities. Further, in contrast with other commitments, parenthood is irrevocable. Rossi notes that we can have ex-spouses and ex-jobs but not ex-children.

Rossi argues that failures in mothering should be blamed not on individual women but on the isolated nuclear-family structure and the failure of society to provide institutionalized substitutes for the extended kin to assist in the care of infants and young children. Pohlman likewise concludes that since so many women have dreary reactions to their first ten or twelve years of motherhood, a society-wide problem seems to be present, and he calls for a society-wide solution.

It seems illogical that each one of many thousands of mothers should conclude she has some peculiar individual problem, and should go through a period of soul-searching and hostility and repression and guilt in her relations to her children. A culture-wide problem suggests the need for national leadership to try to rearrange matters within the culture to alleviate the problem. (Pohlman, 1969, p. 153)

TABLE 4   TOTAL COST OF A CHILD, 1969

	Discounted Cost	Undiscounted Cost[a]
Giving birth	$ 1,534	$ 1,534
Raising a child	17,576	32,830
College education	1,244	5,560
Total direct cost	$20,354	$39,924
Opportunity cost for the average woman[b]	39,273	58,437
Total cost of child	$59,627	$98,361

[a]Discounted and undiscounted costs—spending $1,000 today costs more than spending $1,000 over a ten-year period because of the nine years of potential interest on the latter. This fact is allowed for in the discounted figures by assuming interest earned annually on money not spent in the first year. True costs are not accurately reflected in the undiscounted estimates, for these are simply accumulations of total outlays without regard to the year in which they must be made.
[b]Depending on the educational background of the mother, the opportunity costs (earnings foregone by not working) could be higher or lower.
Source: *Population and the American Future*, report of the Commission on Population Growth and the American Future (Washington: U.S. Government Printing Office, 1972), p. 81.

Not only the transition to parenthood but also the continuing financial and psychological costs of raising a child have received recent attention from a number of writers. One estimate arrives at a cost of $40,000 to raise a child from birth to age eighteen. If the income the mother would have made had she been working is counted, the price reaches $100,000. As to the psychological impact, John and Suzanne Clausen report the following findings:

Especially during the early years, children connote broken sleep, noise, confusion, and when there are several, congestion. Mothers of young children put in an inordinately long work week and tend to be confined to the home much of the time. The early years of motherhood are frequently remembered as the period when one constantly yearned for a full night's sleep and for a day free of demands. In our longitudinal data at the Institute of Human Development, mothers with three or more children fairly closely spaced, looking back at the early years of motherhood, from the perspective of the late 40's, are likely to recall those early years as years of extreme exhaustion and discouragement. (1971, p. 7)

Pohlman notes that many parents find interacting with children, especially over long periods of time, a strain:

One reason is the frequent conflict over the child's actions. Parents want the child to do one thing; the child wants to do another. The battle between wills can prove wearying. Demanding strict and unwavering obedience may be the simplest procedure, but even this is a strain on parents. And many parents doubt whether this is the right approach. . . . They may alternate between permissiveness and irritated punitiveness. If they punish physically, they may feel guilty for this; if they fail to do so, they may feel guilty for the omission. (1969, p. 105)

But the strains of parenthood are not the inevitable battle of wills and the temperamental incompatibilities of adults and children. In part, they are the responsibility of social arrangements which make parents solely responsible for children, and which fail to provide even minimal assistance for parents as they go about their daily rounds of work and chores.

Moreover, despite the myth of the child-centered society, we are remarkably adult-oriented, with few places where children can be integrated into adult activities. One mother has described the result as follows:

I have three children, 8, $2\frac{1}{2}$, and 1. They are beautiful children, and most times I delight in them. But there are times when I see them as encumbrances, the objects of my frustration and anger. They are welded to me not only at birth, but by a society that sees them as totally my problem, my burden alone. Wherever I move, they move with me: to the drugstore, to the newsstand, the fish market. Where once I moved on two legs, now I move on eight.

As parents, my husband and I are the sole providers, protectors, entertainers and watchdogs for our young. We have no "extended family" to help care for them, no communal group to share the tasks. . . . When there are errands to be run or places we want to go — even for an hour — the scheduling and logistical arrangements that must be made would spin the most grizzled heads in the Pentagon.

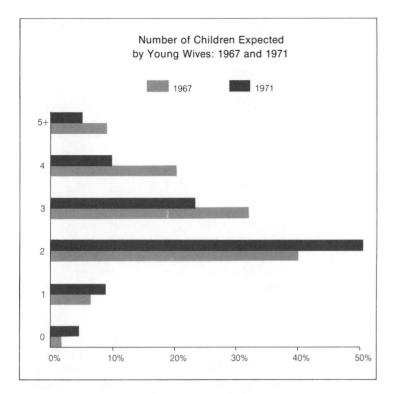

Number of children expected by wives age 18–24 years in the United States, 1967 and 1971. The chart shows the decline in the number of children wanted. For the first time since 1955 the desired number of children has dropped below three. (Based on data in *Population Characteristics*, U.S. Department of Commerce, Bureau of the Census, Series P-20, No. 232, Washington: U.S. Government Printing Office, 1972)

Though free universal community-controlled child care is one goal, child-care service of another sort is equally important. Part-time child care. Hourly child care. Child care provided on sites our dreary but necessary chores lead us to. Dragging the children along to places where adults don't even want to go doubles the frustration . . . and more often than not, turns the children into recipients of our frustrations. (Francke, 1972, pp. 27–28)

The inconveniences this middle-class mother experiences are magnified to greater torment for the poor, who must spend hours waiting with their children in welfare offices, hospital clinics, and the courts.

The everyday trivial strains of parenthood have been increased by changes in American life having nothing to do with children or families. The decline of the urban neighborhood, with its local stores and lively sidewalk life, the suburban automotive way of life, the general feeling that public places are unsafe—all this has resulted in a dehumanization of life in general which makes it harder than ever to integrate children into everyday adult life.

The Future of Parenthood

We have focused so heavily on the dark side of parent-child relations in this chapter because the prevailing views of the subject have been so romantic and unrealistic. It is possible, however, to end on an optimistic note.

As we have emphasized throughout this chapter, the care a child will receive when it comes into the world is not guaranteed by genes, instincts, or societal necessity. The first requirement for adequate child care is this: the child should be wanted by whomever is responsible for it, although loving and wanting a child do not guarantee competence in a parent. Anything that reduces the likelihood of unwanted births can only increase the chances that children who are born will be treated humanely. The ability to exercise control and choice about parenthood must mark a milestone in what Erich Fromm has called the "revolution of the child."

Many other ongoing social changes now—the abortion movement, women's liberation, the concern with overpopulation and the environment, the increasing acceptability of singleness, childlessness, and homosexuality—can only mean that fewer children will be born as a result of carelessness or social pressure. When parenthood is romanticized, when it is assumed that all women are endowed with maternal instincts and innate competence in caring for infants and young children, any alternative means of child care can only be seen as a deprivation for the child. The prevailing myths of parenthood obscure the possibility that child-care facilities may rescue children from physical and emotional mistreatment, and even improve the relationship between the parents and children. After reviewing the literature on the experiences of women during the first ten or twelve years of parenthood, Pohlman suggests that neighborhood child-care and education centers are a vital necessity for the well-being of both mothers and children. He writes:

> We believe that most mothers need to be away from their children for a few hours each day, whether they are employed outside their homes or not. Such a "recess" probably permits a mother to relate to her children with greater zest and effectiveness when she is with them. Many mothers cannot bring themselves to leave their children, because of justifiable concern with the quality of substitute care they will receive. Also many mothers lack even the small initiative needed to arrange to be away from children, under existing circumstances. All of this seems to imply the need for a systematic program of child care and education, a program of excellent quality. (Pohlman, 1969, p. 153)

The prejudice against child-care facilities outside the home has become a self-fulfilling prophecy. The relatively few day-care facilities that do exist are woefully inadequate in terms of both quantity and quality. They are conceived to be places where only a mother in extreme circumstances would consider sending a child. And they are conceived to be total substitutes for family child care, five days a week, eight hours a day, all year long.

Such forms of child care are needed, but there is another kind for which the need is even greater—part-time, drop-in child care for parents to use as they go about their business. Pohlman also mentions the need for visiting nurses or other parent surrogates to help out when parents or children are sick. Such services would relieve the kinds of strains that led the widowed father to break his son's arm in the incident reported earlier in this chapter.

Further, trends within the family itself promise to relieve some of the strains of parenthood, which until now have fallen most heavily on women. In young middle-class families, that segment of the population most sensitive to changes in the intellectual climate, parenthood is coming to be defined more and more as a joint enterprise of both the husband and the wife. (Recently the City College of New York announced a plan to grant both paternity and maternity leaves to its employees.) The trend seems to be motivated not only because the women are insisting that the men share some of the load, but because many young professional men themselves no longer accept as their fate the compulsive male careerism that dominated the 1950's.

Finally, parent-child relations are being affected by far-reaching changes in definitions of both adulthood and childhood. We will consider these changes in the following chapters.

Summary

The prevailing conceptions of parenthood in the social sciences and popular thought have emphasized the naturalness of parenthood and the societal need for children. Early mother-child relations in particular are assumed to be governed by innate processes of mutual attraction, independent of social contexts.

Actually, however, the evolutionary evidence suggests that human infants, in contrast to our primate relatives, are born into a nurturance gap. The same factors that led to the evolution of the human brain resulted in the greater helplessness of human infants, and a greater dependency on learning and culture for carrying out maternal activities.

Parent-child relations cannot be understood apart from specific social, cultural, and historical settings. The feeding and care of young children can be a heavy burden or an easily assumed one, depending on the food supply, cultural attitudes toward infants, and the particular circumstances of individual parents. The fact that infanticide has been widely practiced in Western society and elsewhere is evidence that benevolence toward children is not built into human nature, and is not a societal imperative.

To understand parenthood in our own society, we must realize how modern kinship and work patterns may make parenthood more difficult than in traditional societies. In most cultures and in our own historical past, parenthood is carried out in the midst of the community, and along with economic responsibilities. It is a less self-conscious process because traditional ways can be followed, and the child's future status is already known. Our own society, however, imposes great demands on parents while providing minimal institutional support to replace the kin and community assistance of former times.

THE CONSTRUCTION
OF CHILDHOOD

Chapter 9

Nature wants children to be children before they are men. If we deliberately pervert this order, we shall get premature fruits which are neither ripe nor well flavored. . . . Childhood has ways of seeing, thinking, and feeling, peculiar to itself; nothing can be more foolish than trying to substitute our ways for them.

Jean-Jacques Rousseau, *Emile*

There seems little doubt that, in our . . . culture, a contributing factor to the characteristic features of "child mentality" that we have discovered is the positive efforts we make to keep our children childish.

A. Irving Hallowell, *Culture and Experience*

Chapter Nine   The twentieth century has been hailed as "the century of the child," and American families have been described as child-centered to an extreme degree. Foreign visitors from the nineteenth century on as well as anthropologists who have studied other peoples find our concern with childhood unique. "We have set a new record; no other people seems ever to have been so preoccupied with children, so anxious about them, or so uncertain about how to deal with them" (Goodman, 1970, p. 1).

Despite our reputation for child-centeredness, however, the 1970 White House Conference on Children, whose task was to assess the status and needs of children in America, warned of "national neglect of children" (p. 252). One conference participant argues that the alarm was not made urgent enough:

. . . The evidence indicates that American society, whether viewed in comparison to other nations or to itself over time, is accordingly progressively less attentive to its children. The trend is already apparent when the child is born. America, the richest and most powerful country in the world, stands thirteenth among the nations in combatting infant mortality. (Bronfenbrenner, in White House Conference on Children, 1970, p. 252)

The participants not only had in mind children from disadvantaged families when they wrote of the neglect of children. Children from all classes, the conference report notes, suffer from being isolated from adult society. Within the home there is evidence of a decline in parent-child interaction over the past twenty-five years (Bronfenbrenner, 1970). Further, the parent-child interaction that does occur is not all beneficial to children: one out of four fractures diagnosed in children under three results from physical abuse by parents; two children die every day from parental abuse (Kempe, 1973).

The coexistence of concern and neglect, or worse, in the treatment of children is not unique to our time and place. Perhaps the greatest gap between popular imagery and reality concerning children occurred in the Victorian era when, as Peter Coveney (1967) points out, the *myth* of innocent childhood prevailed along with the *practice* of savagery toward children. Coveney refers not only to the exploitation of children in mines and factories, but also to the severe child-rearing practices approved by Victorian families.

In addition to the gap between ideal and reality in the treatment of children, our attempts to understand the child's place in society are complicated by contrasting images of the child which not only have succeeded each other but have coexisted side by side.

One of the recurring themes of the growing literature on the history of the family is how ideas about children taken for granted in one era come to be regarded as false by the next. In medieval times, for example, children were seen as miniature adults. They wore adult clothing, and when painters gave them adult proportions, no one seems to have noticed that the representations were inaccurate. To later ages such paintings appear quaint and funny.

The image of the child as an incomplete adult was replaced by the demonic child of Calvinism and the Jesuits, a child whose corrupt nature and evil will called for severe discipline, of which whipping was a ritual part, in order to fit him to be a moral citizen. "Spare the rod and spoil the child" was once a literal prescription for child rearing.

The corrupt child in turn became—for the romantic school of writers, such as Blake, Wordsworth, and Rousseau—a noble savage, whose "doors of perception" and capacities for experiences were not yet deadened by an industrial society. The serious social criticism implied by the image of the romantic child wilted away to become the Victorian cult of the innocent child; childhood became a never-never land of fun and games.

Actually, the image of childhood innocence never entirely replaced the demonic child of the Puritans; particularly in England and America, attitudes toward childhood have been marked by "a curious conflict between childhood as innocence and the grim portrait of an evil being who must be scourged to his salvation" (Kessen, 1965, p. 33). At the end of the nineteenth century Freud revived the image of the demonic child, and made it the focus of a new psychology. Freud's theories of infantile sexuality attacked the image of childhood innocence and ushered in the first of the "developmental images" of the child which have dominated the twentieth century. Since that time the leading images of the child have been supplied by scientific professionals—psychologists, psychiatrists, pediatricians—

rather than by religionists and poets. Thus the child is defined by his place on a staircase of development—the child of ages and stages.

In view of the profound changes that have occurred in our culture's theories of childhood, we can hardly rest assured that we have at last discovered childhood as it really is.

What Is a Child?

The enormous variation in the ideas different cultures and historical eras have had about children, their needs, capacities, and the dynamics of growth suggest that the answer is not as obvious as it seems. In this chapter we are going to explore such issues as the following: Is the nature of childhood universal, or do childhood experiences and the characteristics of children vary? To what extent has childhood as we know it been shaped by our family life and other social practices regarding children? Does a society's recognition of the various stages of childhood and youth indicate sensitivity to children's needs? Or does age grading represent a means of segregating children from adult society and exerting greater social control over them? Is the history of childhood one of uninterrupted progress?

In trying to define a child, we face many of the same problems we faced earlier in trying to arrive at a definition of the term "family." The very word "child" carries with it a number of assumptions that get in our way. For example, the term exists in opposition to another term—"adult"—like light and dark, male and female. Thus our language suggests an opposition, a discontinuity between children and adults, which fits with actual social practice in our society. We tend to assume that children have a separate and distinct nature that distinguishes them from adults: adults work and are responsible, children play and are irresponsible; adults are controlled and rational, children are emotional and irrational; adults think abstractly, children think concretely; adults are sexual, children are asexual; and so on.

Above all, we tend to view children through the lenses of the developmental model or paradigm: the assumptions that the child develops naturally by passing through a number of stages, that these stages follow one another in a constant order, that each order is appropriate for a particular age, and that the child has within itself a built-in timetable of development. The essential principles of the developmental paradigm, first elaborated in 1762 by the philosopher Rousseau in *Emile*, continue to guide the field of child study.

In premodern societies, in our own historical past, and in groups outside the middle class, a different concept of childhood has prevailed: the child is seen as a miniature adult. Bennett Berger has contrasted the two conceptions of childhood as follows:

> In viewing the history of how children are conceptualized by adults, social scientists have . . . emphasized the differences between pre-industrial, agricultural, or sometimes lower-class views on the one side, and industrial or middle-class views on the other. In the former view, the status of children is seen as essentially ascribed at birth and rooted in the kinship system. In this view children are seen as simply small or inadequate versions of their parents, totally subject to traditional or otherwise arbitrary parental authority. The "modern" industrial, middle-class view, by contrast, tends to treat the child as a distinctive social category: children have their own special psychology, their own special needs, patterned processes of growth often elaborated into ideas about developmental stages which may postpone advent to "full" adulthood well into a person's twenties, and still later. (Berger et al., 1972, p. 11)

Most professional and popular writings on childhood seem to take for granted that there is a closer fit between the child's special nature and his or her place in modern societies than in the premodern model where children are treated as little adults.

The prevailing assumption is that the discontinuities between adults and children are not recognized, that the child's nature is being violated. For example, we find the fact that young children work in some cultures both anomalous and distasteful. Even a sophisticated anthropologist can express surprise at the failure of Indian mothers, for example, to appreciate children's work:

> . . . Even those children who did work regularly were not accorded recognition. For instance, Narayan's mother, when asked about her son's chores, reported that he did not do very much work. It would seem that walking an average of 12 miles a day, and carrying a load for 6 to 9 of those miles, might be considered a rather arduous undertaking for a slightly built 7-year-old boy, but his mother was not impressed. (B. Whiting, 1963, pp. 356–357)

Other failures to mark off childhood from adulthood also strike us as incongruous — as when children wear adult cloth-

ing—or horrifying—as when, as in many cultures, children are not shielded from sexual knowledge. In general, the failure of preindustrial societies to recognize childhood is taken to be an indicator of the backwardness of primitive peoples. Indeed, anthropologists of the late nineteenth and early twentieth centuries often equated the mentality of adult "savages" with that of the child in Western culture. Hence the failure to separate adulthood from childhood could be interpreted as a sign of arrested development: if children and adults acted in similar ways, it must be because the adults never progressed beyond the earliest stages of mental development. Although anthropologists have rejected the notion that the norms of child development in Western cultures are the measuring rod against which other cultures are to be judged, the equation of preliterate adult with Western child persists as strongly as ever in psychology. Further, psychological concepts of childhood not only are *ethnocentric*—biased in favor of Western culture—but also they may be *chronocentric*—biased in favor of a particular historical period. As Kenneth Keniston has put it:

> Every epoch tends to freeze its own unique experience into an ahistorical version of life in general. Modern developmental psychology witnesses this universal trend. Despite recent advances in our understanding of human development, our psychological concepts have generally suffered from an historical parochialism that takes the patterns, timetables, and sequences of development prevalent among middle-class children in contemporary Western societies as the norm of human development. (1971a, p. 332)

The concepts of childhood that prevail in our culture, particularly among the most educated parts of the public, are those of developmental psychology. Psychologists and psychiatrists are generally conceded to be the experts in the field; most research in human development is carried out by psychologists, and the intellectual giants of the field, Freud and Piaget, have also come from psychology. Both have stressed the biologically based universality of developmental stages; they have assumed, along with psychology as a field, that we need not study development or other psychological phenomena in any other place or time than our own, since developmental laws "transcend both culture and history" (Keniston, 1971a, p. 333).

The Ideology of Childhood and the Developmental Paradigm

The model of the child in psychology reflects the prevailing cultural attitudes and practices concerning children. The psychologist's model also reflects, however, the intellectual traditions of psychology as a field.

The nature of the child became an object of scientific inquiry in the psychology laboratory beginning in the second half of the nineteenth century. A major, if not *the* major, reason for the rise of scientific interest in the child at this time was the work of Darwin. It is almost impossible to overestimate the dramatic impact of Darwin on our notions of children as well as on psychology in general. As Hallowell notes:

Revitalized interest in animal mentality, child mentality, and the mentality of primitive man, all received their impetus from a common source: the concept of evolution. As a consequence of Darwin's work, evolution at once became the skeleton key by means of which attempts were made to unlock, and sometimes to force, new and untried doors of knowledge. Stages of evolutionary development soon were postulated for physical, biological, cultural, and mental phenomena. All kinds of analogies were drawn, new continuities envisaged, and underlying laws of development sought. (1955, p. 14)

One of the most influential concepts to emerge from the new interest in evolution was the recapitulation hypothesis, the notion that the development of the individual repeats the history of the species ("ontogeny recapitulates phylogeny"). The starting point for the recapitulation hypothesis was the development of embryos. Thus it was noted that the human embryo starts out as a single-celled organism, becomes a multicelled organism, then resembles a fish, and so on. Extending this idea beyond the prenatal period, the mental development of the growing child was assumed to repeat the mental development of the human race, reaching its highest point in the adult rational mind of Western man. Thus, as Kessen puts it, there was a "riot of parallel-drawing" between the mind of the child and what was presumed to be earlier historical stages of the human species:

The irreducible contribution of Darwin to the study of children was . . . in his assignment of scientific value to childhood. Species develop, societies develop, man develops. From the publication of *The Origin of Species* to the end of the nineteenth century, there was a riot of parallel-drawing between animal and child, between primitive man and child, between early human history and child. The developing child was seen as a natural museum of human phylogeny and history; by careful observation of the infant and child, one could see the descent of man. (Kessen, 1965, p. 115)

In short, child psychology did not start without preconceived notions about children. It began by equating children with animals and with "savages"; it was not driven to such parallels after amassing a large number of observations which could not be *explained* by any other means. Although psychologists do observe children, child psychology is not and has never been a descriptive or purely observational science like geography or meteorology. As Kessen remarks of the baby biographers who kept diaries of their children's development after Darwin had made child study scientifically important, and as did Darwin himself, psychologists not only see children, they see living expressions of their theoretical positions.

Let us summarize the essential features of developmental theories. Although each theory selects a different aspect of the child as the key to understanding the process of development, they all agree on several things:

1   Development is self-propelled and teleological — that is, the "push" to change comes from within the organism — and the endpoint of the developmental changes is implicit at the beginning. The process of development seems to "know" where it is going.

2   The adult is categorically, or qualitatively, different from the child.

3   The different stages of childhood are also qualitatively different from each other. The endpoint of development is placed at the twenties. Until recently the legal designation of twenty-one as the age of adult status accorded well with developmental theories. The developmental tasks postulated by the theories take that long to complete.

4   Developmental theories are organized around a concept of adult competence. For Freud the endpoint of development is the genital, heterosexual adult, parent to children, with a place in the occupational world. For Piaget the endpoint of development becomes possible at adolescence, when the stage of formal operational thinking — the ability to think hypothetically and abstractly — is attained.

Thus, by definition, developmental theories set up a polar opposition between child and adult nature. If the adult end of the scale is defined as logical and rational, then the child is by definition autistic, irrational, emotional, and lacking in perceptual and cognitive structures. These qualities are conceived of as being appropriate for children, and related to such positive attributes as curiosity, originality, and creativity. A similar polarity is set up between work and play: work is the province of the adult, and play that of the child.

Finally, developmental theories claim to be universal. Freudian theory is notable for its depiction of a series of developmental changes triggered by biological events. The theory allows for different outcomes depending on how the child's development crises are met, but the developmental basics of orality, anality, genitality, and the Oedipal crises are held to be universal. Piaget's progressions are generally thought to be drawn on maturation and encounters between the physical and social environment found in all cultures.

The major developmental theories actually care little and say little about what children really do. The only developmental theorist to concern himself with the specifics of daily life, such as what the eighteen-month-old is likely to be doing at 9:15 A.M., was Arnold Gesell (1943). If most developmental theories are overly general, however, Gesell's is overly specific. He was not concerned with the actual behavior of different children in their particular milieu, but with "the child," whose daily schedule or "behavior day" was taken to be the norm for a particular age. Mothers who were irked by a particular behavior—say a two-and-a-half-year-old's standing in a doorway, unable to decide whether he wants to go in or out—could consult Gesell and find that specific behavior described as characteristic of that stage. Thus Gesell comforts not only because he provides an encyclopedia of children's behavior, but also because he usually does not blame parents for many common problems.

Freud and Piaget   The two giants of developmental theory, Freud and Piaget, are both somewhat removed from the mundane realities of child life—Piaget probably more so than Freud. Both provide striking images of childhood. They throw a bright light on aspects nobody else noticed, yet, paradoxically, their emphasis on novel aspects of the child obscured others. Thus Freud revolutionized the image of the child by pointing out sexual interests that previous generations of adults had refused to notice. The baby at the breast, the toddler on the potty chair, the four-year-old lusting after his mother and wishing murder on his father became the dominant images of the child, replacing, as we noted earlier, the image of the innocent child that had dominated the Victorian era.

In some ways the Piagetian image of the child is the polar opposite of the Freudian image. If the Freudian child is a demonic little beast, seething with lust and aggression,

Piaget's is a scientist bubbling with curiosity; the baby dropping toys out of his crib is revealed to be a little Galileo, observing the behavior of falling bodies. Not only does he exhibit a thirst for knowledge as strong as the sexual urges of the Freudian child—even stronger, because less satiable—but the Piagetian child has an active and independent intellect. In Freud's imagery of the child as well as that of most socialization research, the child is the more or less passive recipient of the demands and teachings of his culture; his only alternative to acceptance is resistance. The choice of weaning and toilet training as the central events in the socialization of the child are significant: these are precisely the areas that allow no room for innovation on the part of the child. All children are eventually weaned and toilet trained; in these struggles the culture always wins, and the child always conforms.

The Piagetian child, however, does not merely internalize the standards of adults as he grows up. Roger Brown summarizes the Piagetian view of socialization as follows:

> The mature persons with whom a child interacts behave in accordance with such systems of norms or rules as are called logic, mathematics, language, morality, aesthetics . . . and so on. For the most part these systems have not been explicitly formulated by the adults whose behavior is governed by them and they will not be explicitly formulated by the child who acquires them. This process is not a simple "passing over" of the systems from one generation to another. What each child extracts at a given age is a function of his idiosyncratic experience and of his present intellectual capabilities. The systems governing the child change as he grows older and they need not, in the end, simply reproduce the rules that prevail in his society. The outcome can be unique and sometimes revolutionary. (R. W. Brown, 1965, p. 193)

Yet the Piagetian child is not so unlike the Freudian one as he appears at first glance. He is curious like a scientist, but his capacity to process information is as yet unsophisticated. His limited thought processes are based on a logic that is egocentric, animistic, and easily tricked by appearances. Show him two equal balls of clay, roll one into a sausage, and he will tell you there is now less clay in it because it is thinner. He has a very long way to go before he is ready to participate in adult life.

The problem with these images of the child is not so much that they are wrong but that they stress particular aspects of development. Parents who have studied Freud before having children are often surprised to find that the very young infant does not seem to spend all his time being "oral" and that toilet training doesn't occupy most of the toddler's days. Robert White has attempted to translate the psychosexual stages of development into terms of the kind of competence the child is trying to achieve at each stage. He compares Gesell's descriptions of infancy with the Freudian models, and writes of the oral stage as follows:

> Somehow, the image has gotten into our minds that the infant's time is divided between eating and sleep. Peter Wolff (1959) is now showing that this is not true even for newborn infants, who show distinct forerunners of what will later become playful exploratory activity. Gesell notes that at four weeks there is apt to be a waking time in the late afternoon during which visual experience begins to be accumulated. At 16 weeks this period may last for half an hour, and the times increase steadily up to one year. Gesell's typical "behavior day" shows an hour of play before breakfast, two hours before lunch, an hour's carriage ride and another hour of social play in the afternoon, and perhaps still another hour after being put to bed. At the age of 12 months, the child is already putting in a six-hour day of play, not to mention the overtime that occurs during meals and the bath. (R. W. White, 1960, pp. 110–111)

Thus, although eating and sucking are important to the child in the first year, the concept of "orality" does not describe all the infant is doing. However, observing the behavior of two-and-a-half-year-old children does not even give the kind of direct support to the idea of an anal stage as looking at a young infant gives to the oral period. White writes:

> To be sure, there is plenty of evidence, even in the pages of the clean-minded Gesell, that children are interested in anal functions, that they play with feces, and that they experience frustration and conflict over the process of toilet training. But direct observation would never suggest that these happenings were the central preoccupations of the second and third year. (p. 115)

White argues that the crisis of autonomy is central at this age and that toilet training is a subsidiary problem. As a result of his new ability to walk and run, the child constantly gets into everything and runs out of bounds. Further, emerging

language skills enable the child to say "no" to parental demands and to issue orders. To the extent that two-and-a-half
is a difficult age, such difficulties derive primarily from the
clash of child power versus parent power. Toilet battles
represent only one instance of this power struggle. Accordingly, White questions whether this period of life should
be termed an "anal" stage.

Piaget's model of the child is as incomplete a description
of everyday activity as Freud's even though it focuses on the
very things that the Freudian theories slight—the child's
will to learn, to explore, and to make sense of the environment. Piaget's work on the first two years of life is rich in
detailed descriptions of actual behavior of infants, but the
incidents are selected to illustrate the stages of intellectual
growth rather than to give a rounded picture of the child
and his day's activities.

Piaget's description of stages after the first two years
serves as an even less useful guide to the activities and
interests of children than his description of infant activities.
When Piaget moves beyond the first two years his focus shifts
away from spontaneous behavior. He becomes more interested in the child's thought processes, as revealed by asking
the child questions—in a clinical or experimental approach.

This gap between interpretation of child behavior as
reported by such developmental theorists as Freud and
Piaget and the everyday life of children has important consequences for our interpretation of children's roles in other
cultures and historical eras. We tend to think, implicitly,
that developmental theories explain why children are children—that is, they explain why the child needs special institutions, plays and goes to school rather than working, and
needs to be cared for by his parents until he has passed adolescence and is ready to get a job and start his own family.
Yet a rather different interpretation is suggested by the
historical analyses of childhood. These studies cast doubt on
the notion of childhood incompetence and the need for
special institutions. They also suggest that much of what we
think of as childishness, or childish nature, at least in children over seven, may be as much a *product* of the special
treatment of children as the *cause* of it.

The Limitations of the Developmental Paradigm   There has been
a persistent objection on the part of some anthropologists

to the sweeping assertions of psychologists concerning human development. In general, the anthropologists have attacked two ideas: the universal developmental stages and the incompetence of children. Mary Ellen Goodman (1970), for example, argues that the data of anthropology refute two fallacies of American child rearing and pedagogy: (1) the fallacy of universal age/stage linkages, and (2) the fallacy of underestimation—the assumption that children are incompetent.

Margaret Mead pioneered in the anthropological critique of the idea of universal maturational stages. Her studies of adolescence in Samoa (1928) shook the notion of adolescence as an inevitable period of emotional crisis. She also challenged one of Piaget's early assumptions about intellectual development. In his early writings Piaget had postulated that children go through a stage of animistic thinking—believing that inanimate objects are alive and try to hurt or help people. Mead's observations of Melanesian children challenged this notion by showing that children were less animistic and more realistic than adults. Another supposedly "universal" stage of development which anthropologists have failed to find in other cultures is that of latency—the period from about six to adolescence which Freud has described as free of sexual drives and interests. In some cultures genital sexual behavior is continuous from infancy through adulthood.

At a more general level Ruth Benedict argued that, although the life cycle from infancy to adulthood rests on physiological nature, the facts of nature are "doctored" in different ways by different cultures. These "doctorings," she writes, should not be read off in any one culture as nature itself. No one of the particular patterns of childhood should be regarded as the "natural" path to maturity. Our culture is distinctive because of the sharp discontinuities between the behavior demanded of the child and that demanded of adults:

> From a comparative point of view our culture goes to great extremes in emphasizing contrasts between the child and the adult. The child is sexless, the adult estimates his virility by his sexual activities; the child must be protected from the ugly facts of life, the adult must meet them without psychic catastrophe; the child must obey, the adult must command this obedience. These are all dogmas of our culture, dogmas which, in spite of the facts of nature, other cultures commonly do not share. In spite of the physical contrasts between adult and child, these are cultural accretions. (Benedict, 1938, pp. 21–22)

Using earlier periods of our own society, rather than other cultures, historians have also challenged the assumption that our current definitions of life's stages are universal. In addition, historians have challenged our prevailing assumptions as to the meaning of age grading in terms of the welfare of the child. It is widely assumed that the history of the child in Western culture, and particularly in America, is one of uninterrupted progress. Kessen, for example, in the history of child study, speaks of the "rise" of the child from his older place as an ill-formed adult at the edges of the society to his present position as "cultural hero" (1965, p. 5).

Yet some historians have questioned whether a high degree of sensitivity to the various stages of childhood and youth really is evidence of concern with the child's welfare. As David Rothman (1971) has pointed out, there is a "darker side" of age grading. Age grading may reflect one form of social control over children, "part of an effort to lock-step

the child into rigid and predetermined modes of behavior."
Thus age grading may reflect an attempt on the part of those
charged with the management of children to make their
tasks easier. The sensitivity to ages and stages may reflect a
"rationalization of childhood" in the interests of making the
child's behavior more predictable and manageable. Speaking
of the schools, colleges, orphan asylums, and other institutions for the socialization of the young that grew up in the
nineteenth century, Rothman writes:

> The spread of common schools, the erection of houses of
> refuge, the multiplication of orphan asylums, and the nature of
> college training did not necessarily indicate improvements and
> reforms. The coercive elements in the pre-Civil War common
> schools, both in practice and in concept, are so obvious that it is a
> testimony to the strength of democratic ideology that historians
> could ignore them for so long. An element of social control runs
> through almost everything that Horace Mann wrote. The houses
> of refuge and orphan asylums were an overt attempt to *infantilize*
> *the young,* to put delinquents, vagrants, and the homeless into a
> rigid and disciplined environment where they would acquire the
> obedience that their parents had failed to inculcate. Behind these
> institutions was the assumption that any manifestation of public
> disorder in the young was evidence of future depravity. (Rothman,
> 1971, p. 376)

Within the family as well, historians have questioned
whether a concern with child rearing is an index of pure concern with the child's welfare. "Enlightened" child rearing
may reflect not so much a decline in parental authority as a
"shift in tactics" from coercion to manipulation (Rothman,
1971). In a review of early nineteenth-century literature on
child rearing, Sunley (1955) suggests that the emergence of
interest in the child and problems of child rearing seems to
have reflected a new emphasis on the child as the agent of
parental ambitions, and as a representative of the parent's
status in society.

The Child's Place: Social Contexts of Childhood

It is misleading to look to the animal models of parents and
children, as some psychologists and naturalists would have
us do, and think of the family as a little enclave of nature set
in the midst of an otherwise artificial man-made environment. The fateful encounter between parents and children
does not occur in a vacuum. From the moment of birth, and

even before, what happens to the child will be determined by the social setting he meets — the culture, the technological level of his society, the social class structure and where he and his family are placed in it, the historical moment, and so forth. These factors impinge on the child in some very specific ways: how he will be fed, and by whom; whether he will be tightly swaddled or allowed to move his arms and legs freely; whether he has three, or twelve, or twenty-one years to live before assuming adult responsibilities; and finally, whether he has a chance to live at all. For many centuries in Western society, and in underdeveloped countries today, most children would not live to their fifth birthday. Most deaths occurred in the first year. These demographic facts of life seem to have a profound effect on the attitudes and feelings people have toward their children, particularly their infants.

The imagery of childhood and the treatment of children indicate the kind of social order prevailing in a particular place and time. The infant and child symbolize two related themes: the impulsive side of human nature and subordination to authority. The larger society has historically impinged on day-to-day encounters between parents and children by assuming that the family is and should be a miniature version of the state. The family represents a "little commonwealth," wrote William Goudge in 1622, where "the first principles and grounds of government and subjection are learned" (see Demos, 1970). Whether it is subjugation or freedom that the child should learn depends of course on whether the writer is conservative or radically liberal, but commentators of both points of view see child rearing as citizenship training.

For the functional sociologist, looking at society as an organism struggling to survive, "needs" of the societal organism determine what shall be made of the new member of society:

It should be evident . . . that the ways in which society meets its imperatives for survival have implications for the individual's socialization and that in actuality the requisites of continuing social life come down to what is largely a set of requirements for individual socialization. (Inkeles, 1968, p. 82)

Somehow his parents and others must indoctrinate him so that the social needs become his own desires. If society needs peasants, parents must produce peasants. If society needs industrial workers, parents will produce them. Some have argued that this is an "oversocialized" view of people. Freudian critics, in particular, have argued that no society is completely successful in rearing children to do what they have to do, and not do what they are not supposed to do. The more orthodox Freudians see a constant war between the forces of sexual and aggressive "instincts" and civilization. In this battle "civilization" represents the forces of light, and the instincts the forces of darkness. The individual must surrender to the demands of civilization or organized social life becomes impossible. There is a striking parallel, as has often been noticed, between these Freudian views of the child as a creature of impulse and earlier Calvinist notions of innate depravity.

Opposing all the foregoing definitions of the child in relation to society is a tradition beginning with Rousseau and such Romantic writers as William Blake, and finding current expression in the works of Laing, Goodman, Friedenberg, and others. This radical-liberal tradition refuses to see in the struggles of parents and children a battle between civilization and destructive or bestial impulses. Instead of civilization they see particular social and political orders, each with its own patterns of injustice and oppression. And they see impulse, when it is not suppressed and thereby warped by society, as benign rather than bestial and as self-limiting rather than insatiable.

Obviously, this is an issue deeply enmeshed with personal attitudes and values and not easily resolved by factual evidence. Most people either know in their hearts that people are basically cruel and lascivious, that only society holds the monster in man in check, or else they believe along with Rousseau, Blake, Reich, and others that the eroticism and aggression of the child are themselves innocent until they have been suppressed and corrupted by society.

There is some evidence that actual child-rearing patterns and the personality and behavior of children, particularly obedience behavior, is influenced by the political order within which the family lives. William Stephens (1963, pp. 322–339) notes that societies vary considerably in terms of how much the father is a domineering patriarch. In some societies, for example, children are supposed to kneel or bow when greeting their father, speak to him in a soft voice, never argue or dispute with him, and never address him by his personal name. Furthermore, where societies demand such signs of deference and obedience from children to fathers, there are usually similar deference relationships toward older people in general, especially elder males, and from wives toward husbands as well. Stephens calls this the "patriarchal pattern."

What determines whether or not a society will have autocratic family patterns? Stephens finds "the most powerful original cause" in political organization: autocratic states beget autocratic families. In an earlier chapter we described the change from the simple, relatively democratic hunting tribes to the more centralized kingdom characteristic of agricultural societies. Stephens argues that as tribes were taken over by other tribes, who then became the nobles in a kingdom, or by kingdoms, their deference customs and child-rearing practices changed. Then as kingdoms gave way to democratic states, families became more egalitarian.

Evidence supporting Stephens' thesis has emerged recently in studies of changes in child-rearing practices in Western culture. Aries and others have argued that child rearing in the Middle Ages was an erratic, un-self-conscious process. During early modern times child discipline became an object of public and family concern: children were to be trained for obedience and respect for authority. The child came to be seen as having a will that had to be broken to teach him the proper subservience. Beatings, ritualistically administered, were the preferred means (D. Hunt, 1970, pp. 133–136). These child-rearing changes occurred while the political order was changing from feudalism to centralized monarchism, and the cultural climate was dominated by religious movements emphasizing the sinfulness of human nature:

A good child was a fearful child. This view of the nature of childhood agreed with the authoritarian concept of the family which was a cornerstone of royal absolutism. On this point the Catholic Reformers agreed with English Puritans and Dutch and German priests. Child-parent relations thus responded to the major societal problem of the age, to create a more disciplined population than had existed in the Middle Ages and the Renaissance. All three institutions, family, church, and absolute monarch, attempted to break the willfulness of the individual. (Moller, 1971, p. 16)

How is it that the political order comes to be reflected in families, and vice versa? We do not know. The author of the preceding quotation makes it sound a bit too purposive — that "society needed" a more disciplined population and therefore rewrote the rules of child rearing. More likely the process is a complex one involving ideological changes and psychological pressures which are then transmitted into ways of handling children. The process is likely to be circular, with much feedback between one sort of influence and another — economic, social, and political changes making certain ideologies more plausible, the ideologies in turn facilitating the social change, and so on. The question of how child-rearing practices articulate with the political and social order is a complex one that calls for a lot more research.

The Invention of Childhood   The premodern period in Europe did not mark off "childhood" as a separate status requiring separate institutions. Somewhere between the ages of four and seven, children entered adult life. Before this integration into the world of adults, the medieval child as an infant was regarded with what Aries calls "indifference." Parents did not become emotionally attached to their babies, and the death of an infant was not the occasion for great grief. Aries attributes this indifference to the brutal demographic realities of the time: as we noted earlier, most children were born to die. As late as the first half of the eighteenth century, the odds were three to one against a child living to see his fifth birthday (Kessen, 1965). It is not hard to see why medieval parents failed to feel tender sentiments toward infants. The same attitude of fatalistic resignation toward the death of infants occurs today wherever the infant-mortality rates approach those of medieval times, as in the underdeveloped areas of the world. And, of course, an analogy exists today in the general attitude toward the death of a very old person: such a death is sad, but expected, and therefore not emotionally devastating.

The contrast between the two attitudes toward the death of babies is dramatically illustrated in the report of a Peace Corps worker in Ecuador:

I had become friendly with a farm family who also ran a little cafe out on the road where the buses stopped. One morning I was sitting around waiting for a bus to take me down to the next village when one of the farmer's sons and his wife sat down by me. She was holding a baby in her arms who was dying of pneumonia, and I sat there listening to that unbearable gasping struggle for breath while the family calmly gathered around the child and watched. Only the mother seemed to be uspet.

I was sure that they were waiting for the bus to rush the baby to a doctor, but as the bus came closer and finally into sight they made no move. And suddenly using the most beautiful Spanish of my life, completely out of control I was screaming at them "Your baby's going to die; you've got to get him to a doctor. Now. Now."

The young mother began to pant; her husband looked to his father who simply nodded his head in a sort of permission without saying anything, and the young couple ran down to the road and stopped the bus.

When I got back that night they told me that the baby was dead. (Thomsen, 1965, p. 26)

Later the writer was shocked by what he felt was a lack of seriousness at the funeral. He knew the statistics of the area—three out of five babies die before their third year. And he knew that the religious beliefs of the people made the deaths bearable. But he could not learn to accept calmness in the presence of dying babies.

In medieval and early modern times people saw the infant as existing in a sort of limbo, hanging between life and death, more as a kind of animal than a human being, without mental activities or recognizable bodily shape. Ironically and tragically, the very indifference to infants caused by the death rates seems to have led to child-rearing practices that lessened still further the child's chances to survive. Or as Kessen puts it: "Paradoxically . . . the culture in which child mortality is high does not develop a compassionate and valuing attitude toward young children. . . . It is clear that the medical revaluation of the past two centuries has permitted high valuation of the infant by saving his life" (1965, p. 31).

Even when attitudes toward infants began to change, however, the evidence suggests that they were still not regarded as precious and unique human beings, containing future talents. Rather, the child became an object to be "coddled" (Aries, 1962). The child's image changed from that of an unattractive or not very interesting animal to a cute pet, a little monkey, whose main role in life was to entertain adults. Some aspects of this "coddling attitude" are found today, for example, in adults who pinch the cheeks of strange babies on streets and in stores.

The Middle-Aged Child   The major contrasts between pre-modern societies and our own focus on the middle-aged child, the seven- to twelve-year old. In a worldwide and historical perspective, our culture is decidedly unusual in that children of this age are not involved in productive work.

Stephens points out, for example, that in nearly all the societies in his ethnographic notes, children go to work by the age of ten, after a period of apprenticeship:

> Typically, work begins somewhere between the ages of three and six, the load of duties is gradually increased, and sometime between the ages of nine and fifteen the child becomes—occupationally speaking—a fully functioning adult. (Stephens, 1963, p. 386)

In nearly all instances the work the children do is clearly and specifically an apprenticeship for adult roles, rather than a children's chore such as running errands. The removal of middle-aged children from the work force is a comparatively recent feature of Western society.

If the medieval attitudes toward infants contrast sharply with today's attitudes, the contrast between today's and the earlier attitudes toward the middle-aged or school-aged child is at least as striking, but in the opposite direction. Aries' work sketches the movement of the infant from a limbo outside society to a focal place in the family. But the movement of the middle-aged child, as Aries sees it, was from a secure place in the adult community to a segregated existence outside the world of adults:

> Generally speaking, transmission from one generation to the next was insured by the everyday participation of children in adult life. . . . Everyday-life constantly brought together children and adults in trade and craft. . . . The same was true of the army. . . . In short, wherever people worked, and also wherever they amused themselves, even in taverns of ill repute, children were mingled with adults. In this way they learnt the art of living from everyday contact. (Aries, 1962, p. 368)

The adults with whom the medieval child worked were not always his or her parents. For many centuries in Europe, and in early America, the practice of apprenticeship was

common, although just how widespread it was we do not know. Aries writes of apprenticeships beginning at the age of eight or nine and lasting until fourteen to eighteen. Apprenticeships involved both domestic service and the learning of a trade or profession; there was no separation between work and family life.

Aries' description of medieval culture as "lacking a concept of childhood" may be misleading. As the preceding descriptions suggest, the period seemed equally lacking in a concept of adulthood; it was a society lacking age consciousness as an important definer of role, behavior, and status. Today one's age is almost as much a part of one's identity as one's name—for example, people are identified by names and ages in newspaper stories. People in earlier times were not unaware of age differences, but age consciousness and age grading were simply not that important.

Furthermore, the lifespan was divided differently from the way it is now in Western society. We see life as dividing naturally into infancy, childhood, adolescence, adulthood, middle age, old age. There are further subdivisions; for example, we put an infant into one of the following categories: the baby in arms, the knee baby, the toddler, and the preschooler. In earlier times, however, the lifespan was segmented differently: infancy, which lasted until five to seven; a period of childhood which was only vaguely differentiated from adolescence; adulthood, which evidently lasted until about age fifty; and old age. In this minimally age-graded society, no activities were set aside for children or adults only. Sexual talk and play was not defined as something from which the child had to be protected. Children gambled, drank wine and beer, and carried swords and guns; adults collected dolls, played blind man's buff, and rolled hoops. Fairy tales provided amusement for all ages, as did frequent communal festivals such as May Day, Twelfth Night, the European counterpart of Halloween, and others. In all these festivities children and adolescents participated fully, although sometimes the two age groups had special roles. Further, the polarity of work and play was as lacking as age distinctions.

To realize the importance of games and festivities in the society of old is hard for us today, when for countryman and city dweller alike there is only a very narrow margin between a laborious, hypertrophied professional activity and a demanding, exclusive family vocation. . . .

In the society of old, work did not take up so much time during the day and did not have so much importance in the public mind: it did not have the existential value which we have given it for something like a hundred years. . . . On the other hand, games and amusements extended far beyond the furtive moments we allow them: they formed one of the principal means employed by a society to draw its collective bonds closer. (Aries, 1962, pp. 72–73)

Schooling and Childhood   In our society going to school has replaced childhood work. It is school, more perhaps than the family, that defines the child's place in Western culture. For us school is the "natural habitat" of childhood, the school child is *the* child. Indeed, the very idea of childhood seems to have grown up along with the schools. The concept of childhood, the concept of the private, intense nuclear family, and the idea of the school as part of the "normal" socialization of the child were different aspects of the same ideological change that transformed the medieval world into the modern era.

The assumptions about childhood and education that we regard almost as part of human nature grew up gradually over the past four hundred years. We assume, for example, that stages of education should correspond to the age of the student. Thus we take it for granted that all the children in a class should be the same age, or close to it. Only in college and graduate school is the connection between level of subject matter and age of the student loosened somewhat. But even here there is an appropriate age for a particular level of work, and a person much younger or older than the standard will be noticeable and perhaps feel out of place.

By contrast, in medieval times and for a while after, school was not associated with age. A person attended school whenever he was ready and it was convenient, regardless of age. A seven-year-old could join a class where most other students were fifteen and over. Or a young man could work at a trade during his childhood and begin school at adolescence, without spoiling his chances for a higher-level career.

Furthermore, within the early school the child enjoyed the same status as outside—a free adult in a world of other adults. In fact, school children were frequently armed, and schools established regulations for student firearms and swords.

Old men, young men, adolescents and children could all be found sitting in the same classroom, learning the same lessons. They turned up for classes, but no one cared about the rest of their lives. Sometimes, as we learn from Thomas Platter's story of his school days in the early sixteenth century, groups of students ranging in age from the early twenties to a mere ten would wander in search of learning from France to Germany and back again. They lived like hippies and wandered like gypsies, begging, stealing, fighting; yet they were always hungry for books. Platter was nineteen before he could read fluently, but within three years he mastered Latin, Greek, and Hebrew. And in the end he became rector of Basel's most famous school. (Plumb, 1972, p. 83)

Only gradually did the following ideas emerge: that the different ages ought to be separated, that there is an appropriate age at which students ought to do a certain grade level of work, that the subject matter should be divided into grade levels, that students need to be protected from the vicissitudes of adult life and subjected to a special discipline to develop their characters. Authoritarian regimes, corporal punishment, and constant surveillance replaced student autonomy. Aries argues that these changes in education were developed by moralists who should be sharply distinguished from humanists concerned with spreading intellectual ideas and culture. Aries further argues that the new idea of school as an institution for shaping the moral fiber of children was related to a tightening of social control in general:

These reformers, these moralists, whose influence on school and family we have observed in this study, fought passionately against the anarchy (or what . . . struck them as the anarchy) of medieval society. . . . A positive moralization of society was taking place: the moral aspect of religion was gradually triumphing in practice over the sacred . . . aspect. This was how these champions of a moral order were led to recognize the importance of education. We have noted their influence on the history of the school, and the transformation of the free school into the strictly disciplined college. The religious orders founded at that time, such as the Jesuits or the Oratorians, became teaching orders, and their teaching was no longer addressed to adults like that of the preachers . . . of the Middle Ages, but was essentially meant for children and young people. This literature, this propaganda, taught parents that they were spiritual guardians . . . of their children. (Aries, 1962, p. 412)

In short, the new ideologies of education and the family defined the child as a person not yet ready for life, who had to be given special treatment and placed in a sort of quarantine before he was allowed to join the adults.

The new moral ideology stressed by Aries is but one aspect of the process of modernization that began in Europe at the end of the Middle Ages. An increasingly complex society began to need increasing numbers of skilled and trained men for commerce, law, diplomacy:

The turning point that gave rise to most of the traits peculiar to our culture is essentially to be found between the eleventh and the twelfth centuries when towns grew in number as well as in size and established their predominance over the countryside. . . .

As an urban life based in the main on trade and manufacture developed, the division of labor grew and social structures became progressively more complex. The needs for literacy and literate persons became . . . obvious. Growth of an urban society and growth of schools and literacy were closely related phenomena. The areas that experienced higher rates of economic expansion and more revolutionary social change were also the areas in which schools and teachers were relatively more numerous. (Cipolla, 1969, pp. 41–45)

Imperialism and conquest also increased the demand for skilled manpower: "The great empires—the French, the British, the Spanish and the Dutch—required men with the habit of authority. The proconsuls of empire had to be stamped with the image of gentlemen, aware of obligations as well as privileges. Discipline, best enforced by regular schooling, proved the most efficacious mold" (Plumb, 1972, p. 84). Nor was it only the gentlemanly arts of diplomacy and law that required education. In the sixteenth century one had to be literate to be a gunner, to navigate a ship on the open sea, to be a printer, or maker of maps, clocks, and precision instruments (Cipolla, 1969, p. 49). Although schooling and literacy spread in response to social need, they soon began to acquire an independent value. To be illiterate came to be a mark of social shame.

Although schools, as we noted earlier, began by mixing people of all ages, they gradually developed into private worlds of children, distinct from adult life. There began to be a culture of childhood, developed in part by adult regulations of children's dress, reading, and deportment, and in part by the children themselves. Kept out of the adult world, children began to develop their own "lore and language" (see Opie and Opie, 1959). Among the European upper classes of the nineteenth century, children were separated from adults even within the home. Children lived in their own section of the house, with nurses, governesses, and tutors, visiting their parents only for short periods: ". . . the difference between the life of a sixteenth- and a late nineteenth-century child is so vast as to be almost incomprehensible. Three centuries had created a private world for children" (Plumb, 1972, p. 84).

Childhood: Incubator or Prison?   What are the consequences of the shift in the child's role from young worker to pupil, from economic asset to unemployable dependent? Is the child in a premodern setting "deprived" of childhood and of the opportunity to develop his or her potential? Or is the child in a modern society deprived of a meaningful place in life, and forced into a repressive and artificial world? Do school and family pressures crush the child's creativity and individuality, or do they permit it to flourish? Does the separation of school from everyday practical life result in empty and irrelevant verbalism, or does the very abstractness of school learning make complex and reflective thought possible?

Arguments have been made on all these positions, and the debate is especially lively today as a result of the ferment of youth and the increasing challenge to school systems at all levels. At one extreme the following argument is made:

The revolution of youth has been building for decades because we forced the growing child into a repressive and artificial world — a prison, indeed, that was the end product of four centuries of . . . that gradual exclusion of the maturing child from the world of adults. We can look back with longing to the late medieval world when, crude and simple as it was, men, women, and children lived their lives together, shared the same morals as well as the same games, the same excesses as well as the same austerities. (Plumb, 1972, p. 84)

How can we resolve the contradiction between the "small adult" conception of childhood and psychological developmental theories proposing that a child is not ready for full participation in adult life until he has completed a series of developmental tasks lasting into his twenties? Some psychologists resolve the issue by assuming that development runs its course whether or not children wear adult clothes and take part in adult life. A child in grown-up clothes remains a child, and adults remain adults. According to this view development is a universal process in all cultures and historical periods. Psychologists, of course, have known about some of the historical and anthropological studies revealing a lack of differentiation between adults and children. But these findings have been dismissed as a sign of ignorance in those societies, not as a challenge to a universal process of development.

A second interpretation assumes that development isn't universal, but is cut short in premodern societies. An old but controversial tradition in anthropology looks on the "primitive" adult as psychologically like the child in Western culture. Thus the child in such a society doesn't have so far to go as the child in an advanced society in order to be fully developed. So the similarity of children and adults in medieval and primitive societies is explainable as the retardation of adult development. Adults are thought not to advance mentally much beyond childhood.

. . . We have traditionally seen the human life cycle as an escalator onto which the infant steps at birth and along which he is carried until his death. The view I am proposing here is that human development is instead a very rough road, pitted with obstructions, interspersed with blind alleys, and dotted with seductive stopping places. It can be traversed only with the greatest of support and under the most optimal of conditions. (Keniston, 1971a, pp. 336–337)

In short, medieval people were culturally deprived. They could not ride to the top of the "escalator" because their culture had hampered their capacity for development. What are the conditions which are believed to impede development? The usual explanations of the "cultural deprivation" of primitive and earlier societies include the following: lack of schools and literacy, traditional beliefs and practices that interfere with independent thought and behavior, the practice of teaching by showing how to do real-life tasks rather than verbal explanations out of a real-life context, and finally, the lack of a period of childhood as a time out from real work in order to prepare for higher levels of development. A variation of the arrested-development argument states that simpler cultures possess other skills than the narrow cognitive ones described by Western developmental theories.

Whatever the merits of the argument that people in "simpler" societies are more childlike in their thought processes—and there is good reason to believe this idea is wrong—the question remains whether medieval society can be compared with tribal cultures. Yet it would be wrong to equate premodern European society with subsistence-level tribes. Economically, politically, and culturally, medieval society was more complex than most other cultures. Furthermore, the bulk of the historical data pertains to the upper social classes of the times—people most advanced in such matters as literacy. For the most part Aries does not deal with peasants but with the urban middle and upper classes.

Aries is not arguing that medieval people were ignorant of the nature of childhood. He is saying that putting adult clothes on a seven-year-old and sending him off to work is as compatible with the true "nature" of childhood as seeing the same child as an extension of the baby he was a few years ago, and keeping him walled off from adult society. This segregation of children into schools and society of like-aged peers is no more natural, according to this view, than the child's taking his place as a little adult in a world of other adults.

Precocity   It is important to note that children in earlier
times not only performed such craft occupations as farming,
baking, and shoemaking; they could also be apprenticed to
lawyers, merchants, pharmacists, administrators, and, of
course, the Church. But the strongest evidence against equating the absence of childhood with developmental arrest is
contained in Aries' discussion of the concept of precocity. In
early times children could not only enter apprenticeships
young, but could also enter and complete college at relatively
young ages; for example, it was possible to enter college at
the age of nine or ten, and complete one's studies at thirteen.
Aries notes that up until a certain time, "whether this [pre-
cocity] was the result of talent, as in the case of Descartes, or
of forcing . . . precocity implied a superiority which
opened the way to a great career" (1962, p. 222). Only later
did the idea appear that there was something not quite right
about doing adult things or older child things before one
was "ready."

     In an era when children worked in the midst of adults,
that a child could also be precocious in school was not regarded with today's ambivalent wonder.

We should not forget that schooling was very recent in the mid-sixteenth century and restricted in many cases either to a few years of study or to a few people or classes. Outside school, in the army camps, in the offices of lawyers or administrators, in the courts where politics and diplomacy were conducted by grandees or statesmen, and in the workshops where craftsmen plied their trades, boys between the ages of ten and fourteen mixed with adults in everyday life, and above all in the fellowship of a common occupation. Some of them could show a precocious skill without causing excessive surprise to technicians used to cultivating professional values without regard to age. . . . In these psychological conditions, the precocity of a schoolboy did not seem any more extraordinary than the skills of a little artisan, the agility and courage of a child acrobat, or the virtuosity of a young musician. The school had not yet established a sufficient distinction between its pupils and the rest of the child population. These performances would no longer be tolerated once they were regarded as infractions of the special nature of childhood, and that special nature would be recognized in middle-class school children before it was extended to the children of the lower classes. (Aries, 1962, p. 196)

Not surprisingly, during this time when there was no lower limit on the age of starting school, scholastic precocity was not rare. Not only could nine- and ten-year-olds go to college, but until the late 1800's it was common practice in Western culture to begin teaching children the three R's — reading, writing, and arithmetic — as early as age two or three (Fowler, 1962, pp. 128–129). There have been some famous precocious readers, such as Macauley, John Stuart Mill, Francis Galton, and Norbert Weiner, who grew up to be important intellectual figures. All these thinkers experienced intensive cognitive education from their earliest years. William Fowler is a psychologist who has compiled evidence for the capacities of infants and young children for cognitive learning. He argues that early training may well have developed the capacities of these men to genius levels. He points to a small but significant body of psychological experiments showing that two- or three-year-old children of *average* and *low* I.Q.'s can be taught reading as well as other abstract skills.

The last remaining trace of this tradition of early competence has been in the field of music. In the eighteenth century the fact that the child Mozart was performing at three and composing music at five was not so remarkable. Even in the twentieth century the tradition of the musical child prodigy has not died out entirely—Yehudi Menuhin, who gave violin concerts at the age of five, is a leading example.

We seem to have experienced a massive change in cultural attitudes toward childhood precocity. We tend not only to doubt reports of three-year-olds reading, calculating, learning foreign languages, and performing on musical instruments—although child performers such as Shirley Temple are not so rare—but we find something unhealthy and faintly repugnant about such performances. They seem to be violations of the child's nature, and precocity becomes a kind of deviance.

. . . Public opinion soon ceased to admire child prodigies, in the course of the eighteenth century at the latest. The dislike of precocity marks the first breach in the lack of differentiation between children's ages. (Aries, 1962, p. 238)

Now educators began to eliminate children who were "too young," no matter how gifted they might be. The age of starting college was pushed beyond ten. The idea grew that a certain age and level of maturity were appropriate for each class level. It was felt to be wrong for the pupil to be more advanced than he was "supposed" to be. It began to be considered unwholesome for prepubescent boys to be in classes with older adolescents. Interestingly, the idea that one could also be too old to begin school, and that one could be too old as well as too young for a class level, came later than the notion of being too young. These developments marked the beginnings of the way we now break up the lifespan. The middle-aged child, between six and ten, was distinguished from the adolescent and defined as being closer in competence and dependency to the preschooler. Aries writes:

. . . The first ten years . . . were pushed clear of college life. . . . The reason most commonly advanced to justify the postponement of admission to school was the weakness, "imbecility" or incapacity of little children. . . . (Aries, 1962, p. 238)

The contradictions between such thoughts and the reality of gifted children resemble similar contradictions in racist and sexist arguments. Socially the precocious child is something like the uppity black or unfeminine woman: in each instance the person is deviating from his presumed biologically inferior nature, which is both (a) impossible and (b) bad. Indeed, "race" provides a most useful way of describing changes in attitudes toward children from medieval times to the present. During this period children became a "race," differently endowed than adults.

The argument that critics make against the developmental approach to children is not that the concept of development is wrong and ought to be abandoned. Rather, the point is that the concept should be used sparingly and critically. Susan Isaacs, a psychologist who studied cognitive development in preschool children, sums up her findings by noting that the overall impression one gets from her records is that the cognitive behavior of little children, even in the very early years, is not very different from that of adults:

. . . Allowing for the immense difference in knowledge and experience, they go about their business of understanding the world, and what happens to them in it, very much as we do ourselves. . . .

. . . If we stress maturation in mental growth too strongly, and treat it too readily as literal, organic fact (of the same order as the facts of embryology), we are likely both to overemphasize the difference between children and ourselves, and to underestimate the part played by experience in their development. . . . It would in fact, I suggest, be well if maturation were looked upon as *a limiting concept* . . . and strictly confined to those aspects of growth which cannot be shown to be a function of experience. We should be extremely chary of attributing to it any particular ways of behavior which characterize any given children at particular ages, except upon the basis of searching comparative studies of children in the most widely varying circumstances. (Isaacs, 1966, p. 57)

If there is reason to be sparing in our use of the developmental concepts in speaking of preschool children, we should be still more careful about applying them to children above school age.

Historical studies, Aries' work in particular, suggest that the developmental theories may have wrongly designed their staircases of growth by making the upper steps as steep as the bottom ones. These historical studies make it seem questionable whether it is useful and valid to consider the changes from childhood to adolescence, and from adolescence to adulthood, as fully comparable to the change from infancy to childhood.

Five to Seven as Critical Age   The historical studies report a major transition in the child's social status between the ages of five and seven. This same age is often the point of assuming adult work responsibilities in primitive societies; it is also the age of first communion in the Catholic Church, and used to be the age of legal responsibility for crime. The significance of the five-to-seven period is buttressed by recent findings that the really major changes in cognitive development occur at this age. Not too long ago, Sheldon White, a psychologist, published a general paper on this theme (1965). He pointed out that, in a variety of experiments on children's learning, the experimenters typically find a marked change in children's behavior between the ages of five and seven. "Before this age, the pattern of findings obtained with children resembles those obtained when animals are used in like procedures. After this age, the pattern of findings approximates that found for human adults. The transition is from animal-like to human-like learning" (p. 195).

White was intrigued that different types of learning experiments revealed a marked change in children's performances between five and seven, so he looked for more evidence of such shifts. He lists twenty-one behavior changes from age five to seven gleaned from his survey of the research literature. Perhaps the most striking single item in this list is the finding that the adult I.Q. can be predicted with maximal accuracy at this age. Other changes include the following: becoming more abstract and symbolic, less concrete; responding to stimuli less in terms of physical properties and more in terms of the way they are categorized in terms of language; learning to string together images of the past and of the future, and so plan out behavior in advance; learning to locate oneself in space; knowledge of left and right; memory of where things are in relation to each other. In practical terms this means the child can get from one place to another and back again without getting lost.

At a more general level, theoretical treatments of child development also describe the five-to-seven period as a major turning point. For Piaget this age represents a transitional period between major epochs of thought. For the Russian developmental theorists Vygotsky and Luria, this is the decisive turning point in behavior. Soviet researchers after Pavlov emphasize language (the second signal system) as the basis for higher human thought. They explain the changes at five to seven as resulting from the interiorization of speech; speech becomes the vehicle of thought and the regulator of behavior. For Freud the age of five to seven is a time when infantile sexual impulses are repressed, and parental prohibitions are internalized to form the superego. Finally, for learning theory this is a time when the child's responses to stimuli come to be guided by a mediating response which he makes to the stimulus rather than the stimulus itself.

White concludes his review as follows:

> In one way or another Piaget, the Russian theorists, and the S-R [stimulus-response] theorists appear to share a belief that a widely ramified system of juvenile mental processes gives way to higher mental processes during the transition. Freud, on the other hand, argues that there is a strong new force of inhibition at transition. Vygotsky appears to bridge the two approaches; the parallel between his conception of the internalization of speech and Freud's conception of the internalization of sanctions is striking. Of course, the internalization of speech does not take place under threat; perhaps the internalization of conscience does not either. Perhaps the 5–7 period is a time when some maturational development, combining perhaps with influences in the . . . environment, inhibits a broad spectrum of first-level function in favor of a new, higher level of function. (S. White, 1965, p. 213)

White goes on to describe his conception of the change. Before the transition the child's thinking is "associative" and essentially like that of animals; after the transition it is cognitive and essentially like that of adults. White believes that the first layer of associative functioning does not disappear but is inhibited by the cognitive layer. Under stress or time pressure, adult mental processes give way to the older, more primitive mode. The two layers are "stacked."

In White's model of learning processes we have a picture of human development that is fully compatible with the medieval stages of life as portrayed by the historians. Both suggest that there is essentially one step up from the childhood to the adult level and that the transition takes place at around five to seven. The conception of two major stages of thought does not imply that there are no important changes before or after this major watershed. Particularly during infancy, important developmental changes occur—for example, the change at around two from being a nonverbal person to one who can use language to communicate. But the model does suggest that changes occurring after the age of five to seven are not as momentous and, further, the basis of development changes. Before five to seven, maturation plays a major role in developmental change; after five to seven, learning and culture become major forces promoting psychological development.

Childhood and Social Reform

Although the history of childhood may not fit the model of uninterrupted progress, changing attitudes toward children were often motivated by genuine concern for children's welfare. The brutal exploitation of children in the mines and mills of nineteenth-century England served as a horrible example to discredit the idea of children working. In 1842 a Commission on the Employment of Young Persons and Children included among its findings a report that children sometimes as young as five were employed as beasts of burden in the mines, harnessed to heavy carts which they had to pull through tunnels that were long, low, dark, and wet:

> The child is obliged to pass on all fours, and the chain passes under what, in that posture, might be called the hind legs; and thus they have to pass through avenues not so good as a common sewer, quite as wet, and oftentimes more contracted. This kind of labor they have to continue during several hours, in a temperature described as perfectly intolerable. By the testimony of the people themselves, it appears that the labor is exceedingly severe; that the girdle blisters their sides and causes great pain. "Sir," says an old miner, "I can only say what the mothers say; it is barbarity; absolute barbarity." Robert North says, "I went into the pit at 7 years of age. When I drew by the girdle and chain, the skin was broken and the blood ran down. . . . If we said anything, they would beat us. . . . (Cooper, 1842, p. 49)

The reaction against this exploitation made it difficult to see anything but deprivation in the image of a child doing real work. Women, of course, were exploited in the factories along with children. Again the reaction against this led reformers, even a Karl Marx, to protest against women working outside their homes.

In short, the industrial revolution transformed cultural attitudes toward children and work because it changed the nature of work. Before the rise of factories and other large-scale institutions, as we have noted earlier, there was no separation of workplace and residence. Work went on at

home, as part of family life. Indeed, in the early years of industrialization in England, whole families went to work together in factories. During this time, some evidence suggests, factory work was experienced by the workers as less oppressive than it was later (Smelser, 1968).

Another reformist trend that helped shape our current ideas about childhood was aimed at changing schools. One of the reasons that teaching very little children how to read and write fell into disrepute was the harshness of the early schools. Fowler writes:

. . . At all levels of the infant (ages 2–7) and grammar school systems, many serious deficiencies prevailed which persisted well into the last half of the nineteenth century . . . [references omitted]. Curricula were narrowly restricted to religious dogma and the tool subjects [the three R's], often making use of unsimplified texts, including above all the Bible itself. Authoritarian discipline, enforced by harsh physical punishment, was the rule. Teaching methods were rigid and tedious, being based on rote learning through incessant drills on isolated elements. The lecture system was used freely, making little concession to age differences. Enormous classes were characteristic. Infant schools typically confined immobile for hours from 50 to 200 and sometimes as many as 1,000 undernourished children, crowded into galleries. They were watched over by the petty, severe, and ignorant eyes of monitors only slightly older than the children. Over such a mass only one or two adult teachers presided, who were poorly trained, if at all. (1962, p. 129)

The kindergarten and nursery-school movement arose as a protest against harsh schools. Such reformers as Pestalozzi and Froebel argued that the young child would learn best through his own activities, that he needed sensory-motor experiences rather than rote drills, and sensitive understanding rather than harsh discipline. Although some of the leaders of the nursery-school movement invented ways of combining teaching with play—e.g., in the form of educational toys—the major thrust of the movement was to define early childhood as a time for play and social and emotional development. Thus the school-reform movement tried to liberate children from harsh, repressive, and really anti-educational schools, but it also contributed to the definition of the child as a weak, incompetent, and fundamentally unserious creature. Such institutions as the nursery school and kindergarten widened the gap that separated children from adults.

Thus our present images of the child originated from a complex of trends and conditions. The image of the child as weak and dependent both mentally and physically was constructed by the rise of the bourgeois family, by moralists trying to save his soul from original sin, by schoolmasters rationalizing their institutions, and by reformers trying to save the child's body from industrial slavery and his mind from the shackles of rote learning and authoritarian discipline.

All these influences contributed to the image of the child that took shape in developmental psychology. But the theories and images of the child put forth by the professional specialists amplified and specified the differences between adults and children, and between children of different ages. Further, they replaced religious dogma, educational theories, and sentimental notions as the authoritative source of information concerning the child's nature and competence.

Is Age Grading Obsolete? The argument in these pages is not so much that the descriptions of the psychological traits and capacities of children of various ages are wrong but that they are incomplete. Many adolescents and adults fail to "pass" the cognitive tasks appropriate to their ages. Yet no one has suggested that such failure disqualifies adults for performing complex adult social roles. As Kessen has remarked (1962), Piaget's tasks at the adolescent level seem to require the kind of thinking one would expect only of a graduate student in physics. The child's performances on cognitive tasks may similarly fall short of predicting the child's capacities to participate in the complexities of adult social life.

In general, then, the image of the child in psychological theories reflects the assumptions about the child's place in Western society over the past several centuries. There is evidence, however, that contemporary social changes are altering the child's place, both inside the family and in society at large.

In a variety of ways the norms of conventional age grading appear to be losing their previous decisive influence. Although the adult world is still sharply marked off from the world of the child, there is a certain blurring around the edges. "Adolescence" is spreading at both ends—younger children are absorbing teenage culture and attitudes, and many of those in their twenties and beyond are refusing to progress to "adulthood." Some of the indicators of separate status used by Aries, such as dress and amusements, no longer distinguish children and adults as sharply as they once did. Current clothing styles are not only uni*sex*, they are increasingly uni-*age*. Where fairy tales once were shared by all age groups, now television is.

The future of schooling as the child's place and hence definitions of childhood itself are being changed by the current crisis surrounding education. As we noted earlier, schools helped to invent childhood by creating places and roles for children. Educational change now in prospect seems to be in the process of unmaking such places.

There are at least three major challenges to educational institutions as they are now organized. First, there is the argument made by Ivan Illich (1971) and others that school systems are becoming increasingly large and inefficient, and are failing to provide education. Second, some argue that education is too important to be restricted to people of particular ages. Third, there is the argument that today's children have outgrown the schools as they are presently organized.

As James Coleman (1972) has pointed out, we live in an "information rich" society, in which children at young ages begin to have large amounts of vicarious experience through radio, television, and other media. The schools have lost their historic function of providing the child with facts or expanding his horizons. Coleman argues that the present educational system was designed for societies that were "information poor." A child obtained most of what he knew from direct experience, supplemented by reading. The schools were the community's gateway to information.

Thus, the vicarious experience gained through reading supplemented direct personal experience. For those who read widely, the ratio of vicarious to direct experience grew as their range of reading increased, but the rate of shift was limited by the rate and frequency of reading, which for most people was not high. (Coleman, 1972, p. 72)

Television has altered the ratio between direct and vicarious experience for everyone, but especially for children. Long before he enters a schoolroom the young child has acquired an enormous amount of information about the world. In past ages a child entering school would have the adventure of discovering many simple but exciting facts. Coleman cites the example of a man born in 1870 who wrote in his autobiography of his amazement at hearing in school of a train that could travel sixty miles an hour. Thus, Coleman claims, children have outgrown the schools. On the other hand, more and more adults want and need to continue their learning over the lifespan. Coleman and a number of others, including many of the participants in the 1970 White House Conference on Children, have suggested that the schools should be opened to people of all ages, and that children should be integrated into work activities. "The separation between economic and educational institutions would vanish; a workplace would also be an educational institution. . . . The conception of a full-time education up to a given age, followed by full-time work, would be replaced by a continuing mix that begins at an early age and runs through adulthood" (Coleman, 1972, p. 82).

Coleman and others are also reevaluating traditional notions that work is "bad" for children. The horrendous exploitation of children in the mines and mills of the last century have blinded us to the fact that responsible and productive action may reward the child and aid in his development. A series of studies by Mary Engel and her associates (1967, 1968, 1971) has produced findings that challenge the prevailing assumptions about child work. These researchers found that child work—defined as working part-time for strangers for pay—is much more prevalent among fourth-to eighth-grade boys than is generally believed. (The study did not include girls.) Nor did they find that only boys from the poorest homes worked: child work was most prevalent in the lower-middle and middle-class groups (1971). As for the psychological effects of working, these researchers found that having a part-time job not only was not harmful, but also could actually aid in the development of competence and personality. On the other hand, the prolonged uselessness of children today may be demoralizing and even debilitating. The problem of amusing children and keeping them occupied looms large in many middle-class households; and schools have taken on a baby-sitting function:

> As affluence has increased, the child's environment has become impoverished in opportunities for responsible and productive action, or any action that tests and develops him. He is not needed at home, and there is little place for him there during the day. . . . Some upper-middle-class suburban school districts run a full summer program to occupy children, schools in Beverly Hills are in full swing in July. (Coleman, 1972, pp. 74–75)

Coleman suggests that in the future schools may become communities in which children would carry out responsible service activities, like summer work camps which also include time for learning. He also sees something like a revival of the apprentice system: workplaces would be modified to include the young in productive work; they would divide their time between learning and actual work.

A still more radical proposal has been made by Ivan Illich: that schooling in its present institutional form be abolished altogether. Schooling would no longer be compulsory, nor would there be a standard curriculum everyone must follow. Rather, Illich makes detailed proposals for transforming education into a public resource available so that all who want to learn would have access to educational resources at all times. Illich recognizes that doing away with schooling would do away with childhood also:

> Growing up through childhood means being condemned to a process of inhuman conflict between self-awareness and the role imposed by a society . . . . Neither Stephen Daedalus nor Alexander Portnoy enjoyed childhood, and neither, I suspect, did many of us like to be treated as children.
>
> If there were no age-specific and obligatory learning institution, "childhood" would go out of production. . . . If society were

to outgrow its age of childhood, it would have to become livable for the young. The present disjunction between an adult society which pretends to be humane and a school environment which mocks reality could no longer be maintained. (Illich, 1971, pp. 40–41)

Summary

The concept of childhood as a separate stage of life, having its own psychology and requiring separate institutions, is an invention of modern times. In premodern societies, including Western society several centuries ago, children did not live in a separate world from adults. In the premodern pattern children after the age of infancy participated in the economic life of society. The modern concept of childhood seems to be a product of the process of modernization: a complex occupational structure calls for an educated population.

Schools during the medieval era were for anyone who wanted to learn Latin. There was no sequence of courses and no notion that a person could be too young or too old to study a subject. School was a part of the adult world; schoolboys made their own rules and came and went as they pleased. Precocity, particularly among preadolescent children, was common in school as well as in the professions, arts, and trades.

During this period the nuclear family was unimportant, with blood ties ascendant over conjugal bonds. Parent-child relations were weakened by the practice of apprenticeship, with children often residing and working in other homes by the age of seven.

Over several centuries, definitions of childhood, school, and family changed. Childhood came to include adolescence, being defined as the preparatory stage of life for the not fully socialized. Accordingly, schools became instruments of discipline and character training. Authoritarian regimes, corporal punishment, and constant surveillance replaced student autonomy. The home became a place to nurture children and prepare them for later life. Precocity came to be seen as unwholesome. Adults abandoned the toys, games, and stories they shared with children and became more serious. The work ethic replaced the old sociability, and the nuclear family's importance rose.

SOCIALIZATION:
GENERATIONAL POLITICS

Chapter 10

However desperately the seventeenth-century settlers strove to strengthen and preserve it, the home was not an effective instrument of social control in the New World. The laws with monotonous regularity tried to shore up the institution; the preambles which described the need were a dejected commentary on the failure.

. . . The feverish effort to survive, on the first frontier and at each successive advance, generally left fathers and mothers little energy or patience for the education of their offspring. . . .

Children in America also neglected their duty. Cut off from tradition, deprived of connections with the past, they knew no better; and injunctions to preserve fidelity to the home rang hollow, unpersuasive when voiced by elders who had themselves deserted the places of their birth. Then too, the fathers, fumbling through the forests for paths they did not recognize, lost the ability to assure their sons of the way and thus lost also the authority to lead. The old wisdom did not hold in a land strange in soil and climate. . . .

Oscar and Mary F. Handlin, *Facing Life: Youth and the Family in American History*

Chapter Ten   In the ideal societies of the Utopian writers, the only recurrent threat to changeless tranquility arises out of human mortality. People die and new people are born. The social structure is conceived as a set of roles that must be filled, like the positions on a baseball or football team. The whole society must be duplicated anew in every generation. Utopian writers from Plato on, therefore, have been preoccupied with the regulation of reproduction, the training of the young, and the assignment of young people to their adult places in society. In the literary Utopias these processes are arranged so as to affirm the status quo. The rise of the new generation is conceived to be part of the grand design of the social system.

Ralf Dahrendorf has pointed to striking similarities between sociological theorists and Utopian writers. Like the Utopians the functional sociologists conceive of society as a social system in a state of equilibrium; and they also have been preoccupied with the problem of generational replacement. They conceive of socialization in the same terms as the Utopians, as a regular, patterned process that maintains the status quo:

> The system is the same, however often we look at it. Children are born and socialized, and allocated until they die; new children are born, and the same happens all over again. What a peaceful, what an idyllic world the system is . . . . Things not only happen, but they function, and so long as that is the case, all is well. (Dahrendorf, 1958, p. 121)

Student Protest and Socialization Theory

The rebelliousness of youth in the 1960's posed a problem for such theories of socialization. If conformity to norms is conceived to be the end result of socialization, there is no other way to explain such nonconformity as student protest except as a failure of socialization. A "generation gap" is precisely what should not happen according to theories defining socialization as a direct transmission of the cultural heritage from one generation to another. Kenneth Keniston explains why the youth protests of the last decade have been so upsetting to prevailing social-science assumptions:

. . . No event in this decade was more significant than the rise of a youthful opposition—a dissenting order of the young, a counter-culture of the educated, privileged children of the American dream, who found the society they were to inherit failing and flawed. The emergence of this opposition was totally unexpected. In 1960, the "silence" of youth during the previous decade was taken even by the most revolutionary social critics as evidence that advanced industrial societies had effectively "socialized" the young to their purposes. The intellectual apparatus of sociology, political science, and psychology has organized itself to explain why this was inevitable. Powerful "systems of social control," it was argued, suppressed "deviants" and guaranteed "social equilibrium" and "incremental change" without conflict. . . . (Keniston, 1971b, p. vii)

Were the student protestors of the 1960's psychological misfits? These campus protestors are the most studied rebels in history—not only psychologists but also commissions of distinguished citizens investigated the various student protests and the participants. There is remarkable agreement in findings of a variety of different researchers as to the characteristics of the student protestors. Activists typically have come from the ranks of the better and more serious students. The Cox Commission reported:

The present generation of young people in our universities is the best informed, the most intelligent, and the most idealistic this country has ever known. This is the experience of teachers every-where.

It is also the most sensitive to public issues and the most sophisticated in political tactics, perhaps because they enjoy the affluence to support their ideals; today's undergraduate and grad-uate students exhibit, as a group, a higher level of social conscience than preceding generations.

The ability, social conscientiousness and conscience, political sensitivity, and honest realism of today's students are a prime cause of student disturbances. As one student observed during our investigation, today's students take seriously the ideals taught in schools and churches, and often at home, and then they see a sys-tem that denies its ideals in its actual life. Racial injustice and war in Vietnam stand out as prime illustrations of our society's deviation from its professed ideals. . . . (1968, p. 4)

In relation to both the university and their own parents, the activist students tend to show both continuity and conflict. All the studies of student protest show that activists agreed fundamentally with the values professed by their parents. Yet there tended to be great conflict between parents and children about friends, life styles, student demonstrations, and so forth. In short, student protest cannot be explained simply as a rebellion of the unsocialized young against the older generation. Still, the widespread emergence of an oppositional youth culture challenged the prevailing assumptions about generational continuity.

Generational Conflict and Continuity

There was, and is, a good deal of confusion about the meaning of the generation gap, among the experts as well as the public. For most people the notion of a generation gap refers to parent-child conflict. Thus a spate of theories defined student protestors as being in rebellion against their own parents, and taking it out on school authorities and on society in general.

Some writers argued that the generation gap was a myth because lots of parents got along fairly well with their children. Then it turned out that student protestors often agreed with their parents on values although they had experienced conflicts about *actions* at the same time. It was the hippies, it seemed, not political activists, who were more extreme in rejecting the *actions* and *values* of their parents (Keniston, 1971b). Other writers argued that young people could not be neatly separated into political activists or hippies. Margaret Mead entered the debate by declaring that the generation gap doesn't have anything to do with parents and children at all:

> The generation gap is between all the people born and brought up after World War II and the people who were born before it. It's not at all about children and getting on with parents.
>
> If you happen to be a parent who was born and brought up before World War II, and you happen to have children at the moment, you're on one side of the generation gap and they're on the other. But this is an accident. In about 15 years, there will be parents and children on this side of the generation gap. . . .
>
> What we're talking about as the generation gap happened only once. It isn't about parents not getting along with children, or children rebelling, or changing styles of morality. It's simply that at the time of World War II the whole world became one, so that there is a complete difference between all young people and all older people. (Mead, 1971, p. 50)

In contrast to Margaret Mead's view of the generation gap as something that "happened only once," other observers noted that rebellion has long been recognized as an inevitable part of growing up. It is a "stage," like the temper tantrums of the two-year-old. Piaget, for example, has noted that the newly maturing intellectual powers of the adolescent make him aware of the general moral rules of the society, and enable him to be shocked by the failure of adults to live up to them. He is idealistic because his limited experience has not yet taught him how hard it is to put ideals into practice (Piaget, 1967, pp. 64–68). As he "matures" further he will settle down, give up his youthful ideals, and become a member of adult society. S. M. Lipset has pointed out that almost every country has a version of the saying: "He who is not a radical at twenty does not have a heart; he who is still one at forty does not have a head" (Lipset, 1967, p. 58).

A Multiplicity of Gaps   The profusion of contradictory explanations of "the generation gap" suggests that social-science experts were overtaken by events and caught with their theories in disarray. Many social scientists are aware that the prevailing models of socialization don't fit with the complex realities of generational relations in contemporary society, but have not been able to abandon them. Norma Haan has written of the predicament of developmental psychologists and sociologists in dealing with the generation gap:

> Our befuddlement lies, I think, in the officially abandoned, but furtive, persisting idea that the mind of the young is a tabula rasa (blank slate). Parental power and social countervention are still the foci of much research, as if empty-headed children are automatically stamped with effects or simply duplicate their elders. This supposition continues to determine the research design, and in the realm of common sense, leads the older generation to expect that there *should* be a generational replacement, but to their subsequent chronic dismay, there isn't. (Haan, 1971, p. 260)

On the other hand, the theories of rebellion as an inevitable stage tell us nothing about the rise and fall of youthful protest in particular historical periods; they do not tell us why the college generations of the fifties were the silent generation, why campuses erupted all over America and in many parts of the world during the late sixties, and why they became quiet in the early seventies. Nor do they

explain why large numbers of "youth" have not settled down on reaching thirty or even forty. Margaret Mead is correct in pointing to the social changes going on in society as a whole as a source of "the generation gap," but she seems to underestimate the complications these changes introduce into parent-child relations. The realities that impinge on families may result from conditions having nothing to do with families, but they affect families in profound ways. If the balanced, homogeneous social system is not a tenable model of society, the idea of socialization as smooth replacement is no longer tenable either. "Socialization" then becomes problematic: what is the child being socialized to fit into?

. . . If every society contains within it important internal conflicts, then growing children are exposed not to a stable, self-consistent set of social expectations and cultural values, but to social and cultural contradictions. . . . Furthermore, in times of rapid historical change, the societal conflicts to which one generation is exposed will differ from those of the previous generation; partly for this reason, individuals of different historical generations will typically differ from each other in basic personality. (Keniston, 1971b, p. 390)

In short, if we give up the notion that socialization involves the smooth replacement of one generation by the next, we are driven to the conclusion that some sort of generation gap is inevitable. Yet we must also explain why it appears more acute at some periods rather than others. In fact, there seem to be several kinds of generational cleavage, not just one.

Generational Conflict   To most people the term "generation gap" implies conflict between parents and children. Actually, there can be generational conflict without a generation gap, and a generation gap without conflict. Maybe it is because the assumption of generational continuity is so ingrained that little attention has been paid to the variety of ways generational cleavage can come about.

Let us look at generational conflict first. In its purest form generational conflict does not involve a challenge to the social order; it is simply a power struggle between parents and children. The son, for example, may want to take over the father's position, as in a peasant family where the son remains a "boy" until he has taken over the family farm. In general it seems that tension and hostility follow patterns of inheritance. Thus LeVine notes that in societies with patrilineal inheritance and descent there are antagonisms between father and son; in matrilineal societies, where the son inherits from his mother's brother, tensions occur between uncle and nephew (LeVine, 1965, p. 195). Some societies overtly recognize intergenerational antagonism. Among the Tallensi of northern Ghana, for example:

[A son] does eventually take the place of his father in the life of the community, and could be suspected of wanting to hurry on the day when this will happen. . . . Tallensi themselves make no bones about the matter. "Your oldest son is your rival," . . . the men say bluntly. . . . This candor in fathers is not matched by their sons, who never admit the rivalry. . . .

Tallensi explain the rivalry between father and son by means of the mystical concept of the *Yin* or personal destiny. There is, they say, an inborn antagonism between the *Yin* of a father and the *Yin* of his eldest son. . . . The son's *Yin* wants to destroy the father's *Yin*; but the father's *Yin* wants the father to live and be well and remain master of the house. . . . Therefore it will try to destroy the son's *Yin*, and if it is the stronger *Yin* it will cause misfortune and perhaps death to the son. (Fortes, 1949, pp. 225–227, in LeVine, 1965, p. 199)

Freudian writers have emphasized the sexual aspects of conflicts between parents and children, particularly fathers and sons. Although sexual feelings enter into such struggles, an overemphasis on the Oedipal feeling—the sexual rivalry with the parent of the same sex—has obscured the situational realities of power as a source of generational conflict. Thus we have the Freudian explanation of revolutionary activism as a disguised attack on Father.

In 1940 Kingsley Davis published a still relevant article in which he outlines the sociological reasons why conflict between parents and children is inevitable, and why for most societies in history there has been relatively little awareness of the generation gap. Davis argues that the ingredients for generation conflict exist in any society. In traditional societies, however, these inescapable conflicts between parents and children are counteracted in various ways. Part of the potential for conflict arises out of biological and psychological differences between organisms of differing ages, part from the power relations of child and parents. Davis also sees social complexity and social change as sources of parent-child conflict, but these are best considered separately from the more universal power and organismic differences.

Davis notes that parental power is sociologically one of the most extreme forms of authority. Unlike the authority of boss over worker, for example, parental power is unlimited, personal, and inescapable. In traditional societies, however, the power conflicts inherent in parent-child relations are mitigated by several factors. The authority of the parent is supported by the rest of the kinship group and the community in general. There are no competing authorities, such as schools, the mass media, or peer groups. Another reason for the relative lack of challenge to the older generation in traditional societies is the sense of the unbroken continuity of life—the sureness of all concerned that the lives of the children will duplicate the lives of the parents and grandparents.

Another source of parent-child conflict lies in the contrast between ideals and reality. Parents tend to offer their children idealized versions of the culture during the course of socialization. In daily interaction as well as in more formal teaching situations, the child learns such ideals as: Be sincere, don't lie, don't steal, treat other people as you want to be treated yourself, be kind and generous, love your relatives. Since no society ever observed has lived up to its ideal norms, sooner or later the child discovers that the adults don't practice what they've been preaching.

This credibility gap can become a source of conflict between seemingly hypocritical elders and their children. In traditional, slowly changing societies there is what Keniston has called the "institutionalization of hypocrisy" (1971b, p. 297). Violations of the rules are built into the rules. Children are taught that for certain situations and people, the rules don't apply. Or they are told that what appears to be an inconsistency isn't really that after all. Thus the ideal of honesty may be ignored in business dealings, the ideal of kindness may not be extended to foreigners or war-time enemies. In times of rapid social change, however, the institutionalization of hypocrisy may break down. New rules and ideas come into being, Keniston suggests, but there is a lag in the development of rules to justify hypocrisy. For example, modern parents trying to follow the latest expert advice on child rearing may have no rationalization to fall back on when they fail to live up to the new principles. Instead of being able to explain confidently why they departed from the rule, the parents may feel guilty and anxious. In such a situation, Keniston notes, the children are likely to "see the emperor's nakedness with unusual clarity."

Experience Gaps   Social change increases the likelihood that the potentials for conflict inherent in parent-child relations will emerge in consciousness and behavior. But social change need not lead to conflict; it does, however, add an experience gap to the other, more universal gaps. Margaret Mead has described the sense of timelessness that traditional cultures depend on for continuity:

It depends upon the adults being able to see parents who reared them, as they rear their children, in the way they themselves were reared. . . . The answers to the questions: Who am I? *What is the nature of my life as a member of my culture? How do I speak and move, eat and sleep, make love, make a living, become a parent, meet my death?* are experienced as predetermined. (Mead, 1970, pp. 5–6) (Italics in the original)

Social change breaks up this smooth continuity of generations, no matter how it comes about—whether by immigration, revolution, catastrophe, conquest, new technology, or anything that invalidates the experience of the older generation as a model for the young. The parent can no longer use his or her own youth or present reality as a model for the child. The classic example of discontinuity occurs in the immigrant family. The children can easily grow into natives, but the parents forever bear traces of the old country—in their speech and in their manners and standards of propriety.

It is remarkable how long the social sciences have viewed growing up as a process of psychological and physical changes in individuals, set against a background of social stability. There is, as Keniston points out (1971b, p. 60), a superficial awareness that we live in a changing world; we are used to a steady stream of innovations in fashion, popular music, intellectual trends, and so forth. But we lack an appreciation of how profoundly social change affects us, and how greatly it differentiates American society from more static ones. Margaret Mead has also noted this curious assumption of changelessness in the social sciences:

> In our current thinking about the development of human personality, there is a tendency to discuss the effects of culture change . . . whether between generations, or between the former and present environment, as though it were an interruption, however frequent, in normal development. . . .
>
> The assumption is . . . that the normal course of a human life would be cast under conditions where all the ancestors had lived for several generations in the same place; where social changes as registered in the living habits of two generations was slow enough to be easily assimilable by adults, and where young people would in turn grow up to marry others of almost exactly the same background. (Mead, 1947, p. 633)

Mead and other observers have suggested that today's parents and children are in something of the same position as immigrants. People born before World War II, she writes, are immigrants in time. It is more difficult to adapt to new circumstances when you have to unlearn previous knowledge and attitudes. For example, the parents of today's college students grew up believing that technology and economic growth could produce limitless abundance and solve all problems. They were taught that new products must inevitably be better than older or less processed ones. Disposable products were the wave of the future; when people thought about the year 2000 during the forties and fifties, they thought in terms of plastic or paper clothing and furniture, and electrically controlled weather. Energy seemed to be an unlimited resource that could be called upon to do an ever-increasing variety of jobs. For many people who grew up with these attitudes, the new concerns over environmental pollution, ecology, the problems of waste, the idea that unlimited growth and meddling with nature can lead to catastrophe, are hard to grasp emotionally, even when they can be accepted intellectually.

The Persistence of Generational Continuity   Why has the idea of generational continuity been so persistent in the social sciences? Daily reality, as well as literary tradition, suggests that conflict and discontinuity between the generations are far more common than most theories suggest. Part of the answer probably arises from the fact that much socialization research has been guided, as Danziger (1971) points out, by social policy needs of the moment rather than by purely scientific considerations. Thus socialization researchers have focused on the mentally ill, criminals, juvenile delinquents, the poor. During World War II and the past era, researchers looked into the child-rearing practices of America's adversaries — the Germans, the Japanese, and then the Russians — to find the origins of their belligerent attitudes toward us. Thus war, revolution, and all kinds of deviance seemed to arise from faulty socialization of one kind or another. The field of socialization came to be dominated by a "social engineering" approach (Danziger, 1971, p. 17), which looked for reliable techniques of child rearing, therapy, and correction that would produce well-adjusted individuals who would fit smoothly in society's roles. In short, socialization came to connote something that the powerful do to the powerless in the interests of social order.

The Psychology of Socialization

Psychological theories of socialization have absorbed, sometimes inadvertently, sociological and anthropological emphases on the continuity of generations and the social-control features of socialization. Psychological theories are also based upon assumptions of social stability. The child grows

up to mirror its parents, and it does so through two basic processes of socialization, "social molding" and "impulse taming."

The first emphasizes the plasticity of human nature, and stresses the seeming inevitability that infants in any culture, starting out very much like each other, will end up as little replicas of adults of their cultures—talking like them, doing things like them, thinking like them. Stimulus-response or conditioning psychology is one version of a social-molding theory. The rules and prohibitions of the culture become the rewards and punishments the parents use to shape the child's behavior.

The other view emphasizes the control of impulse. The child is not so much a bit of clay, waiting to be shaped, as a willful, aggressive, dirty little animal who must be tamed. Freudian theory provides the most emphatic expression of a basic conflict between biological drives and the demands of organized social life. The key to successful socialization in the Freudian conception is the child's identification with the parent of the same sex as the resolution of the Oedipus complex. Thus the child acquires the roles, values, and morality of the culture as these are embodied in the parent.

In both of these conceptions socialization is defined as the inculcation of conformity. Although they differ in their estimates of the forces opposing socialization, in both approaches the terms are set by the society and by the family acting as society's agent. One presents an image of human nature easily adapted to any social order, and whose strongest motive is conformity; the other portrays the child in the image of the cruel but clever savages of Golding's *Lord of the Flies*. There is no room in either model for legitimate autonomy, dissent, or conflict, no way to conceive of the forces opposed to socialization in any positive way. Both the social-molding model and the impulse-taming model have to define any behavior that deviates from the norms as representing some defect in childhood experience.

Rethinking Socialization   In sum, then, socialization theorists have been faced with the dilemma of choosing between an oversocialized view of human nature on the one hand, or an antisocial view on the other. This impasse is revealed in a striking way in Dennis Wrong's (1961) widely quoted critique of sociological conceptions of socialization. Wrong attacks the (then) prevailing ideas about the nature of society and human motivation. The overintegrated view of society, he writes, is the counterpart of an oversocialized view of human nature. Thus, if one defines society as stable, consensual, and harmonious, one must go on to assume a psychology in which the need to conform is the most important human motive. Wrong argues that socialization theorists have overlooked the "forces in man that are resistant to socialization." In trying to explore the nature of these forces, Wrong can only point to the Freudian id, powerful drives that resist the restraints that civilization places upon them. At the time he was writing, there was no other body of psychological thought besides Freudian theory to account for the forces in man that are resistant to socialization. Further, the turbulence of the 1960's had not yet broken the silence of the previous decade. The years of dissent and protest were to make many observers dissatisfied, as Wrong had been, with the oversocialized, overintegrated view of society and human nature. But the idea of bodily instincts as the major force opposing social equilibrium also seemed inappropriate as an explanation of social turbulence. Although some writers tried to explain ghetto revolts and student protest in such terms, others felt that psychology simply had nothing to contribute to an understanding of historical realities. But there was, in fact, a new psychological perspective emerging from research and theory, one which was not committed, as the older psychologies had been, to assumptions of social stability and generational continuity.

During the 1960's and into the 1970's the field of psychology as a whole, and child development in particular, has quietly been passing through a conceptual revolution that has received little attention outside the discipline. The insights of the new psychology suggest a different way of conceiving of the socialization process. Instead of defining socialization as the growth of conformity, or as a struggle between the forces of instinct and the forces of civilization, the new vision emphasizes the autonomy and activity of the child.

The Experiencing Child

The prevailing theories of socialization have tended to assume that what the child experiences can be directly inferred from parental behavior or environmental events. Recently there has been a growing realization that socialization cannot be described without taking into account the point of view of the central character in the drama, the child itself. The parents' power is limited by the ability of the child to interpret its experience in its own way.

The child, even in infancy, does not merely reflect the environment. It is impossible to *impose* experience on anyone. Even a young infant is capable of imposing his own order on experience. The most basic generation gap, then, is the gap between the selfhood of the growing child and the attempts of other people to control and define him. Yet the prevailing theories of socialization have tended to ignore a conscious "I." They have, as Erik Erikson puts it, deleted "the core of human self-awareness" (1968, p. 218).

Many psychologists, under the influence of Freud's teachings, believed that the decisive events in a person's life occurred in the first few years of life, and centered around nursing, weaning, and toilet training. A huge number of studies were carried out to show that different patterns of infant care, such as breast or bottle feeding, gradual or abrupt weaning, or strict versus relaxed toilet training led to differences in adult personality. The results of these studies have been disappointing. It is by now generally conceded that specific practices, in and of themselves, have no demonstrable effects on adult personality (Caldwell, 1964; Schaffer, 1971).

H. R. Schaffer observes that these studies were based on the assumption that a particular practice must have the same effects on different children: "The nature of the experiencing child, that is, is left out of consideration. . . . It is probably this factor more than any other which accounted for the failure of the above line of investigations and which have now convinced developmental psychologists of the need to pay attention to the experiencing infant . . ." (Schaffer, 1971, p. 16).

It is significant that Schaffer, an experimental child psychologist, is writing of the first year of life. Even working with infants at this very young age, Schaffer finds he cannot make meaningful statements about the child's behavior without taking into account the child's thoughts, feelings, and representations of reality. Even the newborn shows selective attention. He likes to look at certain patterns more than others. Furthermore, the child is now coming to be seen as a socializer of its own parents. With its cry and smile, the infant has at its command two powerful means of controlling its caretakers. Harriet Rheingold (1969) has described how the infant makes "fathers and mothers" out of "men and women." Even very young infants have the power to reward and punish the parents, and let them know the things that please and displease them. By fretting sounds of impatience and facial expressions, the infant lets its caretakers know what it wants them to continue doing, and when it wants them to stop.

The Tasks of Childhood   Defining socialization as weaning, toilet training, and the control of aggression and sexuality stresses just those aspects of growing up where the child is "wrong," the adult is "right," and conformity is the only outcome. Such an emphasis on what the child must suppress in the course of growing up overlooks the staggering amount of learning the child has to do, starting from birth. Piaget's studies (1952, 1954) of the first two years of life show that the everyday world we live in — the world of things and people, time and space, and cause and effect — is not built into the child's perception but has to be constructed. The child cannot tell the difference between itself and the world beyond its skin. It cannot distinguish its mother from other people, nor can it tell the difference between people and inanimate objects. Piaget has documented the many milestones of learning the child has to pass to acquire such a fundamental concept as that of "object permanence": the realization that an object or a person still exists even when one is not looking at it. Yet, by the end of the first year, the child has accomplished all this:

> The child (as Konrad Lorenz once put it) has now joined the human race. He has learned to distinguish familiar people from strangers, he has developed a repertoire of signaling abilities which he can use discriminatively in relation to particular situations and individuals, and he is about to acquire such social skills as language and imitation. (Schaffer, 1971, p. 13)

Most of this early learning occurs without direct teaching. During the first year and a half, the child learns about causation, objects, space, and time through an active exchange with the environment. Thus Piaget's theories, as well as observational studies of young children, simply do not support the notion that basic knowledge is acquired only socially, from parents or other people.

Language   Learning to speak is the child's next large task, and one with very great consequences. What sets human beings off from animals is their capacity to translate experience into symbols. Language does two things: it makes society and culture possible, and it increases awareness of self. Thus, paradoxically, language both *socializes* and *individualizes*.

Recent discoveries in linguistics have made clear that the child, in learning to speak its native language, faces an enormously complex task. It used to be thought that the child learned to speak through a process of trial and error, imitation and correction by the parents. Bit by bit, according to the same principles as animals learned to perform tricks, the theory went, the child built knowledge of language. The stimulus-response explanation of language learning is not supported by observations of young children. It fails completely to account for the fundamental fact about language: its creativity, the fact that the speaker of a language can understand and produce sentences never heard before. A child learns not words and particular sentences, but a system of rules. Out of the welter of speech sounds, the child constructs the basic principles of grammar.

The new awareness of the complexities of early socialization have, as noted earlier, transformed the image of the young child from that of a seething cauldron of lust, or passive lump of clay, to that of a tireless explorer. The single most characteristic thing about human beings is the will to learn, writes Bruner (1966). Similarly, White (1959) presents evidence for a competence motive, an intrinsic need to deal with the environment. The new views of the child echo the spirit expressed sometime earlier by the Soviet children's poet, Kornei Chukovsky:

> It seems to me that, beginning with the age of two, every child becomes for a short period of time a linguistic genius. . . .
> It is frightening to think what an enormous number of grammatical forms are poured over the poor head of the young child. And he, as if it were nothing at all, adjusts to all this chaos, constantly sorting out into rubrics the disorderly elements of the words he hears, without noticing, as he does this, his gigantic effort. If an adult had to master so many grammatical rules within so short a time, his head would surely burst. . . . Fortunately, he does not even suspect this. (Chukovsky, 1966, pp. 9–10)

Jerome Bruner has pointed out that when the child acquires language, it learns not only to represent the world but to transform it. Transformation of reality is built into the grammar of every language.

> . . . The transformational rules of grammar provide a . . . means of reworking the "realities" one has encountered. Not only, if you will, did the dog bite the man, but the man was bitten by the dog, and perhaps the man was not bitten by the dog, or was the man not bitten by the dog? The range of reworking that is made possible even by the three transformations of the passive, the negative, and the query is very striking indeed. (Bruner, 1964, p. 4)

Bruner does not exhaust the possibilities: after all, there is still "the man bites the dog" as another alternative. Indeed, very young children like to play with language in order to "violate the established order of things," as Chukovsky puts it, as in nursery rhymes, nonsense verse, and so forth. Thus the oversocialized view of human nature overlooks more than bodily impulse as a source of nonconformity. It ignores the possibility of using the cultural rules and tools in nonconforming ways:

Conformity to norms is sometimes said to be the end result of a positive or successful socialization. This is much too narrow a conception. The norms of a language are the rules of pronunciation, spelling, semantics, and grammar. Some who have learned these rules very well—children, poets, the Beatles—elect on occasion to violate them. Others who know them well undertake to reform them: to make spelling consistent, or to strip certain works of ambiguity. Similarly, the moral theory an individual forms by working over his moral experience can lead him to reject some part of the conventional morality. He is likely to argue . . . the change he favors will make the total morality more consistent or . . . will more truly realize the basic values of the culture. . . . Saints and revolutionaries and reactionaries all take some such position. It does not seem correct to consider such persons . . . failures of socialization. (R. W. Brown, 1965, pp. 194–195)

Indeterminism and Paradox   Despite its dependency the infant comes into the world with a certain degree of distance and autonomy from other people and the environment. This view of the child poses problems for theories of socialization. For if the child selectively interprets situations and events, we cannot confidently predict behavior from knowledge of the situation alone. The search for direct and simple cause-and-effect relationships between what the parent does and what the child does is bound to fail.

Parents who turn to "the experts" for advice on how to rear their children are often surprised to learn that the expert may not have very specific advice to offer. If he or she does offer a specific technique, chances are another expert will disagree with the first one. "Children need firmness," says one. "Children need understanding above all," says another. "The worst thing a parent can do is vacillate and be inconsistent," says another.

Jane Loevinger (1959) suggests that one of the reasons for such disagreement is that none of the theories work. She provides an amusing and insightful account of how "the experiencing child" introduces indeterminacy into the child-rearing process. There is no guarantee, she writes, that when a parent tries to get a disciplinary message across to the child, the child will interpret that message in the way the parent wants him to. She offers the following illustrative situation: a mother has come upon her five-year-old son hitting his two-year-old sister. She wants to teach him that this is wrong. How will she do it?

Some mothers believe in strong discipline. They feel that unless the child feels pain for wrong behavior, he will tend to repeat it the next time the impulse arises. Such a mother may spank the offending child. Another mother may feel that the child has to be made to understand why it is wrong to hit his little sister, so she will explain to him the error of his ways. This mother would be following an insight theory of learning, in contrast to the first mother who is following a reinforcement or punishment-and-reward theory. A third kind of mother might resemble the second one with the insight theory, but she might believe that the strongest influence on the child is the example or model provided by the parent's own behavior. Such a mother would hesitate to use physical punishment for fear the child would learn that it is all right for a bigger person to be mean to a littler one.

Thus the inescapable parental dilemma: there is no way for any of the mothers to make sure the child will learn what she tries to teach. This, Loevinger claims, is the fallacy common to all parental learning theories. The mother can decide to spank or not, but she cannot control how the child will interpret her action. Thus the child whose mother spanks for reinforcement may learn according to identification theory that it is all right for a big person to hit a little person if you really feel strongly about something and if nobody bigger is around to get you for it.

The children of the insight- and identification-teaching mothers may learn, according to the reinforcement theory their mothers disavow, that nothing much will happen if you do beat up your little sister. The parent teaches by one theory; there is no guarantee the child will not learn by another.

Thus researchers as well as parents have been frustrated in the search for clear or simple cause-and-effect relationships between things parents do or don't do, and the way children turn out. There are no cookbook recipes for producing a particular kind of child. Although it was widely believed a few years ago that the crucial determining events of a person's life were those that occurred early in infancy, in the ways that the parents handled the infant's oral, anal, and genital impulses, there is little evidence that specific practices such as breast or bottle feeding or early or late weaning or toilet training have any profound influence on later development. The same may be said about different disciplinary practices, such as "strictness" or "permissiveness." Whatever specific techniques the parent may use are influenced by the emotional context—most importantly, whether the parent is relatively warm and loving, or cold and hostile, or ambivalent.

The research literature even documents the idea that certain parental actions may produce quite opposite effects. Wesley Becker (1964), in a review article on the effect of parental discipline, cites studies showing that in boys strict discipline on the part of parents may result either in sons who are extremely nonaggressive or extremely aggressive. Becker also points out (p. 197) that all the different approaches to discipline entail certain costs or risks, even if they do result in the very kind of behavior the parent is aiming at. Strictness may foster well-controlled, obedient behavior, but it may also result in children being fearful, dependent and submissive; further, it may dull their intellectual striving and inhibit their ability to deal with aggression in themselves and others. On the other hand, "permissiveness" may result in children who are outgoing, sociable, assertive, and intellectually striving, but it may also lead to less persistence and more aggressiveness.

Pearlin (1971) has discovered another paradoxical outcome of parental pressure in a different set of circumstances. He found that working-class parents who want their children to reach a level of occupation much higher than their own often urge their children to work hard to succeed in school. The children, however, are likely to respond to these pressures not by working hard but by cheating.

Another instance of socialization pressures leading to paradoxical effects is found in Jessie Pitts' (1968) description of French family life. The upper-middle-class French child is not supposed to make friends with other children. The extended family is a "total society," and no one is supposed to have any relationships outside it. The child is supposed to find friendship among his cousins or among children of adult "friends of the family," who have a family-like status. Nevertheless, the child eventually goes to school and participates with peer groups. This is where the paradox comes in. Because the family does not recognize sociability among unrelated children, whenever peer groups do arise they possess a delinquent, antiadult quality.

By contrast most American parents, who want their children to be popular and to participate in group activities such as sports, often encourage and manage their children's social lives. Parents may even take over and run peer-group activities, such as Little League baseball. But among comparably situated French families, the peer group has no legitimate or constructive meaning. Hence all its activities are directly or indirectly tinged by a subversive, antiadult atmosphere.

Finally, Laing (1969) has described a common family scenario where the parent, trying to produce one kind of behavior in the child, actually succeeds in encouraging the opposite. How many times have we heard parents say something like the following to a child?

"I'm always trying to get him to make more friends, but he is so self-conscious. Isn't that right, dear?"

"He's so naughty. He never does what I tell him. Do you?"

"I keep telling him to be more careful, but he's so careless, aren't you?" (Laing, 1969, p. 81)

Usually the parent is exasperated and confused about why the child persists in being self-conscious, naughty, and careless in the face of such pleadings. Laing argues that such statements as those quoted contain a double message. The child is being told "Do X (the good thing), but you really are the kind of person who does Y (the bad thing)." Being told what you *are*, argues Laing, is a much more powerful message than an order merely to do something. In this way the parents, without realizing it, are inducing the child to play a role in a family drama:

> For example, a naughty child is a role in a particular family drama. Such a drama is a continuous production. His parents tell him he *is* naughty, because he does not do what they tell him. What they tell him he *is* is . . . far more potent than what they tell him to do. . . . We are likely to find that such words as: "You are naughty" are the least of it. One is likely to find that the child is being induced to behave as he is by tactile-kinetic-olfactory-visual signals . . . .
>
> These signals do not tell him to be naughty; they define what he does *as* naughty. In this way he learns that he *is* naughty, and *how* to be naughty in his particular family: it is a learned skill. Some children have a special aptitude for it. (Laing, 1969, p. 80)

Conflict and Growth: Families as Difficult Environments

One reason for the persistence of the idea of the family as a harmonious, balanced social system is a line of thought that goes something like this: (*a*) the society needs stable adults to survive; (*b*) stable adults are produced by warm, harmonious, stable families; (*c*) society is surviving; so (*d*) families *must* be warm, stable, and harmonious. The concept of the family as a difficult environment, which has emerged from the study of family interaction, has been hard to accept because of these assumptions.

One of the central insights of the new family psychiatry involves some notion of a persistent theme or myth or drama or game in which family members act out their parts unaware. Thus a child may play the role of family scapegoat, the bright hope of the family, the smart one, the dumb one, the clumsy one, the loving one, the mean one. Sometimes the role is defined in terms of some relative—the child is "just like" this grandparent or that aunt. The child contributes something to the process, of course; not every child can play every role. Sometimes the person's role outside the family is the same as the role within it: the "dummy" or "bad boy" at home is the same in school; then there seems to be little doubt that the person "is" what he "is." But sometimes a person discovers in school or with friends that he doesn't have to be the way he is in the family. One therapist reports a woman patient who was the clumsy oaf of the family, always dropping things, bumping into furniture, moving awkwardly. In the course of psychotherapy, she came to realize that she didn't "have to" move like that, and actually managed to be graceful. The expectations of the family members that she was a clumsy oaf had exerted a powerful influence that made her move awkwardly.

We do not know how strong a role this sort of induction plays in "normal" socialization; Laing argues that this *is* socialization—a form of hypnotic trance, induced since early infancy (1971, p. 82). But elsewhere Laing has argued that the child need not accept the family views of him:

> Self-identity is a synthesis of my looking at me with my view of others' view of me. These views by others of me need not be passively accepted, but they cannot be ignored in my view of who I am. (Laing et al., 1966, p. 6)

Recently some writers have suggested that we need to rethink the role of conflict in human development. In looking at an individual or a family, the prevailing assumption of most psychologists has been that conflict was neurotic and undesirable. Now, however, it appears that conflict is not necessarily something of which the less one has the better. Rather the optimal dose is somewhere in between — not too much, but not too little either. Piaget and other students of cognitive development have argued that intellectual and moral growth occurs as a result of conflict. The child must feel some "perturbation," some sense that something is wrong with the way he is thinking. For example,

. . . The six- to eight-year-old child . . . thinks the moon moves because it is following him around. He does not question whether or not it also follows other people and whether it therefore is possible that the moon follows anybody. Only between nine and ten years of age does the child consider the idea that if the moon follows him then it might follow other people too. He realizes this is impossible — the moon could not follow everyone at the same time. He therefore deduces that the moon follows no one. . . . (Langer, 1969, p. 30)

Thus intellectual growth occurs not through a smooth process of adding on pieces of knowledge bit by bit, but rather by a constant series of small crises in the way the child looks at the world. The child has a certain idea or interpretation or expectation — the moon follows me, people can see my dreams and thoughts, shadows are a substance, if you pour water into a tall, skinny glass there will be more of it, and so on. If these beliefs were never challenged by experience or other people the child's reasoning processes would remain at this "primitive" level. If we think of what kind of environment is most likely to stimulate intellectual skill, it would be one providing some surprise, contradiction, and challenge rather than a merely bland and pleasant one.

There is reason to believe that the same is true of the child's emotional development. The pleasant, conflict-free family atmosphere idealized in the sentimental model of the family may not prove the optimal environment for child development, even in those rare instances where it occurs. Thus the findings of the new anthropology of the family are not, in the end, as shocking as they seem to be at first glance.

Such notions as the politics of experience, family myths, family rules, paradoxical communication, struggles over definitions of the situation, family secrets that everybody knows but doesn't dare talk about — all these concepts and others as well were found to be characteristics of family life in general, and not unique to schizophrenic families. The very usefulness of the new ways of describing family inter- action led to disillusion with the concept of schizophrenic families. This disillusion could lead in two directions: it could let schizophrenic families off the hook, or put all families on it.

For some writers the failure to find some unique quality specific to schizophrenic families meant that mental prob- lems had to arise from some other cause than family experi- ence—most likely some kind of organic defect (see Frank, 1965). For R. D. Laing the lack of uniqueness meant that all families are guilty of psychological double-dealing and emo- tional blackmail. In his later works Laing comes to look on the schizophrenic as a hero, one who refuses to be cowed by the duplicities in family and society that most of us conform to.

There is a compromise position between these two views. The first one ignores the evidence of problematic aspects of ordinary family interaction. Laing's position seems to ignore differences of degree between families as well as the autonomy of the child and his ability to deal with the "perturbations" of family life in the same way as he deals with the rest of the environment. Laing's concepts may suffer from the same psychiatric fallacy we noted earlier—general- izing from clinical cases to the population at large. The schizophrenics treated by Laing may indeed have experi- enced double binds and other forms of psychological mayhem, but Laing obviously did not observe those people who grew up under similar conditions and managed to sur- vive without coming to the attention of psychiatry. In the next section we look at the surprising findings of a study that did make such observations.

The Uses of Adversity   In Berkeley, California, Jean Mac- farlane and her associates studied, through test and inter- view over a period of thirty years, a group of 166 infants born in 1929. The purpose was to observe physical, mental, and emotional growth in average people.

Over the years this study has generated several signifi- cant research findings, but the most surprising of all was the difficulty of predicting what thirty-year-old adults would be like even after the most sophisticated data had been gathered on them as children. Macfarlane, the director of the project, writes that the researchers experienced shock after shock as they saw the people they had last seen at age eighteen. It turned out that the predictions they had made about the subjects were wrong in about two-thirds of the cases! How could a group of competent psychologists have been so mistaken?

Foremost, the researchers had tended to overestimate the damaging effects of early troubles of various kinds. Most personality theory had been derived from observations of troubled people in therapy. The pathology of adult neurotics and psychotics was traced back to disturbances early in childhood—poor parent-child relations, chronic school difficulties, and so forth. Consequently, theories of personality based on clinical observation tended to define adult psychological problems as socialization failures. But the psychiatrist sees only disturbed people; he does not encounter "normal" individuals who may experience childhood difficulties, but who do not grow into troubled adults. The Berkeley method, however, called for studying such people. Data on the experience of these subjects demonstrated the error of assuming that similar childhood conditions affect every child the same way. Indeed, many instances of what looked like severe pathology to the researchers were put to constructive use by the subjects:

> Our adult outcome data . . . show that for many persons early roadblocks were in time bypassed; or compensatory satisfactions were secured; or changed situations permitted resumption of change in direction of growth. In fact, many of the most outstandingly mature adults in our entire group, many who are well integrated, highly competent, and/or creative, who are clear about their values, who are understanding and accepting of self and others, are recruited from those who were confronted with very difficult situations and whose characteristic responses during childhood and adolescence seemed to us to compound their problems. . . .
>
> From their retrospective accounts at age 30, these individuals were very convincing that behaviors we had regarded as disruptive to growth and stability had, in fact, provided them with essential maturity-inducing benefits. (Macfarlane, 1964, p. 121)

In speaking of their lives at their most troubled, these people do not reveal themselves even then as passive victims of circumstance, or of uncontrollable symptoms or impulses. Rather they seem to have been trying to deal with difficult circumstances, to exercise some degree of choice no matter how extreme the situation, to construct a self of their own choosing, even if that meant engaging in behavior that looked bizarre and meaningless to others. For example, a subject who had been seen as a "full-blown schizophrenic" during adolescence, but who turned into a competent adult, said:

"The only stabilizing aspect of my life during that period was the undeviating and all-enveloping homicidal fantasies against my mother. I believe they prevented my complete disintegration until I could escape my home and achieve other methods of handling my strains." (p. 121)

A man who had been in constant trouble in school, and who was finally expelled at age fifteen, said:

"Granted that my defiance of authority precluded a college education. I desperately needed approval, even if it came from kids as maladjusted as I was. Yet I can see positive results too. To maintain my rebel status called for a commitment that demanded my disciplining *all* of the intelligence and stamina which, I believe, has contributed to my adult strength and to my self-confidence in tackling later tough problems. . . ." (p. 121)

Another subject who defied expectations was a girl who also spent most of her adolescent energies defying authorities. She too was expelled from school at age fifteen. At age thirty she is described as an understanding, compassionate mother. She has had specialized training and works with physically handicapped people. One man described himself as a "listless oddball" in high school. He had been left back three times in elementary school, and graduated from high school at twenty-one without recommendations for college. He left the community, made up his educational deficiencies, and is now a talented architect.

The theoretical predictions of the researchers were also jarred from the other direction by the adult status of the children who had seemed especially blessed by ability, talent, or popularity, or easy and confidence-inducing family lives. Those who had enjoyed admiration, success, and approval as children failed to live up to the expectations that the researchers, along with everybody else, held for them. As adults they seemed strained and dissatisfied, wondering what went wrong and longing for the good old days. This pattern was particularly strong for the boys who had been athletic leaders and girls who had been extremely beautiful and popular in high school.

In conclusion Macfarlane writes:

We had not appreciated the maturing utility of many painful, strain-producing, and confusing experiences which in time, if lived through, brought sharpened awareness, more complex integrations, better skills in problem solving, clarified goals, and increasing stability. Nor had we been aware that early success might delay or possibly forestall continuing growth, richness, and competence. It is not clear whether early success, reinforced by the projections of others trying to identify with success, led to unreal expectations and to a disproportionate draining of energies into maintaining an image, whether early success caused fixation on goals inappropriate to adult demands, or sidetracked development from other needed areas, or whether there was not enough stress to temper strength and induce development. We need to look at and to try to conceptualize the configurations of what kinds of stress, in what graded doses, with what compensating supports, at what developmental periods, and in what kinds of organisms, forestall maturity and strength or facilitate them. (Macfarlane, 1964, pp. 122–123)

Social Status and Family Environment   If we take seriously the notion that family interaction is difficult, it may be that the various modes of child rearing may differ not so much in degree of strain as in what kind of problem they pose for the child growing up in them. Despite the size of the literature on child rearing, and the diversity of the populations studied and measures used, two broad patterns of child rearing appear again and again. These two patterns stand as polar contrasts to each other (see Table 5). One is organized around obedience, the other around the personality of the child. The first pattern is typically called traditional, repressive, or authoritarian socialization; the second is called modern, democratic, or child-centered. The chief characteristics of each style are contrasted in Table 5. Needless to say, these represent ideal types rather than patterns one can observe in every family. At the present time most researchers agree that the traditional style of socialization tends to be found in the working class, whereas the democratic style typifies the middle classes—or at least those segments of it most influenced by the literature on child-rearing advice. In the past, however, the pattern seems to have been reversed, with the middle classes more "repressive" in child rearing (Bronfenbrenner, 1958).

TABLE 5   TWO PATTERNS OF SOCIALIZATION

"Traditional" or Status-Centered	"Modern" or Person-Centered
1 Each member's place in family is a function of age and sex status	1 Emphasis on selfhood and individuality of each member
2 Father is defined as boss and more important as agent of discipline; he receives "respect" and deference from mother and children	2 Father more affectionate, less authoritative; mother becomes more important as agent of discipline
3 Emphasis on overt acts—*what* child does rather than *why*	3 Emphasis on motives and feelings—*why* child does what he does
4 Valued qualities in child are obedience, cleanliness	4 Valued qualities in child are happiness, achievement, consideration, curiosity, self-control
5 Emphasis on "direct" discipline: physical punishment, scolding, threats	5 Discipline based on reasoning, isolation, guilt, threat of loss of love
6 Social consensus and solidarity in communication; emphasis on "we"	6 Communication used to express individual experience and perspectives; emphasis on "I"
7 Emphasis on communication from parent to child	7 Emphasis on two-way communication between parent and child; parent open to persuasion
8 Parent feels little need to justify demands to child; commands are to be followed "because I say so"	8 Parent gives reasons for demands—e.g., not "Shut up" but "Please keep quiet or go into the other room; I'm trying to talk on the telephone"
9 Emphasis on conforming to rules, respecting authority, maintaining conventional social order	9 Emphasis on reasons for rules; particular rules can be criticized in the name of "higher" rational or ethical principles
10 Child may attain a strong sense of social identity at the cost of individuality, poor academic performance	10 Child may attain strong sense of selfhood, but may have identity problems, guilt, alienation

Most writers see the repressive style as creating a less benign environment for the child, and as impairing the child's intellectual and emotional development. It appears, however, that both these environments are best seen as problematic for the child, each in its own way. For example, a number of writers have suggested that predicaments such

as the double bind may not reflect personality traits of parents so much as the built-in structure of the middle-class nuclear family. To understand how the middle-class nuclear family has such strains built into it, it is necessary to contrast this family form with two different ones: the traditional extended family of preindustrial society, and working- or lower-class family patterns in industrial societies. The characteristic of the modern middle-class family that sets it off from both of these others is the emphasis on individualism and autonomy on the part of the child. Paradoxically, individualism represents both the chief glory and the chief source of difficulty in modern middle-class socialization. To the extent that the nuclear family and middle-class values represent the norm to which these other groups will move, the attendant problems will be found in these groups also.

The contrast between socialization in traditional kin groups and in the modern nuclear family has been summarized by Hsu as follows:

> There is . . . [in the nuclear-family system] . . . an inherent tendency to conflict between the generations not known in other types of kinship systems. On the one hand parents view their children as their exclusive possession, since they are given unbridled authority to order the youngsters' lives. On the other hand, privacy and self-reliance keep parents and children apart even before the latter reach majority in ownership of property, correspondence, relationship with friends, romance and in the choice of life partners. Therefore, parents often find it hard to let their

children go their own way as the youngsters advance in age, while children often find it necessary to reject their parents as the most important sign of maturity and independence. As a result, the parent-child tie is not only terminated legally upon the youngster's reaching majority, it may be socially and psychologically broken long before. (Hsu, 1961, p. 418)

In short, Hsu points to a contradiction between the values of independence and self-reliance for children, and two other aspects of the nuclear-family system: the actual power of the parents, due to the absence of the kin groups, and also the emotional significance of children in their parents' lives. Thus modern nuclear parents are both more powerful and more affectionate than traditional parents, although their ideology underplays the parental authority as an ideal.

Behavioral versus Attitudinal Conformity   In traditional societies the child depends less on his parents alone, and individuality and independence are less valued; the child is supposed to conform behaviorally. In middle-class Western society, especially American society, parents don't generally want their children to conform for the sake of conformity. They want them to internalize the rules the parents are trying to teach, to believe in them as the right thing to do. Whereas working-class parents tend to value neatness, cleanliness, and obedience in a child, the middle classes tend to value happiness, considerateness for other people's feelings, curiosity, and self-control. They want not only behavioral conformity but attitudinal conformity (Kohn, 1959). The prototypical working-class parent, as he or she emerges from research findings, is happy when the child obeys and does not mind spanking the child for disobedience. The middle-class parent may actually spank the child sometimes, but disapproves of spanking for two reasons: first, he or she believes in the child-centered, psychologically oriented child-rearing teaching of the experts (Bronfenbrenner, 1958). Second, having to spank the child is in itself proof that the parent has failed to get the child to internalize the parent's values—to want to do the "right thing" because it is right. Kohn argues that the emphasis on different values in different social classes reflects both the circumstances of life in each social class and the qualities necessary for the advancement of the child. For the working-class child, cleanliness, neatness, and obedience may actually be necessary to attain respectability and success. The middle-class family, however, can take these values more for granted. Further, lower-class occupations stress working with the hands; middle-class occupations involve working with symbols and people. Kohn has described the "message" of middle-class socialization as follows:

> The child is to act appropriately, not because his parents tell him to, but because he wants to. Not conformity to authority, but inner control; not because you're told to, but because you take the other person into consideration—these are the middle-class ideals. (Kohn, 1959, p. 351)

Thus modern middle-class socialization is both more permissive and more demanding than traditional, restrictive socialization. As Bronfenbrenner puts it:

> Though more tolerant of expressed impulses and desires, the middle-class parent . . . has higher expectations from the child. The middle-class youngster is expected to learn to take care of himself earlier, to accept more responsibility about the home, and—above all—to progress further in school. (1958, p. 424)

The prevailing emphasis in the literature has been that the middle-class pattern of child rearing is better—and that, in fact, the lower-class pattern is a social problem because it is associated with poor school performance. On the other hand, a number of observers have pointed out the problematic qualities of middle-class socialization. For example, Arnold Green (1946) has contrasted the neurotic tendencies of the middle-class male child with the freedom from guilt of his lower-class peers. The very repressiveness of lower-class parents, Green argues, makes it easier to reject them and assert one's own autonomy.

In a similar vein Rose Coser has pointed out that the "schizophrenogenic" mother who exposes her child to the double bind of love and hostility is none other than the ordinary middle-class mother caught between contradictory demands placed on her by society.

The schizophrenogenic mother is described in the writings of many clinicians as having the following characteristics. She dominates her child and is strongly ambivalent. She is both punitive and overprotective. She shrinks from the child when he tries to get close to her, but if the child withdraws from her, she tries to bring him closer or else punishes him for implying she is not a loving mother. The classic example is Bateson's (Bateson et al., 1956) tale of the mother who comes to visit her schizophrenic son in a mental hospital. He hugs her and she shrinks from his embrace. He withdraws. "Don't you love your mother?" she asks. He blushes. "You mustn't be ashamed of your feelings, dear," she says. He stays with her only a few minutes; after she leaves he assaults an aide.

Coser argues that double binding results from the mother domination and mother-child ambivalence that are built into the middle-class family. Mom is such a dominant force in the middle-class child's life for several reasons. She is the source not only of affection, but of both attitudinal and overt conformity.

As far as the children are concerned, the modern middle-class mother would . . . seem to be overinvolved in their lives. She focuses on their inner dispositions for their personality development . . . . She cannot, however, ignore the details of everyday behavior. It is her task to supervise all the children's activities. [She] occupies a position of control over her children that strongly tends to outweigh any possible control that a busy and absent father may be able to have.

. . . Being interested in the children's attitudes as well as their behavior, her supervision makes it possible to weigh all their acts not only in terms of the immediate situations, but also in terms of their symbolic meaning in regard to attitudes and future development. The scolding phrase, "It's not that I mind you not doing the dishes—I do them myself faster anyway—it's your attitude that I object to" expresses criticism both of the youngster's inability to do the task . . . as well as of his underlying disposition. Such control is aimed at both levels of the personality at the same time. (Coser, 1964, p. 378)

Adding to the magnification of the mother's impact on the children is a child-rearing ideology in which the raising of perfect children offers the chief justification for the mother's life. Thus everything the child does not only validates or invalidates its own inner worth, but that of its mother.

The child is also exposed to contradictions arising out of the mother's various roles. Being a wife, mother, and housekeeper involves opposing demands and pressures. The traditional, obedience-demanding mother has little difficulty in resolving conflicts between household cleanliness and childhood messes, but the modern middle-class mother, faced with finger paint on the walls or a clock broken in the pursuit of intellectual curiosity, may experience personal conflict over whether to scold or praise the child for creativity. Besides the conflict concerning the immediate versus the long-range view of the child's behavior, the mother may also be in conflict between her own interests and what she conceives to be those of the child. The child wants to spend Saturday morning watching those awful cartoons. Should she, in the interests of the child's future development, forbid this? Should she permit it in the name of the child's autonomy to choose its own activities? Or should she let the child watch the awful stuff to gain two or three hours of peace and quiet for herself and her husband?

The role of the father in the modern middle-class family contains paradoxes of its own. On the one hand the cultural script calls for the father to be a warm family man, even a pal to his children. The literature comparing the American father with fathers in other cultures shows how much the distribution of authority and affection within the family contrasts with the stereotypical Victorian family. The father is no longer used as the ultimate threat to enforce obedience: "Wait till your father comes home." This means that the middle-class mother can no longer pretend to be the sheltering buffer between the child and the father's wrath and power. Thus the figure of "Mom" takes on witchlike proportions in the child's eyes, while "Dad" seems to embody the gentler virtues.

On the other hand the middle-class father role competes with occupational demands. The highly career-oriented father may be available to his children hardly at all, partly from necessity and partly because he finds that life in the family is mundane when compared with life outside the home, where the responsibility and the power he can command are exciting (Flacks, 1971, p. 29).

In recent years a third role has complicated the lives of middle-class fathers. The sexual revolution, particularly in its *Playboy* aspects, has added aspects of the single-man's role to that of husband and father.

Still another contradictory aspect of the paternal role concerns achievement. Both parents teach achievement values, but father is supposed to embody them. However, most men in this culture are ambivalent, to say the least, about their work. Work in industrial societies is more often than not burdensome and unfulfilling for all classes:

> Lower-level jobs give little pleasure to most people. However, in the higher-level professional, managerial and creative positions, the standards of performance are not only high but are often without clearly stated limits. The individual is under considerable pressure to perform better than he is able. (Goode, 1963, p. 380)

In short, the system makes failures of most men. They fail if they occupy a low-status job, and in high-status jobs they judge themselves against impossibly high standards of creativity and success. The middle-class father communicates standards that define him as a failure, or else he communicates dissatisfaction with the cultural standards. Thus the middle-class child receives confusing messages about achievement (Flacks, 1971). In the working class, by contrast, the child acquires either a fatalistic attitude—success is all a matter of luck—or else the world of achievement can be held out as a promised land that the child may reach, but the parents may never enter. That world is not discredited through familiarity.

Middle-class socialization may be paradoxical at an even deeper level. For example, the demand that a child internalize a rule creates a double-bind situation. The point has been made in a recent article by Sluzki and Elisco (1971). They gave the following example: a university student in therapy reported that his parents had always stressed the importance of having clean teeth. When he was a child they had emphasized that brushing his teeth regularly, on his own initiative, would be clear proof of his being grown up—that is, independent. Sluzki and Elisco argue that this example represents in effect a pathological double bind or paradoxical communication: "Do just what we say, but do so on your own initiative." The parental demand to brush one's teeth on one's own initiative is a model of the paradoxical nature of all socialization based on internalization rather than obedience.

"If you do not obey, we shall be angry with you, but if you obey only because we are telling you, we shall also be angry, because you should be independent" (that is to *want* to do whatever one *should* do of one's own will). This injunction creates an untenable situation, because it demands that an external source be confused with an internal one. But, on the other hand, it is also the almost ubiq-

uitous model for the internalization of social rules. Its universal occurrence in no way alleviates its paradoxical nature. . . . (Sluzki and Elisco, 1971, pp. 398–399)

In short, middle-class families embody in an acute way the strains in the larger culture. The reason they convey contradictory messages to the child in the course of socialization is that the society itself contains contradictions. Thus, as we noted earlier, the middle-class parent is torn between responding to the child's behavior in the here and now and thinking of its meaning for future development. In the society at large a similar conflict occurs between present and future orientations:

In the schools, the media, and the churches, such contradictory values as self-denial and self-expression, discipline and indulgence . . . are being preached, dramatized, and fostered all at once. On the one hand, television and magazines advocate hedonism, consumption and living it up, while schools and churches continue, uneasily, to embody the Protestant ethic. The economy demands discipline and self-control in order to *make* a living and spending and self-indulgence as a *way* of living. (Flacks, 1971, p. 33)

Contradictions such as these, combined with an unprecedented rate of social change, are considered by many to be the roots of today's unrest among youth.

Origins of Youth Movements   Historically, periods of rapid change and social dislocation give rise to a sense of estrangement between the generations. Young people sense more identification with their own age group than with their elders. Typically, revolutions and wars give rise to a sense of generational consciousness for those at the right age to participate in them. "Bliss was in that dawn to be alive," wrote Wordsworth of the French Revolution, "but to be young was very heaven."

Youth movements appear not only in response to dramatic historical events such as revolutions and wars, but also in response to the social strains that may or may not erupt in such focused ways. Thus student-protest movements typically arise in societies in transition, where tribal or traditional agrarian-based cultures are becoming modernized and industrialized. Thus student movements have been prominent in Russia and central Europe in the nineteenth century, and in Latin America and Asia—the Third World—today. Such societies tend to give rise to dissident student groups for several reasons:

First, traditional values, transmitted by the family, are increasingly irrelevant to participation in the emergent industrial occupational structure. Students are acutely aware of this irrelevance in the relatively cosmopolitan atmosphere of the university and in their training for occupations which represent the emerging social order. Second, although students are ostensibly being trained to constitute the future, more modern elite . . . the established elites continue to represent traditional culture, resist modernizing reform, and refuse to redistribute power. Paradoxically, established elites typically sponsor the formation of the university system to promote technical progress while simultaneously resisting the political, social and cultural transformations such progress requires. (Skolnick, 1969, p. 83)

In short, it has been relatively easy to explain student movements in underdeveloped countries where traditional values and practices are being questioned. Traditional, pre-scientific, or authoritarian beliefs are obviously incompatible with the teachings students encounter in a university. Indeed, there is reason to think that literacy itself, along with the experience of going to school, even at the primary level, undermines traditional culture and its transmission from one generation to another. For example, the teacher constitutes another authority in the child's life who must to some degree dilute familial influences. Further, the child is likely to be judged on achievement rather than merely on family status. Evidence suggests that even a little schooling has dramatic effects on the cognitive performances of a tribal child in contrast to his unschooled peers (Bruner et al., 1966). Merely taking the child out of the real world and placing him in a situation where he must think about things in their absence, even if he is only memorizing a text he doesn't understand, seems to enhance his ability to think abstractly and independently.

If student movements result then from the collision between traditional cultures and modernization, and the skills and values it promotes, it is not surprising that the most advanced countries historically have not had mass student movements. Thus, although England and America have had much unrest and dissent, these have not typically been student or youth movements. Richard Flacks has written:

In these societies, the established culture was already rationalistic, democratic, and otherwise modern when the universities began to assume any central social significance. Consequently, most university students in such societies have been conservative, fully integrated into the social order, and ready to assume elite roles without significant strain. Youths who have felt estranged or radical have expressed their dissatisfaction not by revolt of the *youth* but by joining movements of political reform and cultural renovation led by adults. Tension between parents and offspring, although common, has been expressed only rarely through social conflict and mass movement; rather, the young have achieved independence from their elders by striking out on their own, using the opportunities for geographical and social mobility which were widely available. (Flacks, 1971, p. 15)

Since the 1920's and 1930's, there have been pockets of bohemianism and radicalism on American campuses, but the rise of a youthful counterculture was unprecedented and totally unanticipated by social theorists. It couldn't happen here, but it did—and not only here, but in France, Germany, Japan, Sweden, and eastern European nations such as Poland and Czechoslovakia. How? If the emergence of youth movements has been an indicator of social dislocation and resulting modernization, what could it indicate in societies that were not only already modern, but at the forefront of technological development? As Kenneth Keniston has pointed out, there have been two kinds of reactions to the protest movements of the 1960's: simple denunciations of the protestors as spoiled brats, pinheads, ingrates, and so forth (even writing by some rather reputable scholars falls into this category); on the other hand there have been more thoughtful attempts to analyze the reasons why dissent and countercultural trends arose in the 1960's. These analytic interpretations, although they differ in their appreciation of countercultural styles and values, agree on one fundamental point: that the emergence of a youthful opposition in the advanced countries indicates profound societal change, just as it does in societies experiencing the cultural and political crises of modernization. In the advanced countries, however, the shift is from industrial to postindustrial, postmodern society. The shift seems to involve major changes not only in technology and work, but in the psychological makeup of human beings, and the stages of the lifespan. We will consider some of these changes in the next chapter.

Summary

Social scientists have tended to look on socialization as a process by which new generations replace their elders; the social system itself remains the same, like a long-run play performed by a succession of different actors. Some social theorists have regarded socialization as a process of shaping and molding; others have emphasized "internalization" as the key: the child takes into his own personality the norms and values of his culture. In spite of their differences, however, the prevailing theories have tended to define the end result of socialization as conformity to social norms.

This view of socialization has been undermined by several recent developments. First there is the rise of a youthful opposition in the United States and the other industrially advanced countries. The wide-scale dissent of upper-middle-class youth could not be accounted for simply as failures of socialization. Rather, the dissent seemed to arise from taking all too seriously the ideas that had been taught in schools, churches, and homes. Thus it became clear that rebellion and dissenting behavior as well as conformity could be the outcome of otherwise successful socialization.

The turbulence of the 1960's undermined theories of social stability and consensus as the normal state of social life; many scholars became persuaded that change and conflict were the rule rather than special circumstances in need of explanation. If society were not stable and consensual, however, then growing children would be exposed to social and cultural conflicts and inconsistencies. The idea that stable societies are maintained by stable families passing the cultural heritage from one generation to the next becomes increasingly untenable.

The demise of theories of socialization based on stability and consensus brought to the fore a number of concepts which had been anticipated earlier but which became analyzed and developed more fully in the 1960's. These include: the idea that generation gaps are inevitable in any culture; that the child is an active and autonomous agent in its own socialization; that the child is an experiencing self that interprets events in its own way; that conflict may be useful for emotional and intellectual development.

Ultimately, patterns of socialization reflect the technology, organization, and dynamics of society. The process should not be regarded as a constant, and new societies may produce socialization patterns for children and adults that are as yet unimagined.

THE FAMILY:
PROSPECTS AND POLICIES

Chapter 11

Every age, every culture, every custom and tradition, has its own character, its own weakness and its own strength, its beauties and ugliness; accepts certain sufferings as matters of course, puts up with certain evils. Human life is reduced to real suffering, to hell, only when two ages, two cultures and religions overlap.

Hermann Hesse, *Steppenwolf*

Chapter Eleven   Before the mid-1960's, American life seemed to provide living evidence that the family—the nuclear family— was both the fundamental human group and a highly satisfying and beneficent environment. Social scientists in various fields assumed that mother, father, and child formed the basic human group, held together by interlocking needs built into human nature. The nuclear trinity was found in every society and declared to be the basis of social structure. Any attempt to tamper with its division of labor between the sexes or patterns of child rearing was said to be highly dangerous and could result in the downfall of "civilization." Family textbooks could state unapologetically that they were based on the American middle class because that was the ideal norm toward which everyone was striving. The underlying conception of America among most social scientists, not just those in the family field, was that of a "middle-class society in which some people were simply more middle-class than others" (Bottomore, 1966, p. 105). The term "family problems" seemed to refer to marital unhappiness, divorce, illegitimacy, truancy, and conflicts between parents and children—alien growths on a basically sound structure. Deviation from the standard nuclear pattern was attributed to psychopathology, poverty, or just misfortune. Little or no consideration was given to the possibility that different life styles might be functional alternatives to the nuclear-family life style.

Each field—sociology, anthropology, and psychoanalytic psychology—made its own contribution to the evidence supporting the idea of the family as a necessary and therefore universal institution. Some scholars did object to the general consensus. Like the little child who pointed out that the emperor wore no clothes, one sociologist complained that the social scientists, "despite all their elaborate theories and technical research devices, are doing little more than projecting certain middle-class hopes and ideals onto a refractory reality" (Moore, 1958, p. 408). But the climate of opinion and the prevailing social life did not support such critical views.

The Family in Postwar Perspective

The Family in the Fifties   The functionalist theory of the nuclear family, with its two-by-two division into age and sex roles, seemed to fit the prevailing realities of the America of the 1950's. The ambitious, careerist, middle-class husband of the fifties fulfilled the model of the "instrumental" male role. The suburban housewife and mother fulfilled her assigned "expressive" role as socializer of children and domestic mainstay. The baby boom and the popular preoccupation with child-rearing experts confirmed the family's role as a social institution whose primary function was to "integrate" individuals into society.

The prediction of an earlier generation of sociologists that the coming of large-scale urban industrial society would cause the disintegration of the family seemed to be refuted by statistics showing that more people than ever were marrying, that they were marrying younger and producing record numbers of babies. Fewer women were choosing childless careers. Most new housing was of the single-family type. Even the rising divorce rates were interpreted as showing the importance of the family; people were not rejecting marriage, only trying to perfect it, as indicated by the prevalence of remarriages. The "natural habitat" of the mid-century city dweller alternated between work and home. At-homeness or togetherness was more than an ideology, it was a statistical reality as well (Grazia, 1962).

Studies of the mushrooming metropolitan areas in the United States and other advanced societies revealed a social order centered around "the single-family dwelling unit, the conjugal family, selected kinfolk, the job, and the mass media — the latter consumed in the home" (S. Greer, 1962, p. 94). The earlier theorists of the city had seen the city dweller as a sophisticated cosmopolitan, participating in the rich cultural and public life that cities made possible, or else as a rootless person drifting through a fragmented and anonymous life, devoid of intimate human relationships. Yet few urban areas and relatively few individuals lived up to either the cosmopolitan or the fragmented version of the urban stereotype. Summarizing the findings of a number of studies, Greer wrote:

The picture that emerges is of a society in which the conjugal family is extremely powerful among all types of population. This small, primary-group structure is one basic area of involvement; at the other pole is work, a massive absorber of time, but an activity that is rarely related to the family through "outside" friendship with on-the-job associates. Instead, the family, its kin, and its friendship group, is relatively free-floating, within the world of large-scale secondary associations. (S. Greer, 1962, pp. 93–94)

Yet the earlier theorists were confirmed in their assertions concerning the weakening of the community life that existed in earlier times and still exists within the small town and some neighborhoods. In the metropolitan areas where most Americans live (approximately 70 percent of the population according to the 1960 census, 74 percent according to the 1970 census), the community "as a solid phalanx of friends and acquaintances does not exist; if individuals are to have a community in the older sense of *communion*, they must make it for themselves" (S. Greer, 1962, p. 94). Thus family and friends fill the sociability gap created by the decline of the community and old kind of neighborhood. Even in the most "neighborly" neighborhoods, Greer notes, the family tends to be weakly identified with the local community:

. . . "It neighbors," but strictly within bounds. *By and large, the conjugal family group keeps to itself;* outside is the world—formal organizations, work and the communities. . . . The family retires to its domain . . . to work in the garden, listen to radio or television, care for children and read the products of mass media. (S. Greer, 1962, p. 94) (Italics added)

The factual realities of an inward-turning, intensifed family life of the fifties and early sixties were assimilated to a general mood of complacency and celebration in the social sciences as well as the mass media. America was an "affluent society" characterized by "high standards of private consumption, effective maintenance of public order and security, freedom from most of the uncertainties of life that plagued our ancestors, and relatively high levels of humanitarianism" (Nisbet, 1961, p. 5). In comparison with the Depression years, the postwar era of 1945–1960 was a time of unprecedented and remarkable affluence. Family income more than doubled between 1939 and 1969. For the first time a majority of Americans no longer had to worry about being able to obtain the basic necessities of food, clothing, and shelter. Instead, they could take these for granted, and indulge in expenditures on a spectacular scale for items that had once been luxuries: new homes, television sets, wall-to-wall carpeting, cars, boats, hi-fi sets, travel, and so on (Grazia, 1962; S. Greer, 1962; Miller, 1965).

The general prosperity overshadowed in both popular awareness and the social sciences the poverty of a considerable minority of the population. The disadvantaged received very little attention. The eye of the social scientist was firmly focused on the middle-class majority and its remarkable affluence. It was easy for a social scientist to slip from description to celebration. Here is Greer, for example, commenting on the freedom and affluence of modern urban man:

> Though his commitments to the job and the family are constant and have priority in time and energy, he exercises freedom of choice—in the market, the large sphere which Riesman calls consumership. He also has a freedom in the symbol spheres that has never been widespread before in any society. There are some one thousand television hours available each week to the Los Angeles resident. His relative wealth, literacy and privacy allow an exploration of meaning never before possible to the rank and file of any society. In his home life he experiments with leisure. The hobby industries, the do-it-yourself industries, the flood of specialized publications and programs, bear testimony to the increasing use the urbanite makes of this opportunity. He is part of the *nouveaux riches* of leisure. (S. Greer, 1962, pp. 104–105)

Admittedly, social problems had not all been solved. There were still slums, bigotry, poverty, sudden eruptions of violence. But in the perspective of the fifties, these seemed to be peripheral matters. Compared to such problems as had existed in the past—scarcity, mass unemployment, ethnic and class conflict, political instability, epidemics—these difficulties seemed trivial. Even when poverty was "discovered" in the early sixties and became big news, the answer to the problem seemed obvious and easy. Mainly, the solution seemed to be a technical one: to incorporate the disadvantaged and culturally deprived into the general affluence and well-being. The middle-class family pattern was held up as the model for the disadvantaged to follow. Indeed, the "inadequate" family life of the poor, particularly the black poor, was held to be the major reason why those groups had not yet "made it" into the great middle class.

Looking to the future, social scientists saw more of the same—an extension of affluence and middle-class life styles to those "left out" or "left behind" in their pockets of poverty, more technology, more economic growth, all leading to a more stable and balanced social order. The "age of ideology" was over, would not return.

And Then the Deluge   This mood of complacency and consensus was shattered by the outbreak of social unrest in the mid-1960's—the growth of black militancy, the emergence of student dissent, the antiwar movement, the rise of the counterculture, riots and fighting in the streets. In the tranquility of the fifties no one had foreseen anything like these developments. Even more unlikely in those days than the "politics of protest" was the emergence of a politics of the family. At the beginning of the sixties it was only the universality of the middle-class family life style that was called into question with the discovery of poverty. By 1970 there was widespread disenchantment with the prevailing family patterns. The validity of the family was challenged by rebellious students, the commune movement, women's liberation, gay liberation, and the spread of nonmarital cohabitation. Within a relatively short time such notions as the "obsolescence" and "crisis" of the nuclear family passed from being heresies of the counterculture to mass-media clichés.

Everything that used to be taken for granted as part of human nature—definitions of masculinity and femininity, the necessity of marriage, the desirability of having children, the rights and obligations of children and parents to each other—became open to question and debate. Thus ideas deriving from the women's liberation movement have been quietly spreading among suburban housewives and high-school students, and on the pages of women's magazines. The women's liberation perspective is already being credited with reducing birth and marriage rates. Even more unprecedented historically than the women's movement is the rise of the homosexual as a protestor claiming minority rights. What is remarkable here is not the number involved, but the loud proclamation of what was formerly unspeakable and morally dreadful. The open flouting of previous taboos may also be seen in the sudden emergence of unwed pregnancy and motherhood as a viable social role rather than a shameful secret. There is probably no corner of America completely unaffected by the current ferment, even if all that has been provoked is a backlash affirmation of the old morality.

The present mood of uncertainty about family life, however, results not only from the activities of rebels and protestors. The increasing public awareness of problems of overpopulation and environmental pollution also have produced profound implications for the standard nuclear-family

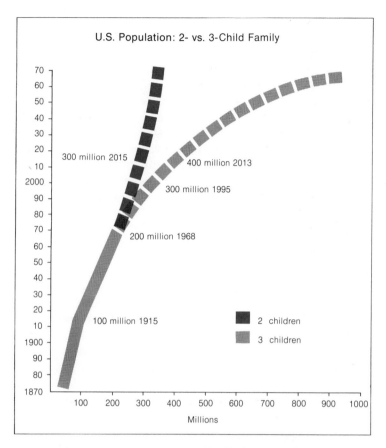

U.S. Population: 2- vs. 3-Child Family

300 million 2015

400 million 2013

300 million 1995

200 million 1968

100 million 1915

2 children
3 children

Millions

The population of the United States passed the 100-million mark in 1915 and reached 200 million in 1968. If families average two children in the future, growth rates will slow and the population will reach 300 million in the year 2015. At the three-child rate the population would reach 300 million in this century and 400 million in the year 2013. (Projections assume small future reductions in mortality and future immigration at present levels.) (From *Population and the American Future*, Washington: U.S. Government Printing Office, 1972)

way of life. The emergence of overpopulation as a problem — not only for underdeveloped countries and the poor, but also for affluent middle-class Americans — has transformed the decision to bear a child from the purely personal realm to the political and social.

The social need for population control is a powerful support for the personal reasons women have always had for limiting childbirth. In the past women were subjected to tremendous social pressure to have many children. Even women who felt temperamentally unsuited, who didn't really like children, had to have some. Now we are reaching the point where no woman need have a child she doesn't want, nor be a mother at all if she feels unsuited to the job. As this is being written the Census Bureau reports the birth rate has reached an all-time low. The prediction of an earlier generation of family theorists concerning the demise of the family suddenly seemed an idea whose time had come. A conservative President opened the 1970 White House Conference on Children with the following statement:

> Never has this White House Conference come at a time of greater national questioning. Long-held attitudes on such subjects as family planning, pornography, health services, school curricula, sex education, family structure, drug abuse, moral standards, governance of higher education, responsiveness of government— all are now openly challenged and debated. (1970, p. 5)

The Family Today   In an earlier chapter we noted how social science in practice scarcely fits the model of value-free inquiry. Every social scientist and, indeed, every natural scientist must start out with certain assumptions about reality. For the natural scientist these assumptions have to do with natural reality, the nature of matter and space, the structure of molecules. For the social scientist these assumptions have to do with the nature of human beings, institutions, and society. There is much less consensus among social scientists as to the nature of social reality than there is among natural scientists about nature. The lack of consensus is especially evident when the social scientist deals with matters of current controversy, such as youthful protest, women's liberation, or any current social problems:

> Social scientists . . . study social problems from the vantage point of committed people striving to make sense of their society. There is nothing wrong with that, but it should not be advertised as disinterested inquiry. We do not advocate the replacement of a fake objectivity with a mindless rejection of scientific standards. But the scientific value of a work of social analysis lies in the quality

of its arguments and evidence, not in the credentials of an "expert" who claims a false detachment. (Skolnick and Currie, 1973, p. 11)

No issue is more controversial than the current ferment surrounding sexuality, sex roles, the generation gap, the counterculture, and the future of the family. Such issues involve not only basic assumptions about the nature of social reality, but also personal notions as to how people ought and ought not to live. In viewing the variety of statements and analyses that have been made, one can discern several general approaches or perspectives. These are not necessarily explicit and well-worked-out theoretical positions, and they do not always focus on the same issues. Roughly, these approaches are the following: (1) a breakdown or liberation perspective; (2) a continuity perspective; (3) a contextual-strain perspective; and (4) a future-adaptation perspective.

Breaking Down or Breaking Free

The first position, the breakdown-liberation perspective, is actually two opposed points of view—one conservative and one radical. What they have in common is a sense of a sharp break with the moral and family traditions of the past. There is not, it should be noted, a perfect correlation between the conservative-radical dimensions we are considering here, and political conservatism or radicalism. It is rare for a political conservative to be a moral radical, although the "swinging" couples studied by Bartell (1971) and others seem to have combined conservative political preferences with a radical sexual style. On the other hand many people with leftist politics have conservative sexual and family attitudes.

The conservative looks at the increases in divorce, sexuality outside marriage, pornography, youthful rebelliousness, the increasing openness about homosexuality, and sees moral breakdown and decadence. The instinctual radical, however, sees not a breaking down but a breaking free, an overthrow of artificial, repressive restraints. Both agree that basic impulses are being unleashed, but they differ drastically as to the nature of impulse. To the conservative, impulses are dangerous, uncontrollable, and rather ugly; to the radical, they are beautiful and innocent.

Similarly, the conservative looks at parent-child relations and sees *Lord of the Flies*. Children are cruel, ignorant, but clever savages who must be restrained by moral and rational adults. The radical, by contrast, sees the moral tables turned the other way. The child has a clarity of perception and moral sensitivity which has been corrupted in adults: socialization is a "almost complete holocaust of the child's experience on the altar of conformity" (Laing, 1971, p. 101).

The "breakdown" perspective includes many popular writers who are fond of alluding to the fall of Rome. It also includes the older generation of family scholars such as Zimmerman who predicted that the decline of the traditional patriarchal family and the rise of the individualistic nuclear family would lead to the general erosion of moral and responsible behavior.

> The extinction of faith in the familistic system is identical with the movements in Greece during the century following the Peloponnesian Wars, and in Rome from about A.D. 150. In each case the change and belief in family systems was associated with rapid adoption of negative reproduction rates and with enormous crises in the very civilizations themselves. (Zimmerman, 1970, p. 34)

In 1935 Zimmerman had written of the "atomistic" family emerging in the twentieth century. He aligned himself with the writings of Frederick Le Play, the nineteenth-century writer who stressed that the good domestic unit — by which he meant the patriarchal stem family — was the fountainhead of citizenship. In 1971, in the Burgess award address to the National Council on Family Relations, Zimmerman offered his interpretation of the turmoil of the 1960's. He saw the emergence of the "no-family," and an anarchic society where irrationality, mob rule, and public fornication are the order of the day:

> . . . In some of the recent rallies and encampments of the youth, young boys and girls fornicate nakedly and openly in the middle of crowds in broad daylight. This type of reversion has not been seen before since the twelfth century except in revolutionary demoralization or in war combat. . . .
> . . . Our present family system is becoming a very extreme type. Its . . . system of values . . . is being challenged successfully by persons who deny the social needs for and validity of any restraints. Out of this has arisen a great deal of confusion and anarchy. The revolution has penetrated the churches, the schools, the social welfare institutions, the public law, the mores, the domestic institutions as well. . . . The public schools are not . . .

allowed to discipline the children. The parents do not ordinarily uphold the teachers or inculcate the needed discipline at home. . . . (Zimmerman, 1972, pp. 327, 331)

Zimmerman suggests that periods of revolution and family breakdown give rise to a counterrevolution. "Good" family behavior emerges when the anarchy becomes so extreme people once again come to value the family virtues. He points to the Soviet experience as an example of family "demoralization" after 1917, and "remoralization" in the new family policies of the 1930's.

A somewhat similar position on the breakdown of the contemporary American family has been taken by Urie Bronfenbrenner, a leading child psychologist. Bronfenbrenner is not concerned with sexual morality, but with a breakdown in socialization. He contrasts child-rearing patterns in America and Russia and concludes that, though Soviet child rearing produces responsible citizens, American child rearing consists of "the unmaking of the American child" (1970, p. 95). Bronfenbrenner writes that there has been a decline in the interaction of parents and children over a twenty-five-year period in the United States. The "vacuum" left by the parents is filled by peers and television, resulting in "antisocial," "alienated" attitudes and behavior. In milder forms this alienation expresses itself as cheating, lying, "playing hooky," teasing; in stronger form it emerges as drug abuse, delinquency, violence, and the counterculture of alienated youth. Bronfenbrenner explicitly refers to the imagery of *Lord of the Flies* as a model of the antisocial peer group:

But as is frequently the case, it is literature which provides us with the most revealing picture of psychological process and effect. In *Lord of the Flies*, William Golding describes the course of events among a group of pre-adolescent boys marooned on an island. Patterns of civilized relationships, epitomized in the person of "Piggy," are as yet too shallowly rooted, and are soon destroyed by the quickly rising sadism of peer power. Piggy is brutally killed just before the adult rescuers arrive. Their first question: "Are there any adults—any grown-ups with you?"

The message of the allegorical ending is clear, and in our view, dictated no less by literary insight than the independent data of behavioral science. If adults do not once again become involved in the lives of children, there is trouble ahead for American society. (Bronfenbrenner, 1970, p. 118)

The antithesis of the breakdown perspective is the liberation or breaking-free interpretation of the family and sexual revolution. The most extreme as well as the most widely known advocate of this point of view is David Cooper. In *The Death of the Family* (1970) Cooper asserts, along with Zimmerman and Bronfenbrenner, that the contemporary family is in a state of extreme decline. Unlike them he applauds rather than denounces its passing. For Cooper the family, schools, universities, and other social institutions are enemies of the individual. He sees the family as an "ideological conditioning device" to regiment its members and prepare them for psychological exploitation. The commune movement, the counterculture, hippies, runaways, dropouts, and LSD users represent the vanguard of the liberation revolution.

Continuity

The classic response on the part of most sociologists to popular assertions of change such as family breakdown and sexual revolution may be summed up in the old French proverb: "The more it changes, the more it is the same thing" (*Plus ça change, plus c'est la même chose*). This stance seems to be based on both statistics and theoretical assumptions. Most sociologists tend to see society as a balanced social system where change is gradual and incremental, rather than sharp and discontinuous. Pointing to statistics on divorce rates, premarital sexuality, and illegitimacy, sociologists are likely to comment that at no point in time were all brides virgins or all marriages harmonious and faithful, whereas today there are significant numbers of people who do not have premarital sex, who are faithful, and who remain married. The following excerpts illustrate this point of view:

. . . Each new generation smiles with amusement at the courtship patterns of the preceding generation, and each generation of parents looks with some consternation on the innovations introduced by its children. In this way, intergenerational change calls attention to itself so that our interests are focused on the differences. . . . The similarity from one generation to the next is ignored. . . . Yet studies of attitudes and behavior covering all the generations of the century show only relatively minor changes in basic patterns between continuous generations. Each generation introduces some new twist to an old theme. Statistical averages change slightly: A few more girls have intercourse with their fiancees before marriage, men get married a fraction of a year younger on the average, a few more couples practice contraception, a few more women are employed in outside jobs. . . . (Udry, 1971, pp. 25–26)

. . . The popular notion that America is undergoing a sexual "revolution" is a myth. The belief that our more permissive sexual code is a sign of a general breakdown of morality is also a myth. (Reiss, 1970, p. 43)

. . . The available data indicate that since World War II, there has not been a mass retreat from chastity standards among the advantaged groups. . . . (Pope and Knudsen, 1965, p. 322)

With regard to divorce, some writers argue that marriage is no less an imposing social institution than it used to be, since more people are getting married more times than ever. Similarly, many family sociologists argue that a sexual revolution is not taking place. Behavior, it is said, has not really changed all that much since the 1920's; it is just that people have become more open about their behavior. Finally, there are those who describe the generation gap as an illusion and the women's liberation movement as a passing fad.

The continuity perspective is undoubtedly correct in its challenge to those who see breakdown and revolution in current changes. Where the latter writers see only anarchic impulse and normlessness, the former group sees new norms emerging. For example, Reiss (1970) argues that premarital sexual behavior reflects a new norm of "permissiveness with affection"; he suggests that young people are assuming more responsibility for their own sexual standards and behavior, rather than simply overthrowing their parents' morality in the name of no restraints or standards.

In a similar vein some of the more thoughtful writers on the generation gap have pointed out continuities in beliefs and attitudes between young people and their parents. Further, where there are generational differences it is the younger generation that shows more social concern than their elders. Citing a number of national surveys of younger and older adolescents and their parents, John Conger concludes:

Although only a small minority, especially of younger adolescents, are militant activists on social or political issues, most do appear to have a greater concern than their parents did at the same ages, or do now, with such issues as socioeconomic discrimination and racial prejudice. Thus, for example, adolescents are far more willing than their parents to have increased school integration and to have blacks and other minority group members as neighbors. . . .

While they are more tolerant than their parents of premarital sexual relationships in which love and commitment are present, they appear generally opposed to promiscuity. . . . Three out of four believe that though a double standard of sexual behavior exists, it is wrong.

Most are interested in job success as conventionally defined, but they are, at least relatively, less concerned with achieving status and recognition by society in their future jobs than earlier generations were, and more concerned with finding work that is "meaningful" and enjoyable and in which they can have pride. Three out of four say they would not work for a company that causes substantial pollution. . . . (Conger, 1971, pp. 1114–1115)

Recently a number of women's magazines have been surveying their readers' attitudes on women's liberation issues. Here too there is evidence that fits the model of incremental change; as in youth attitudes there is a reluctance to identify with radicalism or far-out life styles, coupled with acceptance of many of the principles being advocated by the militants:

. . . These women are far from being radicals or feminists. As the profile of those who replied to the questionnaire shows, they tend to be political moderates, to acknowledge a religious affiliation and to have chosen the conventional life-style of marriage and motherhood.

These rather conventional women, however, harbor some very unconventional attitudes about their status in American society. The overwhelming majority believes that women are, indeed, second-class citizens, a notion that as recently as several years ago was held only by a small minority of women. For example, three women in four concur that the communication media "degrade women by portraying them as sex objects or mindless dolls," virtually all are aware that women earn less than men for doing the same work, fully 94% oppose the argument that women deserve less pay than men because women are not reliable as workers. . . . Almost two in three disagree that "the special privileges that men extend to women more than offset any discrimination they practice against women. . . ." (Tavris and Jayaratne, 1973, p. 68)

In general, then, in looking at any aspect of the current family scene — sexuality, sex roles, generational relations — it is possible to find elements of continuity and stability as well as discontinuity and change. One of the limitations of the continuity point of view, however, is that it plays down historical change in sex and family patterns, and overlooks what may be novel in the present situation.

More recent statistical evidence is documenting marked changes in premarital sexual behavior (see Sorenson, 1973); and rates of marriage and of fertility have been declining. The dramatic drop in ideal family size since 1967 also suggests discontinuous sharp breaks. The general tendency of sociologists to look at family and sexual behavior as constants in society is also being undermined by historical studies.

For example, as opposed to the sociologist's notion that premarital sexuality represents a small, relatively constant proportion of the population, historians have recently been documenting marked rises and falls of premarital sexuality over the past two centuries (Hindus, 1971; Shorter, 1971). Not only illegitimacy but also sexuality within marriage seems to vary over time. The explanations for these changes are, of course, less well established, but historians find heightened sexual activity to be associated with periods where there is an ideology of individual liberation, and a decline in sexuality in periods of conservatism. Similarly, historians find that generational conflict and the roles and status of women vary, as does women's acceptance of their subordinate roles.

Even if the proponents of no essential change were correct on the numbers issue, the arguments about continuity of overt behavior miss the essential point about the norms or the mores—that is, their force rests in their being unchallenged. True, deviant acts carried out secretly or shamefully do not challenge normative standards. But when college girls live openly with young men, unwed movie actresses publicize their pregnancies, homosexuals picket in support of gay liberation, or women's liberationists denounce marriage and advocate masturbation—this is a challenge. The open violation of conventional norms, and the publicity lavished on famous violators by the media, affects even the conservative elements of society. As Sumner pointed out long ago, much of the force of moral rules rests in the unthinkability of their being questioned, and in the assumption, sometimes unconscious, that terrible things will happen if they are violated.

The Sexual Revolution as a Paradigm Change   What the advocates of incremental change dismiss as merely a change in attitudes and norms is, it can be argued, the heart of the matter. The sexual revolution fits the model of Thomas Kuhn's scientific revolution: it is a paradigm change, a transformation of the way the world and the objects in it are viewed:

> . . . When paradigms change, the world itself changes with them. Led by a new paradigm, scientists adopt new interests and look in new places. Even more important, during revolutions scientists see new and different things when looking with familiar instruments in places they have looked before. . . . (Kuhn, 1962, p. 111)

Thus the revolutionary aspect of sexuality today is not to be found in increased amounts of sexual behavior so much as in changed definitions of social reality. Today a significant number of young people "see new and different things" when looking at sexuality, as well as at marriage, illegitimacy, and so forth. The reason these attitude changes seem to fit the model of a paradigm rather than a gradual-change model is that they involve what Kuhn calls "incommensurate views of the world." For the pre-Copernican astronomer the earth was a fixed, immovable body by *definition*. Similarly, when we hear about Einstein's curved space, our minds rebel because our definition of space does not admit the possibility of its being curved. In the same way each definition of sexuality excludes the possibility of the other definitions.

The shift from Victorian morality to the "enlightened" Freudian morality was another such conceptual as opposed to behavioral revolution. In the more extreme version of Victorian or Puritan morality, the impulsive side of human nature is dangerous and abhorrent. Masturbation could drive a person insane. Too much intercourse, even in marriage, could ruin one's health. A single indiscretion could ruin a girl's reputation and turn her into a "fallen women." Even thinking about sex was forbidden to a normal, respectable person. The Freudian revolution changed the definition of sexuality. Sex was still a powerful drive — even stronger than the Victorians had believed — but it could be acknowledged, understood, and controlled. Indeed, Freud argued that "civilization" itself was made possible only through the harnessing of sexual drives. Thus sexuality was opened to rational discussion and rational control, with the emphasis on control. Freudian paradigms substituted another set of restraints for the Victorian ones: normal sex was adult genital sex within marriage; it was also responsible, warm, and loving. Anything else would put one's claims to be a normal, mature person into serious question. In the Freudian paradigm there was tolerance for and understanding of sexual deviance, but only as pathology—something to be cured, if possible.

By contrast the post-Freudian paradigm defines most variant sexual appetites as matters of private preference— "whatever turns you on," "do your own thing," "if it doesn't harm anybody, why not do it?" This attitude derives from the general tendency of the counterculture to rely on feelings and spontaneity as the basis for actions. Edgar Friedenberg has contrasted the attitudes between the generations on the issue of impulses as guides to action:

What tends to distinguish the generations is . . . their feeling about feeling and what people should do about their feelings. In our society, people over 30 are likely to look upon their feelings as a problem rather than a resource or a reliable guide. We try to compensate for them, so as to remain unbiased; to control ourselves and our impulses so they will not lead us into temptation or *liaisons dangereuses* or even into behavior that, granted other people's expectations of persons in our role, would be embarrassing or disruptive. When this process becomes unbearably depriving we seek therapeutic help in strengthening the rational component of our psyche. . . .

The young, by contrast, are more likely to look upon their feelings as a guide to what is good, and certainly to what is good for them, and to view the demands of society and the expectations of others—as the problem. (Friedenberg, 1971, pp. 2–3)

As Friedenberg himself points out, to speak about "generations" in this manner is a distortion. By and large, working-class youth do not participate in the counterculture. But significant numbers of middle-class youth do adhere to the new paradigms.

Similar analyses could be made of the concepts of love and marriage. During the nineteenth century and in most traditional cultures, "love" is not a spontaneous experience forming the basis for a marriage. Marriages are arranged on the basis of social and economic considerations. Although the intended spouses might have some degree of influence on the choice of spouse, they are not expected to love each other before marriage. "Love" would develop later.

As we have noted earlier, the psychoanalytic models of love and marriage coincide with the modern ideology of romantic, conjugal love: for Freud the test of mental health was the ability to work and to love. Love in this paradigm is a deep, lifelong commitment to one's spouse, involving intimacy as well as respect and concern for the other person. In the newer paradigm love cannot be so easily contained within a one-to-one, lifelong relationship.

What difference does it make whether current changes are interpreted in terms of continuity or discontinuity? Philip Slater has argued for a discontinuity interpretation in terms of two different cultures—an old scarcity-oriented culture and an amorphous counterculture based on affluence. He argues that this perspective provides a better understanding of the internal logic of each position. Each "culture" is built on a set of assumptions that hangs together. Further, Slater argues, the two-cultures notion points out the limits to compromise and negotiation when conflict occurs between the two sides:

> I speak of two cultures because we no longer have one. Mixing the two that exist does not add up to the American way of life. They cannot be mixed. . . .
>
> For the older generation, the ultimate moral reference is the far right—authoritarian, puritanical, punitive. Such views are considered extreme . . . but they are accorded an implicit and unquestioned *moral* validity. . . .
>
> For middle-class college students the ultimate moral reference group tends . . . to be the new left, with its emphasis on equalitarianism, radical democracy, social justice, and social commitment. Once again the moderate majority among the young tend to view the proponents of their own moral code as extreme, moralistic and fanatic. . . . (Slater, 1970, pp. 97–98)

The key to understanding the difference between the two cultures, Slater argues, is the concept of scarcity; in the old culture both economic and sexual gratification are in short supply:

> The core of the old culture is scarcity. Everything in it rests on the assumption that the world does not contain the wherewithal to satisfy the needs of its human inhabitants. From this it follows that people must compete with each other for these scarce resources—lie, swindle, steal, if necessary. These basic assumptions create the danger of a "war of all against all.". . . (Slater, 1970, p. 103)

By contrast the "new culture" believes that human wants are easy to satisfy, and the means for doing so plentiful.

Contextual Strain and Future Adaptation

Thus far we have looked at the situation of the family in contemporary society from the point of view of changes in the values, attitudes, and behavior of individual family members. There is another way of looking at what is happening to the family. Rather than viewing values and ideologies as causal, this perspective views family change as a product of changes in the society at large. Again, there are two variations in this perspective: rising divorce rates may be said to show that society is placing greater strains on marriage than the institution can bear; or, high divorce rates may be viewed as an indicator of a new pattern of marriage, more adaptive to modern social conditions (see Farber, 1964; Toffler, 1970).

In Chapter 4 we noted that the same authors who stressed the fit between the nuclear family and industrial society also pointed out certain built-in strains in the modern family. Parsons had noted that when the family lost its economic functions and the home was no longer a workshop or a business, the women, children, and old people were left in an ambiguous position outside the occupational world. For children the shift to industrial work and the removal of the father from the home also meant that the mother played a much larger role in growing up than ever before. Little boys could no longer observe and participate in father's work. Goode, who looks at family change in countries now undergoing modernization, does not stress the family's loss of economic functions so much as the separation of the nuclear unit from the extended kin group. Goode notes a number of contradictions between the ideology of the conjugal family and the realities of life in an urban industrial society. He sees the woman's role as a particular point of strain in the system: "modernism" offers woman equality and liberation from the restrictions of the kin group, yet it leaves her in an isolated household with increased burdens of child rearing.

These authors do not see the male role in modern society as free of strain either. Under constant pressure to produce, achieve, and support, most men spend their lives at work they do not like. At the higher levels of the occupational scale, work is often intrinsically rewarding, but life at the top has its own discontents: the scientist, the artist, the com-

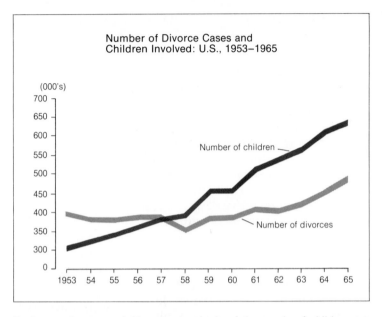

Number of Divorce Cases and
Children Involved: U.S., 1953–1965

Each year, because of divorces, hundreds of thousands of children are added to those living in one-parent families. In addition, uncounted numbers live in homes broken by separation other than divorce. (From *Profiles of Children*, White House Conference on Children 1970, Washington: U.S. Government Printing Office)

pany manager, the professor may judge themselves in relation to heroes of achievement farther up the scale than themselves, rather than by their distance from those below. Thus the home and family are assigned the role of refuge and retreat from the harshness of the occupational world, a difficult if not impossible assignment.

In the theorizing of Parsons, Goode, and others, these strains seemed insignificant aspects of the total picture of life in contemporary society. During the period of social tranquility between World War II and the mid-1960's, to point to such built-in strains in family life seemed merely an academic exercise. Indeed, for "Middle America," today's so-called "silent majority"—the nonpoor, the nonblack, the nonyoung, and, we should add, the not-rich and the not-highly-educated—such questions are still academic. The contradictions of family life are most apparent among the well-educated, technically and professionally skilled part of

the population. It is largely this group that has given rise to student dissenters, hippies, the communal and encounter-group movement, and sexual experimentation. On the other side of Middle America is the third major style of life—that of the poor, the disadvantaged, and the excluded. This group has yet to experience the affluence and family life styles that Middle America enjoys and professional classes are trying to transcend.

It is easy to understand why the poor and disadvantaged should take part in protest movements. But how can we account for the fact that it is the most affluent and privileged groups in America—or, more precisely, their children—who show so much dissatisfaction with society in general and family life in particular? One reason is this: only in the most privileged groups do these strains become clear. For example, the middle-class woman is more likely than her working-class sister to experience the contradiction between the ideology that men and women are equal and the realities of life, particularly of marriage. After receiving the same education, middle-class young men and women often go in very different directions: he participates in the larger world and, despite complaints about the rat race, finds some degree of daily social interaction and stimulation in his work; she retreats into the home. The contrast is greatest when the husband is a professional who really enjoys his work or a businessman who travels to interesting places and indulges in expense-account living. The wife of a factory worker, however, has less cause for envy. In the same way the middle-class child who has been raised "democratically" is sensitized to discrepancies between the ideal of treating young people as "persons," human beings whose views are to be taken seriously, and the actual powerlessness of the dependent young in families, schools, and the larger society.

Alternatively, current ferment may well be interpreted as an adaptation to future social needs. America and other advanced societies are in a transition to a postindustrial or postmodern form of society, and it is mainly the most educated and most technically skilled segment of the middle class that belongs to that era. Thus the women's movement can be seen as a response to the need for women to define themselves as something other than mothers in a world with a very low birthrate and extended lifespans. From this perspective homosexuality can be interpreted as an adaptation to the need for population control. The hippie life style, as Fred Davis (1971) has suggested, with its emphasis on do-it-yourself crafts and music, on being rather than doing, may provide an incipient solution to future problems of work, leisure, and identity in a postindustrial society. The "new poverty" and antimaterialism of the counterculture may be interpreted as an adaptation to the need for a more modest standard of living in the face of the environmental crisis.

If the industrial era with which the nuclear family seemed to fit so well is in the process of changing, it is worthwhile to examine the transition to postindustrialism in more detail.

Postindustrial Society   The central feature of the postindustrial era is the scientific-technological revolution in which automation and electronics have transformed industry. Daniel Bell, who coined the term "postindustrial," argues that the new technology brings about an era in which scientists and other highly trained professionals increase in numbers and gain great prominence and prestige. Learning and knowledge become major growth industries, and the prime sources of an accelerating rate of social change. Brzezinski (1970) has written of the onset of a "technetronic" era symbolized by new complexes of learning research and development which become the principle agents of change in technology, social structure, values, and mores. Yet even in the most advanced countries, the postindustrial era has arrived only partially.

Bell, Brzezinski, and others write approvingly of the dawning new era dominated by a scientific-technological elite. The new society in their view will be highly rational and affluent. There will be unprecedented opportunities for jobs that are inherently interesting—work will tend to be synonymous with play—and there will be increased leisure time, stimulating increased interest in the fine arts and culture. The technetronic society demands close links between the universities, government, and business. The university, the laboratory, the research center, and the computer symbolize the new era as the big factory with its streaming smokestacks symbolized the industrial era. These authors see student dissent and the counterculture as a pathetic revolt against the new age. Once the transition to the new era has been completed, society will be balanced again and there will be no more youthful dissidence. Socialization will once again become a smooth instrument for the replacement of generations.

A similar version of the postindustrial era is looked at with horror by observers from a different perspective. The vision of a computerized society dominated by a small group of experts who hold a monopoly on knowledge becomes, in this view, a totalitarian nightmare. They see in the technetronic society a threat of social control more complete than any despotism that ever existed in the past. Computers and other electronic devices will make surveillance of individuals possible to an unprecendented degree, and psychological and physical controls over the human mind can create docility in the masses of the population.

It is of course impossible to predict the future with any degree of specificity, as the events of the last decade have shown. So it is possible that the smooth-running technetronic society will come about, in the same shape as its admirers and detractors have predicted. But there is a diametrically opposed vision of the postindustrial society, which seems to have the preponderance of evidence in its favor.

Knowledge and Dissent   Instead   of   seeing   postindustrial society as a smoothly functioning scientific Utopia where dissent and conflict have been engineered out of existence, the alternative view argues that such a society will inevitably create dissenters and nonconformists in large numbers. This view argues that the very dependency of the key institutions on an intelligentsia of educated professionals poses a growing dilemma for the ruling elites. For this same intelligentsia is just as likely to provide the major critics and rebels of the social order, along with the trained manpower. Thus student protestors, insurgent intellectuals who protest government policies, as well as "phone phreaks"—electronics experts who use their expertise in opposition to the owners and managers who depend on them—symbolize the contradictions of postindustrial society. Dissent in the postindustrial society arises not from the failures of socialization but from its successes. The critical faculties required by highly educated professionals lead them to question the very legitimacy of the order they serve.

There are at least two versions of this point of view, a sociological and psychological one. The sociological version, which is more direct and simply stated, has recently been set forth by Lipset and Dobson (1972):

Intellectuals and their apprentices, university students, have never been as numerous as they are today. Given the increased requirement of postindustrial society for university-trained people and continuing high levels of innovative research, the university is needed more than ever before. . . .

. . . The growth of critical intelligentsia disposed to support the "adversary culture" and reject the worth of dominant political and economic systems is undermining the capacity of governing systems in modern societies to maintain equilibrium. Leadership itself . . . is under question by intellectuals everywhere. Castro, Mao, Tito, Franco, the Greek colonels, the leaders of western Europe, no less than those who head the governments of the United States and the Soviet Union, find themselves at odds with their intellectuals.

. . . The basic tensions, the contradictions within the system, come increasingly from within the elite itself—from its own intellectual leaders supported by large segments of its student children. . . . The contradiction of post-industrial society, whether Communist or non-Communist, may be its dependence on trained intelligence, on research and innovation, which requires it to bring together large numbers of intellectuals and students on great campuses and in a few intellectual communities located at the centers of communication and influence. (Lipset and Dobson, 1972, p. 184)

Lipset and Dobson present some dramatic statistics documenting how the occupational structures of such advanced countries as the United States and the Soviet Union have changed in recent years. Between 1930 and 1965, for example, while the general work force in the United States increased by half, the number of engineers almost quadrupled and the number of scientists increased almost ten times over. In addition to the increases in people engaged in science and technology, there has been expansion in the numbers and influence of other kinds of knowledge and cultural workers—teachers, artists, writers, journalists, people in the media.

Why are there such strong tendencies for intellectuals to constitute a dissenting force, to bite the hand that feeds them? The answer seems to be that creative work of any kind—scientific or artistic—seems to call for a certain skepticism, a critical detachment from prevailing ideas. This skepticism is a basic part of the scientific attitude—the scientist is supposed to suspend judgment until all the evidence is in. Once a person develops the habit of critical or independent thinking in work, he will likely be critical also in matters outside his special field of work.

When existing bodies of knowledge change rapidly, it is not possible to train young persons with skills that will last a lifetime. Even students who are not aiming to be research scientists must be taught to be skeptical about current solutions to problems and ways of doing things. An engineering student, a computer programmer, a student of business administration—none of these can simply be taught a set of techniques that will remain valid from then on. Rather, they must be taught to be flexible and innovative—that there have been different ways of looking at the problem in the past, and that the future will bring still more innovation. The more broadly a person has been educated, the easier it will be for him or her to change occupations or skills several times over. In addition, only liberal education can adapt to what may be a more serious problem of postindustrial society than the changing occupational demands produced by new technologies: the problem of abundance and leisure.

The Postindustrial Personality   The increased numbers and prominence of intellectual workers is only one aspect of postindustrial or technetronic society. Another and perhaps more profound aspect is the possibility of the end of scarcity and of the grim necessity for men to labor by the sweat of the brow. At first glance it might seem that a society where scarcity no longer exists, and the traditional idea of drudgery work must be drastically curtailed, is a Utopian dream. As a matter of fact such a society is not a dream but a reality now in the process of emerging. Furthermore, the prospect of a drastically reduced necessity for work profoundly unsettles many people. For four centuries at least, the most fundamental economic, social, and religious assumptions of Western life centered around the necessity and sanctity of hard work, self-denial, and thrift. As Michael Harrington has put it:

> To this day, the West believes that a man establishes his worth in the eyes of his neighbor, and even before God, through industry and drudgery and saving. In its most acutely American form, as the poet William Carlos Williams once observed, this attitude asserts itself in the conversational opening, "What do you do?" . . . One, is, it implies, what one does. One is one's work.
>
> What would happen if technology rendered work and the work ethic decadent? (Harrington, 1966, p. 257)

A number of observers have pointed out that the United States today is in an uncomfortable transition between the work ethic, which remains the official ideology, and a not yet clearly worked out ethic appropriate for the postindustrial age. Since World War II the American economy has required high levels of spending and consumption to maintain prosperity. There has been a growing emphasis on immediate rather than deferred gratification. The credit-card economy stresses leisure-time activities—boating, fishing, skiing, camping, hi-fi music—as providing the central meaning of life and definitions of self. Thus the hedonism of the youth culture can be interpreted as a continuation of, rather than a revolt against, the larger culture.

The emergence of both student dissent and the counterculture can be traced to tensions in society at large and in families between the industrial work ethic and newer postindustrial ethic. Keniston, for example, suggests young people growing up in affluent middle-class families simply

do not experience the social and psychological imperatives that led to the industrial type of personality. People brought up in relative economic security, political freedom, and affluence simply take these for granted as facts of life rather than as goals or values to organize their lives around. Moreover, we encounter the paradox that affluence itself, and the ideology surrounding it, is a powerful stimulant to discontent on a mass scale. Advertising constantly bombards us to be dissatisfied with what we already own, and tries to stimulate appetites for more, bigger, better, and newer things. Accordingly, material possessions create new appetites and often prove unable to provide contentment or security.

Kurt Back has suggested that the emergence of the encounter-group movement in America is one expression of the discontents of affluence:

The necessity for survival and fulfillment of such basic needs as food, shelter, and clothing have throughout history engaged the full efforts of man, and the ambition not to have to worry about their adequate fulfillment has been realized by only a few. . . . People have expected that achievement of these needs could bring happiness or lasting satisfaction.

Many who were able to achieve such a fortunate state found that it did not bring happiness or even satisfaction, however. The newly affluent discovered other needs were not satisfied; these needs were less easy to define, but frustration was manifested in boredom, feelings of worthlessness, lack of excitement, and other indicators stereotyped as the symptoms of affluent suburbia. (Back, 1972, p. 37)

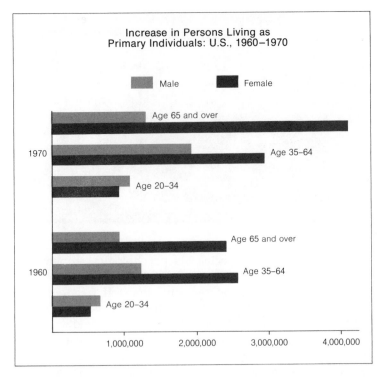

Increase from 1960 to 1970 in persons living as primary individuals—that is, persons who maintained their own households while living alone or with persons not related to them. The greatest *percent* increase since 1960 occurred in the 20–34 age groups for both men and women. Among women in 1970, however, the greatest *number* of primary individuals was in the 65 and older age group, whereas the greatest number of men who were primary individuals was in the 35–64 age group. (Based on data in *Population Characteristics,* U.S. Department of Commerce, Bureau of the Census, Series P-20, No. 233, Washington: U.S. Government Printing Office, 1972)

That the malaise of affluence is confined to the most favored segments of the population does not make it less real.

Another reason affluence fails to satisfy is that it is based on a "fun morality," as Martha Wolfenstein (1954) describes it, that contains a paradoxical injunction: one is obligated to have a good time. Although the Protestant Ethic could give rise to feelings of guilt and worthlessness that one could never undo, still it offered the possibility of trying to satisfy one's conscience through hard work. Fun morality is more elusive. Play becomes permeated by the work ethic; one asks, am I having enough fun, a good enough orgasm, a happy enough marriage? Not only does happiness tend to elude such introspection, but being permitted to satisfy impulses may weaken the pleasure of anticipation:

> In the past when work and play were more sharply isolated, virtue was associated with one and the danger of sin with the other. Impulse gratification presented possibilities of intense excitement as well as of wickedness. Today we have attained a high degree of tolerance of impulses, which at the same time no longer seem capable of producing such intense excitement as formerly. (Wolfenstein, 1954, p. 75)

The Transformation of the Lifespan Beyond the changing definitions of work and play the postindustrial society changes the definitions of the ages and stages of the lifespan. Anthropology and history have shown that such stages of life as childhood and adolescence are largely a matter of social conventions. How the lifespan is divided depends on the existence of social institutions that create places for particular age groups. Thus childhood was not a clearly distinguished concept until the school and the family created a specific place or role for children.

More recently, during the nineteenth century, adolescence became added to childhood as a "second childhood," as David Bakan (1971b) has put it, to meet certain changes in the urban industrial society of that period. The high school contributed to the "invention" of adolescence just as the primary school had contributed to the invention of childhood. The high school seems to have come into being in part because of a lessened need for child labor, an increased need on the part of industry for trained and reliable workers, and agitation by unions against child labor and for more schooling for their own children in the hopes of social mobility.

Now, as we enter the postindustrial era, it appears that a third childhood has been added to the other two. Just as primary school and then high school have spread from the elite to broader segments of the population, so did higher education expand on a mass scale in the postwar era in the advanced countries. By the beginning of the 1970's a majority of high-school graduates were entering college. Keniston has argued that this dramatic increase in higher education has created a new stage of the lifespan—"youth"—on a mass scale:

> Today, in more developed nations, we are beginning to witness the recognition of still another stage of life. Like childhood and adolescence it was initially granted only to a small minority but is now being rapidly extended to an ever-larger group. I will call this stage "youth" and by that I mean both a further phase of disengagement from society and the period of psychological development that intervenes between adolescence and adulthood. This stage, which continues into the twenties and sometimes into the thirties, provided opportunities for intellectual, emotional and moral development that were never afforded to any other large group in history. (Keniston, 1971a, p. 309)

Although Keniston prefers to speak in developmental terms, and speaks of youth as a "psychological stage," he warns that not all college students are in this stage—that some are "adolescents" psychologically and some are adults. Nor are affluence and education necessary for the experience of youth: ". . . There are poor and uneducated young men and women, from Abraham Lincoln to Malcolm X, who have had a youth, and rich educated ones who have moved straightaway from adolescence to adulthood" (p. 17).

In view of all these reservations about the use of the term "stage," it might be more useful to think of "youth" not so much in developmental terms but as a particular kind of cultural outlook or world view or psychological perspective. Keniston writes of youth as merely another stage on the way to adulthood, but there is no evidence that the generation who are now experiencing "youth" will progress toward adulthood in anything like the old sense. Indeed, it may well be that the psychological themes of youth are not so much a postponement of adulthood as a redefinition of it. What Keniston describes as youth may well be an experience that for many people will extend over most of the lifespan.

Keniston's stage of youth resembles what Robert J. Lifton has called the "protean" life style. It used to be that socialization resulted in a finished product, a person whose character was set by the end of adolescence, and who would change only under the most extreme conditions, such as a religious conversion. Now Lifton argues not only that we live in an age of identity crises that may last a lifetime, but that settled identities may change to other settled identities, and more than once. Thus the conditions of life in the twentieth century have produced a new kind of individual, whom Lifton calls "protean man," after the mythological figure who could take the form of any living thing.

Redefinition of Adulthood   The concept of the protean style suggests that we may now be witnessing not so much the invention of a new stage of life as the demise of an old one — adulthood. The tensions between self and society which Keniston posits as being at the core of youth need not, as he seems to assume, result in a stable resolution. Rather, the values a person holds as a "youth" may persist over the lifespan — such values as openness to experience and change, cultivating one's own individual selfhood, and the explora- tion of inner sensibilities.

Adulthood in the old sense was attained when a person's growth and learning had been finished; his place in and relation to society had been set. The conception of childhood as a stage of life exists as a contrast to the idea of adulthood. In the postindustrial era it seems likely that the institutional and psychological basis for conceiving childhood and adult- hood as distinct stages of life may no longer exist. Concep- tions of the stages of life may resemble those of the medieval era more than the industrial age, in that adults and children will not be seen as so sharply different from each other. Yet the postindustrial child, unlike the medieval or the tribal child, will not be seen simply as a smaller version of the parent, heir to the parent's place in society, and subject to parental authority until the death of the parent.

Bennett Berger's research into communal child rearing suggests a third model of childhood, one that may point the way to future patterns of the larger society. Having rejected middle-class notions of maturity, Berger notes, communards have to "rethink the definitions of childhood, adulthood, and the relations between them." He continues:

. . . Like the big "kids" who are their parents, communal children seem to be just littler kids, less skilled, less experienced, and only perhaps less wise.
    . . . "Young people" are regarded as independent of the fam- ily, but not as members of an autonomous category of "children"; instead, their status is likely to be ascribed as that of "person," a development which can be understood as part of an equalitarian

ethos, as complementary to parallel developments in the status of females, from "women" (or even "mothers") to "people," and in the status of men, from being characterized in invidious status terms to being characterized as, above all, a "human being." . . . (Berger, 1972, pp. 11–12)

Berger observed a transition from infancy to "person" status after the age of four, as in Aries' description of medieval times. When children grow past physical dependence on adults, "they are treated and tend to behave as just another member of the extended family — including being offered (and taking) an occasional hit on a joint of marijuana as it is passed around the family circle" (1972, p. 12). Berger believes that the single most important belief governing adult-child relations in the communes is that the behavior of the children does not reflect on the parents in any way. In contrast to both preindustrial and middle-class child rearing, adults are not characterized by what they do or do not do with or to their children.

Such adult-child relations may well become the future pattern in the larger society. This development would not depend on everyone joining a rural commune. Rather, such an outcome seems implicit in a variety of trends now going on in society at large. First, the prevailing conceptions of childhood and adulthood impose disabilities on children and burdens on parents. The role of the incompetent, dependent, subordinate child, whether at home or at school, has become increasingly burdensome to adolescents in particular, but to younger children as well. Subordination has never come naturally to children — "they have to be carefully taught," as the song goes. Today the counterculture of adolescents and youth provides a powerful socializing influence on younger children, as evidenced in part by the extension of the youth cultural styles of music, dress, and even protest into the lower school grades. Besides, the trend in middle-class families toward democratic, psychologically oriented child rearing, however inconsistently carried out, makes it hard for children to accept irrational or bureaucratic authority later on. If one has been treated as a person at home, it is hard to accept being treated as something less at school or at work.

Further, the prescriptions for child rearing that have prevailed in the middle classes impose heavy burdens on parents, particularly mothers. These prescriptions demand that the parent, particularly the mother, provide intellectual stimulation, emotional self-fulfillment, and autonomy for the child. If, however, parents also desire such things for *themselves,* they find themselves in conflict with the desire to provide them for the child. As Richard Flacks has noted:

. . . To provide children intellectual stimulation and sensory variety requires intense involvement in the quality of their activities. But if the parents are to provide the quantities of time, energy and patience required to achieve these goals they must limit their own recreation and pursuits and get enough sleep so they will have sufficient energy and patience to allow their offspring to be the central focus of attention. . . . This conflict between the demands of childrearing and the personal needs of the parents constitutes another source of parental inconsistency and undermines the "ideal" character of the modern middle-class family. (Flacks, 1971, p. 26)

If the ideology of women's liberation and personal fulfillment for both parents spreads among the middle classes, as it seems likely to do, then we may find that the child's "place" in the family has changed. The production of perfect children may no longer be a central goal of middle-class parents. Indeed, the experience of the parents of today's teen-agers and youth serves as a warning against parents counting too much on children fulfilling parental dreams.

America as a City   Another aspect of postindustrialism is the spread of urbanism to the entire society. Again it is the high-education, high-skill segment of the population that within America carries these trends to their furthest development. Geographic mobility is a feature of all industrial societies, but America even in preindustrial times has always been a highly mobile society. For three centuries successive waves of immigration from outside have been matched by internal westward migration. This migratory pattern has not diminished in the twentieth century; indeed, each generation of Americans seems to be more mobile than the preceding one (S. Greer, 1962, p. 107). In the last few decades there have been great shifts of population from the cities to the suburbs, from rural to urban areas, from northeast and middle west to west and south.

Mobility in modern society differs from that in the past. The European immigrant or the westward-moving farmer

might be uprooted from his birthplace, but many would settle down to build roots in the new place. Mobility was not necessarily a way of life. Also, in earlier times, to be in a place was to be part of it in a way that is no longer possible; as Philip Slater has pointed out, along with the decline of kinship in modern societies there has also been a loss of the most "primitive and elementary form of association, territoriality," which simply implies that the bonds between two people are a function of their spatial distance from each other (Slater, 1968, pp. 83–84).

The change in America today can be looked at from two aspects of the same process: on the one hand a decline in the functions and power of the local community, and on the other an increase in the scale of the total society. As Greer has argued, all of America has become a big metropolitan area; the visible decline of the central city and the spread of people to suburbs has obscured the fact that the city has come to dominate the entire society in a way that has never been seen before. The cities of the past were small islands of civilization set in oceans of rural hinterland, and containing only a minority of the country's population. The vast increase in the scale of the total society is largely due to improvements in transportation and communication: the electronic revolution brought about instant worldwide communication; the jet engine has brought every place on earth within hours of any other place. McLuhan's concept of the "global village" may be an exaggeration except in moments of international crisis, but the United States as a national community is a more arguable concept:

. . . Technological changes . . . have allowed a mastery of space never known before—one that makes possible rapid and precise communication across and coordination of behavior over great distances. The culture of the large-scale society is urban in its essence; all ears are tuned to the nationwide communication networks, and behavior is ordered by the large-scale agencies of government bureau, corporation, and national market. (S. Greer, 1962, p. 195)

Thus any American today who owns a television set or who works for a large corporation is part of the national community in a way unknown to previous generations. Yet this nation-city is an abstract and bloodless community. It has undermined the basis of the local community without pro-

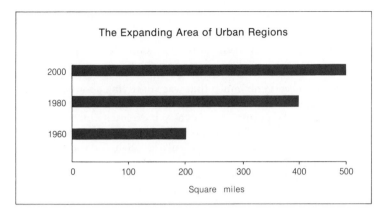

The territory of urban regions is doubling in the period 1960 to 1980. By the year 2000, urban regions will encompass one-sixth of the continental United States land area. (From *Population and the American Future*, Washington: U.S. Government Printing Office, 1972)

viding a substitute for community sociability. The large corporation makes its decisions in terms of the national market rather than local concerns. Walter Cronkite may be a better source of information than the corner newsvendor or grocer, but he cannot nod politely to us and ask after the children, or do an occasional favor. In short, he cannot provide the kind of casual human contact that once formed a daily part of peoples' lives in urban areas.

A number of writers see in the commune movement an attempt to recapture the lost community of neighborhood and home town. For example, Zablocki writes:

For many people, the neighborhood or home town has given way to the community of interest. With the automobile and the telephone, it is probably easier for people of common interests to find one another and spend time together, than ever before in history. Such communities of interest are a kind of intentional community, but they fall short of satisfying the human need for communal relationships. . . . Relations between members of . . . interest groups tend to be segmental and transitory, their members tend to avoid becoming deeply dependent on one another. (Zablocki, 1971, pp. 293–294)

Such writers as Zablocki and Slater see here a tragic dilemma of freedom versus community. On the one hand human relationships are freed from external constraints such as

kinship and territory and can be based on individual qualities of interest, taste, and temperament. On the other hand
this freedom and individuality is "paid for" by a loss of
security, stability, and permanence:

> There was certainly much that was stultifying about the neigh-
> borhood, home-town and village life of previous generations.
> Privacy and the opportunity to develop individual differences were
> hard to achieve. . . . Superstition, narrowness, and intolerance —
> were common. It would be difficult to wish for the return of
> such communities.
> Yet here is the paradox: for all their narrowness these were real
> communities, while communities of interest are not. (Zablocki,
> 1971, p. 294)

The loss of community is also a side effect of affluence.
Affluence increases family privacy: from the apartment house
to the single-family home in the suburbs; from the mixed
neighborhood of stores, garages, and high-density housing
to the green-lawned residential area; from the corner laun-
dromat to the home laundry; from the public swimming area
to the backyard pool; from the daily stop at the local butcher,
baker, and grocer to the weekly visit to the supermarket; from
the bus or subway to the private car — all these are the luxuries of convenience and privacy which large sectors of America's urban population have been able to buy for themselves.
Yet in so doing they have lost the multiple points of social
contact that help contribute to a sense of community.

Not only stable, long-term relationships with people in
the local community have declined, but also a more transitory
sort of sociability that used to be part of daily life has
declined — unplanned meetings of acquaintances and neighbors in local shops or on the street, greeting rituals, occasional favors, or just plain people-watching.

Again there is a dilemma — privacy and abundance versus community and poverty:

> In communities that are poor, or in times of scarcity, sharing
> between individuals and families is a *necessary* element of sur-
> vival. . . . It is the hallmark of abundance that the need for such
> sharing disappears. Each family has its own vacuum cleaner, its
> own set of pots and pans, its own transport . . . etc. Thus the
> necessity of social interaction, the necessity to share, is no longer a
> driving force in communities of abundance; men can withdraw into
> their self-contained, self-sustaining homes. This means that the

feeling of community, of being related and bound together in some way, is cut off from a region that in the past furnished communal experience. (Sennett, 1970a, pp. 48–49)

While noting the loss of sociability that affluence brings, we should not glamorize poverty and sharing: irritation, suspicion, and conflict are, as Oscar Lewis points out, also part of the togetherness of the poor.

The Intensification of Family Life   The demise of the local community has meant that people turn increasingly to home and family. As Parsons has theorized, the family is more important than ever in modern societies, despite its loss of economic and educational functions. Its remaining psychological functions — child nurturance and maintaining the psychological balance of adults — are crucial because the nuclear family is the only group left that carries these out. The question is whether the family can bear the burden that these demands place on it. The high rates of marriage and remarriage can be interpreted as signs that the family is healthy and vital. Even divorce, as we have noted earlier, can be interpreted as a "healthy symptom of the desire of individuals to obtain happiness in marriage" (Butterworth and Weir, 1972, p. 75).

On the other hand the high rates of marriage and divorce can be interpreted as a sign of desperation: that people are looking to marriage to fulfill needs that cannot be met there. One cannot say that a straw is an effective life preserver merely because a drowning man will grab for one. As Slater has observed, in stable and permanent social contexts, married people can require very little from each other. In working-class areas and ethnic enclaves of large cities, husbands and wives often lead rather separate lives; the wife may be intensely involved with her kin, the husband with his work, friends, and his relatives. The shift to middle-class status or suburban living loosens the ties with others outside the nuclear family, and marriage becomes more intense, more intimate, and at the same time more difficult:

In a nonmobile society one expects of marriage only a degree of compatibility. Spouses are not asked to be lovers, friends, and mutual therapists. But it is increasingly true of our society that the marital bond is the closest, deepest, most important, and putatively most enduring relationship of one's life. Therefore it is increasingly likely to fall short of the demands on it and to be dissolved. As emotional alternatives are removed, its limitations become less and less tolerable. The social ties of modern Americans are becoming so ephemeral that a permanent point of reference seems essential, and this perhaps accounts for the heroic effort made in our society — through marriage manuals, counselors, psychotherapists, magazine articles, and so on — to find ways of enabling the marriage relationship to bear the enormous burdens placed on it. (Slater, 1968, p. 90)

Family ties in modern societies have been both intensified and strained by still another factor outside the family itself — the control of disease and the resulting prolongation of life. It has been estimated that a couple marrying in preindustrial times in Europe would expect to have, on the average, about twenty-five years of married life together (P. Laslett, 1965, p. 100). Today people marry younger and live longer; a couple can look forward to forty or fifty years of life together. In other words the length of marriage has almost doubled over the past several centuries.

Another difference between preindustrial times and our own is the presence of three and even four generations of the same families at the same time. In earlier times the newly married couple would probably not live to see their children married. Indeed, it was often necessary for young people to wait until the death of their parents in order to be able to afford marriage. As Laslett sums it up, "You could not with any confidence expect to see your grandchildren in the world we have lost" (1965, p. 98).

We have come to take it so much for granted that death is natural in old age that it is hard to grasp what life must have been like when death was a constant presence that could overtake anyone at any time. In one English village in the seventeenth century, for example, more than a third of all the children had lost a parent. The stepmother and stepfather were common figures, as were lonely old widowed women:

In the face of facts like these it may become difficult for us to go on being sorry for ourselves because of the vast numbers of broken homes and solitary neglected people, which we think of as characteristic of high industrialism in our day. . . . (P. Laslett, 1965, p. 95)

The Future: Is the Nuclear Family Obsolete?

Events of the past fifteen years should threaten anyone who would dare to predict social futures. Those who foresaw a continuation of the public turbulence of the sixties turned out to have been as mistaken as those who thought of the tranquility of the fifties as the permanent and natural state of an advanced technological society. Yet the prediction that the seventies will turn out to be a revisitation of the fifties may also be wrong.

Part of the reason for the seeming tranquility now is that we have become accustomed to many of the attitudes and behavior that seemed shocking and revolutionary when they first appeared. For example, long hair on men no longer looks as strange as it did when it first appeared. People may dislike it intensely, but it has lost the shock value of novelty. The same is true of some of the ideas of the counterculture.

In a remarkably short span of time, the sentimental model of the nuclear family that had dominated the mass media as well as much professional writing on the family during the fifties had turned into its opposite. The family group that had been described as universal and natural was suddenly said to be in a state of crisis, or decline, or misery. There were numerous suggestions for alternative family forms to replace the nuclear family: the commune, the group marriage, the abolition of the nuclear family as a legal status, the nonmonogamous or "swinging" marriage—all dutifully reported on by the mass media. Needless to say these ideas were and are very much minority views, but nevertheless they are now part of the social landscape.

Along with their novelty these views have also lost much of their claim to be the instant solution to the problems that beset the family. To the extent that these alternatives have been tried, it is fair to state that none of them has proved as workable in practice as their originators had hoped. It was the commune more than any other alternative family form that was looked to as the hope and model of the future. Yet as we noted in Chapter 4 the vision of a harmonious, warm, loving, supporting community did not emerge very easily or very often from attempts at group living. In part, the difficulties of building communes could be attributed to problems inherited from the larger society—the inability of people reared in a materialistic, individualistic environment to adapt to a life of sharing and deep commitment to a group. In part, some of the difficulties of communes occurred because some communal values contradicted other values.

A more basic problem with the communal idea may lie in its resemblance to the sentimentalized model of the nuclear family which it apparently rejects—a resemblance which a number of authors have pointed out. Bennett Berger, as we noted earlier, has pointed out the similarities between the ideology of the rural commune and the middle-class flight to the suburbs of the postwar years: both seek to withdraw from the problems of urban life, and define happiness in terms of a perfected family life based on togetherness. Jeffrey (1972) has pointed out how dominant American ideas about home and family in the nineteenth century and today resemble the ideas of Utopian planners. He notes two flaws in the Utopian idealization of the home: first, the difficulties of putting into practice the ideas of a blissful and harmonious family life.

> Indeed, it even appears that the aspirations were so high as to breed greater frustration with family life than they might otherwise have been forced to endure. Internally, the perfectionist expectations place heavy burdens of guilt upon both sexes. (Jeffrey, 1972, p. 37)

Besides leading to unrealistic expectations, the turning away from the problems of the larger society may have made those problems worse. Writing of the nineteenth century, Jeffrey observes:

> In terms of the relationship between family and community, the middle-class yearning for a small corner of peace in the form of a happy family may actually have furthered the social trends which Americans deplored and which caused them to turn inward in the first place: the misgovernment of the city, the frantic race for status through conspicuous consumption, the degradation of politics in the Jacksonian era. . . . (Jeffrey, 1972, p. 37)

One of the most useful outcomes of the recent social ferment is the undermining of the perfectionist expectations about the home and family that have persisted in America through the twentieth century. Although the sentimental gush of the nineteenth-century writers gave way to the "scientific" concern with psychological needs and mental health, a similar romanticization of family life persisted.

The vehemence of the attack on the family today is probably an expectable reaction to the sentimental exaggerations that persisted for so long. But it may be as unrealistic to look at the nuclear family as the cause of our troubles as to look up to it as our salvation. Nor is the restoration of the extended family the solution either. If Utopianism is one pitfall to avoid in trying to deal with the problem of the family, *familism* — the tendency to see in family forms themselves either the cause or solution to family problems — is another. The sentimentalization of the extended family is often as extreme as that of the nuclear family. Every family system has its own set of strains, its costs as well as its benefits.

In any event the idea that the disappearance of the extended-family household is to blame for modern family strains is wrong. Despite the persistence of the stereotyped "classical family of Western nostalgia," as Goode puts it, there is no evidence in America or Europe that the large household bursting with kin was ever the prevailing form of the family. In the past as now, most houses were small and most families nuclear, although servants or apprentices might be part of the household too. What has changed is the surrounding social context. Many of the problems of the family can be attributed to strains placed on it by the changes accompanying industrialization: the separation of work from the household and the consequences flowing from that separation — the removal of men from households during the day, the removal of women, children, and older people from the occupational world and their shift to a dependent status, the decline of the local community as a source of sociable interaction, the rise of the private family with its accompanying loneliness and regressive dangers, the discontents of affluence and fun morality. Thus the most promising solutions for problems of the family are those that propose ways of dealing with these points of strain rather than with structural reorganization of the family itself.

The Dialectics of Intimacy There is good reason to believe that some problems of the family may never be solved. Even after the problems of poverty, inequality, racism, sexism, and imperialism have been solved, the family will still be problematic, assuming it exists at all. As we have emphasized in a previous chapter, there are some cogent reasons for believing that social life in general is never in a steady state of conflict-free equilibrium. There is always change, conflict, disagreement over means and ends, and gaps between ideal norm and the activities of everyday life. Rather than being the exception to the general state of social life, the family is best seen as a model of conflict, change, and ambivalence. Indeed, as Freud and Simmel have argued, the more intimate social relations are, the more they are likely to give rise to conflict (see Coser, 1956). Yet the norms that people bring to family life cannot be left out of the picture either. The struggles between the sexes and the generations cannot be understood as power struggles pure and simple. Even the most extreme instances of physical violence between family members usually arise from a complex mixture of hate and love rather than cold, uncaring hostility. Indeed, as Freud has taught us, love and hate are closely linked—we do not love *or* hate, but love *and* hate.

David Schneider has noted that when kinship is stripped of its economic and political functions, it remains as a symbol of a particular quality of human relationship. Kinship ties symbolize love or, in sociological jargon, "enduring diffuse solidarity":

> They symbolize those kinds of interpersonal relations which human beings as biological beings *must* have if they are to be born and grow up. They symbolize . . . a special kind of trust which is not contingent and which does not depend on reciprocity. (Schneider, 1968, p. 116)

It is significant that no revolutionary movement, however opposed to conventional forms of the family, has dispensed with the symbolism of kinship as an ideal form of human relatedness. Revolutionaries may wish to abolish the family, but only in the name of brotherhood or sisterhood.

In a very real sense the family has stood for the best in human feeling between people. Marx, for example, took the natural relation between man and woman as the ideal model of human relatedness. Brotherhood, sisterhood, motherly love, fatherly concern—we still use family terms when we want to describe good relationships between people, even though these terms have often been abused. A most striking example of this paradox is found in David Cooper's often brilliant and more often outrageous book, *The Death of the Family* (1970). Cooper proclaims "the end of the age of relatives," and declares that a family is a trap, the ideological conditioning device of an exploitive society, and a destroyer of all autonomous initiative and spontaneity. Yet he dedicates the book to his brother and sister-in-law and their children, who, during a mental and physical crisis that occurred while he was writing the book, treated him with "immense kindliness and concern . . . just as a true family should."

The need for intimacy and commitment seems to persist after the traditional ideologies of the family have lost their validity. Each model of the family has its own set of virtues, but also a set of liabilities. Thus it is currently popular to romanticize the traditional extended family—the communes, in fact, base themselves on this model of the family—but when this form of the family prevails it is experienced by many of those in it, especially by women and young people, as highly oppressive. In looking at extended-family systems in other societies, Western observers tend to be highly impressed by their benefits and to overlook their strains. The anthropologist Robert LeVine (1965) points out that the extended family is seen as providing care for the aged, the sick, and the unemployed. It seems to provide security for all its members, ensuring that no one will have to face life's troubles alone. Yet, LeVine notes, a growing body of anthropological evidence indicates that extended families confer not only benefits on family members but considerable fear and hostility as well:

We hear of the frequency of suicide among the desperate young married women of traditional China seeking to escape their tyrannical mothers-in-law. From North India it is reported that young wives develop hysterical seizures when marital obligations force their return to residence with their husbands' families. Assassins are hired to help settle internal family quarrels in Egyptian villages. Fraternal tensions within domestic groups are extremely widespread from China to West Africa. . . . Accusations of witchcraft and sorcery—a common medium for the expression of hostility —tend to be concentrated among kinsmen in East African societies. Parricide is a marked phenomenon in at least one Uganda tribe. . . . The burden of such disparate fragments of data is that the very structures which entail kinship obligations beyond the nuclear family engender antagonisms which may ultimately be registered in homicide, suicide, litigation, and other forms of interpersonal conflict. (LeVine, 1965, p. 189)

In general, then, it appears that the tensions that arise in family systems are not separate and distinct from their benefits. The intimate environments of the extended family provide security because of each member's lifelong obligation to the other members, but these very commitments often give rise to intense conflicts that cannot be expressed in an open and direct way. If conflict does occur it often takes an explosive and disruptive form, such as witch-craft accusations.

In short, the search for some ideal form of the family may be futile. Every principle of family organization, whatever its benefits, entails certain costs. The anthropologist Paul Bohannan (1971) has stated the point in terms of household structure. Every family system, he notes, must solve the problem of how to organize households. There are a variety of possible solutions, but each one incurs a number of problematic side effects. Bohannan examines three types of household structure: where the father-son relationship pro-vides the cornerstone, as in the Tiv; the mother-daughter-based household that prevailed among the Iroquois Indians in the eighteenth and early nineteenth centuries; and finally the American nuclear-family household, grounded on the husband-wife relationship.

We have already noted structural problems of the nuclear-family household: it places a great burden on the marital relationship and it is vulnerable to disruption through divorce and death. By contrast, among the Tiv both parenting and spousing are highly diffuse activities, leading to a seemingly idyllic stability, continuity, and calm. Bohan-nan writes:

> A Tiv child has several "mothers." His father's mother and her linked co-wives, if she has any, are his mothers when he is in his own compound. His mother's mother and her linked co-wives are his mothers when he is with his non-agnatic close kinsmen. More-over, there is a whole household full of people to whom one is a "child"; all the adult women married into the compound call one "my child" — the reciprocal term is "our wife," and is the only place in which spouse terms are used in parenting relationships. (Bohannan, 1971, p. 59)

But the security and continuity provided by the ex-tended-family household also entail certain costs not imme-diately evident in an idealized version of extended-family life. In Tiv and Iroquois societies, parent-child conflicts are not expressed directly; instead they emerge in the form of preoccupations with witchcraft.

If a solution exists to the problem of family and house-hold organization, it is probably to be found in some com-bination of systems. Rather than search for some idyllic form of family life it might be both intellectually more interesting and humanly much more beneficial to think of how the normal conflicts, strains, and power imbalances of family living can be compensated for; to say that all families are coercive and prone to conflict is merely another way of saying that the family is no Utopia.

Bohannan notes that the prevailing "solutions" to the household organization problem are rarely if ever backed up by another "solution" to deal with failures. Thus there is no backup institution to take over the tasks of the American home broken by divorce. The Tiv who had broken off with his father or his brothers tended to be socially "crippled." The reason why there are no parallel institutions to back up the main ones has to do with the moral principles surrounding family life. In most societies the prevailing form of the family is deemed to be the only one and the best one. There is a fear that if another way of doing things were available it would undermine the morality of the first system. Thus President Nixon recently vetoed a day-care bill because it would weaken the nuclear family by providing mothers with an "out" from the responsibilities of child care. Such reasoning ignores the costs to children of failing to provide an "out" for mothers who wish to have one. It also ignores the reality of millions of children who are left without care because their mothers must work and there are no facilities for them.

Basically the problem is the tendency to think that one family system must replace another, rather than coexist with it. Ultimately the significance of the communes may lie in their opening up a variety of possibilities for household organization. Before the communes the only way most people could enjoy the intimate environment of a household was through marriage. Now that is no longer true, and divorce may be losing some of its disastrous sting as a result. Communes are emerging as a kind of backup institution for failed marriages, and marriage may be taking on new life as a backup institution for failed communes. Crash pads, drop-in clinics, encounter groups, switchboards for people to call in a crisis—all these may be viewed as fail-safe systems to deal with breakdowns in family functioning.

Modest Proposals   At the White House Conference on Children in 1970 a number of proposals (pp. 428–429) were made which, if adopted, could help ease the strain on the family.

Many of the suggestions fit the model of backup institutions which help sustain family life by providing alternative ways of performing family functions. Some recommendations pertinent to the family include:

1 Comprehensive family-oriented child-development programs including health services, day care, and early childhood education

2 Development of a program to eliminate the racism that cripples all children

3 Reordering of national priorities beginning with a guaranteed basic family income adequate for the needs of children

4 Improvement of the nation's system of child justice so law responds in timely, positive ways to the needs of children

5 A federally financed national child health-care program that assures comprehensive care for all children

6 A system of early identification of children with special needs that delivers prompt and appropriate treatment

As with many government commissions dealing with social problems, the difficulty is not in finding solutions but in implementing them. For example, the three top-priority recommendations of the conference called for day care, programs to eliminate racism, and a guaranteed family income. But the President vetoed a bill calling for day care two years after the conference; busing school children has emerged as a greater concern in the country than the racism it is supposed to counteract; and a bill for a guaranteed annual income, a revolutionary concept put forth by a conservative President without much enthusiasm, died in Congress. It seemed clear that the mood of the country was against such a proposal at that time. Yet perhaps such proposals serve some purpose if they educate.

Last Words

All fixed, fast-frozen relations, with their train of venerable prejudices and opinions, are swept away, all new-formed ones become antiquated before they can ossify. All that is solid melts into air, all that is holy is profaned, and man is at last compelled to face, with his sober senses, his real conditions of life and his relations with his kind.

In these words Marx described the destruction, by the modernizing forces of capitalism, of the myths that had sustained traditional society. It is a description that few students of modernization would dispute.

What a chilling prospect—to face the real conditions of life and our relations with others with sober senses! The other side of liberation from the constraints of religion, family, hereditary status, and small community has been described as alienation. As Peter Berger (1973) points out, the alienation or "homelessness" of modern social life is most clearly seen in the fate of religion in the shift from traditional to modern society. For most of human history, religion has provided an "overarching canopy" of symbols that explained the meaning of life, death, suffering, and one's place in the universe. Religious beliefs in traditional societies are experienced as certain and real because they are taken for granted by everyone. In modern societies religion is pluralized and certainty is lost. The individual encounters others who do not share his or her beliefs. Religion is no longer socially given, but becomes a matter of individual choice or perference. Yet, although religion in modern society suffers from a "crisis of plausibility," the experiences that called for the comforts of religion are still with us— sickness, death, loss and pain.

Much of the same sort of analysis can be applied to the family today. For most of human history, intimacy and community were the by-products of kinship systems and economic necessity. The conjugal family—the freedom to choose one's spouse—was the first step in the liberation of family life from these restraints. In our own day we are witnessing a further pluralization of family life; one chooses not merely a spouse, but one of a variety of competing life styles. The change is a liberating one, but we should not lose sight of the costs. Like death and sickness, the need for intimacy and enduring commitment has outlasted the social institutions that provided for them in the past.

BIBLIOGRAPHY

Ackerman, N. (1958). *The psychodynamics of family life: Diagnosis and treatment of family relationships.* New York: Basic Books.

Adams, Alice (1971). Ripped off. *New Yorker,* 47:14.

Adams, B. N. (1968). *Kinship in an urban setting.* Chicago: Markham.

Alland, A., Jr. (1967). *Evolution and human behavior.* Garden City, N.Y.: Natural History Press.

_____ (1972). *The human imperative.* New York: Columbia Univ. Press.

Allport, G. W. (1968). The historical background of modern social psychology. In G. Lindzey and E. Aronson (eds.), *The handbook of social psychology,* 2nd ed., pp. 1–80. Reading, Mass.: Addison-Wesley.

Anthony, E. J., and Therese Benedek (1970). *Parenthood: Its psychology and psychopathology.* Boston: Little, Brown.

Arensberg, C. M., and S. T. Kimball (1968). *Family and community in Ireland.* 2nd ed. Cambridge, Mass.: Harvard Univ. Press.

Aries, P. (1962). *Centuries of childhood: A social history of family life.* Robert Baldick (trans.). New York: Knopf.

Back, K. W. (1972). *Beyond words: The story of sensitivity training and the encounter movement.* New York: Russell Sage.

Bakan, D. (1971a). *Slaughter of the innocents: A study of the battered child phenomenon.* San Francisco: Jossey-Bass.

——————— (1971b) Adolescence in America: From idea to social fact. *Daedalus*, Fall, 979–995.

Ball, D. W. (1972). The "family" as a *sociological* problem: Conceptualization of the taken-for-granted as prologue to social problems analysis. *Social Problems, 19*:3, 295–307.

Bandura, A. (1969). Social-learning theory and identificatory processes. In D. A. Goslin (ed.), *Handbook of socialization theory and research*, pp. 213–262. Chicago: Rand McNally.

Barry, H., I. L. Child, and M. K. Bacon (1959). Relations of child training to subsistence economy. *American Anthropology, 61,* 51–63.

Bart, Pauline (1970). Mother Portnoy's complaint. *Transaction, 8,* 69–74.

Bartell, G. D. (1971). *Group sex.* New York: Wyden.

Bateson, G., D. D. Jackson, J. Haley, and J. Weakland (1956). Towards a theory of schizophrenia. *Behavioral Science, 1,* 251.

Beach, F. A. (1956). Characteristics of masculine "sex drive." In M. R. Jones (ed.), *Nebraska symposium on motivation 1956*, pp. 1–32. Lincoln: Univ. of Nebraska Press.

Beauvoir, Simone de (1949). *The second sex.* Paris: Gallimard. New York: Knopf, 1953.

——————— (1968). Cited in A. Memmi, *Dominated man.* New York: Orion.

Becker, W. C. (1964). Consequences of different kinds of parental discipline. In M. L. Hoffman and Lois Wladis Hoffman (eds.), *Review of child development research*, vol. 1, pp. 169–208. New York: Russell Sage.

Bem, Sandra L., and D. J. Bem (1970). Training the woman to know her place: The power of a non-conscious ideology. In D. J. Bem, *Beliefs, attitudes, and human affairs.* Belmont, Ca.: Brooks/Cole.

Bender, D. R. (1967). A refinement of the concept of household: Families, co-residence, and domestic functions. *American Anthropologist, 69*:5, 493–504.

Benedict, Ruth (1938). Continuities and discontinuities in cultural conditioning. *Psychiatry, 1*:2, 161–167.

Berger, B., B. M. Hackett, and R. M. Millar (1972). Child-rearing practices in the communal family. Unpublished progress report to National Institute of Mental Health.

Berger, P., Brigitte Berger, and H. Kellner (1973). *The homeless mind.* New York: Random House.

Berkner, L. K. (1972). The stem family and the developmental cycle of the peasant household: An eighteenth-century Austrian example. *American Historical Review, 77,* 398–418.

Bernard, Jessie (1964). The adjustments of married mates. In H. T. Christensen (ed.), *The handbook of marriage and the family*, pp. 675–739. Chicago: Rand McNally.

——————— (1971). *Women and the public interest.* Chicago: Aldine.

——————— (1972). Paper presented at symposium on sex role learning in children and adolescence. American Association for the Advancement of Science meetings, Washington, D. C., December 1972. Reported in *Science,* *177,* 1128.

Birdwhistell, R. L. (1966). The American family: Some perspectives. *Psychiatry,* *29,* 203–212.

Blau, P. M. (1964). *Exchange and power in social life.* New York: Wiley.

Blood, R. O., Jr., and R. L. Hamblin (1958). The effect of the wife's employment on the family power structure. *Social Forces, 36,* 347–352.

——————, and D. M. Wolfe (1960). *Husbands and wives: The dynamics of married living.* New York: Free Press.

Blumberg, Rae Lesser, and R. F. Winch (1972). Societal complexity and familial complexity: Evidence for the curvilinear hypothesis. *American Journal of Sociology, 77:* 5, 898–920.

Bohannan, P. (1963). *Social anthropology.* New York: Holt.

—————— (1971). Dyad dominance and household maintenance. In F. L. K. Hsu (ed.), *Kinship and culture,* pp. 42–65. Chicago: Aldine.

Boszormenyi-Nagy, I., and J. L. Framo (eds.) (1965). *Intensive family therapy.* New York: Harper & Row.

Bott, Elizabeth (1957). *Family and social network.* London: Tavistock.

Bottomore, T. B. (1966). *Classes in modern society.* New York: Pantheon.

Bowlby, J. (1969). *Attachment and loss.* New York: Basic Books.

Boyers, R., and R. Orill (eds.) (1969). *R. D. Laing and anti-psychiatry.* New York: Harper & Row.

Broderick, C. B. (1971). Beyond the five conceptual frameworks: A decade of development in family theory. *Journal of Marriage and the Family, 33:*1, 139–159.

Bronfenbrenner, U. (1958). Socialization and social class through time and space. In Eleanor E. Maccoby, T. M. Newcomb, and E. L. Hartley (eds.), *Readings in social psychology,* 3rd ed., pp. 400–425. New York: Holt.

—————— (1970). *Two worlds of childhood: U.S. and U.S.S.R.* New York: Russell Sage.

Brown, D. G. (1958). Sex role developments in a changing culture. *Psychological Bulletin, 55,* 232–242.

——————, and D. B. Lynn (1966). Human sexual development: An outline of components and concepts. *Journal of Marriage and the Family, 28,* 155–162.

Brown, R. W. (1965). *Social psychology.* New York: Free Press.

Bruner, J. S. (1964). The course of cognitive growth. *American Psychologist, 19,* 1–15.

——————, Rose R. Olver, Patricia M. Greenfield, et al. (1966). *Studies in cognitive growth.* New York: Wiley.

Brzezinski, Z. K. (1970). *Between two ages: America's role in the technetronic era.* New York: Viking.

Burgess, E. W. (1926). The family as a unity of interacting personalities. *The Family, 7,* 3–9.

Burton, R. V., and J. W. M. Whiting (1961). The absent father and cross-sex identity. *Merrill-Palmer Quarterly, 7,* 85–95.

Butterworth, E., and D. Weir (1972). *Social problems of modern Britain.* London: Fontana/Collins.

Caldwell, Bettye M. (1964). The effects of infant care. In M. L. Hoffman and Lois Wladis Hoffman (eds.), *Review of child development research,* vol. 1, pp. 9–87. New York: Russell Sage.

Cernea, M. (1970). *Changing society and family change: The impact of the cooperative farm on the peasant family.* Stanford, Ca.: Center for Advanced Study in the Behavioral Sciences.

Chapple, E. D. (1970). *Culture and biological man: Explorations in behavioral anthropology.* New York: Holt.

Chesler, Phyllis (1971). Patient and patriarch: Women in the psychotherapeutic relationships. In Vivian Gornick and Barbara K. Moran (eds.), *Woman in sexist society,* pp. 362–392. New York: Basic Books.

Chomsky, N. (1968). *Language and mind.* New York: Harcourt, Brace & World.

Chukovsky, K. (1966). *From two to five.* Miriam Morton (trans. and ed.). Berkeley: Univ. of California Press.

Cipolla, C. M. (1969). *Literacy and development in the West.* Baltimore: Penguin.

Clausen, J. A., and Suzanne Clausen (1971). The effects of family size on parents and children. Unpublished ms., Institute of Human Development, Univ. of California, Berkeley. To be published in James Fawcett (ed.), *Psychological perspectives on population.* New York: Basic Books.

Coleman, J. S. (1972). The children have outgrown the schools. *Psychology Today, 5:9,* 72–75, 82.

Comfort, A. (1967). *The anxiety makers.* New York: Dell (Delta).

Conger, J. J. (1971). A world they never knew: The family and social change. *Daedalus,* Fall, 1105–1138.

Cooper, A. A. (1842). A speech before the House of Commons, U.K., June 7, 1842. Reprinted in *Speeches of the Earl of Shaftesbury, K.G.,* pp. 31–58. London: Chapman & Hall, 1968.

Cooper, D. G. (1970). *The death of the family.* New York: Vintage.

Coser, L. A. (1956). *The functions of social conflict.* New York: Free Press.

Coser, Rose Laub (1964). Authority and structural ambivalence in the middle-class family. In Rose Laub Coser (ed.), *The family: Its structure and functions,* pp. 370–383. New York: St. Martin's.

Coveney, P. (1967). *The image of childhood.* Baltimore: Penguin.

Cox Commission (1968). *Crisis at Columbia.* New York: Vintage.

Crozier, Blanche (1935). Constitutionality of discrimination based on sex. *Boston University Law Review,* 1935, 723, 727–728. Cited in L. Kanowitz, *Women and the law.* Albuquerque: Univ. of New Mexico Press, 1969.

Cuber, J. F. (1970). Alternate models from the perspective of sociology. In H. A. Otto (ed.), *The family in search of a future,* pp. 11–23. New York: Appleton-Century-Crofts.

_____, and Peggy Harroff (1965). *Sex and the significant Americans.* Baltimore: Penguin.

Dahrendorf, R. (1958). Out of Utopia: Toward a reorientation of sociological analysis. *American Journal of Sociology, 64*:2, 115–127.

D'Andrade, R. (1966). Sex differences and cultural institutions. In Eleanor E. Maccoby (ed.), *The development of sex differences.* Stanford, Ca.: Stanford Univ. Press.

Danziger, K. (1971). *Socialization.* Baltimore: Penguin.

Davis, F. (1971). Why all of us may be hippies someday. In E. Z. Friedenberg (ed.), *The anti-American generation,* pp. 61–80. Chicago: Aldine (Transaction).

Davis, K. (1940). The sociology of parent-youth conflict. *American Sociological Review, 5,* 523–535.

Davis, Natalie (1971). The reasons for misrule: Youth groups and charivari in sixteenth-century France. *Past and Present, 50,* 41–75.

Demos, J. (1970). *A little commonwealth.* New York: Oxford Univ. Press.

Deutsch, Helene (1944). *The psychology of women: A psychoanalytic interpretation.* New York: Grune & Stratton.

Diamond, M. (1965). A critical evaluation of the ontogeny of human sexual behavior. *Quarterly Review of Biology, 40,* 147–173.

Drake, Emma (1901). *What a young wife ought to know.* Cited in A. Comfort, *The anxiety makers.* New York: Dell (Delta), 1967.

Edmonds, V. H. (1967). Marriage conventionalization: Definition and measurement. *Journal of Marriage and the Family, 29,* 681–688.

_____, G. Withers, and Beverly Di Batista (1972). Adjustment, conservatism, and marital conventionalization. *Journal of Marriage and the Family, 34*: 1, 96–104.

Ellenberger, H. (1970). *The discovery of the unconscious.* New York: Basic Books.

Emmerich, W. (1959). Parental identification in young children. *Genetic Psychological Monographs, 60,* 257–308.

Engel, Mary, G. Marsden, and Sylvia Woodaman (1967). Children who work and the concept of work style. *Psychiatry, 30,* 392–404.

_____, _____, and _____ (1968). Orientation to work in children. *American Journal of Orthopsychiatry, 38,* 137–143.

_____, _____, and Sylvia Woodaman Pollock (1971). Child work and social class. *Psychiatry, 34*:2, 140–155.

Erikson, E. H. (1963). *Childhood and society,* 2nd ed. New York: Norton.

_____ (1964). Inner and outer space: Reflections on womanhood. *Daedalus,* Spring.

_____ (1968). *Identity: Youth and crisis.* New York: Norton.

Eshelman, J. R. (1971). *Perspectives in marriage and the family: Text and readings,* 3rd ed. Boston: Allyn and Bacon.

Fallers, L. A. (1965). The range of variation in actual family size: A critique of Marion J. Levy's argument. In A. J. Coale, L. A. Fallers, M. J. Levy, Jr., D.

Schneider, and S. S. Tomkins, *Aspects of the analysis of family structure*, p. 77. Princeton, N.J.: Princeton Univ. Press.

Farber, B. (1964). *Family organization and interaction*. San Francisco: Chandler.

_____ (1966). *Kinship and family organization*. New York: Wiley.

Feldman, H. (1962). Unpublished research. Cited in E. H. Pohlman, *Psychology of birth planning*. Cambridge, Mass.: Schenkman, 1969.

Firestone, Shulamith (1970). *The dialectic of sex: The case for feminist revolution*. New York: Morrow.

Flacks, R. (1971). *Youth and social change*. Chicago: Markham.

Flavell, J. H. (1963). *The developmental psychology of Jean Piaget*. Princeton, N.J.: Van Nostrand.

Fontana, V. J. (1964). *The maltreated child*. Springfield, Ill.: Thomas.

Ford, C. S., and F. A. Beach (1951). Human sexual behavior in perspective. In C. S. Ford and F. A. Beach, *Patterns of sexual behavior*. New York: Harper.

Fortes, M. (1949). *The web of kinship among the Tallensi*. London: Oxford Univ. Press.

_____, R. W. Steel, and P. Ady (1947). Ashanti survey, 1945–46: An experiment in social research. *Geographical Journal, 110*, 149–179. Cited in D. R. Bender, 1967.

Fowler, W. (1962). Cognitive learning in infancy and early childhood. *Psychological Bulletin, 59*:2, 116–152.

Fraiberg, Selma (1959). *The magic years*. New York: Scribner.

Framo, J. L. (1965). Systematic research on family dynamics. In I. Boszormenyi-Nagy and J. L. Framo (eds.), *Intensive family therapy*, pp. 407–462. New York: Harper & Row.

_____ (1972). *Family interaction: A dialogue between family researchers and family therapists*. New York: Springer.

Francke, Linda (1972). Tot lots: Integrating children into everyday life. *Ms.*, 1:1, 27ff.

Frank, G. H. (1965). The role of the family in the development of psychopathology. *Psychological Bulletin, 64*, 191–205.

Freeman, Jo (1970). The building of the gilded cage. Unpublished ms., University of Chicago. Reprinted in *Green Hearings*, U.S. House of Representatives, Sect. 10. Washington: U.S. Government Printing Office, 1970.

Fremont-Smith, F. (1970). Comment cited by I. C. Kaufman, Biologic considerations of parenthood. In E. J. Anthony and Therese Benedek, *Parenthood: Its psychology and psychopathology*. Boston: Little, Brown, 1970.

Freud, S. (1898). *The future of an illusion*. Garden City, N.Y.: Doubleday (Anchor), n.d.

_____ (1909). *Analyse der Phobie eines S-jährigen Knaben*. Vienna: Deuticke.

Friedenberg, E. Z. (1971). *The anti-American generation*. Chicago: Aldine (Transaction).

Fromm, E. (1970). *The crisis of psychoanalysis*. New York: Holt.

Gagnon, J. H. (1965). Sexuality and sexual learning in the child. *Psychiatry, 28,* 212–228.

—————, and W. Simon (1970). *The sexual scene.* Chicago: Aldine (Transaction).

Geertz, C. (1965). The impact of the concept of culture on the concept of man. In J. R. Platt (ed.), *New views of the nature of man,* pp. 93–118. Chicago: Univ. of Chicago Press.

Gesell, A., and Frances L. Ilg (1943). *Infant and child in the culture of today.* New York: Harper.

Gibson, G. (1972). Kin family network: Overheralded structure in past conceptualizations of family functioning. *Journal of Marriage and the Family,* 34:1, 13–23.

Gil, D. G. (1968). Incidence of child abuse and demographic characteristics of persons involved. In R. E. Helfer and C. H. Kempe (eds.), *The battered child.* Chicago: Univ. of Chicago Press.

—————— (1970). *Violence against children.* Cambridge, Mass.: Harvard Univ. Press.

—————— (1971). Violence against children. *Journal of Marriage and the Family,* 33:4, 637–648.

Gilman, Charlotte Perkins (1903). *The home: Its work and influence.* New York: McClure Phillips.

Ginott, H. (1972). Being a parent. King Features Syndicate, 1972. Reprinted in *San Francisco Sunday Examiner and Chronicle,* Feb. 11, 1973.

Goffman, E. (1959). *The presentation of self in everyday life.* Garden City, N.Y.: Doubleday.

Goode, W. J. (1956). *Women in divorce.* New York: Free Press.

—————— (1963). *World revolution and family patterns.* New York: Free Press.

—————— (1964). *The family.* Englewood Cliffs, N.J.: Prentice-Hall.

—————— (1971). Force and violence in the family. *Journal of Marriage and the Family,* 33:4, 624–636.

Goodman, Mary Ellen (1970). *The culture of childhood: Child's-eye views of society and culture.* New York: Teachers College Press.

Goody, J., and I. Watt (1962). The consequences of literacy. *Comparative Studies in Society and History, 5,* 304–326, 332–345.

Gough, Kathleen E. (1959). The Nayars and the definition of marriage. *Journal of the Royal Anthropological Institute of Great Britain and Ireland,* 89:1. Reprinted as "Is the family universal?—The Nayar case," in N. W. Bell and E. F. Vogel (eds.), *A modern introduction to the family,* pp. 76–93. New York: Free Press.

—————— (1971). The origin of the family. *Journal of Marriage and the Family,* 33:4, 760–771.

Gouldner, A. W. (1970). *The coming crisis of Western sociology.* New York: Basic Books.

Gove, W. R., and Jeanette F. Tudor (1973). Adult sex roles and mental illness. *American Journal of Sociology, 78*:4, 812–835.

Grazia, S. de (1962). *Of time, work, and leisure*. New York: Twentieth Century Fund.

Green, A. W. (1946). The middle-class male child and neurosis. *American Sociological Review, 11*, 31–41.

Greer, Germaine (1971). *The female eunuch*. New York: McGraw-Hill.

Greer, S. (1962). *The emerging city: Myth and reality*. New York: Free Press.

Greven, P. (1970). *Four generations: Population, land and family in colonial Andover, Massachusetts*. Ithaca, N.Y.: Cornell Univ. Press.

Haan, Norma (1971). Moral redefinition in families as the critical aspect of the generational gap. *Youth and Society, 2*:3, 259–283.

_____ (1972). Personality development from adolescence to adulthood in the Oakland Growth and Guidance Series. *Seminars in Psychiatry, 4*:4.

_____, and N. Livson (1972). Sex differences in the eyes of expert personality assessors: Blind spots. Unpublished ms., Institute of Human Development, Univ. of California, Berkeley.

Hale, N. (1971). *Freud and the Americans*. New York: Oxford Univ. Press.

Haley, J. (1963). *Strategies of psychotherapy*. New York: Grune & Stratton.

Hallowell, A. I. (1955). *Culture and experience*. Philadelphia: Univ. of Pennsylvania Press.

Handlin, O., and Mary F. Handlin (1971). *Facing life: Youth and the family in American history*. Boston: Little, Brown.

Hardy, K. R. (1964). An appetitional theory of sexual motivation. *Psychological Review, 71*, 19–26.

Hareven, Tamara (1971). The history of the family as an interdisciplinary field. *Journal of Interdisciplinary History, 2*:2, 399–414.

Harlow, H. F. (1962). The heterosexual affectional system in monkeys. *American Psychologist, 17*, 1–9.

_____, M. K. Harlow, and E. W. Hansen (1963). The maternal affectional system in infant monkeys. In Harriet J. Rheingold (ed.), *Maternal behavior in mammals*. New York: Wiley.

Harrington, C., and J. W. M. Whiting (1972). Socialization process and personality. In F. L. K. Hsu (ed.), *Psychological anthropology*, pp. 469–507. Cambridge, Mass.: Schenkman.

Harrington, M. (1966). *The accidental century*. New York: Macmillan.

Harris, M. (1964). *The nature of cultural things*. New York: Random House.

_____ (1968). *The rise of anthropological theory: A history of theories of culture*. New York: Thomas Y. Crowell.

Hauser, P. M. (1970). Comments in *The Millbank Memorial Fund Quarterly, 48*:2, part 2.

Hawkes, Jacquetta (1963). *Prehistory*. In *History of mankind: Cultural and scientific development*, vol. 1, part 1. New York: New American Library (Mentor).

Henry, J. (1963). *Culture against man.* New York: Random House.

——————— (1971). *Pathways to madness.* New York: Random House.

Herschberger, Ruth (1948). *Adam's rib.* New York: Pellegrini & Cudahy.

Hess, R. D., and G. Handel (1959). *Family worlds.* Chicago: Univ. of Chicago Press.

Hicks, Mary W., and Marilyn Platt (1970). Marital happiness and stability. *Journal of Marriage and the Family, 32,* 553–574.

Hill, R., and D. A. Hansen (1960). The identification of conceptual frameworks utilized in family study. *Marriage and Family Living, 22,* 299–311.

Himes, N. E. (1963). *Medical history of contraception.* New York: Gamut.

Hindus, M. (1971). Historical trends in American pre-marital pregnancy. Paper presented at American Historical Association, New York, December 1971.

Hochschild, Alene R. (1973). A review of sex role research. *American Journal of Sociology, 78*:4, 1011–1029.

Hoffman, Lois Wladis (1972). Early childhood experiences and women's achievement motives. *Journal of Social Issues, 28*:2, 129–155.

Hooker, Evelyn (1965). Gender identity in male homosexuals. In J. Money (ed.), *Sex research.* New York: Holt.

Horney, Karen (1932). The dread of women. *International Journal of Psycho-analysis, 13,* 359.

Hsu, F. L. K. (ed.) (1961) *Psychological anthropology.* Homewood, Ill.: Dorsey.

Hunt, D. (1970). *Parents and children in history: The psychology of family life in early modern France.* New York: Basic Books.

Hunt, M. (1969). *The affair.* New York: World.

Ichheiser, G. (1970) *Appearances and realities: Misunderstandings in human relations.* San Francisco: Jossey-Bass.

Illich, I. (1971). *Deschooling society.* New York: Harper & Row.

Inkeles, A. (1968). Society, social structure, and child socialization. In J. Clausen (ed.), *Socialization and society,* pp. 75–129. Boston: Little, Brown.

Isaacs, Susan (1966). *Intellectual growth in young children.* New York: Schocken.

Janeway, Elizabeth (1971). *Man's world, woman's place.* New York: Morrow.

Jeffrey, K. (1972). The family as utopian retreat from the city: The nineteenth-century contribution. In Sallie TeSelle (ed.), *The family, communes, and utopian societies,* pp. 21–41. New York: Harper & Row.

Kanowitz, L. (1969). *Women and the law: The unfinished revolution.* Albuquerque: Univ. of New Mexico Press.

Kanter, Rosabeth M. (1968). Commitment and social organization: A study of commitment mechanisms in Utopian communities. *American Sociological Review, 33,* 499–518.

——————— (1972). *Commitment and community: Communes and utopias in sociological perspective.* Cambridge, Mass.: Harvard Univ. Press.

Kempe, H. (1973). Quotes from personal interview. *Woman's Day,* March 1973, p. 62.

Keniston, K. (1971a). Psychosocial development and historical change. *Journal of Interdisciplinary History*, 2:2, 329–345.

_____ (1971b). *Youth and dissent: The rise of a new opposition.* New York: Harcourt Brace Jovanovich (Harvest).

Kerr, Madeline (1958). *The people of Ship Street.* London: Routledge.

Kessen, W. (1962). "Stage" and "structure" in the study of children. In W. Kessen and C. Kuhlman (eds)., *Thought in the young child*, pp. 65–82. *Monographs of the Society for Research in Child Development*, no. 83.

_____ (1965). *The child.* New York: Wiley.

Klemesrud, Judy (1971). Happy duos aren't so rare. *San Francisco Chronicle*, June 8, 1971. (Copyright 1971, N.Y. Times News Service.)

Kohlberg, L. (1966). A cognitive-developmental analysis of children's sex-role concepts and attitudes. In Eleanor E. Maccoby (ed.), *The development of sex differences*, p. 91. Stanford, Ca.: Stanford Univ. Press.

Kohn, M. L. (1959). Social class and parental values. *American Journal of Sociology, 64,* 337–351.

_____ (1963). Social class and parent-child relationships. *American Journal of Sociology, 68,* 471–480.

Komarovsky, Mirra (1967). *Blue-collar marriage.* New York: Vintage.

Kuhn, T. (1962). *The structure of scientific revolutions.* Chicago: Univ. of Chicago Press.

Laing, R. D. (1969). *Self and others.* Baltimore: Penguin.

_____ (1971). *The politics of the family.* New York: Random House.

_____, H. Phillipson, and A. R. Lee (1966). *Interpersonal perception: A theory and a method of research.* New York: Harper & Row.

Lambert, W. W. (1971). Cross-cultural backgrounds to personality development and the socialization of aggression: Findings from the six-culture study. In W. W. Lambert and Rita Weisbrod (eds.), *Comparative perspectives on social psychology*, p. 433. Boston: Little, Brown.

Langer, J. (1969). Disequilibrium as a source of development. In T. Mussen, J. Langer, and M. Covington (eds.), *Trends and issues in developmental psychology*, pp. 22–37. New York: Holt.

Langer, W. L. (1972). Checks on population growth: 1750–1850. *Scientific American, 226,* 93–100.

Lantz, H. R., and Eloise C. Snyder (1969). *Marriage,* 2nd ed. New York: Wiley.

Lasch, C. (1965). *The new radicalism in America.* New York: Vintage.

Laslett, Barbara (1973). The family as a public and private institution: A historical perspective. Unpublished ms., Univ. of Southern California, Los Angeles, September 1972. To be published in shortened version in *Journal of Marriage and the Family*, August 1973.

Laslett, P. (1965). *The world we have lost: England before the industrial age.* New York: Scribner.

Lee, R., and I. DeVore (1968). *Man the hunter.* Chicago: Aldine.

LeMasters, E. E. (1957). Parenthood as crisis. *Marriage and Family Living, 19;* 352–355.

_____ (1970). *Parents in modern America: A sociological analysis.* Homewood, Ill.: Dorsey.

Lennard, H. L., and A. Bernstein (1969). *Patterns in human interaction.* San Francisco: Jossey-Bass.

Le Play, F. (1866). *La réforme sociale.* In C. C. Zimmerman and M. E. Frampton, *Family and society,* Princeton, N.J.: Van Nostrand, 1935. Cited in B. Farber (1966), pp. 14–23.

Levenson, E. A. (1972). *The fallacy of understanding: An inquiry into the changing structure of psychoanalysis.* New York: Basic Books.

LeVine, R. A. (1965). Intergenerational tensions and extended family structures in Africa. In Ethel Shanas and G. F. Streib (eds.), *Social structure and the family: Generational relations,* pp. 188–204. Englewood Cliffs, N. J.: Prentice-Hall.

_____ (1970). Cross-cultural study in child psychology. In P. H. Mussen (ed.), *Carmichael's manual of child psychology,* 3rd ed., pp. 559–612. New York: Wiley.

Levy, M. J., Jr. (1955). Some questions about Parsons' treatment of the incest problem. *British Journal of Sociology,* 6, 277–285.

_____ (1965). Aspects of the analysis of family structure. In A. J. Coale, L. A. Fallers, M. J. Levy, Jr., D. Schneider, and S. S. Tomkins, *Aspects of the analysis of family structure.* Princeton, N. J.: Princeton Univ. Press.

Lewis, O. (1951). *Life in a Mexican village: Tepoztlán á restudied.* Urbana: Univ. of Illinois Press.

_____ (1965). The folk-urban ideal types. In P. M. Hauser and L. F. Schnore (eds.), *The study of urbanization,* pp. 491–503. New York: Wiley.

Lidz, T. (1963). *The family and human adaptation.* New York: International Universities Press.

Lifton, R. J. (1965). Woman as knower. In R. J. Lifton (ed.), *The woman in America.* Boston: Houghton Mifflin.

_____ (1969). Protean man. *Yale Alumni Review,* January, 14–21.

Lindzey, G., and E. Aronson (1968). *The handbook of social psychology,* 2nd ed. Reading, Mass.: Addison-Wesley.

Linton, R. (1959). The natural history of the family. In Ruth N. Anshen (ed.), *The family: Its function and destiny,* rev. ed., pp. 30–52. New York: Harper & Row.

Lipset, S. M. (1960). Student activism. *Current Affairs Bulletin,* 42.

_____ (1967). *Student politics.* New York: Basic Books.

_____, and R. B. Dobson (1972). The intellectual as critic and rebel: With special reference to the United States and the Soviet Union. In Intellectuals and change. *Daedalus,* Summer, 137–198.

Litwak, E. (1965). Extended kin relations in an industrial democratic society. In Ethel Shanas and G. F. Streib (eds.), *Social structure and the family: Generational relations.* Englewood Cliffs, N.J.: Prentice-Hall.

Loevinger, Jane (1959). Patterns of child rearing as theories of learning. *Journal of Abnormal and Social Psychology, 59,* 148–150.

Lomax, A., and N. Berkowitz (1972). The evolutionary taxonomy of culture. *Science, 177,* 228–240.

Lyness, Judith L., M. E. Lipetz, and K. E. Davis (1972). Living together: An alternative to marriage. *Journal of Marriage and the Family, 34:2,* 305–311.

McCall, M. M. (1966). Courtship as social exchange: Some historical comparisons. In B. Farber (ed.), *Kinship and family organization,* pp. 190–200. New York: Wiley.

McClelland, D. C., J. W. Atkinson, R. A. Clark, and E. L. Lowell (1953). *The achievement motive.* New York: Appleton-Century-Crofts.

Macfarlane, Jean W. (1963). From infancy to adulthood. *Childhood Education, 39,* 336–342.

_____ (1964). Perspectives on personality consistency and change from the guidance study. *Vita Humana, 7,* 115–126.

Malinowski, B. (1964). The principle of legitimacy: Parenthood, the basis of social structure. In Rose Laub Coser (ed.), *The family: Its structure and functions,* pp. 3–19. New York: St. Martin's.

Maspetiol, R. (1970). Sociologie de la famille rura de type traditionnel en France, in *Sociologie comparée de la famille contemporaire.* Cited in M. Cernea, *Changing society and family change: The impact of the cooperative farm on the peasant family.* Stanford, Ca.: Center for Advanced Study in the Behavioral Sciences.

Masters, W. H., and Virginia Johnson (1970). *Human sexual inadequacy.* Boston: Little, Brown.

Mead, Margaret (1928). *Coming of age in Samoa.* New York: Morrow.

_____ (1935). *Sex and temperament in three primitive societies.* New York: Morrow.

_____ (1947). The implications of culture change for personality development. *American Journal of Orthopsychiatry, 17,* 633ff.

_____ (1949). *Male and female.* New York: Morrow.

_____ (1957). Changing patterns of parent-child relations in an urban culture. *International Journal of Psychoanalysis, 38,* 369–378.

_____ (1966). Marriage in two steps. *Redbook,* July.

_____ (1970). *Culture and commitment.* New York: Natural History Press/Doubleday.

_____ (1971). Future family. *Transaction,* September, 50–59.

Memmi, A. (1968). *Dominated man.* New York: Orion.

Miller, H. (1965). *Income of the American people.* New York: Wiley.

Mills, C. W. (1959). *The sociological imagination.* New York: Oxford Univ. Press.

Minturn, Leigh, and W. W. Lambert (1964). *Mothers of six cultures: Antecedents of child rearing.* New York: Wiley.

Mitchell, G. D. (1969). Paternalistic behavior in primates. *Psychological Bulletin,* 71, 399–417.

Modell, J. (1972). Strangers in the family: Boarding and lodging in industrial America. Paper read at National Conference on the Family, Social Structure and Social Change, April 27–29, 1972, Clark Univ., Worcester, Mass.

Moller, H. (1971). Childhood before the enlightenment. *Psychotherapy and Social Science Review,* 5:9, 16–18.

Money, J. (1961). Sex hormones and other variables in human eroticism. In W. C. Young (ed.), *Sex and internal secretions.* Baltimore: Williams & Wilkins.

——————— (1972). Paper presented at symposium on sex role learning in childhood and adolescence. American Association for the Advancement of Science Meetings, December 1972, Washington, D.C.

———————, Jean Hampson, and J. Hampson (1957). Imprinting and the establishment of gender role. *Archives of Neurological Psychiatry,* 77, 333–336.

Moore, B. M., Jr. (1958). Thoughts on the future of the family. In *Political power and social theory.* Cambridge, Mass.: Harvard Univ. Press, 1958. Cited in S. G. McNall (ed.), *The sociological perspective,* pp. 407–417. Boston: Little, Brown, 1968.

Morgan, E. S. (1944). *The Puritan family.* Boston: Public Library.

Morgan, L. H. (1870). *Systems of consanguinity and affinity of the human family.* Washington: Smithsonian Institution.

——————— (1877). *Ancient society.* New York: Holt. Modern edition by E. Leacock (ed.), *Ancient society.* New York: World (Meridian), 1963.

Murdock, G. P. (1949). *Social structure.* New York: Macmillan.

Murphy, R. F. (1971). *The dialectics of social life: Alarms and excursions in anthropological theory.* New York: Basic Books.

Myrdal, J. (1968). *Confessions of a disloyal European.* New York: Pantheon.

Negrea, A. G. (1936). *The sociological theory of the peasant household.* Bucharest: 1936, p. 45. Cited in M. Cernea, *Changing society and family change: The impact of the cooperative farm on the peasant family,* p. 114. Stanford, Ca.: Center for Advanced Study in the Behavioral Sciences, 1970–71.

Nimkoff, M. F., and R. Middleton (1960). Types of family and types of economy. *American Journal of Sociology,* 66, 215–225.

Nisbet, R. A. (1961). The study of social problems. In R. K. Merton and R. A. Nisbet (eds.), *Contemporary social problems.* New York: Harcourt, Brace & World.

Opie, Iona, and P. Opie (1959). *The lore and language of school children.* London: Oxford Univ. Press.

Orwell, G. (1946). The art of Donald McGill. In *A collection of essays,* p. 107. New York: Harcourt, Brace, 1953.

Otto, H. A. (1970). *The family in search of a future.* New York: Appleton-Century-Crofts.

Parish, W. L., and M. Schwartz (1972). Household complexity in nineteenth century France. *American Sociological Review, 37,* 154–173.

Parsons, T. (1949). *Essays in sociological theory: Pure and applied.* Glencoe, Ill.: Free Press.

_____ (1951). *The social system.* Glencoe, Ill.: Free Press.

_____ (1955). The American family: Its relations to personality and the social structure. In T. Parsons and R. F. Bales, *Family socialization and interaction process,* pp. 3–21. Glencoe, Ill.: Free Press.

_____ (1965). The normal American family. In S. M. Farber, P. Mustacchi, and R. H. L. Wilson (eds.), *Man and civilization: The family's search for survival,* pp. 31–50. New York: McGraw-Hill.

_____ (1971). Kinship and the associational aspect of social structure. In F. L. K. Hsu (ed.), *Kinship and culture,* pp. 409–438. Chicago: Aldine.

_____, and R. F. Bales (1955). *Family socialization and interaction process.* Glencoe, Ill.: Free Press.

Payne, G. H. (1916). *The child in human progress.* New York: Putnam.

Pearlin, L. I. (1971). *Class-context and family relations: A cross-national study.* Boston: Little, Brown.

Piaget, J. (1952). *The origin of intelligence in children.* New York: International Universities Press.

_____ (1954). *The construction of reality in the child.* New York: Basic Books.

_____ (1967). *Six psychological studies.* New York: Random House.

_____, and B. Inhelder (1969). *The psychology of the child.* New York: Basic Books.

Pierce, Christine (1971). Natural law, language and women. In Vivian Gornick and Barbara K. Moran (eds.), *Woman in sexist society: Studies in power and powerlessness,* pp. 242–258. New York: Basic Books.

Pilbeam, D. (1972). Evolutionary anthropology. Review of *The brain in hominid evolution* by P. V. Tobias. *Science, 175,* 1011.

Pilpel, Harriet F., and Theodora Zavin (1964). *Your marriage and the law.* New York: Macmillan (Collier Books).

Pineo, P. C. (1961). Disenchantment in the later years of marriage. *Marriage and Family Living, 23,* 3–11.

Pitts, J. (1968). The family and peer groups. In N. W. Bell and E. F. Vogel, *A modern introduction to the family.* New York: Free Press.

Plumb, J. H. (1972). The great change in children. *Intellectual Digest, 2,* 82–84. (Originally in *Horizon,* Winter 1971.)

Pohlman, E. H. (1969). *Psychology of birth planning.* Cambridge, Mass: Schenkman.

Poloma, Margaret M., and T. N. Garland (1971). The married professional woman: A study in the tolerance of domestication. *Journal of Marriage and the Family, 33:3,* 531–540.

Pope, H., and D. Knudsen (1965). Premarital sex norms: The family and social change. *Journal of Marriage and the Family,* August, 314–323.

Rabkin, R. (1970). *Inner and outer space: Introduction to a theory of social psychi-atry.* New York: Norton.

Reiss, I. L. (1970). How and why America's sex standards are changing. In J. H. Gagnon and W. Simon (eds.), *The sexual scene,* pp. 43–57. Chicago: Aldine (Transaction).

Rheingold, Harriet L. (1969). The social and socializing infant. In D. A. Goslin (ed.), *Handbook of socialization theory and research,* pp. 779–790. Chicago: Rand McNally.

Riesman, D. (1960). The oral and written traditions. In E. Carpenter and M. McLuhan (eds.), *Explorations in communication,* pp. 109–124. Boston: Beacon.

——————— (1964). Two generations. *Daedalus,* Spring, 711–735.

Rodman, H. (1965). The textbook world of family sociology. *Social Problems, 12,* 450.

Rogers, C. (1972). *Becoming partners: marriage and its alternatives.* New York: Delacorte.

Rosow, I. (1965). Intergenerational relationships: Problems and proposals. In Ethel Shanas and G. F. Streib, *Social structure and the family: Generational relations,* pp. 341–378. Englewood Cliffs, N.J.: Prentice-Hall.

Rossi, Alice S. (1968). Transition to parenthood. *Journal of Marriage and the Family, 30,* 26–39.

Rothman, D. J. (1971). Documents in search of a historian: Towards a history of childhood and growth in America. *Journal of Interdisciplinary History,* 2:2, 368–377.

Rousseau, J. J. (1762). *Emile* or *On education.* London: Dent, 1911. (Original French edition in 1762.)

Ruesch, J., and G. Bateson (1968). *Communication: The social matrix of psychiatry,* 2nd ed. New York: Norton.

Ryder, R. G. (1966). The factualizing game: A sickness of psychological research. *Psychological Reports, 19,* 563–570.

——————— (1967). Compatibility in marriage. *Psychological Reports, 20,* 807–813.

——————— (1970a). Dimensions of early marriage. *Family Process, 9,* 51–68.

——————— (1970b). A topography of early marriage. *Family Process, 9,* 385–402.

Ryle, A. (1967). *Neurosis in the ordinary family: A psychiatric survey.* London: Tavistock.

Safilios-Rothschild, Constantina (1970). The study of family power structure: A review of 1960–1969. *Journal of Marriage and the Family, 32,* 539–552.

——————— (1972). *Toward a sociology of women.* Lexington, Mass.: Xerox College Publishing.

Sahlins, M. (1968). In R. Lee and I. DeVore, *Man the hunter.* Chicago: Aldine.

Sartre, J. P. (1963). *Search for a method.* New York: Knopf.

Schacter, S. (1964). The interaction of cognitive and physiological determinants of emotional state. In L. Berkowitz (ed.), *Advances in experimental social psychology,* vol. 1, pp. 49–80. New York: Academic Press.

Schaffer, H. R. (1971). *The growth of sociability.* Baltimore: Penguin.

Schmalenbach, H. (1961). The sociological categories of communion. In T. Parsons et al. (eds.), *Theories of society,* vol. 1. New York: Free Press.

Schneider, D. (1965). Kinship and biology. In A. J. Coale, L. A. Fallers, M. J. Levy, Jr., D. Schneider, and S. S. Tomkins, *Aspects of the analysis of family structure.* Princeton, N.J.: Princeton Univ. Press.

_____ (1968). *American kinship: A cultural account.* Englewood Cliffs, N.J.: Prentice-Hall.

Sears, R. R., Eleanor E. Maccoby, and H. Levin (1957). *Patterns of child rearing.* Evanston, Ill.: Row, Peterson.

Sennett, R. (1970a). *Families against the city: Middle class homes of industrial Chicago, 1872–1890.* Cambridge, Mass.: Harvard Univ. Press.

_____ (1970b). *The uses of disorder: Personal identity and city life.* New York: Knopf.

Shaefer, Leah Cahan (1964). Sexual experiences and reactions of a group of thirty women as told to a female psychotherapist. An unpublished Ph.D. thesis, Teachers College, Columbia Univ., 1964. Cited in E. M. Brecher, *The sex researchers.* Boston: Little, Brown, 1969.

Shaffer, J. B. P. (1970). Review of recent books on marriage. *Harvard Education Review, 40,* 165–174.

Shainess, Natalie (1971). "New" views of female sexuality. A book review of *Female sexuality: New psychoanalytic views* by J. Chasseguet-Smirgel et al. *Psychiatry and Social Science Review,* 5:4, 13–19.

Shorter, E. (1971). Illegitimacy, sexual revolution and social change in modern Europe. *Journal of Interdisciplinary History,* 2:2, 237–272.

_____ (1973). Infanticide in the past. A review of *Slaughter of the innocents* by David Bakan. *History of Childhood Quarterly,* 1:1 178–180.

Shulman, Alix (1970). A marriage agreement. *Out from Under,* 1:2, 5–8.

Simmel, G. (1950). In K. Wolff (ed.), *The sociology of Georg Simmel.* New York: Free Press.

Simpson, G. (1960). *People in families.* New York: Thomas Y. Crowell.

Sjoberg, G. (1965). Cities in developing and in industrial societies: A cross-cultural analysis. In P. M. Hauser and L. F. Schnore (eds.), *The study of urbanization,* pp. 213–263. New York: Wiley.

Skolnick, J. H. (1969). *The politics of protest.* New York: Simon & Schuster.

_____, and E. Currie (1973). *Crisis in American institutions,* 2nd ed. Boston: Little, Brown.

Slater, P. E. (1963). On social regression. *American Sociological Review, 28,* 339–364.

_____ (1968). Some social consequences of temporary systems. In W. G. Bennis and P. E. Slater, *The Temporary Society,* pp. 77–96. New York: Harper & Row.

_____ (1970). *The pursuit of loneliness.* Boston: Beacon.

_____, and Dori I. Slater (1965). Maternal ambivalence and narcissism: A cross-cultural study. *Merrill-Palmer Quarterly, 2,* 241–259.

Sluzki, C. E., and V. Elisco (1971). The double bind as a universal pathogenic situation. *Family Process, 10*:4, 397–410.

Smelser, N. J. (1963). *Social change.* Englewood Cliffs, N.J.: Prentice-Hall.

_____ (1968). *Essays in sociological explanation.* Englewood Cliffs, N.J.: Prentice-Hall.

Smith, R. T. (1956). *The Negro family in British Guiana: Family structure and social status in the village.* London: Routledge.

Sorenson, R. C. (1973). *Adolescent sexuality in contemporary America.* New York: World Publishing.

Spencer, H. (1946). *Essays on education.* New York: Dutton.

Speck, R. V., et al. (1972). *The new families: Youth, communes and the politics of drugs.* New York: Basic Books.

Spiegel, J. (1971). *Transactions: The interplay between individual, family, and society.* New York: Science House.

Spiro, M. E. (1954). Is the family universal? *American Anthropologist, 56,* 840–846.

_____ (1956). *Kibbutz: Venture in utopia.* Cambridge, Mass.: Harvard Univ. Press.

Steele, B. F. (1970). Parental abuse of infants and small children. In E. J. Anthony and Therese Benedek, *Parenthood: Its psychology and psychopathology,* pp. 449–477. Boston: Little, Brown.

_____, and C. B. Pollock (1968). A psychiatric study of parents who abuse infants and small children. In R. E. Helfer and C. H. Kempe (eds.), *The battered child.* Chicago: Univ. of Chicago Press.

Stephens, W. N. (1963). *The family in cross-cultural perspective.* New York: Holt.

Stone, L. (1960). Marriage among the English nobility. *Comparative Studies in Society and History, 3,* 182–206.

Sullerot, Evelyne (1971). *Woman, society and change.* New York: McGraw-Hill.

Sullivan, H. S. (1953). *The interpersonal theory of psychiatry.* New York: Norton.

Sumner, W. G. (1960). *Folkways.* New York: New American Library (Mentor).

Sunley, R. (1955). Early nineteenth-century American literature on child rearing. In Margaret Mead and Martha Wolfenstein (eds.), *Childhood in contemporary cultures,* pp. 150–167. Chicago: Univ. of Chicago Press.

Sussman, M. B. (1959). The isolated nuclear family: Fact or fiction. *Social Problems, 6,* 333–339.

_____ (1965). Relationships of adult children with their parents. In Ethel Shanas and G. F. Streib (eds.), *Social structure and the family: Generational relations.* Englewood Cliffs, N.J.: Prentice-Hall.

Szasz, T. S. (1961). *The myth of mental illness.* New York: Harper & Row.

Tavris, Carol, and Toby Jayaratne (1973). What 120,000 young women can tell you about sex, motherhood, menstruation, housework—and men. *Redbook, 140*:3, 67–69, 127–129.

Taylor, G. R. (1954). *Sex in history.* New York: Ballantine.

Teele, J. E., and W. M. Schmidt (1970). Illegitimacy and race: National and local trends. *Millbank Memorial Fund Quarterly,* April 1970, 48:2, 127–144.

Thomsen, M. (1965). The culture shock of quiet death. *San Francisco Chronicle,* April 25, 1965, p. 26. Cited in L. Broom and P. Selznick, *Sociology: A text with adapted readings.* New York: Harper & Row, 1973.

Toffler, A. (1970). *Future shock.* New York: Random House.

Tomkins, S. S. (1965). The biopsychosociality of the family. In A. J. Coale, L. A. Fallers, M. J. Levy, Jr., D. Schneider, and S. S. Tomkins, *Aspects of the analysis of family structure.* Princeton, N.J.: Princeton Univ. Press.

Trexler, R. C. (1973). Infanticide in Florence: New sources and first results. *History of Childhood Quarterly, 1:1,* 98–116.

Troll, Lillian E. (1969). Issues in the study of the family. A review of *The psychosocial interior of the family,* Gerald Handel (ed.). *Merrill-Palmer Quarterly, 15:2,* 221–226.

Turnbull, C. (1961). *The forest people.* New York: Simon & Schuster.

Udry, J. R. (1971). *The social context of marriage,* 2nd ed. Philadelphia: Lippincott.

Waller, W. W., and R. Hill (1951). *The family: A dynamic interpretation,* rev. ed. New York: Holt.

Washburn, S. L., and I. DeVore (1961). In S. L. Washburn (ed.), *Social life of early man.* Chicago: Aldine.

Watzlawick, P., Jane H. Beavin, and D. D. Jackson (1967). *Pragmatics of human communication: A study of interactional patterns, pathologies and paradoxes.* New York: Norton.

Weisstein, Naomi (1971). Psychology constructs the female. In Vivian Gornick and Barbara K. Moran (eds.), *Woman in sexist society: Studies in power and powerlessness,* pp. 207–224. New York: Basic Books.

White, R. W. (1959). Motivation reconsidered: The concept of competence. *Psychological Review, 66,* 297–333.

———— (1960). Competence and the psychosexual stages of development. In Marshall R. Jones (ed.), *Nebraska Symposium on Motivation,* pp. 97–141. Lincoln: Univ. of Nebraska Press.

White, S. (1965). Evidence for a hierarchical arrangement of learning processes. In L. P. Lipsitt and C. C. Spiker (eds.), *Advances in child development and behavior,* pp. 184–220. New York: Academic Press.

White House Conference on Children (1970). *Profiles of children.* Washington: U.S. Government Printing Office.

Whiting, Beatrice B. (1963). *Six cultures: Studies of child rearing.* New York: Wiley.

Whiting, J. W. M. (1961). Socialization process and personality. In F. L. K. Hsu (ed.), *Psychological anthropology.* Homewood, Ill.: Dorsey.

————, R. Kluckhohn, and A. Anthony (1958). The function of male initiation ceremonies at puberty. In Eleanor E. Maccoby, T. M. Newcomb, and E. L. Hartley (eds.), *Readings in social psychology,* 3rd ed. New York: Holt.

Willis, Ellen (1972). Open marriage: A fantasy. *San Francisco Chronicle,* November 8, 1972.

Winch, R. F. (1968). Some observations on extended familism in the United States. In R. F. Winch and L. W. Goodman (eds.), *Selected studies in marriage and the family*, 3rd ed. New York: Holt.

_____, and Rae Lesser Blumberg (1968). Societal complexity and familial organization. In R. F. Winch and L. W. Goodman (eds.), *Selected studies in marriage and the family*, 3rd ed. New York: Holt.

Wolfenstein, Martha (1954). *Children's humor: A psychological analysis.* Glencoe, Ill.: Free Press.

_____ (1955). Fun morality: An analysis of recent American child-training literature. In Margaret Mead and Martha Wolfenstein (eds.), *Childhood in contemporary cultures*, pp. 168–178. Chicago: Univ. of Chicago Press.

Wrigley, E. A. (1972). The process of modernization and the industrial revolution in England. *Journal of Interdisciplinary History*, 3:2, 225–260.

Wrong, D. (1961). The oversocialized conception of man in modern sociology. *American Sociology Review*, 26, 183–193.

Zablocki, B. (1971). *The joyful community: An account of the Bruderhof, a communal movement now in its third generation.* Baltimore: Penguin.

_____ (1972). Lecture presented at symposium on middle class communes. Univ. of California, Berkeley, February 12, 1972.

Zelditch, M., Jr. (1964). Cross-cultural analyses of family structure. In H. T. Christensen (ed.), *Handbook of marriage and the family*, pp. 462–500. Chicago: Rand McNally.

Zimmerman, C. C. (1947). *The family and civilization.* New York: Harper.

_____ (1970). Statement quoted in The American family: Future uncertain. *Time*, December 28, 1970, 34–39.

_____ (1972). The 1971 Burgess Award Address: The future of the family in America. *Journal of Marriage and the Family*, 34:2, 323ff.

NAME INDEX

SUBJECT INDEX